Southern Arabia

Theodore Bent and
Mrs. Theodore Bent

SOUTHERN ARABIA

BY

THEODORE BENT, F.R.G.S., F.S.A.

AUTHOR OF 'THE RUINED CITIES OF MASHONALAND' 'THE
SACRED CITY OF THE ETHIOPIANS' 'THE CYCLADES, OR LIFE
AMONG THE INSULAR GREEKS' ETC.

AND

MRS THEODORE BENT

WITH A PORTRAIT, MAPS, AND ILLUSTRATION

LONDON

SMITH, ELDER, & CO., 15 WATERLOO PLACE

1900

Lafayette, photo. — —Walker & Boutall ph. sc.

Signature: Theodore Bent

PREFACE

If my fellow-traveller had lived, he intended to have put together in book form such information as we had gathered about Southern Arabia. Now, as he died four days after our return from our last journey there, I have had to undertake the task myself. It has been very sad to me, but I have been helped by knowing that, however imperfect this book may be, what is written here will surely be a help to those who, by following in our footsteps, will be able to get beyond them, and to whom I so heartily wish success and a Happy Home-coming, the best wish a traveller may have. It is for their information that I have included so many things about the price of camels, the payment of soldiers and so forth, and yet even casual readers may care to know these details of explorers' daily lives.

Much that is set down here has been published before, but a good deal is new.

My husband had written several articles in the *Nineteenth Century*, and by the kindness of the editor I have been able to make use of these; also I have incorporated the lectures he had given before the Royal Geographical Society and the British Association. The rest is from his note-books and from the 'Chronicles' that I always wrote during our journeys.

I thought at first of trying to keep our several writings apart; but, to avoid confusion of inverted commas, I decided, acting on advice, just to put the whole thing into as consecutive a form as possible, only saying that the least part of the writing is mine.

The bibliography is far from complete, as I can name only a few of the many books that my husband consulted on all the districts round those which we were going to penetrate.

As to the spelling of the Arabic, it must be remembered that it is a very widely spread language, and there are naturally many different forms of the same word—*e.g. ibn, ben, bin*—and such very various ways of pronouncing the name of the Moslem prophet, that I have heard it pronounced Memet, Mamad and Mad.

I must give hearty thanks in both our names to all who helped us on in these journeys, and especially to Mr. Headlam, who has given me much assistance by going through the proofs of this book. Mr. W. C. Irvine has kindly provided the column of literary Arabic for the vocabulary.

MABEL VIRGINIA ANNA BENT.

13 Great Cumberland Place, W:

October 13, 1899.

CONTENTS

Bibliography

SOUTHERN ARABIA

MASKAT

THE HADHRAMOUT

DHOFAR AND THE GARA MOUNTAINS

AN AFRICAN INTERLUDE: THE EASTERN SOUDAN

THE MAHRI ISLAND OF SOKOTRA

BIBLIOGRAPHY

Abu'lfida Ismael ibn Ali Imad ed din, Prince or King of Hamar.— *Géographie d'Aboulfida*, traduite de l'Arabe et accompagnée de notes et d'éclaircissements par M. Reinaud, par M. S. Guyard. Paris, 1848-83.

Baros, João de.—*Dos feitos que os Portugueses fizeram*. 1778-80.

Binning, Robert.—*A Journal of Two Years' Travel in Persia, Ceylon, &c.* 1857.

Bunbury, Sir E. H.—*Ancient Geography among the Greeks and Romans.* 1879.

Cartas de Alfonzo de Albuquerque.—*Commentaries of Albuquerque*, Hakluyt Society, translated by W. de G. Birch. 1875.

Carter, Dr.—*Paper in the Journal of the Asiatic Society.* Bombay branch.

Chabas, Joseph.—*Les Inscriptions des Mines d'or.* 1862.

Correa, Gaspar.—*Three Voyages of Vasco da Gama.* Hakluyt Society, 1869.

Fernan Lopes de la Castanbeda.—*Historia do descubrimento e conquista da India pe los Portugueses.* Lisbon, 1833.

Glaser, Eduard.—*Skizze der Geschichte der Geographie Süd-Arabiens.* Berlin, 1890.

Goeje, J. de.—*Bibliotheca geographicorum Arabicorum.* 1870-85. *Mémoires d'histoire et de géographie orientales.* 2nd edition, 1886.

Helps to the Study of the Bible.

Hommel, Fritz—*Süd-Arabische Chrestomathie und Minæo-Sabäischen Grammatik*. München, 1893.

India Directory, Part I. 1874.

Miles, Colonel.—*Report of the Administration of the Persian Gulf Residency*, 1884-88. *Journey through Oman and Dhakrireh*. Blue Book, ccxx.

Muhamad ibn Muhamad, *Geographie d'Edrisi*.—Traduite de l'Arabe. Paris, 1836-40.

Muhammad ibn Abdallah, called Ibn Batuta.

Muhammad ibn Muhammad.—*Geographia Nubiensis*, 1619, 4º.

Müller, D. H.—*Epigraphische Denkmäler aus Arabien* (Denkschriften der K.K. Ak. der Wissenschaften Wien). *Phil. Hist.* Cl. 37, 1894. *Himyarische Studien* (Z. D. M., § 30). 1870.

Palgrave, W. G.—*Narrative of a Year's Journey through Central Eastern Arabia*. 1865.

Pollak, Dr. J. E.—*Das Land und seine Bewohner*. 1865.

Sprenger Aloys.—*Bürger und Schlösser Süd-Arabiens. Die Alte Geographie Arabiens*.

Vincent, W.—*The Commerce and Navigation of the Ancients in the Indian Ocean*. 1886.

Wellsted, Lieut.—*Visit to Dhofar in the 'Philomel.'* 1883. *Rough notes of a visit to Nakhl and Jebel Akhdar*.

Ali Ibn al Husain, El Masudi, Abu al Hasan, Diodoros, Marco Polo, Sir John Maundeville, Pliny, the *Periplus*, Strabo, Ebn Said, Ptolemy, and others; but, as many of these names have been copied by me from rough notes of my husband's, I cannot be certain about the editions. I hope the imperfections of this bibliography will be excused.

ILLUSTRATIONS

MAPS

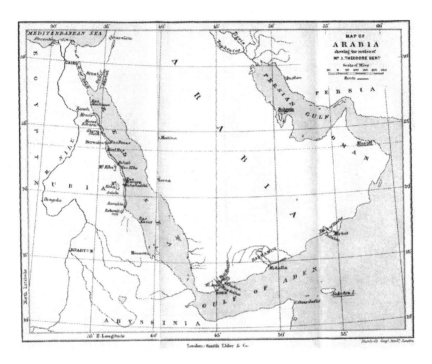

Map of ARABIA

showing the routes of

Mr. J. THEODORE BENT.

Stanford's Geog.ˡ Estab.ˡ, London

London: Smith, Elder & Co.

CHAPTER I

MANAMAH AND MOHAREK

The first Arabian journey that we undertook was in 1889, when we visited the Islands of Bahrein in the Persian Gulf; we were attracted by stories of mysterious mounds, and we proposed to see what we could find inside them, hoping, as turned out to be the fact, that we should discover traces of Phœnician remains.

The search for traces of an old world takes an excavator now and again into strange corners of the new. Out of the ground he may extract treasures, or he may not—that is not our point here—out of the inhabitants and their strange ways he is sure, whether he likes it or not, to extract a great deal, and it is with this branch of an excavator's life we are now going to deal.

We thought we were on the track of Phœnician remains and our interest in our work was like the fingers of an aneroid, subject to sudden changes, but at the same time we had perpetually around us a quaint, unknown world of the present, more pleasing to most people than anything pertaining to the past.

The group of islands known as Bahrein (dual form of Bahr, *i.e.* two seas) lies in a bay of the same name in the Persian Gulf, about twenty miles off the coast of El Hasa in Arabia.

Bahrein is really the name of the largest of the islands, which is twenty-seven miles long by ten wide. The second in point of size is Moharek, which lies north of Bahrein, and is separated from it by a strait of horse-shoe form, five miles in length, and in a few places as much as a mile wide, but for the greater part half a mile.

The rest of the group are mere rocks: Sitrah, four miles long, with a village on it of the same name; Nebi Saleh, Sayeh, Khaseifa, and, to the east of Moharek, Arad, with a palm-grove and a large double

1

Portuguese fort, an island or a peninsula according to the state of the tide.

It was no use embarking on a steamer which would take us direct from England to our destination, owing to the complete uncertainty of the time when we should arrive, so we planned out our way *viâ* Karachi and Maskat; then we had to go right up to Bushire, and again change steamers there, for the boats going up the Gulf would not touch at Bahrein. At Bushire we engaged five Persians to act as servants, interpreter, and overseers over the workmen whom we should employ in excavating.

A Mosque at Manamah, Bahrein

We had as our personal servant and interpreter combined a very dirty Hadji Abdullah, half Persian, half Arab. He was the best to be obtained, and his English was decidedly faulty. He always said *mules* for meals, *foals* for fowls, and any one who heard him say 'What time you eat your mules to-day, Sahib?' 'I have boiled two foals for dinner,' o'r 'Mem Sahib, now I go in bazaar to buy our perwisions of grub,' or 'What place I give you your grub, Mem Sahib?' would have been surprised.

He had been a great deal on our men-of-war; he also took a present of horses from the Sultan of Maskat to the Queen, so that he could boast 'I been to Home,' and alluded to his stay in England as 'when I was in Home.'

Abdullah always says *chuck* and never *throw*; and people unused to him would not take in that 'Those peacock no good, carboys much better,' referred to pickaxes and crowbars.

He used to come to the diggings and say: 'A couble of Sheikhs come here in camp, Sahib. I am standing them some coffee; shall I stand them some mixed biscuits, too?'

I must say I pity foreigners who have to trust to interpreters whose only European language is such English as this.

With the whole of our party we embarked on the steamer which took us to Bahrein, or rather as close as it could approach; for, owing to the shallowness of the sea, while still far from shore we were placed in a baggala in which we sailed for about twenty minutes. Then when a smaller boat had conveyed us as near to the dry land as possible, we were in mid-ocean transferred, bag and baggage, to asses, those lovely white asses of Bahrein with tails and manes dyed yellow with henna, and grotesque patterns illuminating their flanks; we had no reins or stirrups, and as the asses, though more intelligent than our own, will not unfrequently show obstinacy in the water, the rider, firmly grasping his pommel, reaches with thankfulness the slimy, oozy beach of Bahrein.

Manamah is the name of the town at which you land; it is the commercial capital of the islands—just a streak of white houses and bamboo huts, extending about a mile and a half along the shore. A few mosques with low minarets may be seen, having stone steps up one side, by which the priest ascends for the call to prayer. These mosques and the towers of the richer pearl merchants show some decided architectural features, having arches of the Saracenic order, with fretwork of plaster and quaint stucco patterns.

On landing we were at once surrounded by a jabbering crowd of negro slaves, and stately Arabs with long, flowing robes and twisted camel-hair cords (akkal) around their heads.

Our home while in the town was one of the best of the battlemented towers, and consisted of a room sixteen feet square, on a stone platform. It had twenty-six windows with no glass in them, but pretty lattice of plaster. Our wooden lock was highly decorated, and we had a wooden key to close our door, which pleased us much. Even though we were close upon the tropics we found our abode chilly enough after sunset; and our nights were rendered hideous— firstly, by the barking of dogs; secondly, by cocks which crowed at an inordinately early hour; and, thirdly, by pious Mussulmans hard at work praying before the sun rose.

From our elevated position we could look down into a sea of bamboo huts, the habitations of the pearl-fishers: neat enough abodes, with courtyards paved with helix shells. In these courtyards stood quaint, large water-jars, which women filled from goat-skins carried on their shoulders from the wells, wobbling when full like live headless animals; and cradles, like hencoops, for their babies. They were a merry idle lot of folk just then, for it was not their season of work: perpetually playing games (of which tip-jack and top-spinning appeared the favourite for both young and old) seemed to be their chief occupation. Staid Arabs, with turbans and long, flowing robes, spinning tops, formed a sight of which we never tired. The spinning-tops are made out of whelk-shells, which I really believe must have been the original pattern from which our domestic toy was made. The door-posts of their huts are often made of whales' jaws; a great traffic is done in sharks; the cases for their swords and daggers are all of shagreen. The gulf well deserves the name given to it by Ptolemy of the *Ichthyophagorum sinus*.

Walking through the bazaars one is much struck by the quaint, huge iron locks, some of them with keys nearly two feet long, and ingeniously opened by pressure of a spring. In the commoner houses the locks and keys are all of wood. In the bazaars, too, you may find that queer El Hasa money called Tawilah, or 'long bits,' short bars of copper doubled back and compressed together, with a few characters indicating the prince who struck them.

The coffee-pots of Bahrein are quite a specialty, also coming from El Hasa, which appears to be the centre of art in this part of Arabia. With their long beak-like spouts and concentric circles with patterns on them, these coffee-pots are a distinct feature. In the bazaars of Manamah and Moharek coffee-vendors sit at every corner with some huge pots of a similar shape simmering on the embers; in the lid are introduced stones to make a noise and attract the attention of the passers-by. Coffee-shops take the place of spirit and wine shops, which in the strict Wahabi country would not be, for a moment, tolerated. In private houses it is thought well to have four or five coffee-pots standing round the fire, to give an appearance of riches.

Besides the coffee-pots, other objects of El Hasa workmanship may be seen in Bahrein. Every household of respectability has its wooden bowl with which to offer visitors a drink of water or sour milk; these are beautifully inlaid with silver in very elaborate patterns. The guns used by Bahreini sportsmen are similarly inlaid, and the camel saddles of the sheikhs are most beautifully decorated on the pommels in the same style.

The anvils, at which the blacksmiths in the bazaars were squatting, were like large nails with heads about six inches square, driven into the ground and about a foot high.

The old weapons of the Bedouin Arabs are still in use in Bahrein: the long lance which is put up before the tent of the chief when he goes about, the shield of camel-skin decorated with gold paint and brass knobs, the coat of mail, and other objects of warfare used in an age long gone by. Every other stall has dates to sell in thick masses, the chief food of the islanders. Then you may see locusts pressed and pickled in barrels; the poorer inhabitants are very fond of this diet, and have converted the curse of the cultivator into a favourite delicacy. As for weights, the stall-holders would appear to have none but stones, whelk shells, and potsherds, which must be hard to regulate.

An ancient Arab author states that in Oman 'men obtain fire from a spark, by rolling the tinder in dry Arab grass and swinging it round till it bursts into flame.' We often saw this process and bought one of the little cages, hanging to a long chain, which they use in Bahrein.

Of course pearl-fishing is the great occupation of the islands, and Manamah is inhabited chiefly by pearl merchants and divers. Bahrein has in fact been celebrated for its pearl-fishing ever since the days of the Periplus of Nearchus, in the time of Alexander the Great.

Albuquerque, in his commentaries, thus speaks of Bahrein pearl-fishing in 1510:—'Bahrein is noted for its large breeding of horses, its barley crops, and the variety of its fruits; and all around it are the fishing grounds of seed pearls, and of pearls which are sent to these realms of Portugal, for they are better and more lasting than any that are found in any other of these parts.' This is also the verdict of the modern pearl merchants, who value Bahrein pearls, as more lasting and harder than those even of Ceylon. Evidently Albuquerque got an order from his sovereign for pearls, for he writes, in 1515, that he is getting the pearls which the king had ordered for 'the pontifical of our lady.' To this day in their dealings the pearl merchants of Bahrein still make use of the old Portuguese weights and names.

The pearl oyster is found in all the waters from Ras Mussendom to the head of the Gulf, but on the Persian side there are no known banks of value. They vary in distance from one to ninety miles from the low-lying shore of 'Araby the Blest,' but the deep sea banks are not so much fished till the 'Shemal' or nor'westers of June have spent their force. The three seasons for fishing are known as 'the spring fishing' in the shallow water, 'the summer fishing' in the deep waters, and 'the winter fishing' conducted principally by wading in the shoals. The pearls of these seas are still celebrated for their firmness, and do not peel. They are commonly reported to lose one per cent. annually for fifty years in colour and water, but after that they remain the same. They have seven skins, whereas the Cingalese pearls have only six. The merchants generally buy them wholesale by the old Portuguese weight of the *chao*. They divide them into different sizes with sieves and sell them in India, so that, as is usually the case with specialties, it is impossible to buy a good pearl on Bahrein.

Diving here is exceedingly primitive; all the necessary paraphernalia consists of a loop of rope and a stone to go down with, a curious horn thing to hold the nose, and oil for the orifice of the ears. Once a merchant brought with him a diving apparatus, but the divers were highly indignant, and leaguing against him refused to show the best banks. In this way the fisheries suffer, for the best pearls are in the deeper waters, which can only be visited late in the season. The divers are mostly negro slaves from Africa; they do not live long, poor creatures, developing awful sores and weak eyes, and they live and die entirely without medical aid.

At present the pearl-fisheries employ about four hundred boats of from eight to twenty men each. Each boat pays a tax to the sheikh. The fishing season lasts from April to October.

Very curious boats ply in the waters between Manamah and Moharek; the huge ungainly baggalas can only sail in the deeper channels. The Bahrein boats have very long-pointed prows, elegantly carved and decorated with shells; when the wind is contrary they are propelled by poles or paddles, consisting of boards of any shape tied to the end of the poles with twine, and the oarsman always seats himself on the gunwale.

Perhaps the way these boats are tied and sewn together may have given rise to the legend alluded to by Sir John Maundeville when he saw them at the Isle of Hormuz. 'Near that isle there are ships without nails of iron or bonds, on account of the rocks of adamants (loadstones), for they are all abundant there in that sea that it is marvellous to speak of, and if a ship passed there that had iron bonds or iron nails it would perish, for the adamant, by its nature, draws iron to it, and so it would draw the ship that it should never depart from it.'

Many of the boats have curious-shaped stone anchors, and water casks of uniform and doubtless old-world shape. The sheikh has some fine war vessels, called *batils*, which did good execution about fifty years ago, when the Sultan of Oman and the rulers of El Hasa tried to seize Bahrein, and a naval battle took place in the shallow sea off the coast in which the Bahreini were victorious. Now that the Gulf is practically English and piracy at an end, these vessels are more ornamental than useful. His large baggala, which mounted ten tiny guns and was named the *Dunijah*, is now employed in trade.

Then there are the bamboo skiffs with decks almost flush with the side, requiring great skill in working. Boats are really of but little use immediately around the islands. You see men walking in the sea quite a mile out, collecting shellfish and seaweeds, which form a staple diet for both man and beast on Bahrein.

The shallowness of the sea between Bahrein and the mainland has contributed considerably to the geographical and mercantile importance of the Bahrein. No big vessels can approach the opposite coast of Arabia; hence, in olden days, when the caravan trade passed this way, all goods must have been transhipped to smaller boats at Bahrein.

Sir M. Durant, in a consular report, states it as his opinion that, 'under a settled government, Bahrein could be the trading place of the Persian Gulf for Persia and Arabia, and an excellent harbour near the warehouses could be formed.'

If the Euphrates Valley Railway had ever been opened, if the terminus of this railway had been at Koweit, as it was proposed by the party of survey under the command of Admiral Charlewood and General Chesney, the Bahrein group would at once have sprung into importance as offering a safe emporium in the immediate vicinity of this terminus. Bahrein is the Cyprus of the Persian Gulf, in fact. This day is, however, postponed indefinitely until such times as England,

Turkey, and Russia shall see fit to settle their differences; and with a better understanding between these Powers, and the development of railways in the East, the Persian Gulf may yet once more become a high road of commerce, and the Bahrein Islands may again come into notice.

The Portuguese, who were the first Europeans after the time of Alexander to visit the Gulf, recognised the importance of Bahrein. Up to their time the Gulf had been a closed Mohammedan lake. The history of their rule in that part has yet to be written, but it will disclose a tale of great interest, and be a record of marvellous commercial enterprise. It was Albuquerque who first reopened the Gulf to Europeans.

Early in the sixteenth century (1504), he urged the occupation of the Gulf. In 1506 three fleets went to the East under the command of Tristan d'Acunha, with Albuquerque as second in command. Tristan soon took his departure further afield, and left Albuquerque in command. This admiral first attacked and took Hormuz, then governed by a king of Persian origin. Here, and at Maskat, he thoroughly established the Portuguese power, thereby commanding the entrance into the Gulf. From de Barros' account it would appear that the king of Bahrein was a tributary of the king of Hormuz, paying annually 40,000 *pardaos*, and from Albuquerque's letters we read that the occupation of Bahrein formed part of his scheme. 'With Hormuz and Bahrein in their hand the whole Gulf would be under their control,' he wrote. In fact, Albuquerque's scheme at that time would appear to have been exceedingly vast and rather chimerical— namely, to divert the Nile from its course and let it flow into the Red Sea, ruin Egypt, and bring the India trade *viâ* the Persian Gulf to Europe. Of this scheme we have only the outline, but, beyond establishing fortresses in the Gulf, it fell through, for Albuquerque died, and with him his gigantic projects.

The exact date of the occupation of Bahrein by the Portuguese I have as yet been unable to discover; but in 1521 we read of an Arab insurrection in Bahrein against the Persians and Portuguese, in which the Portuguese factor, Ruy Bale, was tortured and crucified.

Sheikh Hussein bin Said, of the Arabian tribe of Ben Zabia, was the instigator of this revolt. In the following year the Portuguese governor, Dom Luis de Menezes, came to terms with him, and appointed him Portuguese representative in the island.

A few years later, one Ras Bardadim, *guazil*, or governor of Bahrein, made himself objectionable, and against him Simeon d'Acunha was sent. He and many of his men died of fever in the expedition, but the Portuguese power was again restored.

Towards the close of the sixteenth century the Portuguese came under the rule of Spain, and from that date their power in the Persian Gulf began to wane. Their soldiers were drafted off to the wars in Flanders instead of going to the East to protect the colonies; and the final blow came in 1622, when Shah Abbas of Persia, assisted by an English fleet, took Hormuz, and then Bahrein. Twenty years later a company of Portuguese merchants, eager for the pearls of these islands, organised an expedition from Goa to recover the Bahrein, but the ships were taken and plundered by the Arabs before ever they entered the Gulf.

Thus fell the great Portuguese power in the Gulf, the sole traces of which now are the numerous fortresses, such as the one on Bahrein.

From 1622 to the present time the control over Bahrein has been contested between the Persians and Arabs, and as the Persian power has been on the wane, the Arabian star has been in the ascendent. In 1711 the Sultan bin Seif wrested Bahrein from Persia; in 1784 the Uttubbi of El Hasa conquered it. They have held it ever since, despite the attempts of Seyid Said of Oman, of the Turks and Persians, to take it from them. The Turks have, however, succeeded in driving them out of their original kingdom of El Hasa, on the mainland of Arabia opposite, and now the Bahrein is all that remains to them of their former extensive territories.

The royal family is a numerous one, being a branch of the El Khalifa tribe. They are the chiefs of the Uttubbi tribe of Arabs.

Most of them, if not actually belonging to that strict sect of Arabians known as Wahabi, have strong puritanical proclivities. Our teetotalers are nothing to them in bigotry. If a vendor of intoxicating liquor started a shop on Bahrein, they would burn his house down, so that the wicked who want to drink any intoxicating liquor have to buy the material secretly from ships in the harbour. Many think it wrong to smoke, and spend their lives in prayer and fasting. Church decoration is an abomination to the Wahabi; therefore, in Bahrein the mosques are little better than barns with low minarets, for the very tall ones of other Mohammedan sects are forbidden. The Wahabi are fanatics of the deepest dye; 'there is one God, and Mohammed is his prophet,' they say with the rest of the Mohammedan world, but the followers of Abdul Wahab add, 'and in no case must Mohammed and the Imams be worshipped lest glory be detracted from God.' All titles to them are odious; no grand tombs are to be erected over their dead, no mourning is allowed; hence the cemetery at Manamah is but a pitiful place—a vast collection of circles set with rough stones, each with a small uninscribed headpiece, and the surface sprinkled with helix shells.

The Wahabi would wage, if they dared, perpetual war not only against the infidel, but against such perverted individuals as those who go to worship at Mecca and other sacred shrines. The founder of this revival is reported to have beaten his sons to death for drinking wine, and to have made his daughters support themselves by spinning, but at the same time he felt himself entitled to give to a fanatical follower, who courted death for his sake, an order for an emerald palace and a large number of female slaves in the world to come.

In 1867 the Shah of Persia aimed at acquiring Bahrein, though his only claim to it was based on the fact that Bahrein had been an appanage of the Persian crown under the Suffavian kings. He instituted a revolt on the island; adopted a claimant to the sheikhdom, and got him to hoist the Persian flag. Our ships blockaded Bahrein, intercepted letters, and obliged the rebel sheikh to quit. Then it was that we took the islands under our protection. In 1875 the Turks caused trouble, and the occupation of Bahrein formed part of their great scheme of conquest in Arabia. Our ship the *Osprey* appeared on the scene, drove back the Turks, transported to India several sheikhs who were hostile to the English rule, and placed Sheikh Isa (or Esau) on the throne under British protection, under which he rules happily to this day.

We went to see him at Moharek, where he holds his court in the winter-time. We crossed over in a small baggala, and had to be poled for a great distance with our keel perpetually grating on the bottom. It was like driving in a carriage on a jolting road; the donkeys trotted independently across, their legs quite covered with water. We were glad when they came alongside, and we completed our journey on their backs.

The courtyard of the palace, which somewhat recalls the Alhambra in its architecture, was, when we arrived, crowded with Arab chiefs in all manner of quaint costumes. His majesty's dress was exceedingly fine. He and his family are entitled to wear their camel-hair bands bound round with gold thread. These looked very regal over the red turban, and his long black coat, with his silver-studded sword by his side, made him look every inch a king.

He is most submissive to British interests, inasmuch as his immediate predecessors who did not love England were shipped off to India, and still languish there in exile; as he owes his throne entirely to British protection, he and his family will probably continue to reign as long as the English are virtual owners of the Gulf, if they are willing to submit to the English protectorate.

We got a photograph of a group of them resting on their guns, and with their kanjars or sickle-shaped daggers at their waists. We took Prince Mohamed, the heir-apparent, and the stout Seid bin Omar, the prime minister of Bahrein. But Sheikh Esau refused to place his august person within reach of our camera.

During our visit we were seated on high arm-chairs of the kind so much used in India, and the only kind used here. They were white and hoary with old age and long estrangement from furniture polish.

For our sins we had to drink the bitterest black coffee imaginable, which tasted like varnish from the bitter seeds infused in it; this was followed by cups of sweet syrup flavoured with cinnamon, a disagreeable custom to those accustomed to take their coffee and sugar together.

Moharek is aristocratic, being the seat of government; Manamah is essentially commercial, and between them in the sea is a huge dismantled Portuguese fort, now used as Sheikh Esau's stables.

The town of Moharek gets its water supply from a curious source, springing up from under the sea. At high tide there is about a fathom of salt water over the spring, and water is brought up either by divers who go down with skins, or by pushing a hollow bamboo down into it. At low tide there is very little water over it, and women with large amphora and goat-skins wade out and fetch what water they require; they tell me that the spring comes up with such force that it drives back the salt water and never gets impregnated. All I can answer for is that the water is excellent to drink.

This source is called Bir Mahab, and there are several of a similar nature on the coast around: the Kaseifah spring and others. There is such a spring in the harbour of Syracuse, about twenty feet under the sea.

The legend is that in the time of Merwan, a chief, Ibn Hakim, from Katif, wished to marry the lovely daughter of a Bahrein chief. His suit was not acceptable, so he made war on the islands and captured all the wells which supplied the towns on the bigger island; but the guardian deity of the Bahreini caused this spring to break out in the sea just before Moharek, and the invader was thus in time repulsed. It is a curious fact that Arados or Arvad, the Phœnician town on the Mediterranean, was supplied by a similar submarine source.

Sheikh Esau's representative at Manamah—his prime minister or viceroy, we should call him, though he is usually known there by the humble-sounding title of the 'bazaar master,' by name Seid bin Omar, is a very stout and nearly black individual, with a European cast of countenance. He looked exceedingly grand when he came to see us, in his under-robe of scarlet cloth, with a cloak of rustling and stiff white wool with a little red woven in it. Over his head floated a white cashmere shawl, with the usual camel-hair rings to keep it on, and sandals on his bare feet. He was deputed by his sovereign to look after us, and during the fortnight we were on the island he never left us for a single day. Though outwardly very strict in his asceticism, and constantly apt to say his prayers with his nose in the dust at inconvenient moments, we found him by no means averse to a cigarette in the strictest privacy, and we learnt that his private life would not bear European investigation. He is constantly getting married. Though sixty years of age he had a young bride of a few weeks' standing. I was assured that he would soon tire of her and put her away. Even in polygamous Arabia he is looked upon as a much-married man.

CHAPTER II

THE MOUNDS OF ALI

And now behold us excavators on the way to the scene of our labours. Six camels conveyed our tents, a seventh carried goat-skins full of water. Four asses groaned under our personal effects; hens for consumption rode in a sort of lobster-pot by the side of clattering pickaxes and chairs; six policemen, or *peons*, were in our train, each on a donkey. One carried a paraffin lamp, another a basket of eggs on the palm of his hand, and as there were no reins and no stirrups, the wonder is that these articles ever survived. As for ourselves, we, like everybody else, rode sideways, holding on like grim death before and behind, especially when the frisky Bahrein donkeys galloped at steeplechase pace across the desert.

For some distance around Manamah all is arid desert, on which grow a few scrubby plants, which women cut for fodder with sickle-like saws, and carry home in large bundles on their backs. Sheikh Esau's summer palace is in the centre of this desert—a fortress hardly distinguishable from the sand around, and consisting, like Eastern structures of this nature, of nothing but one room over the gateway for his majesty, and a vast courtyard 200 feet long, where his attendants erect their bamboo huts and tents. Around the whole runs a wall with bastions at each corner, very formidable to look upon. Passing this, the palm-groves, which are exceedingly fine, are soon reached, and offer delicious shade from the burning sun. Here amongst the trees were women working in picturesque attire, red petticoats, orange-coloured drawers down to their heels, and a dark blue covering over all this, which would suddenly be pulled over the face at our approach, if they had not on their masks, or *buttras*, which admit of a good stare.

The *buttra* is a kind of mask, more resembling a bridle than anything else. In shape it is like two diamond-frames made of gold and coloured braids, fastened together by two of their lower edges. This middle strip comes down the nose and covers the mouth, and the sides come between the ears and eyes. It affords very little concealment, but is very becoming to most of its wearers, particularly if they happen to be negresses. On their heads would be baskets with dates or citrons, and now and again a particularly modest one would dart behind a palm-tree until that dangerous animal man had gone by.

About half way to the scene of our labours we halted by the ruins of the old Arab town, Beled-al-Kadim.

This ancient capital, dating from a period prior to the Portuguese occupation, still presents some interesting ruins. The old mosque (Madresseh-i-abu-Zeidan), with its two slender and elegant minarets, so different from the horrible Wahabi constructions of to-day, forms a conspicuous landmark for ships approaching the low-lying coasts of these islands. Around the body of the mosque runs a fine inscription in Kufic letters, and from the fact that the name of Ali is joined with that of the Prophet in the profession of faith, we may argue that this mosque was built during some Persian occupation, and was a Shiite mosque. The architecture, too, is distinctly Persian, recalling to us in its details the ruins of Rhey (the Rhages of Tobit) and of Sultanieh, which we saw in the north of Persia, and has nothing Arabian about it.

Ruins of houses and buildings surround this mosque, and here in the open space in the centre of the palm-groves the Bahreini assemble every Thursday for a market; in fact the place is generally known now as Suk-el-Khamis, or Thursday's Market.

On our journey out not a soul was near, but on our return we had an opportunity of attending one of these gatherings.

Sheikh Esau has here a tiny mosque, just an open *loggia*, where he goes every morning in summer-time to pray and take his coffee. Beneath it he has a bath of fresh but not over-clean water, where he and his family bathe. Often during the summer heats he spends the whole day here, or else he goes to his glorious garden about a mile distant, near the coast, where acacias, hibiscus, and almonds fight with one another for the mastery, and form a delicious tangle.

Another mile on, closer to the sea, is the fine ruined fortress of the Portuguese, Gibliah, as the natives call it now, just as they do one of the fortresses at Maskat. It covers nearly two acres of ground, and is built out of the remains of the old Persian town, for many Kufic inscriptions are let into the wall, and the deep well in the centre is lined with them. It is a regular bastioned fortification of the sixteenth century, with moat, embrasures in the parapets, and casemented embrasures in the re-entering angles of the bastions, and is one of the finest specimens of Portuguese architecture in the Gulf, an evidence of the importance which they attached to this island.

Amongst the rubbish in the fort we picked up numerous fragments of fine Nankin and Celadon china, attesting to the ubiquity and commerce of the former owners, and attesting, also, to the luxury of the men who ruled here—a luxury as fatal almost as the Flanders wars to the well-being of the Portuguese in the East.

Our road led us on through miles of palm-groves, watered by their little artificial conduits, and producing the staple food of the island. Seid bin Omar talked to us much about the date. 'Mohammed said,' he began, 'honour the date-tree, for she is your mother,' a true enough maxim in parched Arabia, where nothing else will grow. When ripe the dates are put into a round tank, called the *madibash*, where they are exposed to the sun and air, and throw off excessive juice which collects below; after three days of this treatment they are removed and packed for exportation in baskets of palm leaves. The Bahreini, for their own consumption, love to add sesame seeds to their dates, or ginger powder and walnuts pressed with them into jars. These are called *sirah*, and are originally prepared by being dried in the sun and protected at night, then diluted date-juice is poured over them. The fruit which does not reach maturity is called *salang*, and is given as food to cattle, boiled with ground date-stones and fish bones. This makes an excellent sort of cake for milch cows; this, and the green dates also, are given to the donkeys, and to this food the Bahreini attribute their great superiority. The very poor also make an exceedingly unpalatable dish out of green dates mixed with fish for their own table, or, I should say, floor.

Nature here is not strong enough for the fructification of the palm, so at given seasons the pollen is removed by cutting off the male spathes; these they dry for twenty hours, and then they take the flower twigs and deposit one or two in each bunch of the female blossom. Just as we were there they were very busy with the spathes, and in Thursday's Market huge baskets of the male spathes were exposed for sale. The palm-groves are surrounded by dykes to keep the water in.

The date-tree is everything to a Bahreini. He beats the green spadix with wooden implements to make fibre for his ropes; in the dry state he uses it as fuel; he makes his mats, the only known form of carpet and bedding here, out of it; his baskets are made of the leaves. From the fresh spathe, by distillation, a certain stuff called *tara* water is obtained, of strong but agreeable smell, which is much used for the making of sherbet. Much legendary lore is connected with the date. The small round hole at the back is said to have been made by Mohammed's teeth, when one day he foolishly tried to bite one; and in some places the expression 'at the same time a date and a duty,' is explained by the fact that in Ramazan the day's fast is usually broken by first eating a date.

Amongst all these date-groves are the curious Arab wells, with sloping runs, and worked by donkeys. The tall poles, to which the skins are attached, are date-tree trunks. Down goes the skin bucket as the donkey comes up a steep slope in the ground, and then, as he goes down, up it comes again full of water, to be guided into the channel, which fertilises the trees, by a slave, who supports himself going up, and adds his weight to that of the descending donkey, by putting his arm through a large wooden ring hung at the donkey's shoulder. Day after day in our camp we heard the weird creaking from these wells, very early in the morning and in the evening when the sun had gone down, and we felt as we heard it what an infinite blessing is a well of water in a thirsty land.

Leaving the palm-groves and the Portuguese fortress behind us, we re-entered the desert to the south-west; and, just beyond the village of Ali, we came upon that which is the great curiosity of Bahrein, to investigate which was our real object in visiting the island: for there begins that vast sea of sepulchral mounds, the great necropolis of an unknown race which extends far and wide across the plain. The village of Ali forms as it were the culminating point; it lies just on the borders of the date-groves, and there the mounds reach an elevation of over forty feet, but as they extend further southward they diminish in size, until miles away, in the direction of Rufa'a, we found mounds elevated only a few feet above the level of the desert, and some mere circular heaps of stones. There are many thousands of these tumuli extending over an area of desert for many miles. There are isolated groups of mounds in other parts of the islands, and a few solitary ones are to be found on the adjacent islets, on Moharek, Arad, and Sitrah.

Complete uncertainty existed as to the origin of these mounds, and the people who constructed them, but, from classical references and the result of our own work, there can now be no doubt that they are of Phœnician origin. Herodotus[1] gives us as a tradition current in his time that the forefathers of the Phœnician race came from these parts. The Phœnicians themselves believed in it: 'It is their own account of themselves,' says Herodotus; and Strabo[2] brings further testimony to bear on the subject, stating that two of the islands now called Bahrein were called Tyros and Arados. Pliny follows in Strabo's steps, but calls the island Tylos instead of Tyros, which may be only an error in spelling, or may be owing to the universal confusion of r with l.

Ptolemy in his map places Gerrha, the mart of ancient Indian trade and the starting-point for caravans on the great road across Arabia, on the coast just opposite the islands, near where the town of El Katif now is, and accepts Strabo's and Pliny's names for the Bahrein Islands, calling them Tharros, Tylos or Tyros, and Arados. The fact is that all our information on the islands prior to the Portuguese occupation comes from the Periplus of Nearchus. Eratosthenes, a naval officer of Alexander's, states that the Gulf was 10,000 stadia long from Cape Armozum, *i.e.* Hormuz, to Teredon (Koweit), and the mouth of the Euphrates. Androsthenes of Thasos, who was of the company of Nearchus, made an independent geographical survey of the Gulf on the Arabian side, and his statements are, that on an island called Ikaros, now Peludji, just off Koweit, he saw a temple of Apollo. Southwards, at a distance of 2,400 stadia, or 43 nautical leagues, he came on Gerrha, and, close to it, the islands of Tyros and Arados, 'which have temples like those of the Phœnicians,' who were (the inhabitants told him) colonists from these parts. From Nearchus, too, we learn that the Phœnicians had a town called Sidon or Sidodona in the Gulf, which he visited, and on an island called Tyrine was shown the tomb of Erythras, which he describes as 'an elevated hillock covered with palms,' just like our mounds, and Erythras was the king who gave his name to the Gulf. Justin accepts the migration of the Phœnicians from the Persian Gulf as certain; and M. Renan says, 'The primitive abode of the Phœnicians must be placed on the Lower Euphrates, in the centre of the great commercial and maritime establishments of the Persian Gulf.'[3] As for the temples, there are no traces of them left, and this is also the case in Syrian Phœnicia; doubtless they were all built of wood, which will account for their disappearance.

As we ourselves, during the course of our excavations, brought to light objects of distinctly Phœnician origin, there would appear to be no longer any room for doubt that the mounds which lay before us were a vast necropolis of this mercantile race. If so, one of two suppositions must be correct, either firstly, that the Phœnicians originally lived here before they migrated to the Mediterranean, and that this was the land of Punt from which the Puni got their name, a land of palms like the Syrian coast from which the race got their distorted Greek appellation of Phœnicians; or secondly, that these islands were looked upon by them as a sacred spot for the burial of their dead, as the Hindoo looks upon the Ganges, and the Persian regards the shrines of Kerbela and Meshed. I am much more inclined to the former supposition, judging from the mercantile importance of the Bahrein Islands and the excellent school they must have been for a race which was to penetrate to all the then known corners of the globe—to brave the dangers of the open Atlantic, and to reach the shores of Britain in their trading ventures; and if nomenclature goes for anything, the name of Tyros and the still-existing name of Arad ought to confirm us in our belief and make certainty more certain.

Our camp was pitched on this desert among the tumuli. The ground was hard and rough, covered with very sharp stones; though dry, it sounded hollow, and it seemed as though there were water under it.

Our own tent occupied a conspicuous and central place; our servants' tent was hard by, liable to be blown down by heavy gusts of wind, which event happened the first night after our arrival, to the infinite discomfiture of the bazaar-master, who, by the way, had left his grand clothes at home, and appeared in the desert clad in a loose coffee-coloured dressing-gown, with a red band round his waist. Around the tents swarmed turbaned diggers, who looked as if they had come out in their night-gowns, dressing-gowns, and bath-sheets. These lodged at night in the bamboo village of Ali hard by, a place for which we developed the profoundest contempt, for the women thereof refused to pollute themselves by washing the clothes of infidels, and our garments had to be sent all the way to Manamah to be cleansed. A bamboo structure formed a shelter for the kitchen, around which, on the sand, lay curious coffee-pots, bowls, and cooking utensils, which would have been eagerly sought after for museums in Europe. The camel, which fetched the daily supply of water from afar, grazed around on the coarse desert herbage; the large white donkey which went into the town for marketing by day, and entangled himself in the tent ropes by night, was also left to wander at his own sweet will. This desert camp was evidently considered a very peculiar sight indeed, and no wonder that for the first week of our residence there, we were visited by all the inhabitants of Bahrein who could find time to come so far.

It was very weird to sit in our tent door the first evening and look at the great mound we were going to dig into next morning, and think how long it had stood there in the peace its builders hoped for it. There seemed to be quite a mournful feeling about disturbing it; but archæologists are a ruthless body, and this was to be the last night it would ever stand in its perfect shape. After all, we were full of hope of finding out the mystery of its origin.

The first attack next morning was most amusing to behold. My husband headed the party, looking very tall and slim, with his legs outlined against the sky, as he, with all the rest, in single file and in fluttering array, wound first round the mound to look for a good place to ascend, and then went straight up.

They were all amazed when I appeared and gave orders to the division under my command.

They looked very questioningly indeed, but, as the Persians had learnt to respect me, the Bahreini became quite amenable.

Theodore Bent Receiving Visitors at The Mounds, Bahrein

The dimensions of the mound on which we began our labours were as follows: 35 feet in height, 76 feet in diameter, and 152 paces in circumference. We chose this in preference to the higher mounds, the tops of which were flattened somewhat and suggested the idea that they had fallen in. Ours, on the contrary, was quite rounded on the summit, and gave every hope that in digging through it we should find whatever was inside in *statu quo*. At a distance of several feet from most of the mounds are traces of an outer encircling wall or bank of earth, similar to walls found around certain tombs in Lydia, as also round a tumulus at Tara in Ireland, and this encircling wall was more marked around some of the smaller and presumably more recent tombs at the outer edge of the necropolis; in some cases several mounds would appear to have been clustered together, and to have had an encircling wall common to them all.

We dug from the top of our mound for 15 feet, with great difficulty, through a sort of conglomerate earth, nearly as hard as cement, before we reached anything definite. Then suddenly this close earth stopped, and we came across a layer of large loose stones, entirely free from soil, which layer covered the immediate top of the tombs for two feet. Beneath these stones, and immediately on the flat slabs forming the roof of the tomb, had been placed palm branches, which in the lapse of ages had become white and crumbly, and had assumed the flaky appearance of asbestos. This proved that the palm flourished on Bahrein at the date of these tombs, and that the inhabitants were accustomed to make use of it for constructive purposes.

Six very large slabs of rough unhewn limestone, which had obviously come from Jebel Dukhan, lay on the top of the tomb, forming a roof. One of these was 6 feet in length, and 2 feet 2 inches in depth.

The tomb itself was composed of two chambers, one immediately over the other, and approached by a long passage, like the dromos of rock-cut Greek tombs, which was full of earth and small stones. The entrance, as was that of all the tombs, was towards the sunset. This passage was 53 feet in length, extending from the outer rim of the circle to the mouth of the tomb. Around the outer circle of the mound itself ran a wall of huge stones, evidently to support the weight of earth necessary to conceal the tomb, and large unhewn stones closed the entrance to the two chambers of the tomb at the head of the passage.

We first entered the upper chamber, the floor of which was covered with gritty earth. It was 30 feet long, and at the four corners were recesses 2 feet 10 inches in depth, and the uniform height of this chamber was 4 feet 6 inches. The whole surface of the interior to the depth of two or three inches above the other *débris* was covered with yellow earth composed of the tiny bones of the jerboa, that rat-like animal which is found in abundance on the shores of the Persian Gulf. There was no sign of any recent ones and only a few fragments of skulls to show what this yellow earth had been. We then proceeded to remove the rubbish and sift it for what we could find.

The chief objects of interest consisted in innumerable fragments of ivory, fragments of circular boxes, pendants with holes for suspension (obviously used as ornaments by this primitive race), the torso of a small statue in ivory, the hoof of a bull fixed on to an ivory pedestal, evidently belonging to a small statue of a bull, the foot of another little statue, and various fragments of ivory utensils. Many of these fragments had patterns inscribed on them—rough patterns of scales, rosettes, encircling chains, and the two parallel lines common to so many ivory fragments found at Kameiros, and now in the British Museum. In fact, the decorations on most of them bear a close and unmistakable resemblance to ivories found in Phœnician tombs on the shores of the Mediterranean, and to the ivories in the British Museum from Nimrud in Assyria, universally accepted as having been executed by Phœnician artists: those cunning workers in ivory and wood whom Solomon employed in the building of his temple, and, before the spread of Egyptian and Greek art, the travelling artists of the world. The ivory fragments we found were given into the hands of Mr. A. S. Murray, of the British Museum, who wrote to my husband as follows: 'I have not the least doubt, judging from the incised patterns, from bull's foot, part of a figure, &c., that the ivories are of Phœnician workmanship.'

The pottery found in this tomb offered no very distinctive features, being coarse and unglazed, but the numerous fragments of ostrich egg-shells, coloured and scratched with rough patterns in bands, also pointed to a Phœnician origin, or at least to a race of wide mercantile connection: and in those days the Phœnicians were the only people likely to combine in their commerce ostrich egg-shells and ivory. We also found small shapeless pieces of oxidised metal, brass or copper. There were no human bones in the upper chamber, but those of a large animal, presumably a horse.

The chamber immediately beneath was much more carefully constructed; it was exactly the same length, but was higher, being 6 feet 7 inches, and the passage was wider. It was entirely coated with cement of two qualities, the upper coat being the finest, in which all round the walls at intervals of two feet were holes sloping inwards and downward. In similar holes, in one of the other tombs we opened, we found traces of wood, showing that poles on which to hang drapery had been inserted. The ground of this lower chamber was entirely covered with a thin brown earth of a fibrous nature, in appearance somewhat resembling snuff; it was a foot in depth, and evidently the remains of the drapery which had been hung around the walls. Prior to the use of coffins the Phœnicians draped their dead,[4] and amongst this substance we found traces of human bones.

Thus we were able to arrive at the system of sepulture employed by this unknown race. Evidently their custom was to place in the upper chamber broken utensils and the body of an animal belonging to the deceased, and to reserve the lower chamber for the corpse enshrouded in drapery. For the use of this upper chamber our parallels are curiously enough all Phœnician. Perrot gives us an example of two-storied tombs in the cemetery of Amrit, in Phœnicia, where also the bodies were embedded in plaster to prevent decay prior to the introduction of the sarcophagus, reminding us of the closely cemented lower chambers in our mounds. A mound containing a tomb with one chamber over the other was in 1888 observed in Sardinia, and is given by Della Marmora as of Phœnician origin. Here, however, the top of the tomb is conical, not flat, as in our mounds, which would point to a later development of the double chamber which eventually blossomed forth into the lofty mausolea of the later Phœnician epoch, and the grandiose tombs of Hellenic structure.

Also at Carthage, that very same year that we were in Bahrein, *i.e.* 1889, excavations brought to light certain tombs of the early Phœnician settlers which also have the double chamber. In answer to Perrot's assertion that all early Phœnician tombs were *hypogea*, we may say that as the Bahrein Islands offered no facility for this method of sepulture, the closely-covered-in mound would be the most natural substitute.

Before leaving the tombs we opened a second, and a smaller one of coarser construction, which confirmed in every way the conclusions we had arrived at in opening the larger tomb. Near the village of Ali, one of the largest mounds has been pulled to pieces for the stones. By creeping into the cavities opened we were able to ascertain that the chambers in this mound were similar to those in the mound we had opened, only they were double on both stories, and the upper story was also coated with cement. Two chambers ran parallel to each other, and were joined at the two extremities.

Sir M. Durand also opened one of the mounds, but unfortunately the roof of the tomb had fallen in, which prevented him from obtaining any satisfactory results; but from the general appearance, it would seem to have been constructed on exactly the same lines as our larger one. Hence we had the evidence of four tombs to go upon, and felt that these must be pretty fair specimens of what the many thousands were which extended around us.

[1] II. 89.

[2] XVI. iii. 4.

[3] *Hist. des langues sémitiques*, ii. 183.

[4] Perrot, *History of Art in Phœnicia*.

CHAPTER III

OUR VISIT TO RUFA'A

During the time that we spent at Ali we had numerous visitors. The first day came five camels with two riders apiece, and a train of donkeys, bringing rich pearl merchants from the capital; these sat in a circle and complacently drank our coffee and ate our mixed biscuits, without in any way troubling us, having apparently come for no other object than to get this slender refreshment.

Next day came Sheikh Mohammed, a young man of seventeen, a nephew of Sheikh Esau, who was about to wed his uncle's daughter, and was talked of as the heir-apparent to the throne; he was all gorgeous in a white embroidered robe, red turban, and head rings bound in royal gold. He played with our pistols with covetous eyes, ate some English cake, having first questioned the bazaar-master as to the orthodoxy of its ingredients, and then he promised us a visit next day.

He came on the morrow, on a beautifully caparisoned horse, with red trappings and gold tassels. He brought with him many followers and announced his intention of passing the day with us, rather to our distress; but we were appeased by the present of a fat lamb with one of those large bushy tails which remind one forcibly of a lady's bustle, and suggests that the ingenious milliner who invented these atrocities must have taken for her pattern an Eastern sheep. This day 'Prince' Mohammed handled the revolver more covetously than ever, and got so far as exchanging his scarlet embroidered case, with red silk belt and silver buckle, for my leathern one.

Sheikh Mohammed was very anxious to see how I could shoot with my revolver, so a brown pot containing about half a pint of water was put on a lump of rock as a mark. I was terrified; for I knew if I missed, as I surely expected, I should bring great discredit on myself and my nation, and there was such a crowd! My husband said I must try, and I am sure no one was more astonished than I was that I shattered the pot. If I had not it would have been said that I only carried the revolver for show.

That afternoon a great cavalcade of gazelle huntsmen called upon us. The four chief men of these had each a hooded falcon on his arm, and a tawny Persian greyhound, with long silky tail, at his side. They wore their sickle-like daggers in their waistbands; their bodies were enveloped in long cloaks, and their heads in white cloths bound round with the camel-hair straps; they were accompanied by another young scion of the El Khalifa family, who bestrode a white Arab steed with the gayest possible trappings. Thus was this young prince attired: on his head a cashmere kerchief with gold akkal; he was almost smothered in an orange cloth gown trimmed with gold and lined with green, the sleeves of which were very long, cut open at the ends and trimmed; over this robe was cast a black cloth cloak trimmed with gold on the shoulders, and a richly inlaid sword dangled at his side, almost as big as himself, for he was but an undersized boy of fifteen. The sportsmen made a very nice group for our photography, as did almost everything around us on Bahrein.

Any excavator would have lost patience with the men of Bahrein with whom we had to deal; tickets had to be issued to prevent more men working than were wanted, and claiming pay at the end of the day; ubiquity was essential, for they loved to get out of sight and do nothing; with unceasing regularity the pipe went round and they paused for a 'drink' at the bubble-bubble, as the Arabs express it; morning, noon-tide, and evening prayers were, I am sure, unnecessarily long. Accidents would happen, which alarmed us at first, until we learnt how ready they were to cry wolf: one man was knocked over by a stone; we thought by his contortions some limb must be broken, and we applied vaseline, our only available remedy, to the bruise; his fellow-workmen then seized him by the shoulders, he keeping his arms crossed the while, shook him well 'to put the bones right again,' as they expressed it, and he continued his work as before.

The bazaar-master and the policeman would come and frantically seize a tool, and work for a few seconds with herculean vigour by way of example, which was never followed. 'Yallah!' 'hurry on' (*i.e.* Oh God); 'Marhabbah!' 'very good,' the men would cry, and they would sing and scream with a vigour that nearly drove us wild. But for the occasional application of a stick by the bazaar-master and great firmness, we should have got nothing out of them but noise.

One day we had a mutiny because my husband dismissed two men who came very late; the rest refused to work, and came dancing round us, shouting and brandishing spades. One had actually got hold of a naked sword, which weapon I did not at all like, and I was thankful 'Prince' Mohammed had not yet got the revolver. For some time they continued this wild weird dance, consigning us freely to the lower regions as they danced, and then they all went away, so that the bazaar-master had to be sent in search of other and more amenable men. Evidently Sheikh Esau, when he entrusted us to the charge of the bazaar-master and sent policemen with us, was afraid of something untoward happening. Next day we heard that his majesty was coming in person with his tents to encamp in our vicinity, and I fancy we were in more danger from those men than we realised at the moment, fanned as they are into hatred of the infidel by the fanatical Wahabi; thirty years ago, I was told, no infidel could have ventured into the centre of Bahrein with safety.

Another important visitor came on Saturday in the shape of Sheikh Khallet, a cousin of the ruling chief, with a retinue of ten men, from Rufa'a, an inland village. We sat for awhile on our heels in rows, conversing and smiling, and finally accepted an invitation from Sheikh Khallet to visit him at his village, and make a little tour over the island. Accordingly, on Sunday morning we started, accompanied by the bazaar-master, for Rufa'a, and we were not a little relieved to get away before Sheikh Esau was upon us, and escape the formalities which his royal presence in our midst would have necessitated.

We had an exceedingly hot ride of it, and the wind was so high that our position on our donkeys was rendered even more precarious than usual. The desert sand whirled around us: we shut our eyes, tied down our hats, and tried to be patient; for miles our road led through the tumuli of those mysterious dead, who once in their thousands must have peopled Bahrein; their old wells are still to be seen in the desert, and evidences of a cultivation which has long ago disappeared. As we approached the edge of this vast necropolis the mounds grew less and less, until mere heaps of stones marked the spot where a dead man lay, and then we saw before us the two villages of Rufa'a. Of these, one is known as Rufa'a Shergeh, or South-western Rufa'a; the other, which belongs to the young Prince Mohammed, is called Rufa'a Jebeli. The Rufa'a are much older than Moharek, or Manamah; they are fortified with castellated walls of mud brick. Many of the El Khalifa family reside here in comfortable houses. South-western Rufa'a is quite a big place, and as our arrival became known all the village turned out to see us. The advent of an English lady among them was something too excessively novel: even close-veiled women forgot their prudery, and peered out from their blue coverings, screaming with laughter, and pointing as they screamed to the somewhat appalled object of their mirth. 'Hade bibi!' ('there goes the lady'), shouted they again and again. No victorious potentate ever had a more triumphant entry into his capital than the English 'bibi' had on entering South-western Rufa'a.

Sheikh Khallet was ready to receive us in his *kahwa* or reception-room, furnished solely by strips of matting and a camel-hair rug with coarse embroidery on it; two pillows were produced for us, and Arabs squatted on the matting all round the wall, for it was Sheikh Khallet's morning reception, or *majilis*, just then, and we were the lions of the occasion. Our host, we soon learnt, rather to our dismay, was a most rigid ascetic—a Wahabi to the backbone. He allows of no internal decorations in his house; no smoking is allowed, no wine, only perpetual coffee and perpetual prayers; our prospects were not of the most brilliant. Some of the Wahabi think even coffee wrong. After a while all the company left, and Sheikh Khallet intimated to us that the room was now our own. Two more large pillows were brought, and rugs were laid down; as for the rest we were dependent on our own very limited resources. We had brought our own sheets with us.

The Interior of Sheikh Saba's House at Rufa'a, Bahrein

Sheikh Saba, who had married Sheikh Khallet's sister, was a great contrast to our host; he had been in Bombay and had imbibed in his travels a degree of worldliness which ill became a Wahabi. He had filled his house, to which he took us, with all sorts of baubles—gilt looking-glasses hanging on the walls; coloured glass balls in rows and rows up to the ceiling, each on a little looking-glass; lovely pillows and carpets, Zanzibar date baskets, Bombay inlaid chests, El Hasa coffee-pots, and a Russian tea-urn—a truly marvellous conglomeration of things, which produced on us a wonderful sense of pleasure and repose after the bareness of our host's abode. Sheikh Saba wore only his long white shirt and turban, and so unconventional was he that he allowed his consort to remain at one end of the room whilst my husband was there.

The courtyards of these houses are architecturally interesting: the Saracenic arch, the rosettes of open-work stucco, the squares of the same material with intricate patterns—great boons in a hot land to let in the air without the sun. There is also another contrivance for obtaining air; in building the house a niche three feet wide is left in the outer wall, closed in on the inner side except for about a foot. It is funny to see the heads of muffled women peering out of these air-shafts, into which they have climbed to get an undisturbed view. Here some of the women wear the Arabian *buttra* or mask, which, while it hides their features, gives their eyes full play. They are very inquisitive. Some of the women one meets on Bahrein are highly picturesque when you see them without the dark-blue covering.

I was fetched to one harem after the other, always followed by a dense crowd, to the apparent annoyance of my hostesses, who, however, seemed powerless to prevent the intrusion. I saw one woman holding on to the top of the door and standing on the shoulders of one who was squatting on the floor. One good lady grew enraged at the invasion, and threw a cup of hot coffee in an intruder's face.

In the afternoon we rode over to Mountainous (and, it might be added, ruinous) Rufa'a.

It is built on a cliff, 50 feet above the lowest level of the desert; from here there is a view over a wide, bleak expanse of sand, occasionally relieved by an oasis, the result of a well and irrigation, and beyond this the eye rests on Jebel Dukhan, 'the mountain of mist,' which high-sounding name has been given to a mass of rocks in the centre of Bahrein, rising 400 feet above the plain, and often surrounded by a sea-fog; for Bahrein, with its low-lying land, is often in a mist. Some mornings on rising early we looked out of our tent to find ourselves enveloped in a perfect London fog—our clothes were soaking, the sand on the floor of our tent was soft and adhesive; then in an hour the bright orb of heaven would disperse all this, for we were very far south indeed, on the coast of Arabia. Alas! on arrival we found that our young friend Sheikh Mohammed was out, for he had to be in attendance on his uncle, Sheikh Esau, who had just arrived at his tent near our encampment, and he had to provide all his uncle's meals; we saw a donkey with a cauldron on its back large enough to boil a sheep in, large copper trays, and many other articles despatched for the delectation of the sovereign and his retinue. Sheikh Mohammed's mother, quite a queenly-looking woman, was busying herself about the preparation of these things, and when she had finished she invited us to go into the harem. My husband felt the honour and confidence reposed in him exceedingly, but, alas! all the women were veiled; all he could contemplate was their lovely hands and feet dyed yellow with henna, their rich red shirts, their aprons adorned with coins, their gold bracelets and turquoise rings. However I assured him that with one solitary exception he had lost nothing by not seeing their faces. In one corner of the women's room was the biggest bed I ever saw: it had eight posts, a roof, a fence, a gate, and steps up to it; it is a sort of daïs, in fact, where they spread their rugs and sleep, and high enough to lay beds under it too. Occasionally we got a good peep at the women as they were working in the fields, or cutting with semi-circular saws the scrub that grows in the desert for their cattle.

Half-way between the two Rufa'as we halted at a well, the great point of concourse for the inhabitants of both villages. It was evening, and around it were gathered crowds of the most enchanting people in every possible costume. Women and donkeys were groaning under the weight of skins filled with water; men were engaged in filling them, but it seems to be against the dignity of a male Arab to carry anything. With the regularity of a steam crane the woodwork of the well creaked and groaned with a sound like a bagpipe, as the donkeys toiled up and down their slope, bringing to the surface the skins of water. It was a truly Arabian sight, with the desert all around us, and the little garden hard by which Sheikh Saba cultivates with infinite toil, having a weary contest with the surrounding sand which invades his enclosure.

The sun was getting low when we returned to our bare room at Sheikh Khallet's, and to our great contentment we were left alone, for our day had been a busy one, and a strain on our conversational powers. Our host handed us over to the tender mercies of a black slave, Zamzam by name, wonderfully skilled at cooking with a handful of charcoal on circular stoves coloured red, and bearing a marked resemblance to the altars of the Persian fire-worshippers. He brought us in our dinner: first he spread a large round mat of fine grass on the floor; in the centre of this he deposited a washing basin filled with boiled rice and a bowl of *ghi* or rancid grease to make it palatable; before us were placed two tough chickens, a bowl of dates, and for drink we had a bowl of milk with delicious fresh butter floating in it. Several sheets of bread about the size and consistency of bath towels were also provided, but no implements of any kind to assist us in conveying these delicacies to our mouths. With pieces of bread we scooped up the rice, with our fingers we managed the rest, and we were glad no one was looking on to witness our struggles save Zamzam with a ewer of water, with which he washed us after the repast was over, and then we put ourselves away for the night.

Very early next morning we were on the move for our trip across the island. The journey would be too long for donkeys, they said, so Sheikh Khallet mounted us on three of his best camels, with lovely saddles of inlaid El Hasa work, with two pommels, one in front and one behind, like little pillars, capped and inlaid with silver. We—that is to say my husband and I and the bazaar-master—ambled along at a pretty smart pace across the desert in the direction of a fishing village called Asker, on the east coast of the island, near which were said to exist ancient remains; these, of course, turned out to be myths, but the village was all that could be desired in quaintness; the houses were all of bamboo, and the floors strewn over with little white helix shells; in one of them we were regaled with coffee, and found it delicious after our hot ride; then we strolled along the shore and marvelled at the bamboo skiffs, the curiously-fashioned oars and water casks, the stone anchors, and other primitive implements used by this seafaring race. The bazaar-master would not let us tarry as long as we could have wished, for he was anxious for us to arrive before the midday heat at a rocky cave in the 'mountain of mist,' in the centre of the island. We dismounted from our camels, and proceeded to examine Jebel Dukhan, an escarped mass of limestone rocks with rugged outline and deep caves. From the gentle elevation of the misty mountain one gets a very fair idea of the extent and character of Bahrein. The island has been likened to a sheet of silver in a sea of pearl, but it looked to us anything but silvery, and for all the world like one of the native sheets of bread—oval and tawny. It is said to be twenty-seven miles long and twelve wide at its broadest point. From the clearness of the atmosphere and the distinctness with which we saw the sea all around us, it could not have been much more. There are many tiny villages dotted about here and there, recognisable only by their nest of palm trees and their strips of verdure. In the dim distance, to our left, arose the mountains of Arabia; beyond, the flat coast-line of El Hasa, encircling that wild, mysterious land of Nejd, where the Wahabi dwell—a land forbidden to the infidel globe-trotter.

Yet another sheikh of the El Khalifa family was introduced to us, by name Abdullah; he owns the land about here, and having been advised of our coming, had prepared a repast for us, much on the lines of the one we had had the evening before.

We much enjoyed our cool rest and repast in Abdullah's cave, and for two hours or more our whole party lay stretched on the ground courting slumber, whilst our camels grazed around. Another sheikh was anxious to take us to his house for the night, but we could not remain, as our work demanded our return to camp that night, so we compromised matters by taking coffee with him on a green oasis near his house, under a blazing sun, without an atom of shade, and without a thing against which to lean our tired backs. Then we hurried back to Rufa'a, to take leave of our friend, Sheikh Khallet, and started off late in the evening for our home.

Soon we came in sight of Sheikh Esau's tent; his majesty was evidently expecting us, for by his side in the royal tent were placed two high thrones, formed of camel saddles covered with sheepskins, for us to sit upon, whilst his Arabian majesty and his courtiers sat on the ground. As many as could be accommodated sat round within the walls of the tent. Those for whom there was no room inside continued the line, forming a long loop which extended for some yards outside the tent. Here all his nephews and cousins were assembled. That gay youth Sheikh Mohammed, on ordinary occasions as full of fun as an English schoolboy, sat there in great solemnity, incapable of a smile though I maliciously tried to raise one. When he came next morning to visit us he was equally solemn, until his uncle had left our tent; then his gaiety returned as if by magic, and with it his covetousness for my pistol. Eventually an exchange was effected, he producing a coffee-pot and an inlaid bowl, which had taken our fancy, as the price.

On the surrounding desert a small gazelle is abundant. One day we came across a cavalcade of Bahreini sportsmen, who looked exceedingly picturesque in their flowing robes and floating red kaffiehs, and riding gaily caparisoned horses, with crimson trappings and gold tassels. Each had on his arm a hooded falcon and by his side a Persian greyhound. When the gazelle is sighted the falcon is let loose; it skims rapidly along the ground, attacks the head of the animal, and so confuses it that it falls an easy prey to the hounds in pursuit. Albuquerque in his 'Commentaries' says: 'There are many who hunt with falcons about the size of our goshawks, and take by their aid certain creatures smaller than gazelles, training very swift hounds to assist the falcon in catching the prey.'

In their ordinary life the Bahrein people still retain the primitiveness of the Bedouin.

There are about fifty villages scattered over the islands, recognisable from a distance by their patch of cultivation and groups of date-palms. Except at Manamah and Moharek they have little or nothing to do with the pearl fisheries, but are an exceedingly industrious race of peasants who cultivate the soil by means of irrigation from the numerous wells with which the island is blessed. There are generally three to six small wheels attached to the beam, which is across the well, over which the ropes of as many large leathern buckets pass. When these buckets rise full they tilt themselves over, the contents is then taken by little channels to a reservoir which feeds the dykes, transferred thence to the palms in buckets raised by the leverage of a date-trunk lightly swung by ropes to a frame, and balanced at one end by a basket of earth into which it is inserted; it is so light to lift that women are generally employed in watering the trees.

To manure their date-groves they use the fins of a species of ray fish called *awwal*, steeped in water till they are putrid; *awwal*, by the way, was an ancient name of the Island of Bahrein, perhaps because it was the first island of the group in size, *awwal* in Arabic meaning *first*.

The area of fertility is very rich and beautiful; it extends all along the north coast of the island, and the fishing village of Nayim, with its bamboo huts nestling beneath the palm-trees, is highly picturesque; and all this fertility is due to the number of fresh-water springs which burst up here from underground, similar, no doubt, to those before alluded to which spring up in the sea. The Arabs will tell you that these springs come straight from the Euphrates, by an underground channel through which the great river flows beneath the Persian Gulf, doubtless being the same legend alluded to by Pliny when he says, 'Flumen per quod Euphratem emergere putant.' There are many of them—the Garsari well, Um-i-Shaun, Abu Zeidan, and the Adari, which last supplies many miles of date-groves through a canal of ancient workmanship. The Adari well is one of the great sights of Bahrein, being a deep basin of water 22 yards wide by 40 long, beautifully clear, and full of prismatic colours. It is said to come up with such force from underground that a diver is driven back, and all around it are ruins of ancient date, proving that it was prized by former inhabitants as a bath. The water is slightly brackish, as is that of all these sources, so that those who can afford it send for water to a well between Rufa'a Jebeli and Rufa'a Shergeh— called Haneini, which is exceedingly good, and camels laden with skins may be seen coming into Manamah every morning with this treasure. We obtained our water supply thence. The other well, Abu Zeidan, is situated in the midst of the ruins known as Beled-al-Kadim, or 'old town.'

Two days later our camp was struck, and our long cavalcade, with Seid-bin-Omar, the bazaar-master, at its head, returned to Manamah. He had ordered for us quite a sumptuous repast at his mansion by the sea, and having learnt our taste for curiosities, he brought us as presents a buckler of camel-skin, his 8-foot-long lance, and a lovely bowl of El Hasa work—that is to say, minute particles of silver inlaid in wonderful patterns in wood. This inlaying is quite a distinctive art of the district of Arabia along the north-eastern coast known as El Hasa; curious old guns, saddles, bowls, and coffee-pots, in fact everything with an artistic tendency, comes from that country.

The day following was the great Thursday's Market at Beled-al-Kadim, near the old minarets and the wells. Mounted once more on donkeys, we joined the train of peasants thither bound; I being as usual the object of much criticism, and greatly interfering with the business of the day. One male starer paid for his inquisitiveness, by tumbling over a stall of knick-knacks, and precipitating himself and all the contents to the ground.

The minarets and pillars of the old mosques looked down on a strange scene that day. In the half-ruined, domed houses of the departed race, stall-holders had pitched their stalls: lanes and cross lanes of closely-packed vendors of quaint crockery, newly-cut lucerne, onions, fish, and objects of European fabric such as only Orientals admire, and amongst all was a compact mass of struggling humanity; but it was easy to see that the date-palm and its produce formed the staple trade of the place. There were all shapes and sizes of baskets made of palm-leaves, dates in profusion, fuel of the dried spathes, the male spathes for fructifying the palm, and palm-leaf matting—the only furniture, and sometimes the only roofing of their comfortless huts.

The costumes were dazzling in their brilliancy and quaintness. It was a scene never to be forgotten, and one of which a photograph, which I took from a gentle eminence, gives but a faint idea. It was our last scene on Bahrein—a fitting conclusion to our sojourn thereon.

MASKAT

CHAPTER IV

SOME HISTORICAL FACTS ABOUT OMAN

On two separate occasions we visited Maskat. The first time was in 1889 on our way to Persia, and the second in 1895 when we were starting for Dhofar, on the journey which I shall describe later.

On each occasion we had to reach it by way of India, for like all the rest of the Persian Gulf Maskat is really an outlying portion of our Indian Empire. By just crossing a range of mountains in Persia you cross the metaphorical watershed between our India and Foreign Offices. At Shiraz you hesitate between India and England. You ask the question, 'Shall I send my letters *viâ* Bombay, or *viâ* Russia?' You hasten to get rid of your rupees, for this is the last place where their merit is recognised. North of Shiraz you are in a distinctly foreign country. Our officials hail from the Foreign Office and belong to the legation of Teheran. You are no longer under British protection, you are in the dominions of the Shah.

But so long as you are on the shores of the Gulf you are, so to speak, in India. The officials receive their pay in degenerate rupees instead of pounds sterling, they live in 'bungalows,' they talk of 'tiffin,' and eat curry at every meal.

We keep a British ship of war in the Gulf. We feel that it is a matter of the first importance that those countries should remain under our protection, and that the Turks should not build forts at Fao and otherwise interfere with our trade in the Karoun, and that no other power should have a foothold thereon. The last generation talked much about a Euphrates Valley Railway, with its terminus at Koweit; we now hear a great deal about the opening up of the Karoun, but it is the lordship of the Gulf which is the chief matter of importance just at present both for India and for ourselves.

In this district Maskat is the most important point; the kingdom of Oman, of which it is nominally the capital, commands the entrance to the Gulf. In the ninth century of the Christian era ships trading from Sherif to China took in water at Maskat from the wells which still supply the town. Between Aden and the Persian Gulf it is the only harbour where ships of any size can find anchorage, and it may, in fact, be said to play much the same part with respect to the Persian Gulf that Aden does to the Red Sea. In many other ways the places are strikingly similar. They are both constructed on arid, volcanic rocks, which produce the smallest amount of verdure and reflect the greatest amount of heat; water in both of them is the scarcest of commodities. Of all places in the world Maskat has the reputation of being the hottest, facing, as it does, the Indian Ocean, and protected from every cooling breeze by rugged volcanic hills, without a blade of cultivation upon them, and which reflect and intensify the scorching rays of the burning sun. Aden is said to have but a piece of brown paper between it and the infernal fires. Maskat would seem to want even this meagre protection, and 'gives,' as a Persian poet has expressed it, 'to the panting sinner a lively anticipation of his future destiny.'

The approach to the cove of Maskat is highly striking. Many-coloured volcanic rocks of fantastic form protect the horseshoe-shaped harbour, whilst behind the white town, as far as the eye can reach, stretch deeply serrated, arid mountains, which culminate in the heights of Jebel Akhdar, or the 'Green Mountains,' some fifty miles, as the crow flies, inland, reaching an elevation of 9,000 feet. We were told that snow sometimes falls in the winter-time on Jebel Akhdar, and it rejoices in a certain amount of verdure, from which it derives its name. This range forms the backbone of Oman, and at its foot lie Nezweh and Rostok, the old capitals of the long line of imams of Oman, before Maskat was a place of so much importance as it is at present. The streams which come down from these mountains nowhere reach the sea, but are lost in the deserts, and, nevertheless, in some places they fertilise oases in the Omani desert, where the vegetation is most luxuriant and fever very rife. Grapes grow on the slopes of Jebel Akhdar, and the inhabitants, despite the strictures of Mohammed, both make and drink wine of them, and report says (how far it is true I know not) that the Portuguese exported thence the vines to which they gave the name of muscatel. The inhabitants of this wild range are chiefly Bedou and pastoral, and it is from this quarter that the troubles which beset the poor sultan, Feysul, generally emanate.

The harbour of Maskat is full of life. The deep blue sea is studded with tiny craft: canoes painted red, green, and white, steered by paddles, swarm around the steamer; fishermen paddling themselves about on a plank or two tied together, or swimming astride of a single one, hawk their wares from boat to boat. The oars of the larger boats are generally made with a flat circular piece of wood fastened on to a long pole, and are really more like paddles than oars. In the northern corner lie huddled together large dhows, which, during the north-east monsoons, make the journey to Zanzibar, returning at the change of the season. Most of these belong to Banyan merchants in Maskat, and are manned by Indian sailors. Close to them is the small steamer *Sultanieh*, which was presented by the Sultan of Zanzibar to his cousin Sultan Tourki of Maskat, now a perfectly useless craft, which cannot even venture outside the harbour by reason of the holes in its side. From its mast floats the red banner of Oman, the same flag that Arab boats at Aden fly. It was originally the banner of Yemen, to which place the Arabs who rule in Oman trace their origin; for early in our era, according to Arab tradition, Oman was colonised and taken possession of by descendants of the old Himyarites of Yemen.

The shore of the town is very unpleasant, reeking with smells, and at low tide lined with all the refuse and offal of the place. At high tide shoals of fish come in to feed on this refuse, and in their train follow immense flocks of seagulls, which make the edge of the water quite white as they fly along and dive after their prey. Here and there out of the sand peep the barrels of some rusty old cannon, ghostly relics of the Portuguese occupation.

In the middle of the beach is the sultan's palace, but it is immeasurably inferior to the new residency of the British political agent, which stands at the southern extremity of the town, just where it can get all the breeze that is to be had through a gap in the rocks opening to the south; here we were most hospitably entertained by Colonel Hayes Sadler on our second sojourn. Even in this favoured position the heat in summer is almost unendurable, making Maskat one of the least coveted posts that the Indian Government has at its disposal. The cliffs immediately round the town are of a shiny schist, almost impossible to walk upon, and reflect the rays of the sun with great intensity.

On either side of the town stand two old Portuguese forts kept up and manned by the sultan's soldiers; in them are still to be seen old rusty pieces of ordnance, one of which bears a Portuguese inscription with the date 1606, and the name and arms of Philip III. of Spain; also the small Portuguese chapel in the fort is preserved and bears the date of 1588. These are the principal legacies left to posterity by those intrepid pioneers of civilisation in a spot which they occupied for nearly a century and a half. These forts testify to having been of great size and strength in former times, and show considerable architectural features, and the traces of a luxuriant and opulent population.

With regard to the ancient history of Oman, there is little known. The empire of the Himyarites, which filled Yemen and the Hadhramout valley with interesting remains, does not appear to have extended its sway so far eastward; no Sabæan remains have as yet been found in Oman, nor are there any that I have heard of further east than the frankincense country of Dhofar, over six hundred miles west of Maskat. Neither Ptolemy nor the author of the 'Periplus' gives us any definite information about the existence of a town in the harbour of Maskat, and consequently the first reliable information we have to go upon is from the early Arabian geographers.

From Torisi we learn that Sobar was the most ancient town of Oman; but that in his day Maskat was flourishing, and that 'in old times the China ships used to sail from there.'

Oman was included in Yemen by these earlier geographers, doubtless from the fact that Arabs from Yemen were its first colonisers; but all that is known with any certainty is that, from the ninth century a.d. a long line of imams ruled over Oman, with their capitals at Nezweh or Rostok, at the foot of Jebel Akhdar. This title, by which the Arab rulers were known, had been conferred on the Arab rulers of Oman for centuries, and signifies a sort of priest-king, like Melchisedek, to whom, curiously enough, is given the same title in the Koran. The election was always by popular acclamation, and inasmuch as the Omani do not recognise the two 'imams' who immediately succeeded Mohammed, but chose their own, they form a separate sect. In olden days the men of Oman were called 'outsiders' by their Mohammedan brethren, because they recognised their own chief solely as the head of their own religion, and are known otherwise as the Ibadiet or Ibadhuyah, followers of Abdullah-bin-Ibadh, as distinct from the Shiahi (Shiites) and Sunni, between which sects the rest of Islam is pretty equally divided. Internecine wars were always rife amongst them; but, at the same time, these early Omani had little or no intercourse with the outer world. Of the internal quarrels of the country, the Omani historian Salid-bin-Ragik has given a detailed account, but for the rest of the world they are of little interest. In those days Oman seems to have had two ports, Sur and Kalhat, on the Indian Ocean, which were more frequented than Maskat. Marco Polo, 1280 a.d., calls the second Calaiati in his 'Journal,' and describes it as 'a large city in a gulf called, also, Calatu,' and the Omani paid tribute to the melek or king of Hormuz for many generations, but with the rise of Maskat, Sur and Kalhat declined.

Oman first came into immediate contact with Europeans in the year 1506, when Albuquerque appeared in Maskat harbour bent on his conquest of the Persian Gulf, and with the object, not even yet accomplished, of making a route to India by way of the Euphrates valley. From Albuquerque's 'Commentaries' we get a graphic description of the condition of the country when he reached it.

At first the Arabs were inclined to receive the Portuguese without a struggle; but, taking courage from the presence of a large army of Bedouin in the vicinity, they soon showed treacherous intentions towards the invaders, so that the Portuguese admiral determined to attack the town and destroy it, and the commentator states that 'within were burned many provisions, thirty-four ships in all, large and small, many fishing barks, and an arsenal full of every requisite for ship-building.'

After effecting a landing, the Portuguese ordered 'three gunners with axes to cut the supports of the mosque, which was a large and very beautiful edifice, the greater part being built of timber finely carved, and the upper part of stucco,' and it was accounted a propitious miracle by the Portuguese that the men who performed this deed were not killed by the falling timber. Maskat was then burnt and utterly destroyed; and 'having cut off the ears and noses of the prisoners he liberated them.' The commentator concludes his remarks on Maskat as follows: 'Maskat is of old a market for carriage of horses and dates; it is a very elegant town, with very fine houses. It is the principal *entrepôt* of the kingdom of Ormuz, into which all the ships that navigate these parts must of necessity enter.'

The hundred and forty years during which the Portuguese occupied Maskat and the adjacent coast town was a period of perpetual trouble and insurrection. The factory and forts of Jellali and Merani were commenced in 1527, but the forts in their present condition were not erected till after the union of Portugal and Spain, in 1580; the order for their erection came from Madrid, and the inscription bears the date 1588. Not only were the Arabs constantly on the look-out to dislodge their unwelcome visitors, but the Turks attacked them likewise, with a navy from the side of the Persian Gulf, and the naval victory gained by the Portuguese off Maskat in 1554 is considered by Turkish historians to have been a greater blow to their power than the better known battle off Prevesa in 1538, when D'Oria defeated Barbarossa and obliged Solyman to relinquish his attempt on Vienna.

When, after the union of Portugal with Spain, the colonial activity of the former country declined, the colonies in the Persian Gulf fell one by one into the hand of the Persians and Arabs.

Out of the kingdom of Oman they were driven in 1620, and confined to the town of Maskat by the victorious imam, Nasir-bin-Murshid, during whose reign of twenty-six years the legend is told that no man in Oman died a natural death. Two years later they were also driven from Maskat itself, and those two forts Jellali and Merani which they had built, the last foothold of the Portuguese on the Omani territory, were taken from them.

The historian Salil tells the amusing story of the final fall of Maskat into the hands of the Arabs. The Portuguese governor, Pereira, was deeply enamoured of the daughter of a Banyan merchant of Maskat; the man at first refused to let him have his daughter, but at length consented, on condition that the wedding did not take place for some months. Pereira was now entirely in the hands of the Banyan and did everything he told him; so the crafty Indian communicated with the Arabs outside Portuguese territory, telling them to be ready when due notice was given to attack the town. He then proceeded to persuade Pereira to clean out the water tanks of the fort, and to clear out the old supplies of food preparatory to revictualling them; then, when the forts were without food and water, and finally having damped all the powder, he gave notice to the Arabs, who attacked and took the town on a Sunday evening, when the Portuguese were carousing.

Captain Hamilton gives another account in his travels,[5] and tells us that the Arabs were exasperated by a piece of pork, wrapped up in paper, being sent as a present to the imam by the governor, Pereira, and he also adds that the Portuguese were all put to the sword, save eighteen, who embraced Mohammedanism; and that the Portuguese cathedral was made the imam's palace, where he took up his residence for a month or two every year.

Since those days these two forts have been regularly used by rival claimants to the sovereignty of Oman as convenient points of vantage from which to pepper one another, to the infinite discomfiture of the inhabitants beneath.

The departure of the Portuguese did not greatly benefit the Omani. Writing in 1624 to the East India Company, Thomas Kerridge speaks of Maskat as 'a beggarly, poor town,' and 'Ormusz,' he says, 'is become a heap of ruins.' At last, in 1737, owing to the jealousies of the rival imams, Seid and Ibn Murshad, Maskat was taken by the Persians. They were, however, soon driven out again by Ahmed-bin-Sayid, or Saoud, a man of humble origin but a successful general; as a reward for his services he was elected imam in 1741, and was the founder of the dynasty which still rules there.

The successors of Ahmed-bin-Sayid found the obligations of being imam, and the oath which it entailed to fight against the infidel, both awkward and irksome, so his grandson, Saoud, who succeeded in 1779, never assumed the title of imam, but was content with that of sultan, and consequently the imamate of Oman has, with one short exception, been in abeyance ever since.

Under the first rulers of this dynasty Oman became a state of considerable importance. During the reigns of Sultan Saoud and his son Sultan Saoud Sayid, a large part of the Arabian mainland was under the rule of Oman, as also Bahrein, Hormuz, Larij, Kishm, Bandar Abbas, many islands and their pearl fisheries, and Linga, also a good part of the coast of Africa; and it was they who established the alliances with England and the United States.

The first political relations between the East India Company and the ruler of Oman took place in 1798, the object being to secure the alliance of Oman against the Dutch and French. A second treaty was made two years later, and it was provided in it that 'an English gentleman of respectability on the part of the Honourable East India Company, should always reside at the port of Maskat.'

An English gentleman of respectability has consequently resided there ever since, and from the days of Sultan Sayid has become the chief factor in the government of the place.

Sultan Sayid-bin-Sayid stands out prominently as the great ruler of Oman, and under his rule Oman and its capital, Maskat, reached the greatest pitch of eminence to be found in all its annals. He ascended the throne in 1804, and reigned for fifty-two years.

He found his country in dire distress at the time of his accession, owing to the attacks of the fanatical Wahabi from Central Arabia, who had carried their victorious arms right down to Maskat, and had imposed their bigoted rules and religious regulations on the otherwise liberal-minded Mohammedans of Eastern Arabia. With Turkish aid on the one hand, and British support on the other, Sultan Sayid succeeded in relieving his country from these terrible scourges, and drove them back into the central province of Nejd, from which they had carried their bloodthirsty and fanatical wars over nearly the whole of the peninsula, and, when all fear from the Wahabi was over, Sultan Sayid extended his conquests in all directions. He occupied several points on the Persian Gulf and the opposite coast of Beluchistan, and materially assisted the Indian Government in putting down the piracy which had for long closed the Gulf to all trade; and finally, in 1856, he added the important Arab settlement of Mombasa and Zanzibar, on the African coast, to his dominion.

During this long reign Maskat prospered exceedingly. It was the great trade centre for the Persian Gulf, inasmuch as it was a safe depôt, where merchants could deposit their goods without fear of piracy; vessels going to and from India before the introduction of steam used frequently to stop at Maskat for water. As a trade centre in those days it was almost as important as Aden, and with the Indian Government Sultan Sayid was always on most friendly terms.

When Sultan Sayid died, the usual dispute took place between his successors. England promptly stepped in to settle this dispute, and, with the foresight she so admirably displays on such occasions, she advocated a division of Sayid's empire. Zanzibar was given to one claimant, Oman to the other, and for the future Oman and Sultan Tourki remained under British protection.

Since the death of Sultan Sayid the power of Oman has most lamentably gone down, partly owing to the very success of his attempts to put down piracy; this, followed by the introduction of steam, has diminished the importance of Maskat as a safe port for the merchants to deposit their wares. It is also partly due to the jealousies which prevail between the descendants of Sayid who rule in Zanzibar and in Maskat. Palgrave in 1863 describes Maskat as having 40,000 inhabitants; there are probably half that number now.

The Sultan of Zanzibar has to pay an annual tribute of 40,000 crowns to his relative of Maskat in order to equalise the inheritance, and this tribute being a constant source of trouble, of late years he has taken to urging the wild Bedouin tribes in Oman to revolt against the present, rather weak-minded sultan who reigns there. He supplies them with the sinews of war, namely money and ammunition, and the insurrection which occurred in February 1895 was chiefly due to this motive power.

One of his sisters married a German, the English conniving at her escape from Zanzibar in a gunboat. On her husband's death, her elder brother having in the meantime also died, she returned to Zanzibar thinking her next brother, the present sultan, to be of a milder disposition, but he refused to take any notice of her and her children.

The present ruler of Maskat, Sultan Feysul, is a grandson of Sultan Sayid and son of Sultan Tourki by an Abyssinian mother. Since his accession, in 1889, he has been vacillating in his policy; he has practically had but little authority outside the walls of Maskat, and were it not for the support of the British Government and the proximity of a gunboat, he would long ago have ceased to rule. When we first saw him, in 1889, he was but a beardless boy, timid and shy, and now he has reached man's estate he still retains the nervous manner of his youth. He lives in perpetual dread of his elder brother Mahmoud, who, being the son of a negress, was not considered a suitable person to inherit the throne. The two brothers, though living in adjacent houses, never meet without their own escorts to protect them from each other.

The way in which Feysul obtained possession of the Sultan's palace on his father's death, to the exclusion of his brother, is curious.

Feysul said his grief for his father was so great that his feelings would not admit of his attending the funeral, so he stayed at home while Mahmoud went, who on his return found the door locked in his face.

The palace is entered by a formidable-looking door, decorated with large spiked bosses of brass. This opens into a small court which contained at the time of our first visit the most imposing sight of the place, namely the lion in his cage to the left, into which Feysul was in the habit of introducing criminals of the deepest dye, to be devoured by this lordly executioner. Opposite to this cage of death is another, a low probationary cage, which, when we were there, contained a prisoner stretched out at full length, for the cage is too low to admit of a sitting posture. From this point he could view the horrors of the lion's cage, so that during his incarceration he might contemplate what might happen to him if he continued, on liberation, to pursue his evil ways. Another door leads into a vaulted passage full of guards, through which we passed and entered into an inner court with a pool in the centre and a wide cloister around it supporting a gallery.

Sultan Feysul was then a very young man, not much over twenty. He was greatly interested in seeing us, for we were the first English travellers who had visited him since his accession. We caught sight of him peeping at us over the balcony as we passed through the courtyard below, and we had to clamber up a ladder to the gallery, where we found him ready to welcome us. He seized our hands and shook them warmly, and then led us with much effusiveness to his *khawah*, a long room just overhanging the sea, which is his reception and throne-room. Here were high, cane-bottomed chairs around the walls, and at one end a red chair, which is the throne; just over it were hung two grotesque pictures of our Queen and the Prince Consort, such as one could buy for a penny at a fair. They are looked upon as objects of great value here, and act as befitting symbols of our protectorate.

The imam fed us with sweets and coffee, asked us innumerable questions, and seemed full of boyish fun. Certainly with his turban of blue and red checked cotton (which would have been a housemaid's duster at home), his faded, greenish yellow cloak, fastened round his slender frame by a red girdle, he looked anything but a king. As we were preparing to depart the young monarch grew apparently very uneasy, and impatiently shouted something to his attendants, and when the servant came in, Feysul hurried to him, seized four little gilt bottles of attar of roses, thrust two of them into each of our pockets, and with some compliments as to our Queen having eyes everywhere, and Feysul's certainty that she would look after him, the audience was at an end.

Sultan Feysul was a complete autocrat as far as his jurisdiction extended. At his command a criminal could be executed either in the lion's cage or in a little square by the sea, and his body cut up and thrown into the waves. The only check upon him was the British Resident. His father, Tourki, not long before sewed up a woman in a sack and drowned her, whereupon a polite message came from the Residency requesting him not to do such things again. Hence young Feysul dared not be very cruel—to offend the English would have been to lose his position.

His half brother, Mahmoud, whose mother was a Swahili, lives next door to his brother, Sultan Feysul, in the enjoyment of a pension of 600 dollars a mouth. The uncles, however, are not so amenable. The eldest of them, according to Arabian custom, claimed the throne and had collected an army amongst the Bedouin to assert his claims, and was then in possession of all the country, with the exception of Maskat and El Matra, for Feysul had no money, and hence he could not get his soldiers to fight. But then it had been intimated to Feysul that in all probability the English would support his claims if he conducted himself prudently and wisely. So there was every likelihood that in due course he would be thoroughly established in the dominions of his father.

When we visited the town for the second time an even more serious rebellion was impending, the Bedouin of the interior, under Sheikh

Saleh, having attacked Maskat itself. The sultan and his brother, who hastily became friends, retired together to the castle, and the town was given up to plunder. There were dead bodies lying on the beach, and but for the kindness of Colonel Hayes Sadler, the British Resident, there would have been difficulties in the fort as regards water. They relied principally on H.M.S. *Sphinx*, which lay in the harbour to protect British interests, and to maintain Sultan Feysul in his position.

This state of terror lasted three weeks, when the rebels, having looted the bazaars and wrecked the town, were eventually persuaded to retire, free and unpunished, with a considerable cash payment; probably intending to return for more when the cooler weather should come, and the date harvest be over. With the consent of, and at the request of, the Indian Government, Sultan Feysul has imposed additional heavy duty on all the produce coming in from the rebel tribes, that he may have a fund from which to pay indemnities to foreigners who suffered loss during the invasion. A good many Banyan merchants, British subjects, suffered losses, and their claim alone amounted to 120,000 rupees. As a natural result of this disaster and its ignominious termination, Sultan Feysul's authority at the present moment is absolutely *nil* outside the walls of Maskat and El Matra, and he is still in a state of declared war with all the Bedouin chiefs in the mountains behind Maskat.

A few British subjects were scared, but not killed, and as all was over in a few weeks no one thought much more about it except those more immediately interested, and few paused to think what an important part Maskat has played in the opening up of the Persian Gulf and the suppression of piracy, and what an important part it may yet play should the lordship of the Persian Gulf ever become a *casus belli*.

Although Maskat has been under Indian influence for most of this century, it has latterly gone down much in the world; the trade of the place has well-nigh departed, and with a weak sultan at the head of affairs, confidence will be long in returning. Unquestionably our own Political Agent may be said to be the ruler in Maskat, and his authority is generally backed up by the presence of a gunboat. There is also an American Consul there, who chiefly occupies himself in trade and steamer agencies, and in 1895 the French also sent a Consul to inquire into the question of the slave trade, which is undoubtedly the burning question in Arabia.

Whilst England has been doing all she can to put slavery down, it is complained that much is carried on under cover of the French flag, obtained by Arab dhows under false pretexts from the French Consul resident in Zanzibar. Sultan Feysul remonstrated with France on this point, and the appointment of a Consul is the result.

The great reason for our unpopularity in Arabia is due without doubt to our suppression of this trade. Slavery is inherent in the Arab; he does as little work as he can himself, and if he is to have no slaves nothing will be done, and he must die. In other parts of South Arabia—Yemen, the Hadhramout, the Mahra country, and Dhofar— slavery is universal; and there is no doubt about it the slaves are treated very well and live happy lives; but here in Oman, under the very eye of India, slavery must be checked. Our gunboat, the *Sphinx*, goes the round of the coast to prevent this traffic in human flesh, and frequently slaves swim out to the British steamer and obtain their liberty. This naturally makes us very unpopular in Sur, where the Jenefa tribe have their head-quarters, the most inveterate slave-traders of Southern Arabia. The natural result is that whenever they get a chance the Jenefa tribe loot any foreign vessel wrecked on their shores and murder the crew. In the summer of 1894, however, a boat was wrecked near Ghubet-el-Hashish, containing some creoles from the Seychelle Islands, after being driven for forty-five days out of their course by south-east monsoons, during which time three or four of them had died. The survivors were much exhausted, but the Bedouin treated them kindly, for a wonder, and brought them safely to Maskat. For doing this they were handsomely rewarded by the Indian Government, though they had kept possession of the boat and its contents; nevertheless, they had saved the lives of the crew, and this, being a step in the right direction, was thought worthy of reward.

The jealousies, however, of other tribes were so great that the rescuers could not return to their own country by the land route, but had to be sent to Sur by sea.

Feysul has had copper coins of his own struck, of the value of a quarter anna. On the obverse is a picture of Maskat and its forts, around which in English runs the legend, 'Sultan Feysul-bin-Tourki Sultan and Imam of Maskat and Oman,' and on the reverse is the Arab equivalent. He has also introduced an ice-factory, which, however, is now closed, and he wished to have his own stamps, principally with a view to making money out of them; but our agent represented to him that it was beneath the dignity of so great a sultan to make money in so mean a way, and the stamps have never appeared. Sultan Feysul had done much in the last few years, since our first visit, to modernise his palace. British influence has abolished many horrors and cruelties, and the lion having died has not been replaced.

For the Indian Government the question of Maskat is by no means pleasant, for, should any other Power choose to interfere and establish an influence there, it would materially affect the influence which we have established in the Persian Gulf.

[5] Pinkerton, vol. viii.

CHAPTER V

MASKAT AND THE OUTSKIRTS

I never saw a place so void of architectural features as the town of Maskat itself. The mosques have neither domes nor minarets—a sign of the rigid Wahabi influence which swept over Arabia. This sect refuse to have any feature about their buildings, or ritual which was not actually enjoined by Mohammed in his Koran. There are a few carved lintels and doorways, and the bazaars are quaintly pretty, but beyond this the only architectural features are Portuguese.

All traces of the Portuguese rule are fast disappearing, and each new revolution adds a little more to their destruction. Three walls of the huge old cathedral still stand, a window or two with lattice-work carving after the fashion of the country are still left, but the interior is now a stable for the sultan's horses, and the walls are rapidly crumbling away.

The interior of Maskat is particularly gloomy: the bazaars are narrow and dirty, and roofed over with palm matting; they offer but little of interest, and if you are fond of the Arabian sweetmeat called *halwa*, it is just as well not to watch it being made there, for niggers' feet are usually employed to stir it, and the knowledge of this is apt to spoil the flavour. Most of the town is now in ruins. Fifty years ago the population must have been nearly three times greater than it is now. There is also wanting in the town the feature which makes most Moslem towns picturesque, namely the minaret; the mosques of the Ibadhuyah sect being squalid and uninteresting. At first it is difficult to distinguish them from the courtyard of an ordinary house, but by degrees the eye gets trained to identify a mosque by the tiny substitute for a minaret attached to each, a sort of bell-shaped cone about four feet high, which is placed above the corner of the enclosing wall. I have already mentioned the Ibadhuyah's views with regard to the imams. I believe they hold also certain heterodox opinions with regard to predestination and free will, which detach them from other Moslem communities; at any rate they are far more tolerant than other Arabian followers of the Prophet, and permit strangers to enter their mosques at will. Tobacco is freely used by them, and amongst the upper classes scepticism is rife. The devout followers of Mohammed look upon them much as Roman Catholics look on Protestants, and their position is similar in many respects.

As elsewhere in Arabia, coffee is largely consumed in Oman, and no business is ever transacted without it; it is always served in large, copper coffee-pots, of the quaint shape which they use in Bahrein. Some of these coffee-pots are very large. An important sheikh, or the mollah of a mosque, whose guests are many, will have coffee-pots two or three feet in height, whereas those for private use are quite tiny, but the bird-like form of the pot is always scrupulously preserved.

The bazaars of Oman do not offer much to the curio-hunter. He may perchance find a few of the curved Omani daggers with handsome sheaths adorned with filigree silver, to which is usually attached, by a leather thong, a thorn extractor, an earpick, and a spike. The belting, too, with which these daggers are attached to the body, is very pretty and quite a specialty of the place; formerly many gold daggers were manufactured at Maskat and sent to Zanzibar, but of late years the demand for these has considerably diminished.

The iron locks in the bazaars are very curious and old-fashioned, with huge iron keys which push out the wards, and are made like the teeth of a comb. These locks are exceedingly cumbersome, and seem to me to be a development of the wooden locks with wooden wards found in the interior of Arabia. Some of them are over a foot long. I have seen a householder after trying to hammer the key in with a stone, at last in despair climb over his own garden wall.

Perchance a shark-skin or wooden buckler may be picked up from a Bedou from the mountains, and there are chances of obtaining the products of many nationalities, for Maskat, like Aden, is one of the most cosmopolitan cities of the East. Here, as in El Matra, you find Banyans from India, Beluchi from the Mekran coast, negroes from

Zanzibar, Bedouin, Persians from the Gulf, and the town itself is even less Arab than Aden.

The ex-prime minister's house, which occupies a prominent position in the principal street, is somewhat more Oriental in character than most, and possesses a charmingly carved, projecting window, which gladdens the eye; and here and there in the intricacies of the town one comes across a carved door or a carved window, but they are now few and far between.

The suburbs of Maskat are especially interesting. As soon as you issue out of either of the two gates which are constructed in the wall, shutting the town off from the outer world, you plunge at once into a new and varied life.

Here is the fish and provision market, built of bamboos, picturesque, but reeking with horrible smells and alive with flies; hard by is a stagnant pool into which is cast all the offal and filth of this disgusting market. The water in the pool looks quite putrid, and when the wind comes from this quarter no wonder it is laden with fever germs and mephitic vapours. Consequently, Maskat is a most unhealthy place, especially when the atmosphere is damp and rain has fallen to stir up the refuse.

The women with their mask-veils called *buttra*, not unlike the masks worn with a domino, pleased us immensely, so that we sought to possess a specimen. They brought us several, which, however, did not quite satisfy us, and afterwards we learnt that an enterprising German firm had made a lot of these *buttra* for sale amongst the Maskat women; but the shape being not exactly orthodox, the women will not buy them, so the owners of these unsaleable articles are anxious to sell them cheap to any unsuspecting traveller who may be passing through.

Outside the walls the sultan is in the habit of distributing two meals a day to the indigent poor; and inasmuch as the Omani are by nature prone to laziness, there is but little doubt that his highness's liberality is greatly imposed on.

In the market outside the walls we lingered until nearly driven wild by the flies and the stench, so we were glad enough to escape and pursue our walk to the Paradise valley and see the favourable side of Maskat. There the sleepy noise of the wells, the shade of the acacias and palms, and the bright green of the lucerne fields, refreshed us, and we felt it hard to realise that we were in arid Arabia.

As you emerge you come across a series of villages built of reeds and palm branches, and inhabited by members of the numerous nationalities who come to Maskat in search of a livelihood. Most of these are Beluchi from the Mekran coast, and Africans from the neighbourhood of Zanzibar. The general appearance of these villages is highly picturesque, but squalid. Here and there palm-trees, almond-trees, and the ubiquitous camelthorn are seen interspersed amongst the houses; women in red and yellow garments, with turquoise rings in their ears and noses, peep at you furtively from behind their flimsy doors, and as you proceed up the valley you find several towers constructed to protect the gardens from Bedouin incursions, and a few comfortable little villas built by Banyan merchants, where they can retire from the heat and dust of Maskat.

The gardens are all cultivated, with irrigation, and look surprisingly green and delicious in contrast with the barren, arid rocks which surround them; the wells are dug deep in the centre of the valley, in the bed of what elsewhere would be a river, and are worked by a running slope and bullocks who draw up and down skin buckets, which, like those in Bahrein, empty themselves automatically into tanks connected with the channels which convey the water to the gardens.

After walking for a mile or two up this valley all traces of life and cultivation cease, and amidst the volcanic rocks and boulders hardly a trace of vegetable life is to be seen. It is a veritable valley of desolation, and there are many such in waterless Arabia.

By ascending paths to the right or to the left of the valley, the pedestrian may reach some exquisite points of view; all the little *cols* or passes through which these paths lead are protected at the summit by walls and forts—not strong enough, however, as recent events have shown, to keep off the incursions of the Bedouin. The views over Maskat and the sea are charming, but one view to the south will be for ever impressed on my mind as one of the most striking panoramas I have ever seen. When the summit of a little pass on the south side of the valley is reached after a walk of about two miles, you look down through a gateway over the small valley and fishing village of Sedad, amongst the reed houses of which are many palm-trees and a thick palm garden belonging to Sayid Yussuf, which gives the one thing wanting to views about Maskat, namely, a mass of green to relieve the eye. A deep inlet of the sea runs up here with its blue waters, and beyond stretch into illimitable space the fantastic peaks of the Oman mountains, taking every form and shape imaginable; these are all rich purples and blues, and the colouring of this view is superb.

From Sedad one can take a boat and row round the headlands back to Maskat. The promontories to the open sea are very fine: beetling cliffs of black, red, and green volcanic rocks, and here and there stand up rocky islets, the home of the cormorant and the bittern. In a small cove, called Sheikh Jabar, half-way between Sedad and Maskat, and accessible only by boat (for none but the most active of the natives can scale the overhanging rocks), is a tiny strand which has been chosen as the Christian burial-place. There are not very many graves in this weird spot, and most of them are occupied by men from the gunboats which have been stationed at Maskat. Among them is the grave of Bishop French, who came to Maskat some years ago with the object of doing missionary work amongst the Omani, but he fell a sacrifice to the pernicious climate before he had been long at his post, and before he had succeeded in making any converts.

About three miles from Maskat lies the town of El Matra, the commercial centre of the kingdom of Oman. It would be the seat of government also were it not exposed to the southern winds. The journey is nearly always made by sea; it takes much longer to go by land, for a ridge of hills has to be crossed. In a canoe it is only half an hour's paddle, and when the weather is favourable the canoe owners drive a rattling trade. The canoes, which they call *houris*, are hollowed out of a tree trunk, double-prowed, and with matting at the bottom. They are not very stable and make one think unpleasantly of sharks.

You pass the Fahl, or Stallion Rock, in the harbour, a name constantly given by Arabs to anything large and uncanny looking, and turning sharp round a rocky corner you see before you El Matra.

The town is governed by a *wali* chosen by the imam, and in the bazaars may be seen, in hopeless confusion, Banyans from India, Omani, Bedouin, Persians and Jews. These nationalities have each their separate wards for living in, walled off to keep them from perpetual brawls, and they only meet one another in the bazaars, where the eye of the bazaar-master is upon them, ready to inflict condign punishment on disturbers of the peace, in which cases the innocent more frequently suffer than the guilty.

The Monday's market is filled with quaint countryfolk, bringing in baskets of fruit and wearing the upper garment of red cotton and the large white girdle and turban.

At El Matra live most of the richest merchants, and it is the point from which all the caravan roads into the interior start; it, too, has a Portuguese castle, and presents a much more alluring frontage than Maskat. In a nice-looking house by the shore dwelt Dr. Jayakar, an Indian doctor, who had lived for twenty-five years at Maskat, combining the post of British Vice-Consul with that of medical adviser to the few Europeans who dwell there. He said he preferred Maskat to any other place in the world, and hoped to end his days there; he was a great naturalist, and his house was filled with curious animals from the interior, and marvels from the deep. He showed us specimens of a rabbit-like animal which the Arabs call 'whabba,' and which he affirmed is the coney of the Bible, and of the oryx, which lives up on the Jebel Akhdar; it has two straight horns which for one instant and from one point of view when it is running sideways look like one, and some say the fact gave rise to the mythical unicorn.

It is, to say the least of it, a great disadvantage to have your medical man at El Matra when you are ill at Maskat; if the weather is stormy boats cannot go between the two places. There is a troublesome road across the headland by which the doctor can come, partly by water and partly on foot, in case of dire necessity, but the caravan road, entirely by land, goes a long way inland, and would take the medical man all day to traverse. Behind El Matra are pleasant gardens, watered by irrigation, which produce most of the fruit and vegetables consumed in these parts.

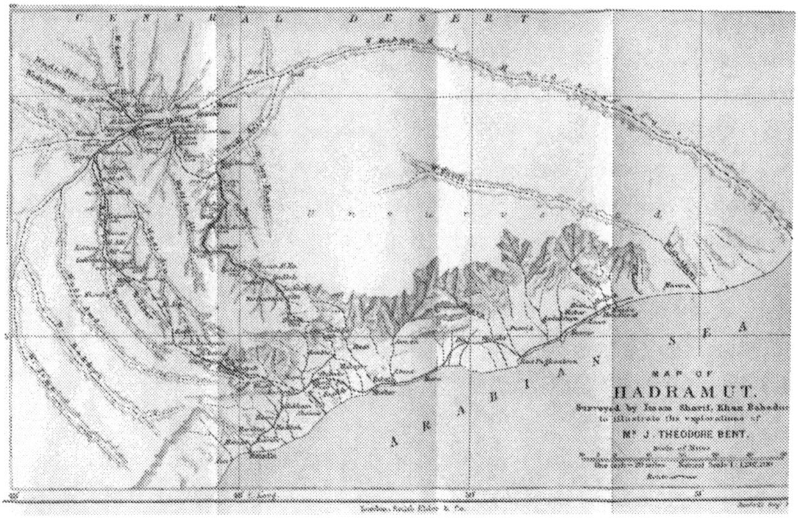

Map of Hadramut

Surveyed by Imam Sharif, Khan Bahadur.

to illustrate the explorations of

Mr. J. THEODORE BENT.

Stanford's Geog.l Estab.t, London

London: Smith, Elder & Co.

During our fortnight's stay at Maskat in 1895, we frequently in the evening coolness rowed about the harbour and examined its bays and promontories. The energetic crews of numerous gunboats of various nationalities stationed here at different times have beguiled their time by illuminating the bare cliffs with the names of their ships in large letters done in white paint. French, Russian, Italian, and German names are here to be read, but by far the largest number are in English. The rocks at the mouth of the harbour are literally covered with delicious oysters, and one of our entertainments was at low tide to land on these rocks and get our boatmen to detach as many of the shellfish as we could conveniently consume.

Such is Maskat as it exists to-day, a spot which has had a varied history in the past, and the future of which will be equally interesting to those who have any connection with the Persian Gulf.

THE HADHRAMOUT

CHAPTER VI

MAKALLA

After our journeys in South Africa and Abyssinia, it was suggested to my husband that a survey of the Hadhramout by an independent traveller would be useful to the Government; so in the winter of 1893-94 we determined to do our best to penetrate into this unknown district, which anciently was the centre of the frankincense and myrrh trade, one of the most famed commercial centres of 'Araby the Blest,' before Mohammedan fanaticism blighted all industries and closed the peninsula to the outer world.

In the proper acceptation of the term, the Hadhramout at the present time is not a district running along the south-east coast of Arabia between the sea and the central desert, as is generally supposed, but it is simply a broad valley running for 100 miles or more parallel to the coast, by which the valleys of the high Arabian table-land discharge their not abundant supply of water into the sea at Saihut, towards which place this valley gradually slopes.

There is every reason to believe that anciently, too, the Hadhramout meant only this valley; we learnt from Himyaritic inscriptions that five centuries b.c. the name was spelt by the Himyars as it is now (namely, t m r d h [Symbol: See page image]), and meant in that tongue 'the enclosure or valley of death,' a name which in Hebrew form corresponds exactly to that of Hazarmaveth of the tenth chapter of Genesis, and which the Greeks, in their usual slipshod manner—occasioned by their inability, as is the case still, to pronounce a pure *h*—converted into *Chatramitæ*, a form which still survives in the Italian word *catrame*, or 'pitch.'

Owing to the intense fanaticism of the inhabitants, this main valley has been reached only by one European before ourselves—namely, Herr Leo Hirsch, in 1893. In 1846 Von Wrede made a bold attempt to reach it, but only got as far as the collateral valley of Doan. My husband and I were the first to attempt (in the latter part of 1893 and the early part of 1894) this journey without any disguise, and with a considerable train of followers, and I think, for this very reason, that we went openly, we made more impression on the natives, and were able to remain there longer and see more, than might otherwise have been the case, and to establish relations with the inhabitants which, I hope, will hereafter lead to very satisfactory results.

Having arrived at Aden with letters of recommendation to the Resident from the Indian Government and the India Office, besides private introductions, we were amazed at all the difficulties thrown in our way. It quite appeared as if we had left our native land to do some evil deed to its detriment, and we were made to feel how thoroughly degrading it is to take up the vocation of an archæologist and explorer.

Many strange and unexpected things befell us, but the most remarkable of all was that when a certain surgeon-captain asked for leave to accompany us, it was refused to him on the ground that 'Mr. Theodore Bent's expedition was not sanctioned by Government,' in spite of the fact that the Indian Government had actually placed at my husband's disposal a surveyor, Imam Sharif, Khan Bahadur. We had no assistance beyond two very inferior letters to the sultans of Makalla and Sheher, which made them think we were 'people of the rank of merchants,' they afterwards said.

Imam Sharif has travelled much with Englishmen, so he speaks our language perfectly, and having a keen sense of humour, plenty of courage and tact, and no Mohammedan prejudices, we got on splendidly together. He was a very agreeable member of the party. My husband paid all his expenses from Quetta *via* Bombay, with three servants, including their tents and camp equipage, and back to Quetta.

Our party was rather a large one, for besides ourselves and our faithful Greek servant Matthaios, who has accompanied us in so many of our journeys, we had with us not only the Indians, but a young gardener from Kew, William Lunt by name, as botanist, and an Egyptian named Mahmoud Bayoumi, as naturalist, sent by Dr. Anderson, whose collections are now in the British Museum of Natural History at South Kensington.

The former was provided with all the requisites for digging up forest trees, and Mahmoud had with him all that was necessary for pickling and preserving large mammals, for no one knew what might be found in the unknown land; and many were the volunteers to join the party as hunters, who promised to keep us in game, whereas if they had come they would only have found reptiles.

As interpreter was recommended to us by the native political agent at Aden, Saleh Mohammed Jaffer, Khan Bahadur—a certain Saleh Hassan. He proved to be a fanatical Moslem, whose only object seemed to be to terrify us and to raise enemies against us, in order to prevent our trampling the holy land where Mohammed was born. Throughout our journey he was a constant source of difficulty and danger.

Our starting-point for the interior was Makalla, which is 230 miles from Aden, and is the only spot between Aden and Maskat which has any pretensions to the name of port. The name itself means 'harbour.' It is first mentioned by Ibn Modjawir; Hamdani calls it El Asa-Lasa, and Masudi gives the name as Lahsa. The harbour is not available during the south-west monsoon, and then all the boats go off to Ras Borum or the Basalt Head.

Here we were deposited in December 1893 by a chance steamer, one which had been chartered and on which for a consideration we were allowed to take passage. I took turns with the captain to sleep in his cabin, but there was nothing but the deck for the others.

Immediately behind the town rise grim, arid mountains of a reddish hue, and the town is plastered against this rich-tinged background. By the shore, like a lighthouse, stands the white minaret of the mosque, the walls and pinnacles of which are covered with dense masses of sea-birds and pigeons; the gate of this mosque, which is really nearly in the sea, is blocked up by tanks, so that no one can enter with unwashed feet. Not far from this rises the huge palace where the sultan dwells, reminding one of a whitewashed mill; white, red, and brown are the dominant colours of the town, and in the harbour the Arab dhows, with fantastic sterns, rock to and fro in the unsteady sea, forming altogether a picturesque and unusual scene.

Beyond the Bab Assab are huts where dwell the Bedouin who come from the mountains. They are not allowed to sleep within the town. There is a praying-place just outside the gate. In the middle of the town is a great cemetery full of tamarisks, and containing the sacred tomb of the sainted Wali Yakoub in the centre.

We were amused by a dance at a street corner to the beating of drums. It consisted of a hot, seething mass of brown bodies writhing about and apparently enjoying themselves.

Stone tobacco pipes are made here of a kind of limestone, very curly silver powder-flasks, rather like nautilus shells, and curious guns without stocks. The Bedou women wear tremendously heavy belts and very wide brass armlets. Their faces are veiled with something like the *yashmak* of Egypt, but it is of plain blue calico, a little embroidered.

Makalla is ruled over by a sultan of the Al Kaiti family, whose connection with India has made them very English in their sympathies, and his majesty's general appearance, with his velvet coat and jewelled daggers, is far more Indian than Arabian. Really the most influential people in the town are the money-grubbing Parsees from Bombay, and it is essentially one of those commercial centres where Hindustani is spoken nearly as much as Arabian. The government of the country is now almost entirely in the hands of the Al Kaiti family, which at present is the most powerful family in the district, and is reputed to be the richest in Arabia.

About five generations ago the Seyyids of the Aboubekr family, at that time the chief Arab family at the Hadhramout, who claimed descent from the first of the Khalifs, were at variance with the Bedou tribes, and in their extremity they invited assistance from the chiefs of the Yafei tribe, who inhabit the Yafei district, to the north-east of Aden. To this request the Al Kaiti family responded by sending assistance to the Seyyids of the Hadhramout, putting down the troublesome Bedou tribes, and establishing a fair amount of peace and prosperity in the country, though even to this day the Bedouin of the mountains are ever ready to swoop down and harass the more peaceful inhabitants of the towns. At the same time the Al Kaiti family established themselves in the Hadhramout, and for the last four generations have been steadily adding to the power thus acquired. Makalla, Sheher, Shibahm, Haura, Hagarein, all belong to them, and they are continually increasing, by purchase, the area of their influence in the collateral valleys, building substantial castles, and establishing one of the most powerful dynasties in this much-divided country. They get all their money from the Straits Settlements, for it has been the custom of the Hadhrami to leave their own sterile country to seek their fortunes abroad. The Nizam of Hyderabad has an Arab regiment composed entirely of Hadhrami, and the Sultan Nawasjung, the present head of the Al Kaiti family, is its general: he lives in India and governs his Arabian possessions by deputy. His son Ghalib ruled in Sheher, his nephew Manassar, who receives a dollar a day from England, ruled in Makalla, and his nephew Salàh ruled in Shibahm, and the governors of the other towns are mostly connections of this family. The power and wealth of this family are almost the only guarantee for peace and prosperity in an otherwise lawless country.

The white palace of the Sultan Manassar is six stories high, with little carved windows and a pretty sort of cornice of open-work bricks, unbaked of course, save by the sun. It stands on a little peninsula, and like Riviera towns, has pretty coast views on either side. The sultan received us with his two young sons, dressed up in as many fine clothes as it was possible to put on, and attended by his vizier, Abdul Kalek; no business was done as to our departure, but only compliments were paid on both sides. After we had separated presents were sent by us, loaves of sugar being an indispensable accompaniment.

The so-called palace in which we were lodged was next to the mosque and close to the bazaar; the smells and noise were almost unendurable, so we worked hard to get our preparations made, and to make our sojourn here as short as possible. This 'palace' was a large building; a very dirty staircase led to a quantity of rooms, large and small, inhabited in rather a confusing manner, not only by our own party, but by another, and to get at our servants we had to pick our way between the prostrate forms of an Arabian gentleman and his attendants. We were the first arrivals, so we collected from the various rooms as many bits of torn and rotten old matting as we could find, to keep the dust down in our own room, which was about 40 feet long by 30 feet wide, so very much covered with dust that no pavement could be seen without digging. It would have been necessary to have 'seven maids with seven brooms to sweep for half a year' before they could have cleared that room. Windows were all round, unglazed of course, and quite shutterless. We set out our furniture and had plenty of room to spread the baggage round us. An enormous packing case from Kew Gardens had little besides a great fork in it, so that case came no farther. Another case, to which the botanist had to resort constantly, had always to be tied up with rope, as it had neither lock nor hinges.

We were six days at Makalla arranging about camels and safe conduct, and wondering when we should get away; so of course we had plenty of time to inspect the town, which on account of the many Parsees had quite an Indian air in some parts. Sometimes one comes upon a deliciously scented part in the bazaars where myrrh and spices, attar of roses, and rose leaves are sold in little grimy holes almost too small to enter; but for the part near the fish market, I can only say that awful stenches prevail, and the part where dates and other fruits are sold is almost impassable from flies.

For our journey inland we were entrusted by the sultan to a tribe of Bedouin and their camels. Mokaik was the name of our Mokadam or head-man, and his tribe rejoiced in the name of Khailiki. They were tiny spare men, quite beardless, with very refined, gentle faces; they might easily have been taken for women, so gentle and pretty were they. They were naturally dark, and made darker still by dirt and indigo. Their long shaggy hair was twisted up into a knot and bound by a long plaited leather string like a bootlace, which was wound round the hair and then two or three times round the head, like the fillet worn by Greek women in ancient times. They were naked save for a loin-cloth and the girdle to which were attached their brass powder flasks, shaped like a ram's horn, their silver cases for flint and steel, their daggers, and their thorn extractors, consisting of a picker and tweezers, fastened together. They are very different from the stately Bedouin of Syria and Egypt, and are, both as to religion and physique, distinctly an aboriginal race of Southern Arabia, as different from the Arab as the Hindoo is from the Anglo-Saxon.

Our ideas as to *Bedouin* and *Bedawi*, which latter word we never heard while we were in Southern Arabia, were that they were tall, bearded men, not very dark in colour, and our imaginations connected them with hospitality and much clothes. None of these characteristics are found among the Bedouin of this district. *Bedouin* is not a word in use, but *Bedou* for both singular and plural. They speak of themselves as *el Bedou*, and when they have seen us wondering at some strange custom, they have said apologetically, 'Ah! Bedou, Bedou!' I have heard them address a man whose name they did not know 'Ya Bedou.' I mean to use *Bedou* for singular and *Bedouin* for plural.

Besides the Bedouin we were accompanied by five soldiers, Muofok-el-Briti, Taisir-i-Fahari, Bariki, and an old man. For the twenty-two camels we paid 175 dollars to Hagarein, a journey, we were told, of twenty days.

It would have been useless to have had riding camels, as one could get no faster than the baggage and soldiers, and travelling so far daily, and up such rocks, one had to go at foot-pace. We should have had to wait longer at Makalla while more camels were collected, and the more camels you have the farther they stray when food is scarce, and the more chance there is of the annoyance of waiting for lost camels to be found, and sometimes found too late to start that day. We need not have had twenty-two camels, and once, later, all the baggage was sent on ten, but this was to suit the purposes of the Bedouin.

Before proceeding further with our journey, I will here say a few words concerning the somewhat complex body politic of this portion of Arabia, the inhabitants of which may be divided into four distinct classes.

Firstly, there are numerous wild tribes of Bedouin scattered all over the country, who do all the carrying trade, rear and own most of the camels, and possess large tracts of country, chiefly on the highlands and smaller valleys. They are very numerous and powerful, and the Arabs of the towns are certainly afraid of them, for they can make travelling in the country very difficult, and even blockade the towns. They never live in tents, as do the Bedouin of Northern Arabia; the richer ones have quite large houses, whilst the poorer ones—those in Shabwa and the Wadi Adim, for instance—dwell in caves.

Secondly, we have the Arabs proper, a decidedly later importation into the country than the Bedouin. They live in and cultivate the lands around the towns; many of them carry on trade and go to India and the Straits Settlements, and some of them are very wealthy. They also are divided into tribes. The chief of those dwelling in the Hadhramout are the Yafei, Kattiri, Minhali, Amri, and Tamimi. The Bedouin reside amongst them, and they are constantly at war with one another, and the complex system of tribal union is exceedingly difficult to grasp.

Thirdly, we have the Seyyids and Sherifs, a sort of aristocratic hierarchy, who trace their descent from the daughter and son of the Prophet. Their influence in the Hadhramout is enormous, and they fan the religious superstition of the people, for to this they owe their existence. They boast that their pedigree is purer than that of any other Seyyid family, even than those of Mecca and Medina. Seyyids and Sherifs are to be found in all the large towns and considerable villages, and even the Arab sultans show them a marked respect and kiss their hands when they enter a room. They have a distinct jurisdiction of their own, and most disputed points of property, water rights, and so on, are referred to their decision. They look with peculiar distrust on the introduction of external influence into their sacred country, and are the obstructionists of the Hadhramout, but at the same time their influence is decidedly towards law and order in a lawless land. They never carry arms.

Lastly, we have the slave population of the Hadhramout, all of African origin, and the freed slaves who have married and settled in the country. Most of the tillers of the soil, personal servants, and the soldiers of the sultans are of this class.

CHAPTER VII

OUR DEPARTURE INTO THE INTERIOR

Never shall I forget the confusion of our start. Mokaik and ten of his men appeared at seven in the morning of the day before in our rooms, with all the lowest beggars of Makalla in their train, and were let loose on our seventy packages like so many demons from Jehannam, yelling and quarrelling with one another. First of all the luggage had to be divided into loads for twenty-two camels, then they drew lots for these loads with small sticks, then they drew lots for us riders, and finally we had a stormy bargain as to the price, which was finally decided upon when the vizier came to help us, and ratified by his exchanging daggers with Mokaik, each dagger being presented on a flat hand. In the bazaars bargains are struck by placing the first two fingers of one contractor on the hand of the other. All that day they were rushing in and weighing, and exhorting us to be ready betimes in the morning, so we were quite ready about sunrise.

We felt worn and weary when a start was made at two o'clock, and our cup of bitterness was full when we were deposited, bag and baggage, a few hundred yards from the gate, and told that we must spend the night amidst a sea of small fish drying on the shore, and surrounded on all sides by dirty Bedou huts. These fish, which are rather larger than sardines, are put out to dry by thousands along this coast. Men feed on them and so do the camels; they make lamp-oil out of them; they say the fish strengthens the camel's back, and they consider it good for camels to go once a year to the sea. Large sacks of them are taken into the interior as merchandise; they are mixed with small leaves like box, and carried in palm-leaf sacks, about 3 feet wide and 1½ feet high, and the air everywhere is redolent of their stench.

At this point we had the first of many quarrels with our camel-men; we insisted on being taken two miles farther on, away from the smells; nothing short of threats of returning and getting the sultan to beat them and put them in prison enabled us to break through the conventional Arab custom of encamping for the first night outside the city gates. However, we succeeded in reaching Bakhrein, where white wells are placed for the benefit of wayfarers, and there beneath the pleasant shade of the palm-trees we halted for the remainder of the day and recovered from the agonies of our start. Among the trees was a bungalow belonging to the sultan where we had hoped to have been able to sleep, but it was pervaded by such a strong smell of fish that we preferred to pitch our tents.

Between this place and Makalla all is arid waste, but near the town, by the help of irrigation, bananas and cocoanut trees flourish in a shallow valley called 'the Beginning of Light.' There are numerous fortresses about Bakhrein, so the road is now quite safe for the inhabitants of Makalla; the sultan has done a good deal to repress the Bedouin who used to raid right into the town. He crucified many of them.

We took a couple of hours over our start next day, the Bedouin again quarrelling over the luggage, each trying to scramble for the lightest packages and the lightest riders. They tried to make me ride a camel and give up my horse to my husband. As he was so tall, he could obtain neither a horse nor a donkey, so had perforce to ride a camel.

He had been able to buy a little dark donkey for Imam Sharif and the sultan gave me a horse, but all the rest were on camels. I thought I should enjoy riding by the camels and talking to everyone, but my hopes were not carried out.

The difficulty of passing the strings of camels was enormous. The country was so very stony that if you left the narrow path it took a long time to pick your way.

I used to start first with Imam Sharif, and then my horse, at foot-pace, got so far ahead that the soldiers said, 'We cannot guard both you and the camels.' I had then to pull in the horse with all my might. Sometimes I went on with Imam Sharif, one soldier and a servant carrying the plane-table. He used to go up some hill to survey, and I, of course, had to climb too for safety. I had to rush down when I saw our *kafila* coming and mount, to keep in front. If I got behind, the camels were so terrified that they danced about and shed their loads, and I was cursed and sworn at by their drivers.

We stopped three hours at Basra (10 miles), where there are a few houses, water, and some cultivation, and where the camels were suddenly unloaded without leave, and there was a great row because we moved the soldiers' guns from the tree, the shade of which we wished to have ourselves. We again threatened to return, but at last, as Taisir fortunately could speak Hindustani, he could make peace, and they ended by kissing hands and saying salaam (peace).

The sun was setting when we reached a sandy place called Tokhum (another 5 miles on), where we camped near some stagnant water. We had to wait for the moon, to find our baggage and get out the lantern. We had travelled over almost leafless plains save that they had little patches of mesembryanthemum, and the inevitable balloon-shrub (*madhar*). Rising and starting by moonlight on Christmas morning, we stopped in Wadi Ghafit (*madhar*), a very pretty side valley, with warm water and palm-trees, and what looked like a grassy sward near the water, but which really consisted of a tiny kind of palm. The camel-men wanted to pass this place and camp far away on the stones, sending skins for water, but somehow my husband found this out after we had passed Wadi Ghafit, and managed to carry off the camels, tied tail after tail to his own camel, so the Bedouin had to follow unwillingly. We gave them some presents, saying it was not an everyday occurrence, but that this was a great feast with us; so we made friends.

The Bedouin were very unruly about the packing. We could not get our most needful things kept handy, and they liked to pack our bread with their fish, and the waterskins anywhere among our bedding.

Mokaik did not seem to have much authority over the various owners of the camels, and they were always quarrelling among themselves, robbing each other of light loads and leaving some heavy thing, that no one wished for, lying on the ground; this often occasioned re-packing. They had for each camel a stout pair of sticks with strong ropes attached, and having bound a bundle of packages to each stick, two men lifted them and wound the ropes round the sticks over a very tiny pack-saddle and a mass of untidy rags. When we arrived they liked to simply loose the ropes from the sticks and let the baggage clatter to the ground and lead away the camels. As they would not be persuaded to sort the things, and as twenty-two camels cover a good deal of space, it was like seeking the slain on a battlefield when we had to wander about having every bundle untied.

Three days' camel-riding up one of the short valleys which lead towards the high table-land offered little of interest beyond arid, igneous rocks, and burnt-up, sand-covered valleys, with distorted strata on either side. Here and there, where warm volcanic streams rise out of the ground, the wilderness is converted into a luxuriant garden, in which palms, tobacco, and other green things grow. One of the scrub trees which clothe the wilderness is called by the Arabs *rack*, and is used by them for cleaning their teeth. It amused us to chew this as we went along: it is slightly bitter, but cleans the teeth most effectually.

There is also a poisonous sort of cucumber, called by the Arabs *madakdak*. They clean out the inside and fill the skin with water, which they drink as a medicine. At Sibeh, which we reached after a very hot ride of twelve or thirteen miles, we found water with scores of camels lying round it, for there were two or three other *kafilas*, or caravans, beside our own. It was dreadfully cold that night, and we could not get at our bag of blankets.

Next we entered the narrow, tortuous valley of Howeri, which ascends towards the highland, in which the midday heat was intense; and at our evening halts we suffered not a little from camel-ticks, which abound in the sand, until we learnt to avoid old camping-grounds and not to pitch our tents in the immediate vicinity of the wells.

We encamped in a narrow, stony river-bed, between walls of rock, near a little village called Tahiya. There is a good deal of cultivation about. The closeness of the situation made the smell of the dried fish we carried for the camels almost unbearable.

These sacks are stretched open in the evening and put in the middle of a circle of camels, their masters often joining in the feast. One of the men was attacked by fever, so he was given quinine, and his friends were told to put him to bed and cover him well. When we went to visit him later we found him quite contented in one of these fish sacks, his head in one corner and his legs all doubled up and packed in; only a bare brown back was exposed, so we had a few of the camel's rags thrown on his back, and he was well next day.

We went on ten miles to Al Ghail, rising to an altitude of 2,000 feet above the sea-level. This word *ghail* begins with the Arabic *ghin*, which is a soft sound between *r* and *g*.

There are two villages near the head of the Wadi Howeri, where there is actually a *ghail*—that rare phenomenon in Arabia, a rill or running stream. Here the Bedou inhabitants cultivate the date palm, and have green patches of lucerne and grain, very refreshing to the eye.

We had come up one of the narrowest of gorges, but with hundreds of palm-trees around Al Ghail, the first of the two villages, which is in the end of the Wadi Howeri. It is an uninteresting collection of stone huts, with many pretty little fields, and maidenhair fern overhanging the wayside. There are little enclosures with walls round them, and small stones in them, on which they dry the dates before sending them to Aden. The rocky river-bed itself is waterless, the *ghail* being used up in irrigation.

At Al Bat'ha, which is just above the tableland, we actually encamped under a spreading tree, a wild, unedible fig called *luthba* by the Arabs, a nickname given to all worthless, idle individuals in these parts. Bedou women crowded around us, closely veiled in indigo-dyed masks, with narrow slits for their eyes, carrying their babies with them in rude cradles resembling hencoops, with a cluster of charms hung from the top, which has the twofold advantage of amusing the baby and keeping off the evil eye. After much persuasion we induced one of the good ladies to sit for her photograph, or rather to sit still while something was being done which she did not in the least understand.

There is very good water at Al Bat'ha, and so much of the kind of herbs that camels like that we delayed our departure till eight, shivering by a fire and longing as ardently for the arrival of the sun as we should for his departure. The road had been so steep and stony that the camel-riders had all been on foot for two days. I am sure that, except near a spring, no one dropped from the skies would dream he was in Arabia the Happy. It is hard to think that 'the Stony' and 'the Desert' must be worse.

CHAPTER VIII

THE AKABA

Having left these villages behind us, we climbed rapidly higher and higher, until at an elevation of over 4,000 feet we found ourselves at last on a broad, level table-land, stretching as far as the eye could reach in every direction. This is no doubt the 'Maratha Mountains' of Ptolemy, the Mons Excelsus of Pliny,[6] which shuts off the Hadhramout, where once flourished the frankincense and the myrrh.

Words cannot express the desolate aspect of this vast table-land, Akaba or the 'going-up,' as the Arabs call it. It is perfectly level, and strewn with black lumps of basalt, looking as though a gigantic coal-scuttle had been upset. Occasionally there rises up above the plain a flat-topped mound or ridge, some 80 feet high, the last remnant of a higher level which is now disappearing. There is no sign of habitation. Only here and there are a few tanks, dug to collect the rain-water, if any falls. These are protected or indicated by a pair of walls built opposite one another, and banked up on the outer side with earth and stones, like shooting butts. The Akaba is exclusively Bedou property, and wherever a little herbage is to be found, there the nomads drive their flocks and young camels.

Of the frankincense which once flourished over all this vast area, we saw only one specimen on the highland itself, though it is still found in the more sheltered gullies; and farther east, in the Mahri country, there is, I understand, a considerable quantity left. We were often given lumps of gum arabic, and myrrh is still found plentifully; it is tapped for its odoriferous sap. It is a curious fact that the Somali come from Africa to collect it, going from tribe to tribe of the Bedouin, and buying the right to collect these two species, sometimes paying as much as fifty dollars. They go round and cut the trees, and after eight days return to collect the exuded sap.

In ancient times none but slaves collected frankincense and myrrh. This fact, taken probably with the meaning of the name Hadhramout (the later form of the ancient name Hazarmaveth), gave rise to the quaint Greek legend 'that the fumes of the frankincense-trees were deadly, and the place where they grew was called the valley or enclosure of death.'

From personal observation it would appear that the ancients held communication with the Hadhramout almost entirely by the land caravan-route, as there is absolutely no trace of great antiquity to be found along the coast-line, whereas the Wadi Hadhramout itself and its collateral branches are very rich in remains of the ancient Himyaritic civilisation.

Though we were always looking about for monuments of antiquity, the most ancient and lasting memorial of far past ages lay beneath our feet in that little narrow path winding over Akaba and Wadi, and polished by the soft feet of millions of camels that had slowly passed over it for thousands and thousands of years.

We found the air of the table-land fresh and invigorating after the excessive heat of the valleys below. For three days we travelled northwards across the plateau. Our first stage was Haibel Gabrein. This is, as it were, the culminating point of the whole district; it is 4,150 feet above the sea. From it the table-land slopes gently down to the northward towards the main valley of the Hadhramout, and eastwards towards the Wadi Adim. After two days more travelling we approached the heads of the many valleys which run into the Hadhramout; the Wadis Doan, Rakhi, Al Aisa, Al Ain, Bin Ali, and Adim all start from this elevated plateau and run nearly parallel. The curious feature of most of these valleys is the rapid descent into them; they look as if they had been taken out of the high plateau like slices out of a cake. They do not appear to have been formed by a fall of water from this plateau; in fact, it is impossible that a sufficient force of water could ever have existed on this flat surface to form this elaborate valley system. In the valleys themselves there is very little slope, for we found that, with the exception of the Wadi Adim, all the valley heads we visited were nearly of uniform height with the main valley, and had a wall of rock approaching 1,000 feet in height, eaten away as it were out of the plateau. We were, therefore, led to suppose that these valleys had originally been formed by the action of the sea, and that the Hadhramout had once been a large bay or arm of the sea, which, as the waters of the ocean receded, leaving successive marks of many strands on the limestone and sandstone rocks which enclosed them, formed an outlet for the scanty water-supply of the Southern Arabian highlands. These valleys have, in the course of ages, been silted up by sand to a considerable height, below which water is always found, and the only means of obtaining water in the Hadhramout for drinking purposes, as well as for cultivation, is by sinking wells. The water of the main valley is strongly impregnated with salt, but is much sweeter at the sides of the valley than in the centre. No doubt this is caused by the weight of the alkaline deposits washed down from the salt hills at Shabwa, at the head of the main valley.

The steep, reddish sandstone cliffs which form the walls of these valleys are themselves almost always divided into three distinct stories or stratifications, which can be distinctly seen on the photographs. The upper one is very abrupt, the second slightly projecting and more broken, and the third formed by deposit from above. The descent into the valley is extremely difficult at all points. Paths down which camels can just make their way have been constructed by the Bedouin, by making use of the stratified formation and the gentler slopes; but only in the case of the Wadi Adim, of all the valleys we visited, is there anything approaching a gradual descent.

It appears to me highly probable that the systematic destruction of the frankincense and myrrh trees through countless generations has done much to alter the character of this Akaba, and has contributed to the gradual silting up of the Hadhramout and its collateral valleys, to which fact I shall again have occasion to refer. The aspect of this plateau forcibly recalled to our minds that portion of Abyssinia which we visited in 1892-93; there is the same arid coast-line between the sea and the mountains, and the same rapid ascent to a similar absolutely level plateau, and the same draining northwards to a large river-bed in the case of Abyssinia, into the valleys of the Mareb and other tributaries of the Nile, and in the case of this Arabian plateau into the Hadhramout. Only Abyssinia has a more copious rainfall, which makes its plateau more productive.

It had not been our intention to visit the Wadi Al Aisa, but to approach the Hadhramout by another valley called Doan, parallel and further west, but our camel-men would not take us that way, and purposely got up a scare that the men of Khoreba at the head of Wadi Doan were going to attack us, and would refuse to let us pass. A convenient old woman was found who professed to bring this news, a dodge subsequently resorted to by another Bedou tribe which wanted to govern our progress.

The report brought to us, as from the old woman, was to this effect: A large body of sheikhs and seyyids having started from Khoreba[7] to meet and repel us, Mokaik's father had left home to help us. As we had now abandoned Khoreba, Mokaik said he was anxious to hurry off to meet his father and prevent a hostile collision. Mokaik was told *he* could not go as he was responsible for our safety, but that some others might go. 'No,' said Mokaik, 'they cannot be spared from the camels; we will get two men from the village.' My husband agreed to this, but when Mokaik proposed that my husband should at once pay these men, he told Mokaik that he must pay them himself, as he was paid to protect us. This attempt at extortion having failed, we passed a peaceful night and subsequently found Mokaik's father, Suleiman Bakran, safe at home, which he had never thought of leaving.

Our first peep down into the Wadi Al Aisa, towards which our Bedouin had conducted us, was striking in the extreme, and as we gazed down into the narrow valley, with its line of vegetation and its numerous villages, we felt as if we were on the edge of another world.

The descent from the table-land to the Wadi is exactly 1,500 feet by a difficult, but very skilfully engineered footpath. The sun's rays, reflected from the limestone cliffs, were scorchingly hot. The camels went a longer way round, nearer the head of the valley, but, so difficult was our short cut that they arrived before us, and the horse, and the donkey.

Having humbly descended into the Wadi Al Aisa, because we were not allowed to go by the Wadi Doan, we found ourselves encamped hard by the village of Khaila, the head-quarters of the Khailiki tribe, within a stone's throw of Mokaik's father's house and under the shadow of the castle of his uncle, the sheikh of the tribe. These worthies both extorted from us substantial sums of money and sold us food at exorbitant prices, and so we soon learnt why we were not permitted to go to Khoreba, and why the old woman and her story had been produced.

We thought Mokaik and his men little better than naked savages when on the plateau, but when we were introduced to their relatives, and when we saw their castles and their palm groves and their long line of gardens in the narrow valley, our preconceived notions of the wild homeless Bedou and his poverty underwent considerable change.

We climbed up the side of the valley opposite Khaila to photograph a castle adorned with horns, but were driven away; too late, for the picture had been taken.

During the two days we encamped at Khaila we were gazed upon uninterruptedly by a relentless crowd of men, women, and children. It amused us at first to see the women, here for the most part unmasked, with their exceedingly heavy girdles of brass, their anklets of brass half a foot deep, their bracelets of brass, their iron nose rings, and their massive and numerous earrings which tore down the lobe of the ear with their weight. Every Bedou, male or female, has a ring or charm of cornelian set in base silver, and agates and small tusks also set in silver.

The root with which the women paint themselves yellow is called *shubab*. It is dried and powdered. It only grows when there is rain. The whole of the poultry at Khaila was carried about in the arms of the women and children who owned them, all the time of our sojourn, in the hopes of selling them. They, at least, were glad of our departure.

Not far from Khaila, we saw a fine village which we were told was inhabited by Arabs of pure blood, so we sent a polite message to the seyyid, or head-man of the place, to ask if we might pay him our respects. His reply was to the effect that if we paid thirty dollars we might come and pass four hours in the town. Needless to say we declined the invitation with thanks, and on the morrow when we marched down the Wadi Al Aisa we gave the abode of this hospitable seyyid a wide berth, particularly as the soldiers told us it was not safe, for the Arabs meant to kill us.

Leaving Khaila, where we remained two nights and saw the New Year in, we passed a good many towered villages: Larsmeh was one, Hadouf another, also Subak and others. We passed the mouth of the Wadi Doan, which runs parallel to Wadi Al Aisa, and has two branches, only the largest having the name Doan. The mouth is about three miles below Khaila; five miles more brought us to Sief, where we halted for a night. It is also inhabited by pure Arabs, who treated us with excessive rudeness. It is a very picturesque spot, perched on a rock, with towers and turrets constructed of sun-dried brick; only here, as elsewhere in these valleys, the houses being so exactly the same colour as the rocks behind them, they lose their effect. The rich have evidently recognised this difficulty and whitewash their houses, but in the poorer villages there is no whitewash, and consequently nothing to make them stand out from their surroundings.

One can pretty well judge of the wealth of the owners of the various towers and castles by the amount of whitewash. Some have only the pinnacles white, and some can afford to trim up the windows and put bands round the building.

At Sief several men came once or twice and begged my husband to let me go out that the women might see me, but when I went out they would not allow me to approach or hold any intercourse with the Arab women, using opprobrious epithets when I tried to make friendly overtures, with the quaint result that whenever I advanced towards a group of gazing females they fled precipitately like a flock of sheep before a collie dog, so we discovered that it was the men themselves who wished to see me. These women wear their dresses high in front (showing their yellow-painted legs above the knee) and long behind; they are of deep blue cotton, decorated with fine embroidery, and patches of yellow and red sewn on in patterns. It is the universal female dress in the Hadhramout, and looks as if the fashion had not changed since the days when Hazarmaveth the Patriarch settled in this valley and gave it his name.[8] The tall tapering straw hat worn by these women when in the fields contributes with the mask to make the Hadhrami females as externally repulsive as the most jealous of husbands could desire.

I am pretty sure that this must be the very same dress which made such an unfavourable impression upon Sir John Maundeville, when he saw 'the foul women who live near Babylon the great.' He says: 'They are vilely arrayed. They go barefoot and clothed in evil garments, large and wide, but short to the knees, long sleeves down to the feet like a monk's frock, and their sleeves are hanging about their shoulders.'

The dress is certainly wide, for the two pieces of which it is composed, exactly like the Greek peplos, when the arms are extended, stretch from finger-tip to finger-tip, so when this dress is caught into the loose girdle far below the waist, it hangs out under the arms and gives a very round-backed look, as is the case with the peplos.

There are a great many Arabs at Sief, a most unhealthy, diseased-looking lot. They are of the yellow kind of Arab, with Jewish-looking faces.

Saleh retired into Sief on our arrival, and we saw him no more till we started next day. He was a very useless interpreter. He used to like to live in the villages, saying he could not bear to live in the camp of such unbelievers as we were, and used to bring his friends to our kitchen and show them some little tins of Lazenby's potted meat, adorned with a picture of a sheep, a cow, and a pig, as a proof that we lived on pork, whereas we had none with us. He always tried to persuade the people that he was far superior to any of us, and when places had to be made amongst the baggage on the camels for my husband and the servants to ride, he used to have his camel prepared and ride on, leaving some of the servants with no seat kept on the camels for them. My husband cured him of this, for one morning, seeing Saleh's bedding nicely arranged, he jumped on to the camel himself and rode off, leaving Saleh an object of great derision.

Once we got down into the valley we had to ride very close together for safety, and I found it most tiresome making my horse, Basha, keep pace with the camels.

The people at Sief were so disagreeable that I told Saleh to remind them that, if our Queen wanted their country, she would have had it long before we were born, and that they were very foolish to fear so small an unarmed party, who had only come to pass the winter in a country warmer than their own; at the same time, unless we had been quite confident that our safety was well secured from behind, such a party, with a woman among them, would never have come.

We set off early next morning for Hagarein. We passed after one hour Kaidoun, with its own private little valley to the west, a tributary of the main one, which in this part is called Wadi Kasr. There is the grave of a celebrated saint, and a very pious seyyid, called Al Habid Taha Ali al Hadad, abides near it. He never goes out of his house, but is so much revered that many thousands of dollars are sent him from India and other parts, and when his son visited Aden he was received with great honour by the merchants there. Then we passed several other villages, including Allahaddi and Namerr. It was at the *ziaret* or pilgrimage to the grave in Kaidoun that Herr von Wrede, who was disguised, was discovered to be a Christian and forced to turn back.

The town of Hagarein or Hajarein is the principal one in the collateral valleys, and is built on a lofty isolated rock in the middle of the Wadi Kasr, about twenty miles before it joins the main valley of the Hadhramout. With its towers and turrets it recalled to our minds as we saw it in the distance certain hill-set, mediæval villages of Germany and Italy. Here a vice-sultan governs on behalf of the Al Kaiti family, an ill-conditioned, extortionate individual, whose bad reception of us contributed to his subsequent removal from office. Internally Hagarein is squalid and dirty in the extreme; each street is but a cesspool for the houses on either side of it, and the house allotted to us produced specimens of most smells and most insects. The days of rest we proposed for ourselves here were spent in fighting with our old camel-men who left us here, in fighting with the new ones who were to take us on to the main valley, and in indignantly refusing to pay the sultan the sum of money which our presence in his town led him to think it his right to demand.

[6] Pliny, xii. 14, 52: 'In medio Arabiae fere sunt Adramitae pagus Saboraeum in monte excelso.'

[7] The town of Khoreba, in the Wadi Doan, may represent the town of Doan itself mentioned by Hamdani, the Θαβάνη of Ptolemy, which Pliny calls Toani. The name Khoreba signifies ruins.

[8] Gen. x. 26.

CHAPTER IX

THROUGH WADI KASR

When we reached the foot of the hill on which Hagarein stands we dismounted; there was tremendous work to get out the sword of the oldest soldier; he had used it so much as a walking-stick that it was firmly fixed in the scabbard. The scabbards are generally covered with white calico. A very steep, winding, slippery road led us to the gate, where soldiers received us and conducted us to a courtyard, letting off guns the while. There stood the Sultan Abdul M'Barrek Hamout al Kaiti, a very fat, evil-looking man, pitted by smallpox. After shaking hands he led us down the tortuous streets to his palace, and then took us up a narrow mud staircase, so dark that we did not know whether to turn to the right or left; we sometimes went one way and sometimes the other. At length we reached a small room with some goat-hair carpets and we and the sultan, the soldiers (his and ours), the Bedouin and my groom, M'barrek, all seated ourselves round the wall, and after a long time a dirty glass of water was handed round as our only entertainment. As we had had nothing to eat since sunrise, and it was about two o'clock, we did not feel cheerful when the sultan abruptly rose and said he must pray. Praying and sleeping are always the excuses when they want to get rid of guests or say 'not at home,' and indeed the sleeping excuse prevails in Greece also.

Some time after, our four chairs were brought, so we sat till near four o'clock homeless, and getting hungrier and hungrier, when the sultan reappeared, telling my husband all our things were locked up in a courtyard and giving him a great wooden key. We hastened to our home, up a long dark stair, past many floors, all used as stalls and stables, &c., only the two top floors being devoted to human habitation. Each floor consisted of one fair-sized room and one very tiny den, a kitchen. The whole Indian party had the lower room, and three of our soldiers the den. I cannot think how they could all lie down at once, and they had to cook there besides. Above that, we had the best room, the botanist and naturalist the den, and Matthaios made his abode on the roof, where he cooked. The Bedouin, having unloaded the camels in the courtyard across the street, refused to help us, and, as no one else could be got, my husband and all his merry men had to carry up the baggage, while I wrestled with the beds and other furniture in our earthy room. The instant the baggage was up the Bedouin clamoured for payment, and it was trying work opening the various packages where the bags of money were scattered, and to begin quarrelling when we were so weary and hungry. We had been told that our journey to Hagarein would take twenty days, whereas it only took thirteen, and that we must take two camels for water, which had proved unnecessary; besides the camels had been much loaded with fish and other goods belonging to the Bedouin. My husband said he would pay for the twenty days and they would thus have thirty dollars as *bakshish*. But, in the end, the soldiers from Makalla said we must pay *bakshish*: it would be an insult to their sultan if we did not and they would go no further with us. The local sultan also insisting, fourteen more dollars had to be produced. Our own soldiers soon came shouting and saying they must have half a rupee a day for food, which my husband thought it wise to give, though the *wazir* at Makalla had said he was to give nothing.

They were hardly gone when the sultan came back personally conducting two kids and saying we need think of no further expense; we were his guests and were to ask for what we wished. All my husband asked for was daily milk. We got some that day, but never again. My groom, M'barrek, then came, saying he must have food money; that being settled, he returned saying the sultan said he must have half a rupee a day for my horse, which became very thin on the starvation he got.

All this time we could get no water, so not till dark could Matthaios furnish us with tea, cold meat, bread, and honey.

We were fortunate in having plenty of bread. We had six big sacks of large cakes of plain bread dried hard, and of this we had learnt the value by experience. We kept it sheltered, if there was any fear of rain, as in Abyssinia, for instance, and before a meal soaked it in water, wrapped it in a napkin a few minutes, and then dried it up to the consistency of fresh bread. We were often obliged to give it to the horses, for the difficulty as to forage makes them unfit to travel in such barren places.

We also took charcoal and found that, with it and the bread, we had our meals long before the Indian party, who had a weary search for fuel before they could even begin with 'pat-a-cake, pat-a-cake, baker's man.' The making of *chupatties* also causes delay in starting. As to the honey it is most plentiful and tastes like orange flowers, but really it is the date-flower which imparts this flavour. It is much more glutinous than ours. It is packed, for exportation and to bring as tribute, in large round tin boxes, stopped up round the edges with mud. It is used in paying both taxes and tribute.

We were quite worn out with this day. The sultan received a present next morning of silk for a robe, a turban, some handkerchiefs, two watches, some knives, scissors, needle-cases, and other things, but he afterwards sent Saleh to say he did not like his present at all and wanted dollars. He got ten rupees and was satisfied.

We again visited him with our servants and soldiers and were given tea while we talked over the future, and all seemed fair. Later the sultan came to visit us and talk about the escort. He said we must take five soldiers, bargained for their wages, food, and bakshish, and obtained the money. My husband inquired about some ruins near Meshed, three hours by camel from Hagarein, and said that if the sultan would arrange that we should dig safely, he should have forty dollars, and he settled to go with my husband next day to see the place. Accordingly next day the sultan came with eight soldiers, singing and dancing all the way, and some men of the Nahad tribe as *siyara*, as we were then in their land.

The sultan showed us two letters in which it was said that we were to have been attacked between Sief and Kaidoun, and we remembered having seen a man on a camel apparently watching for us, but instead of coming forward he galloped away; and thus it appears we got past the place from which they meant to set upon us, before the attacking party could arrive.

During the days we were at Hagarein several weddings were celebrated. To form a suitable place for conviviality they cover over a yard with mats, just as the Abyssinians do, and the women, to show their hilarity on the occasion, utter the same gurgling noises as the Abyssinian women do on a like occasion, and which in Abyssinia is called *ulultà*. From our roof we watched the bridegroom's nocturnal procession to his bride's house, accompanied by his friends bearing torches, and singing and speechifying to their hearts' content.

On our return from the ruins near Meshed, Taisir (our soldier) came to us and was very indignant about the price the sultan charged for his soldiers. He was given ten rupees to attach himself to us, as an earnest of the good bakshish he would get at the coast, as he said all the other soldiers would go back from Shibahm, and really in that case I think he would have been glad of our escort.

Then Saleh, who had 100 rupees a month and ate with everyone, came to demand half a rupee a day for food; this was granted, as we thought it could come off his bakshish, and he soon appeared to make the same request for Mahmoud, the naturalist. Matthaios was furious, as Mahmoud ate partly with him, and no one was angrier with him than Saleh. It was settled that we should give him tea, bread, and four annas, and they all went off bawling. Afterwards we heard Saleh had said, 'Mr. Bent is giving so much money to the sultan, why should we not have some?'

We really thought at first that we should be able to encamp at Meshed and dig, for there was a seyyid who had been in Hyderabad and was very civil to us, but this happiness only lasted one hour. The sultan said it would really not be safe unless we lived in Hagarein, so we had to give it up as it was an impossibility to dig in the heat of the day, with six hours' journey to fatigue us; besides we must have paid many soldiers and we were told no one would dig for us. So much was said about the dangers of the onward road that Saleh was sent with the letters for Shibahm and Sheher and told to hold them tight, and say that if we could not deliver these in person we should return to the wali of Aden and say that the sultan of Hagarein would not let us go on. This frightened him, so he made a very dear bargain for fifteen camels, and we were to leave next day.

We were glad enough to depart from Hagarein, which is so picturesque that it really might be an old, mediæval, fortified town on the Rhine, built entirely of mud and with no water in its river. All the houses are enormously high, and have a kitchen and oven on each floor. The bricks of which they are built are about one foot square and with straw in them. They have shooting holes from every room and machicolations over the outer doors and along the battlements, and what makes the houses seem to contain even more stories than they do, is that each floor has two ranges of windows, one on the ground so that you can only see out if you sit on the floor, and another too high to see out of at all; below every lower window projects a long wooden spout. The narrow lanes are mere drains, and the whole place a hotbed of disease; the people looked very unhealthy: when cholera comes they die like flies. As a wind up to this last evening Mahmoud came into our room and soon began to say his prayers; we could not make out why, but it turned out he had no light in his room.

Altogether we had not a reposeful time in Hagarein. We were told early next day that fourteen men of the Nahad tribe had come as our *siyara*, though we had been told two would be sufficient; so we had to agree to take four. Then we were asked to pay those who had come unbidden. The sultan came himself about it, and his children came to beg for annas. At last the sultan, who had often said he felt as if he were our brother, obtained twelve rupees which he asked for to pay his expenses for the kids and honey, and said my horse had eaten the worth of twice as much money as he had asked before.

When we finally got off we found the old rascal had only sent half the Nahadi and had only sent two soldiers, and so had really made forty dollars out of us over that one item. The Nahad men had ten dollars each. They are not under the sultan of Makalla, but independent. The Nahad tribe occupy about ten miles of the valley through which we passed, and the toll-money we paid to this tribe for the privilege of passing by was the most exorbitant demanded from us on our journey. When once you have paid the toll-money (*siyar*), and have with you the escort (*siyara*) of the tribe in whose territory you are, you are practically safe wherever you may travel in Arabia, but this did not prevent us from being grossly insulted as we passed by certain Nahad villages. Kaidoun, where dwells the very holy man so celebrated all the country round for his miracles and good works, is the chief centre of this tribe. We had purposely avoided passing too near this town, and afterwards learnt that it was owing to the influence of this very holy seyyid that our reception was so bad amongst the Nahad tribe.

All about Hagarein are many traces of the olden days when the frankincense trade flourished, and when the town of Doan, which name is still retained in the Wadi Doan, was a great emporium for this trade. Acres and acres of ruins, dating from the centuries immediately before our era, lie stretched along the valley here, just showing their heads above the weight of superincumbent sand which has invaded and overwhelmed the past glories of this district. The ruins of certain lofty square buildings stand upon hillocks at isolated intervals; from these we got several inscriptions, which prove that they were the high 'platforms' alluded to on so many Himyaritic inscribed stones as raised in honour of their dead. As for the town around them, it has been entirely engulfed in sand; the then dry bed of a torrent runs through the centre, and from this fact we can ascertain, from the walls of sand on either side of the stream, that the town itself has been buried some 30 feet or 40 feet by this sand. It is now called Raidoun. The ground lies strewn with fragments of Himyaritic inscriptions, pottery, and other indications of a rich harvest for the excavator, but the hostility of the Nahad tribe prevented us from paying these ruins more than a cursory visit, and even to secure this we had to pay the sheikh of the place nineteen dollars, and his greeting was ominous as he angrily muttered, 'Salaam to all who believe Mohammed is the true prophet.'

We were warned 'that our eyes should never be let to see Meshed again;' we might camp before we got there, or after, as we wished, so were led by a roundabout way to Adab, and saw no more of the leprous seyyid who told such wondrous tales about the English king who once lived in Hagarein, and how the English, Turks, and Arabs were all descended from King Sam. Also he told the Addite fable of how the giants and rich men tried to make a paradise of their own, the beautiful garden of Irem, and defied God, and so destruction came upon the tribe of Ad, the remnant of whom survive at Aden on Jebel Shemshan, in the form of monkeys. This is the Mohammedan legend of the end of the Sabæan Empire.

We were much amused with what Imam Sharif said to this seyyid. Imam Sharif is himself a seyyid or sherif, a descendant of Mohammed, his family having come from Medina, so he was always much respected. He said to him: 'You think these English are very bad people, but the Koran says that all people are like their rulers; now we have no spots or diseases on our bodies, but are all clean and sound, which shows plainly that our ruler and the rest of us must be the same. Now you, my brother, must be under the displeasure of God, for I see that you are covered with leprosy.' This was not a kind or civil speech, I fear, but not a ruder one than those addressed to us. This leprosy shows itself by an appearance as if patches of white skin were neatly set into the dark skin.

At Adab they would not allow us to dip our vessels in their well, nor take our repast under the shadow of their mosque: even the women of this village ventured to insult us, peeping into our tent at night, and tumbling over the jugs in a manner most aggravating to the weary occupants. The soldiers had abandoned us and gone to sleep in the village.

A dreary waste of sand led past Kerren to Badorah. I arrived first with Imam Sharif, a servant, and a soldier. We dismounted, as there was some surveying to be done. The people were quite friendly, we thought, though they crowded round me shouting to see the 'woman.' I went to some women grouped at a little distance, and we had no trouble as long as we were there. We had left before the camels came and heard that the rest of the party had been very badly received, stones were thrown, and shouts raised of 'Pigs! Infidels!

Dogs! Come down from your camels and we will cut your throats.' We attributed this to Saleh Hassan, for he made enemies for us wherever we went. At this village they were busy making indigo dye in large jars like those of the forty thieves. We were soon out of the Nahad country.

Our troubles on the score of rudeness were happily terminated at Haura, where a huge castle, belonging to the Al Kaiti family, dominates a humble village, surrounded by palm groves. Without photographs to bear out my statement, I should hardly dare to describe the magnificence of these castles in the Hadhramout. That at Haura is seven stories high, and covers fully an acre of ground beneath the beetling cliff, with battlements, towers, and machicolations bearing a striking likeness to Holyrood; but Holyrood is built of stone, and Haura, save for the first story, is built of sun-dried bricks, and if Haura stood where Holyrood does, or in a rainy climate, it would long ago have crumbled away.

Haura is supposed to be the site of an ancient Himyaritic town. We were told that the sultan of Hagarein is not entirely under Makalla, but that he of Haura is.

The castle of the sultan is nice and clean inside, and it was pleasant, after some very reviving cups of coffee and ginger, and some very public conversation, to find our canvas homes all erected on a hard field—a pleasant change from our late dusty places. Mahmoud obtained a fox, which was his first mammal, saving a bushy-tailed rat. We were sent a lamb and a box of honey, and soon after the governor arrived to request a present. He asked thirty rupees but got twenty, and the new soldiers in place of the Nahadi men were to have five rupees on arrival at Koton. We were now nearing the palace of Sultan Salàh-bin-Mohammad al Kaiti of Shibahm, the most powerful monarch in the Hadhramout, who has spent twelve years of his life in India, and whose reception of us was going to be magnificent, our escort told us.

As we were leaving Haura, just standing about waiting to mount, I felt something hard in one finger of my glove which I was putting on. I thought it was a dry leaf and hooked it down with my nail and shook it into my hand. Imagine my terror on lifting my glove at seeing a scorpion wriggling there. I dropped it quickly, shouting for Mahmoud and the collecting-bottle, and then caught it in a handkerchief. This was the way that *Buthia Bentii* introduced himself to the scientific world, for he was of a new species. It turned out that the 'oldest soldier' was father to the sultan of Haura. He went no farther with us.

The next day, three miles after leaving Haura, we quitted the Wadi Kasr and at last, at the village of Alimani, entered the main valley of the Hadhramout. It is here very broad, being at least eight miles from cliff to cliff, and receives collateral valleys from all sides, forming, as it were, a great basin. Hitherto our way had been generally northward, from Makalla to Tokhum, north-east, and then north-west; now we turned westward down the great valley, though still with a slight northward tendency.

We passed Ghanima, Ajlania on a rock to the right, and Henan and the Wadi Menwab behind it on our left. Wellsted, in his list of the Hadhramout towns, mentions Henan as Ainan, and as a very ancient town, on the hill near which are inscriptions and rude sculptures.

For seven hours we travelled along the valley, which from its width was like a plain till we were within a mile of the castle of Al Koton, where the sultan of Shibahm resides. Thus far all was desert and sand, but suddenly the valley narrows, and a long vista of cultivation was spread before us. Here miles of the valley are covered with palm groves. Bright green patches of lucerne called *kadhlb*, almost dazzling to look upon after the arid waste, and numerous other kinds of grain are raised by irrigation, for the Hadhramout has beneath its expanse of sand a river running, the waters of which are obtained by digging deep wells. Skin buckets are let down by ropes and drawn up by cattle by means of a steep slope, and then the water is distributed for cultivation through narrow channels; it is at best a fierce struggle with nature to produce these crops, for the rainfall can never be depended upon.

We had intended to push on to Al Koton, but Sultan Salàh sent a messenger to beg us not to arrive till the following morning, that his preparations to receive us might be suitable to our dignity, as the first English travellers to visit his domains. So we encamped just on the edge of the cultivation, about a mile off, at Ferhud, where under the shade of palm-trees there is a beautiful well of brackish water, with four oxen, two at each side to draw up the water.

Outside the cultivation in its arid waste of sand the Hadhramout produces but little; now and again we came across groups of the camelthorn, tall trees somewhat resembling the holm oak. It is in Arabic a most complicated tree. Its fruit, like a small crab apple, is called b'dom, very refreshing, and making an excellent preserve; its leaves, which they powder and use as soap, are called ghasl, meaning 'washing'; whereas the tree itself is called ailb, and is dearly loved by the camels, who stretch their long necks to feed off its branches.

We wondered what kind of reception we should have, for people's ideas on this point vary greatly. In order not to offend the sultan's prejudices too much, we determined to dissemble, and I decided not to wear my little camera, and Imam Sharif packed the plane-table out of sight. We settled that he should have the medicine chest in his charge and be the doctor of the party, and addressed him as Hakim. Even Saleh feared so much what the future might hold in store, that he removed his drawers and shoes, and advised Imam Sharif to do the same, as Mohammed had never worn such things. Imam Sharif refused to take these precautions, saying that if Mohammed had been born in Cashmere he would have assuredly worn both drawers and shoes. Imam Sharif wore a Norfolk jacket and knickerbockers and a turban when on the march, but in camp he wore Indian clothes. However, we were soon visited by the sultan's two wazirs on spirited Arab steeds: magnificent individuals with plaided turbans, long lances, and many gold mohurs fixed on their dagger handles, all of which argued well for our reception on the morrow by the sultan of Shibahm.

The Castle of the Sultan of Shibahm at Al Koton

We were a good deal stared at, but not disagreeably, for all the soldiers were on their best behaviour. At Khaila and Sief we had to be tied up, airless, in our tents, as if we left them open a minute when the crowd, tired of seeing nothing, had dispersed, and one person saw an opening, the whole multitude surged round again, pressing in, shouting and smelling so bad that we regretted our folly in having tried to get a little light and air. We saw among others a boy who had a wound in his arm, and therefore had his nostrils plugged up; bad smells are said not to be so injurious as good ones. Some women came and asked to see me, so I took my chair and sat surrounded by them. They begged to see my hands, so I took off my gloves and let them lift my hands about from one sticky hand to another. They looked wonderingly at them and said 'Meskin' so often and so pityingly that I am sure they thought I had leprosy all over. Then they wished to see my head, and having taken off my hat, my hair had to be taken down. They examined my shoes, turned up my gaiters, stuck their fingers down my collar, and wished to undress me, so I rose and said very civilly, 'Peace to you, oh women, I am going to sleep now,' and retired.

Arab girls before they enter the harem and take the veil are a curious sight to behold. Their bodies and faces are dyed a bright yellow with turmeric; on this ground they paint black lines with antimony, over their eyes; the fashionable colour for the nose is red; green spots adorn the cheek, and the general aspect is grotesque beyond description.

We stayed in bed really late next morning, till the sun rose, and then prepared ourselves to be fetched.

The two young wazirs, Salim-bin-Ali and Salim-bin-Abdullah, cousins, came again at 7.30 with two extra horses, which were ridden by my husband and Saleh, as Imam Sharif stuck to the donkey which we named Mahsoud (Happy).

CHAPTER X

OUR SOJOURN AT KOTON

Like a fairy palace of the Arabian Nights, white as a wedding cake, and with as many battlements and pinnacles, with its windows painted red, the colour being made from red sandstone, and its balustrades decorated with the inevitable chevron pattern, the castle of Al Koton rears its battlemented towers above the neighbouring brown houses and expanse of palm groves; behind it rise the steep red rocks of the encircling mountains, the whole forming a scene of Oriental beauty difficult to describe in words. This lovely building, shining in the morning light against the dark precipitous mountains, was pointed out to us as our future abode. My horse, Basha, seemed to have come to life again and enjoy galloping once more, for we had left the servants, camels, &c. to follow.

As we approached *feux de joie* announced our arrival, and at his gate stood Sultan Salàh to greet us, clad in a long robe of canary-coloured silk, and with a white silk turban twisted around his swarthy brow. He was a large, stout man, negroid in type, for his mother was a slave, and as generous as he was large, to Arab and European alike. He looked about fifty-five or sixty, but said his age was 'forty-five or forty.' At first, on being seated in his reception-room, we were very cautious in speaking of our plans, as we were surrounded with all sorts and conditions of men.

He placed at our disposal a room spread with Daghestan carpets and cushions, furnished with two tables and three chairs, and not a mouthful of our own food would he allow us to touch, a hospitality which had its drawbacks, for the Arab *cuisine* is not one suited to Western palates.

We were very glad of this hospitality at first as it would give Matthaios a holiday, which he could devote to the washing of clothes, water being so plentiful. I will describe one day's meals, which were invariably the same. At eight o'clock came several cups, all containing coffee and milk, honey, eggs, hard boiled and peeled, and a large thin leathery kind of bread made plain with water, and another large thin kind made with *ghi*, and like pastry.

About 2.30 came two bowls like slop-bowls, one containing bits of meat, vegetables, eggs and spices in sauce, under about an inch of melted *ghi*, the other a kind of soup. They were both quite different, but at the same time very much alike, and the grease on the top kept them furiously hot. There were little pieces of boiled lamb, and little pieces of roast lamb; tiny balls of roast meat and also of boiled; a mound of rice and a mound of dates; and upon requesting some water we were given one large glassful. Identically the same meal came at 9.30, an hour when the *bona-fide* traveller pines to be in his bed. These things were laid on a very dirty coloured cotton cloth, but no plates or knives, &c. were provided.

At several odd times through the day a slave walked in and filled several cups of tea, a few for each of us. The cups were never washed by him.

After struggling for a few days, many of the party having had recourse to the medicine-chest, we were at length compelled humbly to crave his majesty to allow us to employ our own cook. This he graciously permitted, and during the three weeks we passed under his hospitable roof, our cook was daily supplied by the 'sultanas' — most excellent housewives we thought them — with everything we needed.

One of the most striking features of these Arabian palaces is the wood-carving. The doors are exquisitely decorated with it, the supporting beams, and the windows, which are adorned with fretwork instead of glass. The dwelling-rooms are above, the ground floor being exclusively used for merchandise and as stables and cattle stalls, and the first floor for the domestic offices. The men-servants lie about in the passages. We lived on the second floor, the two next stories were occupied by the sultan and his family, and above was the terraced roof where the family sleep during the summer heat. Every guest-room has its coffee corner, provided with a carved oven, where the grain is roasted and the water boiled; around are hung old china dishes for spices, brass trays for the cups, and fans to keep off the flies; also the carved censers, in which frankincense is burnt and handed round to the guests, each one of whom fumigates his garments with it before passing it on. It is also customary to fumigate with frankincense a tumbler before putting water into it, a process we did not altogether relish, as it imparts a sickly flavour to the fluid.

We found the system of door-fastening in vogue a great nuisance to us. The wooden locks were of the 'tumbler' order. The keys were about 10 inches long, and composed of a piece of curved wood: at one end were a number of pegs stuck in irregularly, to correspond with a number of the tumbling bolts which they were destined to raise. No key would go in without a tremendous lot of shaking and noisy rattling, and you always had to have your key with you, for if you did not lock your door on leaving your room there was nothing to prevent its swinging open; and if you were inside you must rise and unbolt it to admit each person, and to bolt it behind him for the same reason.

We got very friendly with Sultan Salàh during our long stay under his roof, and he would come and sit for hours together in our room and talk over his affairs. Little by little he was told of all our sufferings by the way, and was very angry. We also consulted him as to our plans, and told him how badly Saleh was behaving.

We used sometimes to think of dismissing Saleh, but thought him too dangerous to part with. It was better to keep him under supervision, and leave him as much in the dark as possible about our projects.

The sultan took special interest in our pursuits, conducting us in person to archæological sites, and manifesting a laudable desire to have his photograph taken. He assisted both our botanist and naturalist in pursuing their investigations into the somewhat limited flora and fauna of his dominions, and was told by Imam Sharif that his work with the sextant was connected with keeping our watches to correct time.

He would freely discourse, too, on his own domestic affairs, giving us anything but a pleasing picture of Arab harem life, which he described as 'a veritable hell.' Whenever he saw me reading, working with my needle, or developing photographs, he would smile sadly, and contrast my capabilities with those of his own wives, who, as he expressed it, 'are unable to do anything but painting themselves and quarrelling.' Poor Sultan Salàh has had twelve wives in his day, and he assured us that their dissensions and backbitings had made him grow old before his time; his looking so old must be put down to the cares of polygamy. At Al Koton the sultan had at that time only two properly acknowledged wives, whom he wisely kept apart; his chief wife, or 'sultana,' was sister to the sultan of Makalla, and the sultan of Makalla is married to a daughter of Sultan Salàh by another wife; in this way do Arabic relationships get hopelessly confused. The influence of the wife at Al Koton was considerable, and he was obviously in awe of her, so much so that when he wanted to visit his other wife he had to invent a story of pressing business at Shibahm. 'Our wives,' said he one day, 'are like servants, and try to get all they can out of us; they have no interest in their husband's property, as they know they may be sent away at any time.' And in this remark he seems to have properly hit off the chief evil of polygamy. He also told us that, having got all they can from one husband, they go off to a man that is richer, though how they make these arrangements, if they stick to their veils, is a mystery to me.

Then again, he would continually lament over the fanaticism and folly of his fellow-countrymen, more especially the priestly element, who systematically oppose all his attempts at introducing improvements from civilised countries into the Hadhramout. The seyyids and the mollahs dislike him; the former, who trace their descent from the daughter of Mohammed, forming a sort of hierarchical nobility in this district; and on several occasions he has been publicly cursed in the mosques as an unbeliever and friend of the infidel. But Sultan Salàh has money which he made in India, and owns property in Bombay; consequently he has the most important weapon to wield that anyone can have in a Semitic country.

The sultan told us a famous plan they have in this country for making a fortune. Two Hadhrami set out for India together, a father and son, or two brothers. They collect enough money before starting to buy a very fine suit of clothes each, and to start trade in a small way. They then increase the business by credit, and when they have got enough of other people's money into their hands, one departs with it to the inaccessible Hadhramout, while the other waits to hear of his safe arrival, and then he goes bankrupt and follows him.

Sultan Salàh had not a high opinion of his countrymen, and told us several other tales that did not redound to their credit.

'Before I went to India I was a rascal (*harami*) like these men here,' he constantly asseverated, and his love for things Indian and English is unbounded. 'If only the Indian Government would send me a Mohammedan doctor here, I would pay his expenses, and his influence, both political and social, would be most beneficial to this country.' It is certainly a great thing for England to have so firm a friend in the centre of the narrow habitable district between Aden and Maskat, which ought by rights to be ours, not that it is a very profitable country to possess, but in the hands of another power it might unpleasantly affect our road to India, and in complying with this simple request of Sultan Salàh's an easy way is open to us for extending our influence in that direction.

Likewise from a humane point of view, this suggestion of Sultan Salàh's is of great value, for the inhabitants of the Hadhramout are more hopelessly ignorant of things medical than some of the savage tribes of Africa. Certain quacks dwell in the towns, and profess to diagnose the ailments of a Bedou woman by smelling one of her hairs brought by her husband. For every pain, no matter where, they brand the patient with a red-hot iron (*kayya*); to relieve a person who has eaten too much fat, they will light a fire round him to melt it; to heal a wound they will plug up the nostrils of the sufferer, believing that certain scents are noxious to the sore; the pleasant scents being the most harmful. Iron pounded up by a blacksmith is also a medicine.

On an open sore they tie a sheet of iron, tin, or copper with four holes in the corners for strings. We heard of the curious case of a man who for a wager ate all the fat of a sheep that was killed at a pilgrimage. He lay down to sleep under a shady tree and all the fat congealed in his inside. The doctor ordered him to drink hot tea, while fires were lit all around him, and thus he was cured and was living in Shibahm when we were there.

We had a crowd of patients to treat whilst stationed at Al Koton, and I have entered quantities of quaint experiences with these poor helpless invalids in my note-book.

We had many an interesting stroll round the sultan's gardens at Al Koton, and watched the cultivation of spices and vegetables for the royal table, or rather floor; the lucerne and clover for his cattle, the indigo and henna for dyeing purposes, and the various kinds of grain. But on the cultivation of the date-palm the most attention is lavished; it was just then the season at which the female spathe has to be fructified by the male pollen, and we were interested in watching a man going round with an apron full of male spathes. With these he climbed the stem of the female palm, and with a knife cut open the bark which encircles the female spathe, and as he shook the male pollen over it he chanted in a low voice, 'May God make you grow and be fruitful.' No portion of the palm is wasted in the Hadhramout: with the leaves they thatch huts and make fences, the date stones are ground into powder as food for cattle, and they eat the nutty part which grows at the bottom of the spathes, and which they called *kourzan*. On a journey a man requires nothing but a skin of dates, which will last him for days, and, when we left, Sultan Salàh gave us three goat-skins filled with his best dates, and large tins of delicious honey—for which the Hadhramout was celebrated as far back as Pliny's time[9]—which he sent on camels to the coast for us, as well as a large inscribed stone that I now have in my house.

Innumerable wells are dotted over this cultivated area, the water from which is distributed over the fields before sunrise and after sunset. The delicious creaking noise made by heaving up the buckets greeted us every morning when we woke, delicious because it betokened plenty of water: and these early morning views were truly exquisite. A bright crimson tinge would gradually creep over the encircling mountains, making the parts in shade of a rich purple hue, against which the feathery palm-trees and whitewashed castles stood out in strong contrast. All the animals belonging to the sultan are stabled within the encircling wall, and immediately beneath the palace windows; the horses' stable is in the open courtyard, where they are fed with rich lucerne and dates when we should give corn. Here also reside the cows and bullocks, which are fed every evening by women, who tie together bunches of dried grass and make it appetising by mixing therewith a few blades of fresh lucerne; the sheep and the goats are penned on another side, whilst the cocks and hens live in and around the main drain. All is truly patriarchal in character.

The sultan only possesses four horses, and one of these, a large white mare, strangely enough came from the Cape of Good Hope, *viâ* Durban and Bombay. The sultan of Makalla had three. The 'Arab courser' lives farther north.

As for the soldiers, they sent, as if it were a matter of course, for some money to buy tobacco and were given two or three dollars each, and gladly parted from them friends. The sultan of Makalla had paid them for a fortnight's food, and had written to Sultan Salàh to pay what was owing. My groom was dismissed also without bakshish: he was only a rough fellow taken from the mud brick works at Makalla, and my poor Basha would have fared ill if really dependent on M'barrek for care. My entreaties alone saved him from being publicly bastinadoed, as the sultan wished, when he heard of all his rudeness and disobedience.

The sultan was most anxious to arrange for our onward journey, and wrote seven letters to different sheikhs and sultans, and sent them to us to read, but we could not read them ourselves, and would not let

Saleh, so we were none the wiser. The sultans of Siwoun and Terim are brothers, of the Kattiri tribe, but have no real authority outside their towns. We were anxious to proceed along the Hadhramout valley and to reach the tomb of the prophet Houd. The sultan also went to Shibahm to meet some of the arbiters of our fate, and the sultan of Siwoun agreed to let us pass: but others said we had five hundred camels loaded with arms, and all sorts of other fables, and they all quarrelled dreadfully about us, so the sultan returned to Al Koton to await replies to his letters.

The day the sultan was absent, the women were determined to have a little enjoyment from our presence themselves, so a great many servants came bringing the sultan's ten-year-old daughter Sheikha, a rather pretty little girl, with long earrings all round her ears, which, like all the other women's, hang forward like fringed bells. An uneven number is always worn, and a good set consists of twenty-three. They are rings about two inches in diameter, with long drops attached. Her face was painted with large dots, stripes, and patterns of various colours, and she had thick antimony round the eyes. Her neck, arms, and shoulders were yellow, and her hands painted plain black inside and in a pattern like a lace mitten on the back, the nails being red with henna.

I was also asked to pay a visit to the ladies. I went upstairs. Every floor is like a flat, with its bath-room containing a huge vase called *kazbah*, and the bath is taken by pouring over the person, from a smaller utensil, water which runs away down drain-holes to the wooden spouts. I found myself in some very narrow passages, among a quantity of not over-clean women, who all seized me by the shoulders, passing me on from one to the other till I reached a very large carpeted room, with pillows round it, some very large looking-glasses and a chandelier.

I advanced across the room amid loud exclamations from the seated ladies, and was pointed out a position in front of the two principal ones, who were seated against the wall—one was the chief wife of the sultan, and the other a daughter married to a seyyid, whose hand his father-in-law must always kiss. He is a very disagreeable-looking man, who was much offended because Imam Sharif would neither kiss his hand, being a seyyid himself, nor let his own be kissed. I squatted down, and round me soon squatted many more ladies— they were certainly not beautiful, but one, who was nearest to me and seemed to be my guardian or showman, had a very nice, kind, clever face. Her lips were not so large as most.

We seemed all to be presided over, as we literally were, by a kind of confidential maid, who sat on the little raised hearth in the corner, amongst all the implements for the making of coffee and burning of incense, chanting constantly: 'Salek alleh Mohammed' and something more, of which I can only remember that it was about the faith. Sometimes she was quiet a little, and then, above all the din, she raised her shout, accompanying it with an occasional single loud blow with a stone pestle and mortar. There was no difficulty about seeing the gold anklets the ladies wore, for their clothes, as they sat, were well above their knees. Their feet were painted like fanciful black slippers with lace edges. Their examination of me was very searching, even reaching smelling point, and I feel sure I was being exorcised, for so much was being said about Mohammed. At last an old lady said to me, 'There is no god but God!' with which I agreed, and murmurs of satisfaction went round, while she nodded her head triumphantly. Later on she pointed to the ceiling, and asked if I considered this was the direction in which Allah dwells, and seemed glad when I agreed. Of course no infidel would, she thought.

Presently the woman who had prepared the frankincense brought it down in a small chafing dish, continuing the same chant and handing it round. I wondered if I should be left out, or left till the last, but neither happened, and when my turn came, like the rest, I held my head and hands over the fumes, and we were all fumigated inside our garments. I may have been partaking in some unholy rite, but my ignorance will be my excuse, I hope.

I was then told I might go, which I was glad of, as I had been afraid to offend them by going too soon. I was asked, as I left, if I should like to see their jewellery; of course I said 'Yes,' and had hardly got home and recovered from the deafening row, when I was fetched again.

There were crowds more women of all classes, clean and dirty, and as they came trooping in to see me, the room seemed to resound with the twittering sound of their kisses, for the incoming visitor kissed the sitter's hand, while the sitter kissed her own, and there was kissing of foreheads besides.

Numerous little baskets were brought in with immense quantities of gold ornaments, some very heavy, but with few gems in them— absolutely none of value. They consisted of coral, onyx, a few bad turquoises, crooked pearls, and many false stones. Everything was of Indian work. Sheikha came in in a silk dress with a tremendous, much-alloyed silver girdle, and loaded with chains and bracelets of all sorts, clanking and clashing as she came.

We had very good coffee with ginger and cloves in it, and at this time there was a very great deal of religious conversation and argument, and as they were exciting themselves I thought I would go, for I did not feel very comfortable; but the chief lady said to me, in a very threatening and dictatorial voice:

'La illaha il Allah! Mohammed resoul Allah.' I looked as much like an idiot as I could, and pretended neither to notice nor understand, but I was patted and shaken up by all that were near-enough neighbours to do so, and desired to look at that lady.

Again she said 'La illaha il Allah' in the same tone, and I was told I must repeat it. So she said the first part again in a firm tone, and I cheerfully repeated after her, 'There is no god but God.'

Then she continued, 'Mohammed is his prophet.' I remained dumb. Then the name of Issa (Jesus) went round, and I bowed my head.

The coffee woman then called out, 'Issa was a prophet before Mohammed.'

The Castle of the Sultan of Makalla at Shibahm

They then asked me if Issa was my prophet. I could only say that He is, for my Arabic would not allow of a further profession of my faith.

I gladly departed and gave Sheikha afterwards two sovereigns for her necklace.

They said they would show me their clothes, but they never did. I have described the shape of these dresses, but I omitted to say that they are gaily trimmed with a kind of ribbon about two inches wide, made of little square bits of coloured silks and cottons sewn together. This is put round the armholes, over the shoulder, and down to the hem of the garment over the seam, where a curious gusset or gore runs from the front part to the corner of the train. The dress is trimmed round the neck, which is cut square and rather low, and generally hangs off one shoulder, and, across the breast it is much embroidered, beads and spangles being sometimes introduced. These women seem to live in a perpetual noise: they gurgled loudly when we arrived, and we could always hear them playing the tambourine.

Tiny girls wear, as their only garment, a fringe of plaits as in Nubia, and their heads are shaven in grotesque patterns, or their hair done in small plaits. Boys have their heads shaven also, all except locks of long hair dotted about in odd places. I never saw such dreadful objects as the women make of themselves by painting their faces. When they lift their veils one would hardly think them human. I saw eyes painted to resemble blue and red fish, with their heads pointing to the girl's nose. The upper part of the face was yellow, the lower green with small black spots, a green stripe down the nose, the nostrils like two red cherries, the paint being shiny. Three red stripes were on the forehead, and there was a red moustache, there being also green stripes on the yellow cheeks.

There was a delightful, tiny room on the roof, just a little place to take and make coffee in, and we were allowed to clamber up to this, but not without calling a slave and assuring ourselves that there was no danger of my husband meeting any of the ladies, for it commanded the roof, to which we had not access. We liked going up there very much, for the views were splendid, and we could see down into the mosque, which is built like cloisters, open in the middle. I took some photographs from there, and also, with the greatest difficulty, managed to get one of the room itself by tying my camera, without its legs, of course, with a rope to the outside of the fretwork frame of the little window, which was on a level with the floor. It was hard work not to be in the way myself, as I had to put both arms out of the next window to take out the slides, and to guess at the focus.

The sultan, though his Hindustani was getting a trifle rusty, said he greatly liked the company of Imam Sharif, whose uncle had in some way befriended him in India. Intelligent conversation he had not enjoyed for a long time. He was certainly a little scandalised at Imam Sharif's lax ways in religion, for he was one day sitting without his turban when some coffee was brought. The sultan put his hands up to cover Imam Sharif's head, saying:

'My brother, you are drinking with a bare head, and this is contrary to the Koran.' The same remark was often made in camp by people who looked into his tent. They said, 'Look! he is a Christian, his head is bare.' At the same time no one thought anything of the Bedouin's bare heads.

During this period of uncertainty we made several little explorations of the surrounding valleys.

One day we started out with the sultan, who had on his long coat, which made him look like a huge, sulphur-coloured canary. It was lined with light blue. He, my husband, Saleh, and a groom rode the four horses; Imam Sharif and I had our Basha and Mahsoud, and a camel most smartly decorated carried the Wazir Salim-bin-Abdullah and a soldier; other soldiers followed on foot. We went about five miles to Al Agran to see some ruins perched on a rock beneath the high wall of the plateau, prettily situated with palms, gardens, and wells. The ruins, which are those of a well-built fortress, consist of little more than the foundation, but all embedded in modern houses, so that excavations would be impossible. It must once have been a place of considerable importance. There was a scrap of very well cut ornament, which looked as if it might have belonged to a temple. It was from Al Agran or Algran that we obtained a stone with a spout to it, with rather a long Sabæan inscription on it, a dedication to the god Sayan, known to have been worshipped in the Hadhramout. We were given coffee in a very dirty room, which we were all the time longing to tear down that we might dig under it.

[9] Pliny, vi. 28, § 161: 'Mellis ceraeque proventu.'

CHAPTER XI

THE WADI SER AND KABR SALEH

On January 17 we started from Al Koton with only seven of our camels and two of the sultan's packed with forage, to be away several days. The sultan wished to lend his horses, but my husband refused. However, he had to ride one, a grey, for fear of giving offence, and this was given to him as a present afterwards, and he rode it whenever the rocks allowed till we reached the coast. We eventually sent this horse, Zubda (butter), and my Basha back to their respective donors, though they really expected us to take them to Aden. We had two men of the Nahad tribe as our *siyara*.

Our start took a very long time, for the sultan, attended by many people, came a mile on foot. We travelled four hours and a half, partly through land that would have been cultivated had there been rain, and partly through salt desert, till we turned north-west into the Wadi Ser, where there is a sandy desert. From the entrance to Wadi Ser we could see Shibahm in the distance, an unpromising looking spot among sandhills. We were all able to find shelter at Hanya under an enormous thorny *b'dom* tree covered with fruit, and we felt like birds out of a cage, for we never could walk out at Al Koton without a crowd, and the greasiness and spiciness of the food was beginning to pall. We had a delightful camp, but had to be very careful not to drop things in the sand, as they so quickly disappeared. We had a new man called Iselem, who was to take care of the horses, pluck chickens, and help in pitching the camp. His wonder at the unfolding and setting up of the beds, chairs, &c., was great. There was also an old man called Haidar Aboul. He and one of the soldiers could talk Hindustani, so with Imam Sharif's help we were somewhat independent of Saleh, though we had thought it necessary to bring him, to keep him from working us harm.

We continued our way up the Wadi Ser for about five hours and camped at Al Had in a field near a house, close to some high banks which radiated intense heat, and suffered the more that we had to wait a long time for the tea that we always had with our luncheon, as our water had been stolen in the night. We always tried to save some to carry on and start with next day, fearing we might fare worse in the next place we came to.

The well at this spot is the last water in this direction, for we were reaching the confines of the great central desert. Wadi Ser, being such a waste of sand, is very sparsely populated. The Bedouin here, like the Turkomans, live in scattered abodes, little groups of two or three houses dotted about, and solitary homesteads. It belongs to the Kattiri tribe, who are at war with the Yafei. They once owned Sheher and Makalla and took Al Koton, but in a war in 1874 the Yafei were supported by the English; hence their friendship for England. The animosity still continues and there is little intercourse between Siwoun and Shibahm, though only twelve miles apart. The Kattiri have more of the Bedou about them and the Yafei have more of the Arab. Our *siyar* was twenty-five dollars.

The people were preparing for rain, which may never come; they had had none for two years, but if they get it every three years they are satisfied, as they get a sufficient crop. As it comes in torrents and with a rush, each field is provided with a dyke and a dam, which they cut to let the water off. This dyke is made by a big scraper, like a dustpan, called *mis'hap*, harnessed by chains to a camel or bullocks. The camel goes over the existing bank and when the dustpan reaches the summit the men in attendance upset the surface sand or soil, that has been scraped off, and carry the scraper down. When this is done the field is lightly ploughed; there is nothing more to do except to sit and wait for rain. We saw signs of great floods in some parts.

Whenever we found ruins still visible in or near the Hadhramout we found them on elevated spots above the sand level, from which we may argue that all centres of civilisation in the middle of the valleys lie deeply buried in sand, which has come down in devastating masses from the highland and the central desert. The nature of the sand in this district is twofold. Firstly we have the *loess* or firm sand, which can be cultivated; and secondly the disintegrated desert sand, which forms itself into heaps and causes sandstorms when the wind is high.

The mountains diminish in height the farther north one goes. The character of the valleys is pretty much the same as that of those to the south of the main valley, only they are narrower and much lower, and thus the deep indenture of the valley system of the Hadhramout gradually fades away into the vast expanse of the central desert.

The wazir had been given a bag of money to buy fowls and lambs for us, but Saleh came and said, 'The wazir wants some money for a lamb,' so it was sent and returned. It had not been asked for and caused some offence, but that odious little wretch only wished to make mischief.

The Bedouin are rather clever at impromptu verses, and when we were in Wadi Ser they made night hideous by dancing in our camp. The performers ranged themselves in two rows, as in Sir Roger de Coverley; time is kept by a drum and by perpetual hand-clapping and stamping of the feet, whilst two men execute elaborate capers in the centre, singing as they do so such words as these: 'The ship has come from Europe with merchandise; they shot at the minaret with a thousand cannon.' Bedouin women also take part in these dances, and the Arabs think the dances very impious; it was very weird by the light of the moon and the camp-fire, but wearisome when we wanted to sleep, particularly as they kept it up till after we were all astir in the morning, yelling, bawling, singing, and screeching, Iselem being the ringleader. The ground was shaken as if horses were galloping about. A Bedou was playing a flute made of two leg-bones of a crane bound together with iron.

At a distance of half an hour from our camp there is a stone with an inscription. This was visited on the day of our arrival, but we went again next day that I might photograph it, very difficult in the position in which it is. It is a great rough boulder about 10 feet high, that has slipped down from the mountain, with large rough Sabæan letters just punched on the surface, of no depth, but having a whitish appearance. The letters run in every direction—sometimes side by side, sometimes in columns.

The central and most important word which my husband was able to make out, with the help of Professor Hommels' admirable dictionary of hitherto ascertained Himyaritic words, is *Masabam* or Caravan road. The stone seemed to be a kind of sign-post; for as the old Bedou sheikh who was with us said, there was in olden days, about 500 years ago, a caravan road this way to Mecca, before the Bahr-Safi made it impassable. The Bahr-Safi is a quicksand, north of Shabwa, but none of those present had been there, and they all laughed at Von Wrede's story of King Safi and his army being engulfed in it.

The Bedou sheikh with his retinue came to see that we took no treasure out of the stone. There are a good many old stones built into the side of the stream-bed. Having taken a copy and a photograph, which my husband sent later to Dr. D. H. Müller, in Vienna, to decipher, we departed. We were told that the Wadi Ser goes four hours from that stone to the great desert.

We then turned back and followed our *kafila* to Alagoum, at the junction of Wadi Ser and the Wadi Latat, about two hours' journey. Alagoum is a large cluster of high houses, surrounded by stables and houses excavated in the sandhills, where the inhabitants and their cattle live in hot weather. This is quite an idea suited to the Bedouin, who live in caves, when they can find them. The Bedouin in Southern Arabia never have tents.

We found that Saleh had joined the camel-men in resisting our own people, who wanted to encamp under trees. They had unloaded in the open and Saleh and Iselem had then retired into the village till the tents were pitched, so, as we were to remain in this place two days, we had them moved. We had by this time some of the Kattiri tribe with us as *siyara*.

At Al Garun the Wadi Ser is entered by a short collateral valley called the Wadi Khonab, in which valley is the tomb of the prophet

Saleh, one of the principal sacred places of the district. Kabr Saleh is equally venerated with the Kabr Houd, also called the tomb of the prophet Eber (for, from what we could gather from the statements of intelligent natives, Eber and Houd are synonymous terms) which is to be found in the Tamimi country further up the main valley.

The prophet Houd was sent to reclaim the tribe of Ad. The Mahra tribe are descended from a remnant of the Addites, as also are the Hadhrami, according to the legends. Once a man named Kolabeh, when seeking for camels came upon the beautiful garden of Irem-Dhatul-Imad, which is supposed to have been in the desert near Aden; he found and brought away a priceless jewel which came into possession of the first Ommiad Caliph Nourrijaht. Those who embraced Islamism on the preaching of the prophet Houd were spared, but the rest either were suffocated by a stifling wind or survived in the form of apes, whose descendants still inhabit Jebel Shemshan at Aden.

A remnant are also said to have fled to the Kuria Muria Islands.

We again met with considerable opposition from the Bedouin and our escort when we proposed to visit the Kabr Saleh next day. However, this was overcome by threats of reporting the opposition to Sultan Salàh on our return to Al Koton. So next morning we started. The sultan of Shibahm's people were just as anxious to go as we were, for they were delighted to get the chance of making this pilgrimage to so holy a place, which being in an enemies' country they could not have done but for our escort.

A short ride of two hours brought us nearly to the head of the Wadi Khonab, and there, situated just under the cliff, in an open wilderness, is the celebrated tomb. It consists simply of a long uncovered pile of stones, somewhat resembling a potato-pie, with a headstone at either end, and a collection of fossils from the neighbouring mountains arranged along the top. Hard by is a small house where the pilgrims take their coffee, and the house of the Bedou mollah, who looks after the tomb, is about a quarter of a mile off. Beyond this there is no habitation in sight. A more desolate spot could hardly be found. The tomb is from 30 to 40 feet in length, and one of the legends concerning it is that it never is the same length, sometimes being a few feet shorter, sometimes a few feet longer. The Bedouin have endless legends concerning this prophet. He was a huge giant, they said, the father of the prophet Houd, or Eber; he created camels out of the rock, and hence is especially dear to the wandering Bedou; and he still works miracles, for if even unwittingly anyone removes a stone from this grave, it exhibits symptoms of life, and gives the possessor much discomfort until it is returned. Once a domed building was erected over the tomb, but the prophet manifested his dislike of being thus inclosed and it was removed.

Men are said to go blind if they steal anything connected with the tomb; once a man took a cup from the coffee-house, unaware of the danger he incurred, tied it to his girdle, and carried it off. It stuck to him till he restored it. Another man took a stone away and gave it to his children to play with, but it hopped about till taken back again.

At the time of the *ziara* or pilgrimage which takes place in November, crowds of Bedouin, we were told, come from all the valleys and hills around to worship. All our men treated the grave with the greatest respect, and said their prayers around it barefoot.

I do not know what they would have done to Imam Sharif if he had not comported himself as the others did, so that wretched man had to walk barefoot all round on the sharp stones, and thus we obtained the measurements. He got dreadfully pricked by thorns and coveted the fossils very much. The stones of which the tomb is composed are about the size of cannon-balls, and look just as if newly put together and quite weedless. People stroke the upright stone at the head and then rub their hands on their breast and kiss them, and do the same at the foot. The wazir would have led us up close to it; but the Bedouin hated our being there at all, and would by no means let us sleep there, as we wished to do. We overheard our horrid little Saleh Hassan telling the bystanders that we live on pork.

When we first got there, we were permitted to approach within a few yards of the tomb, so that we saw it very distinctly; but when, after eating our luncheon, and taking a siesta under a tree, we again advanced to inspect it, the Bedou mollah attacked us with fierce and opprobrious language, and, fearing further to arouse the fanaticism of these wild people, we speedily mounted our horses and rode away.

We hoped to be able to visit Kabr Houd, the tomb of Nebi Saleh's son, in the main valley, but, as it will appear, we were to be disappointed. I am told, on reliable Arab authority, that it is similar in every way to the Kabr Saleh—just a long pile of stones, about 40 feet in length, uncovered, and with its adjacent mosque. These two primitive tombs of their legendary prophets, zealously guarded and venerated by the Bedouin, are a peculiar and interesting feature of the Hadhramout. It is a curious fact that when one turns to the tenth chapter of Genesis (the best record we have of the earliest populations of our globe) we find the patriarchal names Salah, Eber, and Hazarmaveth (which last, as I previously stated, corresponds to Hadhramout) following one another in their order, though not in immediate sequence. I am at a loss to account for these names being still venerated by the Bedouin, unless one admits a continuity of legendary history almost too wonderful to contemplate, or else one must consider that they were heathen sites of veneration, which have, under Moslem influence, been endowed with orthodox names. Certain it is that these tombs in the midst of the wilderness are peculiarly the property of the Bedouin, and, though visited, and to a certain extent venerated, by the Arabs, the latter do not attach so much importance to them as they do to the tombs of their own walis or saints, which are always covered tombs, near or in the centre of the towns. Another curious point I may mention in connection with these tombs is that the Arab historian, Yaqut, in his 'Mu'gam,'[10] tells us of a god in the Hadhramout, called Al Galsad, who was a gigantic man; perhaps this god may have some connection with the giant tombs of Saleh and Eber. Also Makrisi, who wrote in the tenth century, a.d., speaks of a giant's grave he saw near Shabwa.

Near Al Agoum we saw a quantity of very ancient stone monuments, situated on slightly elevated ground, above the sand. At first we imagined them to be tombs, but on closer inspection we discovered that the erections, which are large unhewn ones of the cromlech type, are decorated inside with geometric patterns somewhat similar to those we found in the Mashonaland ruins, and therefore my husband was more inclined to believe they were originally used for religious purposes. There are traces of letters above the pattern. The buildings are about 20 feet square and several are surrounded by circular walls. They are apparently of extreme antiquity, and doubtless far anterior in date to any other Himyaritic remains that we saw in the Hadhramout.

The wazir joined us as usual on our return from Kabr Saleh, as we sat outside our tent in the moonlight with Imam Sharif and the Indian interpreters, and we had a pleasant evening. We were perfectly charmed to see great preparations for sleep going on among the Bedouin. We thought they really must be tired after dancing the whole night and walking the whole day. They were busy putting themselves to bed in graves which they dug in the loose dust, not sand; turbans, girdles, and so forth being turned into bedclothes. Just as they were still Iselem began capering about and they all got up shouting and screaming, but the wazir, seeing my distress, with the greatest difficulty quieted them, as he did when they broke out again at three o'clock in the morning.

It took us six hours the following day to ride back to Al Koton, where, not being expected, we could not get a meal of even bread, honey, and dates for about an hour and a half, and then had to wait till we were very sleepy indeed for supper. We endured great hunger that day.

Salim-bin-Ali, the other wazir, had not come with us because he was not well. The day of our reception, in curvetting about, he fell from his horse and had suffered various pains ever since.

The sultan had had another stone brought for us from Al Gran; we did not care to take this away as it had very little writing on it, only

[Symbol: See page image] (*al amin*, to the protection). It is circular, 1 foot 4½ inches in diameter, 2½ inches high, made of coarse marble. We saw a similar circular stone at Raidoun.

The wildest reports were going about as to the water-stone we already had. It was almost the cause of an insurrection against the sultan of Shibahm. They said 'It was very wrong to give that stone to a "gavir"' —as they call us (for all the *k*'s are pronounced *g*)—'only think of our carelessly letting him have it. The Englishman has taken fifteen jewels of gold and gems out of it,' and named a high value.

'You are sure of this?' said the sultan to the ringleader.

'Oh, yes! quite certain!' he said.

So the sultan led him to our room, where the stone was, and said:

'Do you know the stone again? Look closely at it. Has anything happened to it but a washing?'

The man looked extremely small. They said my husband's only business was to extract gold from stones. It is extraordinary how widespread this belief is. It is firmly rooted in Greece. Many a statue and inscription has been shivered to atoms because of it, and our interest in inscriptions was constantly attributed to a wish to find out treasure. We once saw two men in Asia Minor industriously boring away into a column—to find gold they told us. They already had made a hole about 8 inches deep and 4 or 5 inches wide. They think that the ancients had a way of softening marble with acid.

We had again at this time a great many patients; for, as we really had effected some cures the first time we were at Al Koton, our fame had spread. We always had Matthaios and Imam Sharif to help us to elicit the symptoms, and also to consult with as to the cures, because some remedies which suit Europeans were by no means suited to the circumstances of our patients. For instance, the worst coughs I ever heard were very prevalent, but it would be useless to ask the sick to take a hot footbath and stay in bed. The one blue garment, which in different shapes was all the men and women wore, was little protection from the chill of the evening. The women's dresses were always hanging off their backs; and the men, who had each two pieces of thick blue cotton about 2 yards long by 1½ yard wide, with fringes half a yard long, wore one as a permanent petticoat and the other as a girdle by day and when cold as a shawl, often put on in a very uncomfortable way—thrown on in front and left hanging open behind—forming no protection to the back of the lungs.

The poor little baby, aged fifteen months, of the Wazir Salim-bin-Abdullah was brought shrieking in agony, gnawing hard at its emaciated little arms, and all covered with sores. Our hearts were wrung at this wretched sight and we longed to help; we even thought of giving it part of a drop of chlorodyne much diluted, but, fortunately for us, dared not do so, for my husband said to them, 'I do not think the child will live long.' It mercifully was released in a few hours. Then an old man came who 'had a flame in his inside.' My husband examined him and decided that he had an abscess, and, to please him, gave him a dessertspoonful of borax and honey, which he swept up with his finger, and I suppose it did relieve him, for after some minutes he said: 'The fire is gone out.'

It grieved us sorely when poor souls came to us so hopefully and so confident of help, with a withered arm or an empty eye-socket. Some with less serious complaints than these last we recommended to go to Aden hospital, a building of which we never thought at that time we should be inmates ourselves. We found the ladies, to whom a plentiful supply of violent pills had been administered, were better, but the sultan, who had an attack of indigestion, had to be taken in hand at once by us doctors. His wife required a tonic, so we got out some citrate of iron and quinine, a bright, shiny, greenish-yellow, flaky thing, which Imam Sharif assured us would be more beneficial and better liked if shown and admired as gold; so after some conversation about pious frauds, I packed the medicine up neatly and wrote in ornamental letters 'Golden Health Giver,' and this name being explained and translated gave great satisfaction. We were glad to be able to give the kind sultan a new bottle of quinine—more acceptable than gold.

While we were away Mahmoud had found two little hedgehogs. One was dead and stuffed; the other we kept alive for some time and it always liked to creep into my clothes and go to sleep—I suppose because I never teased it. In the little book of directions for zoological collectors we saw, that 'little is known of the reproduction of lizards, so special attention is to be paid,' &c. Mahmoud had brought me two little fragile eggs to keep, about half an inch long, and I had put them in a match-box with tow and packed them in my trunk, and on my return to Al Koton I found two little lizards about 1¼ inch long, one alive and the other dead. Both had to be pickled, as we did not understand how to bring so small a lizard up by hand. They proved to be new to science, as was also a large lizard we had found near Haura, whose peculiarity is that he has no holes along his legs to breathe by, like other lizards. His name is *Aporosceles Bentii*. The first lizard's egg I had I was determined should not slip through my fingers; but alack! and well-a-day! my fingers slipped through it.

In the meantime we were terrible bones of contention, and had the Wadi Hadhramout all by the ears. We were very anxious indeed as to whether we could proceed any farther or should have to go back, and whether we could do either safely. We wanted to go right along the Wadi Hadhramout and to see Bir Borhut or Barahout, a *solfatare* as far as we could make out, but Masoudi in the tenth century speaks of it as the greatest volcano in the world, and says that it casts up immense masses of fire and that its thundering noise can be heard miles away. On the heights near is much brimstone, which the Bedouin find useful for gunpowder. They consider this place is the mouth of hell and that the souls of Kafirs go there. In Iceland there is similar accommodation for those souls. Von Wrede thinks it was the Fons Stygis of Ptolemy, but M. de Goeje thinks that Ptolemy alluded to some place farther west and south of Mareb. Certainly the position given by Ptolemy does not coincide with that of Bir Borhut.

From 'Arabian Society in the Middle Ages,' by S. Lane-Poole, I take the following notices of this place:—

El Kaswini says of Bir Borhut: 'It is a well near Hadhramout and the Prophet (God bless and save him) said "In it are the souls of infidels and hypocrites." It is an Addite well in a dry desert and a gloomy valley, and it is related of Ali (may God be well pleased with him) that he said, "The most hateful of districts to God (whose name be exalted) is the valley of Barahout, in which is a well whose waters are black and fœtid, where the souls of infidels make their abode."'

El Asmaï has narrated of a man of Hadhramout that he said: 'We find near Barahout an extremely disgusting and fœtid smell, and then news is brought to us of the death of a great man of the chiefs of the infidels.'

Ajaïb el Makhloukàt also relates that a man who passed a night in the valley of Barahout said: 'I heard all night (exclamatives) of "O Roumèh! O Roumèh!" and I mentioned this to a learned man and he told me that it was the name of the angel commissioned to keep guard over the souls of the infidels.'

Bir Borhut is not far from Kabr Houd, which is said by some to be even longer and wider than Kabr Saleh. The route lies through the territory of the Kattiri, and the Yafei are quite ignorant of it; it would be quite unsafe for them to go to the sea along the valley, and they always use the road over the tableland. The Kattiri tyrannise over the sultan of Siwoun and are enemies to the sultan of Shibahm; beyond them are the Minhali, who are also enemies; then the Amri and the Tamimi, who are friendly, and then come the Mahri. The sultan told us that not even he could prevent us going along the *kafila* path, but we should not be admitted into any villages and should probably be denied water. One source of enmity between the Kattiri and the Yafei is, I believe, a debt which the Kattiri owe and will not pay. The sultan of Siwoun borrowed three lacs of rupees from the grandfather of the present sultan of Makalla; he would not repay them, so after much squabbling the case was referred to the English at Aden, who, after duly considering the papers, gave Makalla and Sheher (bombarding them first) to the Yafei.

In answer to the seven letters there was nothing from the sultan of Siwoun, and the sultan of Terim sent a verbal answer—'Do as you please,' taking no responsibility—to which Sultan Salàh replied, 'I have sent you a letter, send me a letter.' The sheikh of the Kattiri tribe came to Al Koton and said he would take us, but on January 23 we heard that the sultan of Siwoun had made a proclamation in the mosque there, forbidding the people to admit the unbelievers to the town. Though we could easily go by the *kafila* road, leaving the town of Siwoun two miles on one side, the sultan deemed it wiser for us not to attempt it, as brawls might arise, the two tribes being at war; so we then decided to mount on to the akaba, pass the inhospitable Siwoun and Terim, and reach the friendly Tamimi tribe. The Kattiri *kabila*, or tribe, really came to Siwoun to be ready for us, but the seyyids had collected a large sum of money and bribed the sultan to send them away.

We were hoping to get off to Shibahm, but as the sultan was neither well nor in a very good humour, we had to resign ourselves to settling down in Al Koton in all patience. He said he must accompany us, as he could not depend on his wazirs for they were too stupid.

My husband and I were always occupied. He used to sketch in water-colours, and I had plenty of work developing photographs in a delightful little dark room, where I lived and enjoyed as many skins of water as I could use, till I had to stop and pack my celluloid negatives like artificial flowers, for they curled up and the films contracted and split, from the alkaline water. I had to put glycerine on them when I reached Aden. Our botanist nearly died of dulness and impatience; Mahmoud was quite contented to sit quite still, and I do not think the Indian servants minded much. Poor Imam Sharif used to gaze up at half a dozen stars from a yard, but he dared not venture on the roof to see more.

We took a stroll with the sultan one day, no crowd being allowed, and remarked how many things were grown for spices, those spices which were becoming rather wearisome to us. There was *zamouta*, an umbelliferous plant, the seed of which is used in coffee, and *habat-assoba* for putting in bread; coriander, chili, fennel, and *helf*, a plant very like tall cress, which is used in cookery and also raw, and which we liked as a salad; also *attar*, a purple creeping bean, very pretty and good to eat. There was also another low-growing bean, *brinjol* (egg plant), cucumber, water-melon, henna, and indigo. The sultan has besides a private inclosure where he has some lime-trees, not our kind of lime-tree of course, but the one which bears fruit; and I must not forget cotton, from which the place originally took its name, as it is abundant in a wild state.

At last another polite letter came from the Kattiri, and a letter from the sultan of Terim. 'I have both your letters *and you can do as you like,* my answer is the same.' This did away with all hope of progress in that direction.

Our spirits, however, were much cheered by hearing that the sultan had received a letter from a seyyid at Meshed (probably the nice one who had been in India and had leprosy in his legs), telling him how very badly the sultan of Hagarein had behaved about us. As this was spontaneous, we hoped that the negotiation our sultan was going to undertake about our making excavations at Meshed, Raidoun, or Kubar al Moluk (for some part of the ruins is called Tombs of the Kings), would turn out successfully. The sultan of Hagarein was summoned to Al Koton, but we were away before he came. I believe in the end he was turned out of his place, former misdeeds counting against him.

[10] II., 100.

CHAPTER XII

THE CITY OF SHIBAHM

On January 25 we started for Shibahm, carpets having been sent forward the day before. The sultan was to follow us in a day or two, when some sheikhs had been to see him. We started at 8.30 and were at Shibahm in four hours. We had eleven camels only, three horses, and the donkey. We travelled, as soon as we left Al Koton, through sand nearly all the way. We passed the tall white dome of Sheikh Aboubekr-bin-Hassan's tomb, near which the ruling family are buried if the seyyids permit. They are all-powerful, and the sultan can do nothing in this respect without them — not even be buried in his own family tomb. There is a well beside the tomb, or rather the kind of building from which water is obtained in the open valleys. This consists of a small white building 8 or 9 feet square, with a dome resting on an open pattern composed of a herring-bone course of bricks; a little wooden ladle, 4 or 5 inches wide, stands in one of the little openings to dip out the water, which would otherwise evaporate. They drink out of the ladle, and fill the water-skins and the drinking trough for animals, which stands always near. They would never let us drink from the ladles.

As we neared Shibahm we passed through a good deal of ground that had once been irrigated, but it had had its ups and downs, and was now abandoned. First there had been plenty of soil and the palm-trees were planted in it. Then the wind had denuded the roots, some of which had been banked up and walled in with stones; others were standing on bare roots, but at this time the sand was burying the whole place. There were high drifts against many of the walls and among the trees.

Shibahm is twelve miles distant from Al Koton, and is one of the principal towns in the Hadhramout valley. It is built on rising ground in the middle of the narrowest part of the valley, so that no one can pass between it and the cliffs of the valley out of gunshot of the walls. This rising ground has doubtless been produced by many successions of towns built of sun-dried bricks, for it is the best strategical point in the neighbourhood.

Early Arab writers tell us that the Himyaritic population of this district came here when they abandoned Shabwa, early in the Christian era. We succeeded, however, in finding evident traces of an occupation of earlier date than this, both in a seal, which is described further on, and in an inscription in which the name Shibahm occurs, and which certainly dates from the third century b.c. Even if Shibahm were not the site of the original capital it must always, centuries before our era, have been a place of considerable importance as the centre of the frankincense trade, for here must have been made up the caravans which brought the spices westward by the great frankincense road across Arabia. The caravans take twenty-five days on the journey to Saihut, and five to Makalla; they go also to Nejd, but we could not find out how long they take.

Shibahm is now the property of the sultan of Makalla, but was administered by his cousin Salàh, who received 40,000 rupees a year for the purpose. It is now three hundred years since these Yafei left their old home and came to settle in the Hadhramout. They were then a wild predatory race, plundering caravans; now they have become peaceable and rich. They still remain close friends with the Yafei farther west, but are quite independent of them. It is the maintenance of a residence for the Nizam of Hyderabad, and their constant communication with India, that has doubtless made all the difference between the Yafei tribe and others. Building seems to have been their mania. The sultan of Shibahm has numbers of houses at Al Koton and Shibahm, and he was intending to spend 20,000 rupees in rebuilding his father's house, for the castle at Al Koton is not his own but Government property, and the strip of land across the valley, part of it sandy, goes with it. He was buying up land for himself in the Wadi Al Ain and elsewhere. He told us his father left eleven million rupees to divide among his numerous progeny.

Relationships in that family must be a trifle confused. Manassar of Makalla had married two sisters (both now dead) of his cousin Salàh. Salàh had married two of Manassar's sisters. A daughter of Salàh's married Manassar, and another of them was married to one of Manassar's sons, and Manassar's brother Hussein of Sheher married, or was married to, a third daughter of Salàh. Apparently the same complications existed in the generation before this, but into them it is impossible to go. As in India, the favourite marriage that a man can make is to marry his 'uncle's daughter.' Possibly the fact that property goes from brother to brother till a whole generation is dead, instead of from father to son, has something to do with this arrangement.

A Sabæan Altar

The town of Shibahm offers a curious appearance as one approaches; above its mud brick walls, with bastions and watch towers, appear the tall houses of the wealthy, whitewashed only at the top, which make it look like a large round cake with sugar on it. Outside the walls several industries are carried on, the chief of which is the manufacture of indigo dye. The small leaves are dried in the sun and powdered, and then put into huge jars and filled with water. Next morning these are stirred with long poles, producing a dark-blue frothy mixture; this is left to settle, and then the indigo is taken from the bottom and spread out on cloths to drain; the substance thus procured is taken home and mixed with dates and saltpetre. Four pounds of this indigo to a gallon of water makes the requisite and universally used dye for garments, the better class of which are calendered by beating them with wooden hammers on stones. This noise was a great mystery to us till we traced our way to it and found out what it was. They used also to beat the dried leaf of a kind of acacia called *kharrad*, and, when pounded, make of it a paste which has a beautiful pea-green appearance; it is used for giving a polish to leather.

Another industry carried on outside Shibahm is rope-making out of the fibres of the fan palm (*saap*) which grows wild in the narrower valleys; the leaves are first left to soak in water, and then beaten till the fibres separate. Yet another is that of making lime for whitewash kilns—it is curious to watch the Bedouin beating the lime thus produced with long sticks, singing quaint little ditties as they thump, in pleasant harmony to the beating of their sticks.

We entered the town by some very sloping steps, which led through the gateway, passing some wells and the indigo dyers outside; also some horrible pools where they had put the little fish that the camels eat, to drain the oil from them. We entered a sort of square, having the castle on the right-hand side and a ruined mosque in front of us. This huge castle was built by the grandfather of the Sultan Manassar, sultan of Makalla, but, owing to some difference about his wives, he left the two topmost stories unfinished. No one lives in it, so we had the whole of this immense pile of buildings to ourselves. It belongs to Manassar. It is larger than Al Koton by far, and that is also exceeded in size by Haura. It is a most imposing structure and much more florid than the others. The gateway is a masterpiece of carving in intricate patterns. On entering this you turn sharp to the right up a shallow staircase, protected from without, but exposed to fire from the inmates of the castle. The pillars in the lofty rooms are beautifully carved. All the windows are filled with pretty fretwork; bolts, doors, and window frames are also carved. The huge doors are carved on one side only, the outer one, and inside they are rough and ill-grained and splashed with whitewash. There are pretty dado patterns round the walls; and the staircase, as in the other castles, has numerous doors for defence, usually put in the middle of the flights. Shooting-holes are in every direction. We established ourselves in a room about 30 feet by 25 feet, and used to go up and dine in one of the unfinished rooms at the top where there was a little bit of roof and where the cooking was done. We generally thought it wise to dine in our grill-room, in order to have our food hot. We all greatly enjoyed the works of our own cooks, provisions being supplied to us.

We overlooked a huge puddle into which the surrounding houses drain, and it is a proof of the scarcity of water in this part of Arabia, that they carefully carry this filthy fluid away in skins to make bricks with, even scraping up the remaining drops in the pool with their hands. In fact, it scarcely ever rains in the Hadhramout.

From the roof of our lofty castle we had an excellent view straight down the broad Hadhramout valley, dotted with towns, villages, palm groves, and cultivation for fully thirty miles, embracing the two towns of Siwoun and Terim, ruled over by the two brother sultans of the Kattiri tribe. Close to Shibahm several collateral valleys from north and south fall into the Hadhramout, and a glance at the map made by our chartographer, Imam Sharif, Khan Bahadur, will at once show the importance of this situation.

Shibahm is the frontier town of the Yafei tribe, the Kattiri occupying the valley about two miles to the east, and these two tribes are constantly at war. Sultan Salàh's big standard was in one of our dwelling-rooms ready to be unfurled at a moment's notice. He has cannons on his walls pointed in the direction of his enemy—old cannons belonging to the East India Company, the youngest of which bore the date of 1832. From the soldiers we obtained a specimen of the great conch shells that they use as trumpets in battle, and which are hung to the girdle of the watchmen, who are always on the look-out to prevent a surprise.

The Kattiri are not allowed to stay in the town at night, for we heard that seven months before some of them were detected in an attempt to blow up the palace with gunpowder. There was a fight also, about a quarter of a mile outside the town, in which five Kattiri and seven Yafei were killed. There are three or four armed soldiers to protect Shibahm, the sultan has erected bastions and forts all about it, and the walls are patrolled every night.

There are many ruined houses in the plain, relics of the great war forty years ago, when the Kattiri advanced as far as Al Koton and did great damage. The sultan of Siwoun was invited, with seven sheikhs, to the palace of Shibahm on friendly terms and there murdered in cold blood, while forty of his followers were killed outside.

The inhabitants of Shibahm were not at all friendly disposed to us. On the day of our arrival my husband ventured with two of the sultan's soldiers into the bazaar, and through the narrow streets; but only this once, for the people crowded round him, yelled at him, and insulted him, trying their best to trip him up and impede his progress; he was nearly suffocated by the clouds of filthy dust that the mob kicked up, and altogether they made his investigations so exceedingly disagreeable that he became seriously alarmed for his safety, and never tried to penetrate into the heart of Shibahm again. On the whole I should accredit Shibahm with a population of certainly not less than six thousand souls: there are thirteen mosques in it, and fully six hundred houses, tall and gaunt, to which an average population of ten souls is but a moderate estimate. The slave population of Shibahm is considerable; many slaves have houses there, and wives and families of their own. The sultan's soldiers are nearly all slaves or of slave origin, and one of them, Muoffok, whose grandfather was a Swahili slave, and who had been one of our escort from Makalla, took us to his house, where his wife, seated unveiled in her coffee corner, dispensed refreshments to quite a large party there assembled, whilst Muoffok discoursed sweet music to us on a mandoline, and a flute made out of the two bones of an eagle placed side by side.

Taisir and Aboud were also abiding in Shibahm. Taisir when he met us, on the minute asked for bakhshish, saying he had been ill when we parted and had had none though we had sent it to him. Oh! there was such kissing of hands! so we thought it politic to love our enemy and gave him a present. The Wazir Salim-bin-Ali had travelled with us to take care of us in the absence of his master.

Once the Arabs had a good laugh at the expense of three members of our party. One morning our botanist went forth in quest of plants and found a castor-oil tree, the berries of which pleased him exceedingly. Unwilling to keep so rare a treat for himself, he brought home some branches of the tree, and placed the delicacy before two of our servants, Matthaios and, I am glad to say, Saleh, who also partook heartily. Terrible was the anguish of the two victims, which was increased by the Arabs, veritable descendants of Job's comforters, who told them they were sure to die, as camels did which ate these berries. The botanist did not succumb as soon as the others, who, not believing he had eaten any berries himself, vowed vengeance on his head if they should recover, and demanded that, to prove his innocence, he should eat twelve berries in their presence. To our great relief the botanist was at last seized with sickness, and thereby proved his guiltlessness of a practical joke; three more miserable men I never saw for the space of several hours. However, they were better, though prostrate, next day, and for some time to come the popular joke was to imitate the noises and contortions of the sufferers during their anguish.

In consequence of the enmity manifested towards us we were even debarred from walking in that interesting though smelly part, just outside the town under the walls with the well, the brick-works, the indigo, the oil-making, the many lime-kilns, the armourers, and all the industrious people of the town.

We used to take the air on the roof in the evening; there were no mosquitos, but we were never so persecuted with flies. Fortunately our castle was near the wall, for to dwell in the narrow, tortuous, dirty streets must be fearful—most likely the dust does much to neutralise the evils of the defective drainage. The houses are very high and narrow and built of mud brick (*kutcha*), which is constantly though slowly powdering away. There are many houses in ruins.

We had two or three days of slight cold. The temperature was 62° (F.) in the shade, and it was so cloudy that we expected rain, but none came.

Saleh managed to get ten rupees from my husband, who refused any more, though he brought a piece of cloth which he said he wished to buy from the sultan. The money was only wanted for gambling. He went to Imam Sharif and said, 'How is this that Mr. Bent, who at first was like my brother, now is quite changed?' Imam Sharif said, 'If he was kind to you when you were a stranger, and now that he knows you is different, there must be some reason for it.' 'What have I done?' 'You know best,' said Imam Sharif, 'and I advise you to beg pardon.' Saleh exclaimed, 'And you, who are a Moslem, take part against me with these Christians!' This is the keynote of his conduct to us.

We rode two hours one day, without Saleh, to a place called Kamour, on the southern side of the valley, where there is an inscribed stone at the mouth of a narrow slit or gorge leading to the akaba. The words thereon were painted light red, dark red, yellow, and black, and scratched. The decipherable words 'morning light' and 'offerings' point to this having been a sacred stone when sun worship was prevalent. The letters are well shaped, some letters being strange to us. The writing is *boustrephedon*, which means that it runs backward and forward like an unbroken serpent, each line being read in an opposite direction to that preceding or following it. There is no difficulty in seeing this at a glance, as the shapes of the letters are reversed; for instance, if this occurred in English the two loops of a B would be on the left, if the writing were to be read in that direction, [Symbol: See page image]. The Greek name comes from this style of writing being originally likened to cattle wandering about. This at once relegates it, according to the best authorities, to at least the third century before Christ, and we were forcibly reminded of the large stone in the ruins of Zimbabwe and its similar orientation.

We heard of a cave with an inscription in it in the Kattiri country, about six miles off, almost in sight. We longed 'to dance on Tom Tiddler's ground' and make a dash for it, but the forfeits we might incur deterred us, being our lives. The wazir said he would try to arrange for this, but that, even if the seyyids consented, we must take forty soldiers, well armed, pay them as well as *siyar* to the Kattiri, pay the expenses of the *siyara*, and take as short a time about the business as possible.

On the 27th we heard that some of the tribe of Al Jabber, descended from Mohammed's great friend of that name, had passed Shibahm for Al Koton to fetch us, but there was no news of the Minhali or of the Tamimi.

It was said that the Jabberi could not take us over their highland, past the Kattiri and into the Tamimi country, without consulting the Kattiri, who sometimes help them in their wars. It must be remembered that the Kattiri Bedouin were for us (no doubt in view of the payment of *siyar*), while the seyyids and Arabs of that tribe at Siwoun, and their friends at Terim, were against us.

I need not say we were weary of this indecision, so we sent a letter to the sultan of Shibahm by a messenger saying, 'We have been here three days; what are we to do next?' and planned that Imam Sharif should ride over next day, as he could communicate 'mouth to mouth' with the sultan in Hindustani.

We had one consolation in our imprisonment, for the seal of Yarsahal, which has been mentioned before, was brought to us. The stone is in brown and white stripes, and the setting is very pretty. It had been in the bezel of a revolving ring. We began bargaining for it at once, my husband offering ten rupees for the stone and ten for the golden setting, but the seyyid who brought it said it was the property of a man in Siwoun, who wished to keep it for his children, and he must take it back to him. My husband said 'he should like to look at it very quietly by himself and think over the stone,' and therefore asked the seyyid to remain outside the door for a few minutes. I quickly utilised this quiet time to make an impression with sealing-wax, in case we never saw the seal again. In two hours the seyyid appeared again, and said he had had a letter from Siwoun (twenty-four miles off), saying the (imaginary) owner would not part with it under thirty rupees, but he very soon took twenty and laughed most heartily when I said if I had known how near Siwoun was I would have gone myself.

This seal is of particular interest, for on it were the words 'Yarsahal, the Elder of Shibahm'; and in an inscription published by M. Halévy, we have the two Yarsahals and various members of this family described as vassals of the King of the Gebaniti. Now Pliny says that the capital of the country was Thumna; this is quite correct and was confirmed by the seal, for Thumna was the capital of the Gebaniti, who were a Himyaritic tribe, west of the Hadhramout. It is therefore an additional confirmation of the accuracy of the ancient geographers concerning this district.

In old days Shabwat, as it is called in inscriptions, or Sabbatha, Shaba, and Sabota, as it is written in the ancient authors, was the capital of the country. Hamdani tells us in his 'Geography of the Arabian Peninsula' that there were salt works at Shabwa, and 'that the inhabitants, owing to the wars between Himyar and Medhig, left Shabwa, came down into the Hadhramout and called the place Shibahm, which was originally called Shibat.' Times are much changed since Shabwa was a great town, for from all accounts it is now quite deserted save for the Bedouin, and is six days from good water; the water there is salt and bitter, like quinine, the sultan said. The Bedouin work the salt and bring it on camels, as is mentioned by Makrisi. The effect of salt is traceable in the water of all the wells in the main valley. We would gladly have gone into Shabwa, but it was obviously impossible.

There was a great deal of gun-firing when the Jabberi went by with the sheikh of the Kattiri, and our next interest was a letter from Al Koton, saying 'that the Tamimi, who had sworn on their heads and their eyes to do so, had never appeared, and that the Jabberi wanted 110 dollars, exclusive of camel hire, to go with us, the camels only to go a short distance, and then we must change. What did we wish to do?'

Of course we could not start without providing camels for our onward way, so this answer was sent back: 'We have not come to fight; we do not much care when we go, and we await the advice of the sultan when he comes to-morrow.'

Saleh was quite delighted, but we thought any direction would be good for our map and we still had hopes of digging near Meshed, though we began to have fears that a repulse eastward would strengthen the hands of our enemies westward.

On January the 29th a letter was brought to us by the wazir and the governor of the town, attended by Saleh, more pleased than ever. They said the letter had arrived last night and it was to say that the sultan's pain had increased, so he could not come to-day, and adding what we already knew as to the three neighbouring tribes.

We had a council of three, and feeling that the journey to Bir Borhut was out of the question, we determined to beat what we hoped would be a masterly retreat, so the wazir and the governor were summoned and the following answer was sent:

'We cannot understand the letters of the sultan, having no means of communicating with him privately. Therefore we will return to Al Koton to-morrow, and see him face to face.'

The servants were all quite delighted at this, for Saleh told them the letter was to say we and the soldiers were all going to be murdered.

We had stayed five days in Shibahm, and on the first three had taken sundry walks in the neighbourhood, but during the last two we never ventured out, as the inhabitants manifested so unfriendly a disposition towards us. After the Friday's prayer in the mosque, a fanatical mollah, Al Habib Yaher-bin-Abdullah Soumait, alluded to our unwelcome presence, and offered up the following prayer three times: 'O God! this is contrary to our religion; remove them away!' and two days afterwards his prayer was answered. This very gentleman had not long before been imprisoned for praying to be delivered from the liberal-minded Sultan Salàh, but the people had clamoured so much that he was released.

As we halted at the well outside the town, whilst the various members of our caravan collected, we overheard a woman chide a man for drawing too much water from the well, to which he replied,

'We have to wash our town from the infidel this day.' Needless to say we gladly shook the dust of Shibahm off our feet, and returned to the flesh-pots of Al Koton with considerable satisfaction. Of a truth, religion and fanaticism are together so deeply engrained in the Hadhrami, that anything like friendly intercourse with the people is at present next to impossible.

Religion is the moving spirit of the place; without religion the whole Hadhramout would have been abandoned long ago as useless, but the inhabitants look upon it as the most sacred spot on earth, Mohammed having been born in Arabia, and hence their objection to its being visited by unbelievers. The Shafi sect prevails to the exclusion of all others. The men go in crowds to India, Batavia, and elsewhere, sometimes remaining absent twenty years from their wives and families, and indeed we were told of one case in which a husband had been away for forty years. They return at last to spend their gains and die in their native sanctity.

We reached Al Koton on January 30, and found our friend the sultan very well indeed. We had begun to suspect we were being deceived as to his illness, for when the wazir and Saleh, who seemed in league together, heard the seyyid son-in-law, who came straight from Al Koton soon after the letter, telling us that the sultan was much better, they looked disconcerted, whispered together, and the wazir said, 'You should not talk of what you know nothing about.'

We were most anxious to learn all that had gone on in our absence, and what arrangements had been made. It seemed to be considered a mistake our ever having gone to Shibahm, but I do not think it was. Had we not gone we should never have seen that fine and interesting town, and assuredly not have obtained King Yarsahal's seal.

The sultan told us there had been a great uproar about us, and all the Yafei tribe were now considered Kafirs. The Kattiri absolutely refused the Jabberi leave to conduct us, and the Nahadi, through whose lands we had passed from Hagarein, said that if they had known how the Kattiri would treat us, they would have treated us just the same. It would be madness to go to Shabwa, as we should, even if we could get there, be only further hemmed in; the Wadi bin Ali was closed to us, the Nahadi were between us and Meshed; nevertheless, the sultan had actually sent a man to ask if we could dig there a few days, he camping with us. Our very faint hope of this was only founded on the fact that the seyyids of Meshed are at enmity with those of Siwoun.

On February 1, the Tamimi sent to say they had really started to fetch us, but the Kattiri told them they would declare war on them unless they retired.

The following evening we were thrown into some excitement by the arrival of the sultan in our room with seven letters, the general tenor of which was that eight of the Tamimi had come, with the *siyara* of four Amri only, and no *siyara* of Kattiri, as far as Siwoun, and asked to be passed on, but that the Kattiri refused them safe conduct; they asked the sultan of Shibahm to go to Shibahm and arrange for them to reach us. They proposed that we should, without touching Shibahm, turn into the very next wadi and go up on to the akaba; the men who went with us were to stay with us all the way to the coast. The sultan promised to keep hostages till his returning soldiers told of our safety. We had another council with Imam Sharif. We counted up our dollars, for we had to live on our money-bags till we reached the sea, and determined to reach Bir Borhut if we could, saying nothing to the servants to upset their minds till all was settled.

The sultan went away to Shibahm the next day, and, as usual, the women became very noisy, and during his absence we were close prisoners, on account of our fear of being mobbed. The Indian party were generally looked upon as Jews.

In the evening the sultan came back, telling us that the Tamimi wished to bring 400 soldiers unpaid (?) and to take us through their country, but the Kattiri were too strong for them. They said, 'One man came disguised to see us (Herr von Wrede), one man came undisguised (Herr Hirsch), and now a party has come. Next time it will be a larger one still, and then it will be all over with the sacred valley of the Hadhramout.' Saleh, meanwhile, was doing all he could to annoy us. When we were talking over our difficulties with Imam Sharif, he strutted in with a bill for the camels. My husband said:

'It is already paid.'

'I shall see about others then,' Saleh said.

'They are ordered already.'

'Your groom, Iselem, will not go with you,' said Saleh.

So I told him, 'He won't get the chance; we would not have him if we were paid, and though we have paid him beforehand, we willingly lose our money.'

'I must, then, speak to the sultan about him, for you.'

I said, 'The sultan has decided what he will do with him, and I don't think he will like it.'

'Haidar Aboul will not go with you.'

This made us very angry, as we had seen that Saleh had been tampering with him, lending him his donkey and his sandals when he walked, and whispering with him. He tried to separate everyone from us. Haidar had promised to go with us all the way, and later Imam Sharif brought him to me when I was at home alone, and made him repeat his promise, and assurance that he had never told Saleh he would not go.

Saleh also wanted money, but was refused; he got 100 rupees a month, and 200 were prepaid at Aden. He gambled, and my husband wished to keep the contents of our money-bags for our own use. We calculated that at the cheapest, for soldiers and *siyara* and camels, Bir Borhut would cost 130*l*. Saleh had put all the servants in a most terrible fright, and a soldier had told them that if we went beyond Shibahm we should all be killed, and that we should find no water by the way. So we had to explain to them the plan of going by Wadi bin Ali, and to comfort them as well as we could. These people never seem to think that we value our own lives as much as they do theirs.

Meshed was also closed against us. The sultan of Siwoun and the seyyids had sworn on the Koran not to let us proceed on our journey; the Kattiri had also sworn and sent messages to the Tamimi of Bir Borhut, the Jabberi of Wadi bin Ali, and the Nahadi, and they were all against us.

We had another day of anxiety and uncertainty as to when we should really start, as the camels were not collected till late. We watched eagerly from our tower, counting them as they arrived by twos and threes.

We were rather in despair as as we sat dining in a yard, for at this time we were started with our own cookery, and dined near the kitchen, which Matthaios had been able to make in an arched recess of the inclosure, where there were high hills of date-stones, kept to be ground to paste for cattle-food.

He could not be allowed to defile a Mohammedan kitchen.

After a very few minutes, however, my husband had an idea, which was to go to Sheher somehow, and turn up inland from thence; there were plenty of Tamimi there to help us, and we could thus get to the east side of the Kattiri. Saleh was to know nothing till all was settled.

February 7 was a very weary day of waiting; for we had mended and cleaned everything we possessed, and we packed and hoped the camels would come, expecting to be off on the morrow, but it was not till evening that people, I cannot remember of what tribe, came to bargain with us, and the bargaining continued next morning; so we made all baggage ready to be tied into bundles, for we had no doubt we should start on the 8th at latest.

First they said we must go by the Wadi al Ain, their own home, and this we knew was that they might blackmail us; but they told us it was from want of water on the high ground, over which we must travel for six days, and that we must take two camels for water. Then they said we should take seventeen days in all, and were to pay for twenty at more than double the usual fare. We should have to go back on our old road as far as Adab, then three days in the Wadi al Ain region, the same road near Haibel Gabrein, go on to Gaffit, and thence turn eastward to Sheher.

We were perfectly horrified at this plan; the price was great, and the sultan seemed not to think it possible to go against the Bedouin; but far worse in our eyes was the thought of our map, as we should see no new country, instead of taking a turn or a climb that would have added miles to it.

They left us, and we were sitting on our floor in the deepest depths of dark despair, when news came that these camel-men, having made a fresh plan for more extortions, *i.e.* that there was to be no limit to the number of camels, save their will in loading them, the sultan, being indignant, was thinking of sending for other men.

When we heard that we roused up and concocted a new plan, which was to send for the sultan and ask him to get the Jabberi, and make them take us by the Wadi bin Ali; so he came and agreed to this. We were not to go so long over the highland, but to go up and down at least twice, which would suit us and our map. The sultan told us we should find running water, and that it was a shorter way to Sheher.

Besides this, there lurked in the background, not to be revealed till the last moment, a design to get the Tamimi to come to a place in Wadi Adim and take us to Bir Borhut, a name truly terrible to Matthaios and the Indian servants.

We were in high spirits, and agreed that no matter what our fate might be we were having a delightful evening. Truly I think the pleasures of hope are not sufficiently appreciated, for even if your hopes are never realised the hoping has been a great happiness. On the 8th those extortionate men of Wadi al Ain sent to say they would take us by the Wadi bin Ali, turning out of Wadi Hadhramout at Al Gran, crossing the Wadis bin Ali and Adim, and reaching Sa'ah, where we could branch off for Bir Borhut. This offer was declined, for we were watching and waiting for the Jabberi; and at night we heard that the brave Jabberi were at Shibahm, whereas our messenger had been sent to Wadi bin Ali. They said they wondered at not hearing from us, as the sultan had engaged their camels and promised to let them know when they would be wanted. It was a great mystery to us why the Wadi al Ain people had ever been sent for.

The Jabberi thus defied the Kattiri: 'As sure as we come from Jabberi fathers and Jabberi mothers, we will take these people safely to Bir Borhut; and as sure as you come from Kattiri fathers and Kattiri mothers, you may do your worst but still we will keep them safe'; to which the Kattiri replied: 'We do not wish to make war on you, and we do not care where you take them so long as it is not into our country.'

As soon as we had finished our breakfast next day, a message came to say our horses were ready, and we were to go and drink coffee at a little tower the sultan has in the plain. Most of the party walked. There were only horses for five; a donkey carried a water-skin, and our donkey, Mahsoud, carried halters for every animal. There were the two wazirs, the son-in-law, the sultan of Haura, and a good many servants with carpets for us to sit on, and a teapot. We sat there for about two hours doing nothing but look at the green, an occupation for which this house is expressly built. A gun announced the arrival of the men of Al Jabber, and the sultan sent a man to kill a goat and receive them.

Our great joy at their coming was nothing compared to our extreme satisfaction at parting with them later on.

I cannot say much for my skill as a physiognomist, for I have it recorded that I liked the looks of our Mokadam (that is chief of our *kafila*, or leader) Talib-bin-Abdullah, son of the Jabberi sheikh, and that I did not care for the looks of our new groom, Salem. I was quite wrong in both cases. There were also Saleh-bin-Yamani and another Jabberi. We were certainly, this time, to start next day, but with another change in our route, I believe on account of water. Instead of going by Al Gran, we were to go by Wadi Manwab, retracing our steps as far as Furhud.

Very early in the morning Imam Sharif came to us and told us that the Jabberi had not sufficient camels with them and that we must take camels of Mandob the first day or two, and that others would meet us in the Wadi bin Ali, so there was little hope of a move that day. The Jabberi afterwards said the Mandob way was much the longest, so we changed again.

We delayed several days longer at Al Koton, hoping against hope that the sultan of Terim would grant us permission to pass through his territories, that we might prosecute our journey.

CHAPTER XIII

FAREWELL TO THE SULTAN OF SHIBAHM

Our departure from Al Koton on February 12 was almost as serious an affair as our start from Makalla. Sultan Salàh, with the instincts of true hospitality, not only refused to receive remuneration for our entertainment, but loaded us with presents of food for the way and fodder for our animals, intimating that 'bakshish' to some of his dependents would not be altogether unacceptable. With the object of receiving rewards for their services, the grand viziers, the mounshi (a scribe), the hall-porter, the water-carriers, the slaves who had waited on us, were all brought in a bare-faced manner to our room; as we descended the stairs, expectant menials lined the passages; we had to remember the grooms, the soldiers, and the gardeners. Never again will the irksome custom of tipping be half so appalling as when we left the palace of Sultan Salàh.

The sultan wished to fire off seven guns at our departure, but this we declined. He came about a mile with us, and then went to Shibahm, to send an answer to the letter from the Tamimi, saying, 'On their eyes they would meet us at Sa'ah.' He also determined to stay away a few days, as he should find his house very dull when we were gone. It had been such a great break in the monotony of his life having us, and he had so much enjoyed the society of Imam Sharif that he was always promising him houses, wells, lands, slaves, and wives if he would only return and settle down in the Wadi Hadhramout.

An old and confidential relation of his was to accompany us all the way, and the Wazir Salim-bin-Ali came as far as our first camp, two hours off, in the Wadi Hadira. Here we could plainly see the formation of these valleys, abrupt at the end and like a circus, not made by streams descending, but like creeks and bays of a gigantic fiord. There is not much cultivation in the little valley. This is the road to Sheher. There are two approaches to the akaba, one by the Wadi Hadira and one by the Wadi bin Ali, which is the way to

Sheher. We had to enter the Wadi bin Ali sideways by climbing over the akaba from Wadi Hadira, owing to the opposition of the Kattiri, who hold the mouth of Wadi bin Ali. The wazir departed in the morning with a Martini-Henry rifle which my husband sent to the sultan. This gave rise to the report which we heard afterwards 'that we were distributing arms, of which we had five hundred camel-loads.'

That day we had a very tiresome adventure. Starting off early before our caravan with several Jabberi, we intended to ascend to the plateau before the heat of midday came on. We were accompanied by a few soldiers, who it turned out did not know the way, and having ridden for an hour and a half up a narrow gorge with wild figs, wild date, and fan palms growing around us, and really magnificent cliffs 700 to 800 feet high on either side of us, reddish in colour and with fossils in the limestone strata, a truly fearful and awe-inspiring place, we suddenly came to an abrupt termination of our valley, having wormed ourselves along, chiefly on foot, and found that unless Sindbad's roc came to our assistance we could not possibly get out of it. Consequently we were regretfully obliged retrace our steps, having spent three hours and much toil, but glad of having had an opportunity of following one of these valleys to its bitter end. It appeared that our supposed guides had never been there in their lives.

We scrambled down this wadi, and into the wadi to our right; the way truly was difficult, the valley narrowing and nearly blocked up by perfectly perpendicular cliffs. Our caravan and servants were anxiously awaiting us at a curious spot called Mikadèh, about a quarter of the way up the cliff, where the road which we had missed goes through a natural tunnel about twenty yards long, from lovely pools of rain-water preserved in its recesses, with which we eagerly refreshed ourselves. The rest of the ascent to the plateau was marvellously steep. The camels had to be unloaded, and two fell down. All the baggage was carried by men, up crag after crag, and sometimes there was no sign of a path. I never could have imagined it possible for camels to ascend the roof-like slope of rock up which they had to clamber for the last 50 yards, and indeed, one poor animal did fall, and injured itself so that it had to be unloaded and taken back, whereupon those Bedouin who did not own it heartlessly regretted that it had not been killed, as they would have liked some of its flesh for supper. Just at the end everything had to be unloaded again, and the camels literally dragged up to the top, while we sat dangling our legs over the cliff. Such yelling and shrieking I never heard among the Bedouin, our soldiers and our servants all calling each other rascals, and no one doing more than he could help; and inasmuch as we had about five Salehs, four Umbarreks, and other duplicated names amongst our men, the shouts of 'So-and-so, son of so-and-so,' made us fully realise the clumsiness of Arab nomenclature.

When we clambered up on to the akaba it looked dreary and lifeless, silent and lonely and stony, but it soon became lively enough, for we were a large *kafila*, about fifty people and twenty-four camels. We had by very good fortune a great deal of cloud that day, but also some tremendous sun.

We sat eagerly counting the camels as they came into view, and had great anxiety about eight of them, and were obliged to send two soldiers back to search for them. We meant to proceed farther as water was two hours on, and some of the first-arrived camels were reloaded; but, after all, we felt we must wait for those eight camels, and send back to Mikadèh for water. We could not encamp very comfortably, for the camel which had fallen and hurt his chest had our bedding and night-clothes and Imam Sharif's tent-poles, and besides this our kitchen-box was missing and we had had no luncheon. So another camel was sent down to fetch those necessaries.

It was dreadfully windy, much dust blowing, and so stony that we could only have a peg in each corner of our tents. Rain was threatening, so the baggage was all stacked under the outer fly of our tent. The soldiers behaved most helpfully and the brave and bold Jabberi had not yet once mentioned bakshish in our hearing and were most polite. They were better-looking men than others we had seen, all tall, slight, wiry, and very muscular, a higher type than the

Khailiki and much more dressed. The three principal ones wore turbans, red and yellow. They said they were so very sorry for losing the way that 'none of them felt quite well when they thought of our inconvenience.'

I could not sleep that night, so I got up and put on my dressing-gown and sat near the door with my head out, and so was fortunately ready to slip out when I heard a trailing picket, and found Zubda rushing up and down, looking for water I suppose. We were so short of it that we had washed in a very little without soap, and one horse had drunk that, and the other the water the chickens were washed in. I caught him, but as I could not possibly drive in the picket, I tied him to a packing case, and then had to collect his food, which was blown all over the place, and take it there for him.

On February 14, in consequence of the want of water, great was the hurry to start; we were off about half-past six, and travelled till one o'clock without stopping or getting water; the horses only had half a pint each, that we had washed in. We should not have been so extravagant as to wash that much if we had not wanted to let the horses drink.

The plateau here offered features that were new to us. It is as it were in two stories. From the bottom of a wadi you reach first a slope or talus of loose stones, then a cliff, then another slope of loose stones and a cliff, and next comes the main akaba, and on this again a great deal more of the upper story is left than we had hitherto seen. The upper part is from 80 to 100 feet above the lower; sometimes it is in the form of an isolated flat-topped hill, larger or smaller, and sometimes like a kind of centipede, and in the gullies between the legs of these centipedes are to be found whatever remain of frankincense trees, for vegetation is very sparse on the akaba. Showered about everywhere are small bits of black basalt. We had several ups and downs, and passed wadis running in close to us before we began to descend by what must have been a fearful road for the camels, down the two precipices and the two flights of rolling stones, into the Wadi bin Ali. The way was far better than that of the day before; the very Jabberi never saw such a road as that, they said.

When we started descending we saw the village of Bazahel below us—the Jabberi capital. It has a picturesque modern fort, built on old Himyaritic foundations. When we reached it the soldiers fired guns, and we were very kindly received by the inhabitants, who led us to a house they had prepared for us. We excused ourselves from inhabiting it, saying it was better not to have our baggage carried up, but we would gladly rest in it.

The house seemed very clean—it was of mud of course; the walls of it and the stairs had all been scraped into furrows and curves, and also the dados of the staircase and room were decorated with a kind of basket pattern, and the floors were also in a raised pattern. Carpets were spread, water brought, and with great kindness they locked us in that we might not be disturbed. Only our own party were in this room, the soldiers in another. Matthaios had joined himself to the vanguard to see what happened to us, so my husband shared his horse with him; he had been terrified the day before at the fear that we had been carried off. The Indian servants and the botanist joined us just as coffee with ginger and other spices were brought. Our host had long wrestling with the lock before he could open the door, and after this we were desired to bolt it on the inside. We had a pleasant camp, with palm-trees to shade each cooking fire, no starers being allowed. A woman here joined our *kafila* for protection for a few stages. Even I never saw her face: she always wore her mask and her hat, and looked a most ungainly object. I dare say I looked the same to her. The sultan of Shibahm had sent a man on horseback up that dreadful wadi to our last camp to thank us for the gun, and to warn us by all means to keep on the highlands for fear of the hostile Kattiri.

At Bazahel, Abdullah Mareh-bin-Talib-bin-Said, chief of the Jabberi, welcomed us to his own house later in the day, a most unwonted piece of hospitality. He is much stained with indigo, a very elastic and naked sovereign, who bends his fingers back in a way horrible to behold when he wishes to emphasise his remarks, as he did when he spoke of the Kattiri and his wars with them, and his constantly losing men in raids, as is also the case in his fights with the Hamoumi. As we sat around drinking his coffee, he boasted of his direct descent from Jabber of Hiyal, the friend and councillor of Mohammed, and told us that his family pedigree was safely kept at Terim, with those of all the surrounding tribes of Arabs. Somehow or other we did not care for the Jabberi at all afterwards, and for the rest of our journey to the coast our quarrels with Talib, the son of Abdullah, and the difficulties he would throw in our way, were daily sources of annoyance to us.

We left Bazahel at half-past six next morning with the intention of climbing up to the tableland again. The Wadi bin Ali is not very wide and the ground is bare, though there are many villages scattered about. At rather a large one, where the wadi forks, and which we reached at eight o'clock, we were to begin our ascent. To our dismay the camels were made to sit down and the camel-men said we must stay there the night, as there was no water up above. We declared we knew there was, and that we would go on; they must fill the twenty water-skins which we always carried. Some men were inclined to go on, but were overruled by the majority. After half an hour's contention we rode away with a good many people, leaving a few soldiers with the baggage, to show our determination to proceed, we being told that the others would be afraid to stay behind. We sat down once or twice in full view of the village, to survey the camels and wonder if they were coming, and much perplexed were we. We had expected to change camels the following day, and this was the last day with those men, who by delaying us wished to spin out another day's journey at twenty-five rupees. Those soldiers who were with us recommended us to push on round a corner, where the wadi ran in, and conceal ourselves behind rocks, which there stood up between the path and the village, that the camel-men might not think there was any hesitation on our part; so men, and beasts, and I were carefully hidden, and one who peeped without his turban, reported that some camels were rising, and finally, eight starting.

When we reached the tableland we had to go a long way round to avoid a good many little wadis which were all quite steep, before we reached the water. At the edge of the tableland are some little shelters used by hunters to shoot gazelle, which come down the gullies that to us appeared, inaccessible. Near the water the soldiers made us climb down to the first story of a small wadi, where we sheltered under a shelf of rock which overhangs the whole end of it. When I was cool, I clambered up and found a hollow or depression above our heads, with a few tufts of grass and some shrubs, so I took down some bits of shrubs as 'samples on appro' to the horses, and as they did approve, they were sent up to graze. We lay on our saddle-cloths till three, pretty hungry, when the eight camels came, and a good long time after the others arrived also the relation of the sultan Salàh joined us on a riding camel: an old man, Salem-bin-Mohammad by name. He said the camels had been changed, and the money paid in advance for this day, taken from those men. We had a cold, windy night at this place, Farash. No one had tents but our own party; even the sultan and other gentry lie in the open on journeys. Our horses were given a supper of dates, which are considered very strengthening, and which they much enjoyed.

The tribe of Al Jabber possess the parallel Wadis Adim and Bin Ali, and the road between them across the akaba is much traversed and apparently an ancient one. We went across on the level, eight miles, and then descended by a narrow valley leading into the Wadi Adim. The way was made longer by its having to wind about to skirt the wadis, which cut into it like a fringe; sometimes we were only half a mile from our former or future track. Once we heard a gun fired, and looking across, we saw a *kafila* of fifty camels, a much larger one than our own, slipping behind a hill to hide from us, and presently some men climbed up to peep. We—that is to say my husband, Imam Sharif, and I—with the three chief Jabberi, the Relation, and some soldiers and others, all gathered up together and stood at gaze, without returning the gun-fire, which was meant to find out if we had any bad intentions. Our own camels were very near the strange *kafila*, and that party was terribly frightened. I think the fright was mutual. When we had gone some distance, and were out of sight of the strange caravan, we were amused at seeing the soldiers and the Jabberi, all in line, running on at a double, firing guns, and shouting, 'Hohh! Hohh! Hohh!' My husband asked the Relation what chance we had of being robbed, as this seemed a convenient place, but he comfortingly said, 'We need not be much afraid, for we have the chief of the robbers with us.' This was really true.

The place where we were to climb down into the Wadi Adim was tremendously steep. It really seemed very like trying to climb down the sides of a tea-cup, I wondered how we and the camels and horses would ever do it. However we all did, and the valley became first a crack and then a little wider, and the road then was not so very bad in its own wild way. As soon as the valley became a little flat the men wanted to stop and wait for the camels, but we said we would rather be in the village of Ghail Omr, which they said was only just round a near corner.

So we went on, but for fully two miles, till the Wadi Adim crossed our path. It was full of palms on the far side, so we went over there, but were made, whether we would or no, to return to the mouth of our little wadi again; they said on account of food for the camels. There was a fearful row when we crossed the valley, to make us go back, there were daggers out and loud shouts that my husband and I were rascals (harami) and Imam Sharif a dog, and Matthaios and the rest of the servants were in great alarm.

We were now in much anxiety and perplexity, for we were told the Tamimi had not come, and they were to have been at Ghail Omr before us, to fetch us to Bir Borhut. We ourselves were not at the appointed place, for we were kept pent into the little wadi. We were told that two men had been murdered on the way to Sheher, but we never made out who they were; also that a seyyid and a lot of the Amri tribe had come, so the Relation took my horse and went off to investigate them.

Next morning we thought it well to be ready and to look undismayed; the seyyid with the ten Amri joined us, and we all turned into the Wadi Adim to our right and south. The valley is most fruitful and well worth seeing; there are miles of palm woods; it is about 100 feet higher than Wadi bin Ali, the slope is greater and the mountains lower; it is the most frequented caravan route from Sheher to the Hadhramout. We passed plenty of people coming up, and one day we met a caravan of 150 camels from Sheher with Hadhrami merchants returning from India to enjoy the fruits of their rascality, and end their days on the sacred soil of Arabia. There were little tents on the camels for women, and they seemed to us to have very few armed men.

The stream Ghail Omr is the first running one we saw since Al Ghail. It comes from the small Wadi Loban and is very considerable. Wadi Adim is quite the gem of the valleys that we explored. There is a *ziaret* or place of pilgrimage, which attracts many people, to the tomb of a seyyid Omr, called after Omar, one of the four successors to Mohammed. The Jabberi seem, in spite of possessing this rich valley, to be a poor tribe. There is a large population scattered in small homesteads. They have slaves, who live in little huts made of palm branches, with the interstices plastered with mud.

Ten more Jabberi joined us, so when we reached Sa'ah in two hours and a half, we were more than eighty people, with twenty-five camels, two horses, and three donkeys. We dismounted in a dense crowd, in a field of dry earth cut up into squares with hard ridges, so our floors were most uncomfortable. Naturally we dared do no damage by having them dug smooth.

On our arrival at our camping ground and while we were waiting for our tents to be ready, always a weary, irksome time to the wayworn traveller, I was surrounded by women all masked. They seemed highly astonished at a safety-pin I was taking out, so I gave, or rather offered it, to an old woman near me. She wanted to take it, but several men rushed between us and roared at us both, and prevented my giving it to her. I stood there holding it out and she stretching out her hand, and one or two men then asked me for it for her, so I put it down on a stone and she took it away and seemed pleased, but a man soon brought it back to me on the end of a stick, saying 'they did not know these things and were afraid of them.'

There was no news of the Tamimi and many told us they would not come, but we still kept up our vain hopes, as they had promised to come and wait a day or two for us, bringing with them a *siyara* of the

Minhali and of the Hamoumi. However, we were never allowed to get to the trysting-place, as we afterwards thought, because the Jabberi wanted to keep the fleecing of us in their own hands.

Not one of our party, with the exception of Imam Sharif, wished to go to Bir Borhut, and they all encouraged each other in discouraging us.

About a mile before reaching Sa'ah we saw an old fortress on a spur jutting out of the precipice, with a cut road leading to it, so of course we determined to visit it. We accordingly set out about two o'clock, my husband and I, Saleh on the donkey, some soldiers, some of our *siyara* of Jabberi, and my camera. But we came to a standstill when first four, then nine, and at last fourteen men were seen on the top of the ruins, pointing guns at us. They said they would not let us advance without paying, and we feared to come to terms as our Jabberi first said they were Amri, and then a tribe of Jabberi with whom they were at war. In this uncertainty we had to turn back and my husband complained to the sheikh of Sa'ah, who said that this blackmailing had been planned by one of our three best Jabberi, Seid-bin-Iselem, who went with us, and that he would send men of his own with us in the morning. In the morning they came, sure enough, and first asked for a dollar 'to buy coffee,' but my husband said 'No; he would give bakshish if he found writing, but if he found no writing he would give nothing, and in any case, nothing till we returned.' As we heard no more of them after they had retired to think over it, we were sure there could be no inscription. Besides we had seen that the corner-stones were the only cut ones; the others were all rough.

After dinner we and Imam Sharif had another serious council, finding ourselves in a regular fix.

We determined to stay on one more day at Sa'ah to give the Tamimi a chance to join us, for if we were baffled in getting from here to Bir Borhut, we must get to Sheher as quickly as possible and try from there to reach Bir Borhut. We wished to dismiss our camel-men, but they said they would not let us do so, nor allow anyone else to take the loads. They said they would take us for one rupee a day each camel, but we did not know how many days they would take; they had also said that they would stop where we pleased, or go on all day if we liked, but we had had experience which led us to doubt this. They had now been asked to name their stages; *kafilas* can go in seven or eight days.

We determined that our next attempt to go to Bir Borhut should be with fewer camels. It is a great mistake for explorers in dangerous countries to have collectors with them. They are a great drag and an extra anxiety. The preparations they can make are necessarily all made by guesswork, as no one can tell what is to be found in an unknown country. If we had known we should never have carried the huge spade and fork, which were hated all the way by everyone, or the quantities of cases of spirits of wine and receptacles for large animals, and the dozens of gins, snares, and traps of every description for things that we never found. Of course, in the case of our expedition, there are certain plants and reptiles which would not yet have emerged from their primeval obscurity, and it is a great consolation to feel that something was accomplished in that way. For everyone who is added to such an expedition, the leader has one more for whose life and health he feels a responsibility, one more whose little idiosyncrasies must be studied by all the rest, and who may endanger the safety of all by his indiscretions with regard to the natives, and one more who must be made to pack and be ready in time, or willing not to stray away in times of danger. Mere servants do not so much matter, as they are under control, though the fewer of them the better, as they are human beings who must be fed and carried; but those above them, and who, though not entitled to a seat in the council, feel free to make comments, are the hardest to deal with.

Before we went to bed that night, Haidar Aboul, the second interpreter, came and swore on the Koran that the Relation had promised the camel-men two rupees each; still we lay down happy in the assurance that we should be at Sheher in seven days, but after a night much disturbed by guns for a wedding, the first news that greeted us was that those camel-men wished to leave us. They were told that they could not do so: they were bound to take us to Sheher. They then said they would not go in seven days—who had arranged such long stages? They were told their sheikh had. Then we agreed to go in eight days, hoping that in the end they, finding they would lose no money, would allow us to gain time. Some hours after the little crooked sheikh sent to say that if those men would not take us in seven days he would get others.

The Relation was not of much good to us. There is here no law, order, authority, honour, honesty, or hospitality, and as to the people, I can only describe them as hateful and hating one another. It must be an awful life to live for ever unable to stir without *siyara* even a few miles. The rude Carinthian Boor cannot have been as bad as these Arabians.

After this they came and said we should go in thirteen days. Later the sheikh sent to say he would send twenty soldiers, and make them take us in eight days. This my husband declined, as we knew he had no power, even in his own village.

Then the brother of the sheikh came to ask for a present for him, which was refused, and the sheikh said afterwards we could not trust that brother, he was a liar.

At last another list of different stages was brought, and they swore by God and upon the Koran that they would take us in seven days.

All the time we were in Sa'ah we had to remain in our tent, tightly tied in, for if we did not we were quite deprived of air by the crowd, which became thicker and thicker, driving the foremost nearly into the tent headlong. I sewed strings to the extreme edges of our doors, which lapped half a yard, and this extension of size was very welcome. We afterwards found these strings useful and pleasant, but we always called them the 'Jabberi strings' in remembrance of these tormentors. If, thinking the crowd had dispersed, we ventured to open the tent, a scout proclaimed the fact, and we were again mobbed.

Our tent was 7 feet 6 inches square, and we found this quite large enough when it had to be pitched on a slope, or on a narrow, rocky ledge, when trees had to be cut down to make room in a forest, or when it was among the boulders of a river bed. Imam Sharif's tent was larger, and though it looked more stately in a plain, he sometimes had not room to pitch it, and had to sleep with his servants.

CHAPTER XIV

HARASSED BY OUR GUIDES

We never could ascertain whether the Tamimi had come or not, so on February 18, having given up all hope of joining them and changed ten camels, we set out, but not before nine o'clock.

After Sa'ah the Wadi Adim becomes narrow, stony, and uninteresting, and our way lay for a good part along a stony river bed, gradually mounting, but almost imperceptibly. For several days we pursued the course of this valley, and had we known what would befall us as we approached the head of the Wadi Adim, I think nothing would have induced us to take this route. It appears that a very wicked branch of the Hamoumi tribe hold a portion of this valley, and determined that their enemies, the Jabberi, who stole their cattle and plundered their caravans, should not have the exclusive patronage of the lucrative English travellers on their way to the coast. To our surprise at twelve o'clock we stopped at a well, Bir al Ghuz, when our men began to unload the camels. They said they were only just waiting for the Hamoumi siyara to come up, and that they had already arrived at Sa'ah.

The Hamoumi are a small, poor tribe of Bedouin, who occupy the lower end of Wadi Adim. They hire out camels to caravans, and do a great deal of the carrying business. Their villages consist of miserable little hovels gathered round forts, placed at intervals down the valleys, so that they can see from one to another. They have many flocks and herds, for there is actually pasturage for them, and many of the shepherds live in caves, there being plenty in the sides of the valley, which are composed of pudding-stone; they wall up the front.

We considered that, as Talib-bin-Abdullah, the chief of the Jabberi and so notorious a robber, was our Mokadam, we had better keep friends with him, therefore we spoke him fair. He and his companions came and wrote their names after a list of stages, and made a most solemn oath they would do anything we liked; and after we had sat for an hour or more in the sun, waiting for the Hamoumi, they said we must pass the night at Bir al Ghuz, still swearing to the seven days.

We therefore encamped, and very soon the Jabberi came and asked my husband for a sheep, but he said he would not give one now, but later in the journey he would do so if he found we were getting on well; so they went away, but soon came back for twenty-seven dollars, as *siyar* to the Hamoumi. My husband said he had agreed for twenty-five, but they said they had spent two dollars on a messenger to fetch the Hamoumi. The Jabberi were by way of having 110 dollars for their *siyar*, forty first and the rest at Sheher. They would not move next morning (the 20th) without the whole of the money, so they had to be given that and the twenty-seven dollars for the Hamoumi. Besides this they always demanded their camel-hire every evening.

They next said the way was very dangerous, and we must take men from five other tribes (though we could not imagine how so many could be accommodated in that wilderness), and pay twenty dollars. As my husband refused, and asked them to reflect upon the consequences of their conduct, the soldiers came and now said they recommended him to pay and recover the money at Sheher; otherwise they, the soldiers, said they would give up their weapons to the Jabberi as a pledge that they would pay forty dollars at Sheher. We said they might, but Talib told us that if we did not pay they would give the Hamoumi their money and all go back themselves. We then summoned Imam Sharif and had another council of three.

The servants, meanwhile, used often to be leaning in at the tent door, scanning our faces and begging us to do anything the Jabberi wanted, and moaning that we should never see the ocean any more.

The Jabberi had gone away, as my husband said he must think over this; so we consulted together. We at first quite decided to return to Al Koton, and try to reach the coast by Wadi al Ain and, if we could not have the camels, to load our own three animals with necessaries and money, leaving all else behind, and perhaps to slip by Siwoun in the night. So Talib was recalled, and told that we would go back; that we were now convinced of the dangers of this road, as we saw he was afraid himself, and as he had told us of two places where murders were always committed. But afterwards we thought it wiser to consent to pay the extra thirty dollars (in all fifty-seven) as *siyar* to the Hamoumi, all the tribes mentioned being varieties of Hamoumi. The money was to be placed on the Koran and taken thence by Talib, with an oath that, if the sultan of Sheher thought it unnecessary, it should be refunded. Seid-bin-Iselem and three soldiers witnessed this, but Talib would not allow the Hamoumi to be present. Instead of taking Talib's gun as a deposit, the soldiers were to keep the money in their hands. We were still to be at Sheher within the seven days, and not now to wait two or three days for the five tribes.

Though we did unpack a Koran and make Talib-bin-Abdullah swear on it, we did not then understand that merely swearing on the binding is nothing. The Koran must be opened, and some places are better than others. Oaths by the life of a son, or to divorce a favourite wife, are really good. We being, as I say, ignorant, the oaths were broken.

My husband and I now felt quite conquered; and it must be admitted we had reason.

We had a horrible evening of dust-storms and hurricanes, and were dreadfully afraid of the tent being blown down. In the morning we packed, and the baggage was taken out to be tied in bundles, when Talib demanded the eleven dollars camel-hire for the day before. In vain was he told that all was packed, and he should have them at the next stage. No! he would not go away without his money; so at great inconvenience we had to pay on the nail.

We had not gone an hour before we stopped, unloaded, and changed our camels for Hamoumi camels. 'Now all is peace,' said Talib-bin-Abdullah, and in the same breath asked for two dollars for two extra camels, that we had had before we reached Sa'ah. My husband refused, but when we reached our stage Talib asked for that day's pay, and would not take it without the two dollars. Of course my husband refused again, saying we were not responsible for those two camels; that Talib had contracted to take us and our baggage, and that now we had twenty-two camels instead of the fifteen with which we arrived at Al Koton. Equally, of course, he knew he must pay, and did.

We settled ourselves under some thorny trees at Bir bin Aboudan, where there are two wells with good water. It is larger than most Hamoumi villages, and has palm-trees and many large b'dom-trees.

Besides the Hamoumi, Jabberi, and Yafei, there are many small subsidiary tribes, or rather families, forming little independent communities of their own, in this region.

To continue the life of Talib-bin-Abdullah. As soon as he had received the last-mentioned money, he and his companions and the Hamoumi had a great and loud quarrel. Our money, being so bulky, was in bags scattered about among all the baggage, but we always had one store-bag in my box, and my husband had some for current expenses. The camel-men thought all the money was in a certain bag that was solemnly carried into the tent every night. While they shouted we filled the bag with a certain amount of dollars, meant to represent our entire fortune, and placed it on the table. We had become great hypocrites, but now we both decided that sweet words were of no avail. Whenever Imam Sharif was sent for, the servants crowded round, scanning our faces, and in despair themselves, saying 'our lives are sacrificed,' and making great lamentations about their wives and families.

It was very hard sometimes to keep our voices and countenances cheerful while holding counsel with Imam Sharif as to how we ought to act, for sometimes it is right to haggle over fourpence and sometimes it is right to pay through the nose. It is difficult, indeed, when you are cudgelling your brains, not to knit your brows, even if you only wish to decide if you will take your umbrella or not.

Talib had not been absent from us an hour when he again arrived, saying he wanted four dollars to pay a debt he owed in Bir bin Aboudan; 'it was to come out of the thirty dollars still owing for the *siyara*, and to be paid at Sheher,' he said. He was, of course, told that the money for the *siyara* had been fully paid up, seventy dollars before the sultan of Shibahm, and forty at Sa'ah. Talib bawled a good deal, and my husband pointed to the money-bag and said, 'If you want all my money, take it; but call it by no other name than robbery. Take all at once instead of bothering me perpetually, and I will settle with you at Sheher.'

When they heard this they were frightened, and went away, saying 'Oh! No! No! We do not want that.' They were soon back, and said they wanted four dollars on their food money (four annas a day), 'but not at all unless we wished.' They then acknowledged, before the soldiers, that the *siyar* was fully paid up, and that Talib had made a mistake about those two dollars that he had obtained for the camels. In the meantime we had been planning to get our most urgently needed things ready to load on the horses and to walk to Sheher, only sixty-five miles—but such miles! However, we knew our enemies had the advantage of knowing the way and the water-places, which we did not, and could climb like monkeys over places where we could not take horses.

I am sure we should never have found the way over such mountains, where camels sat down and slid, and we did much the same, sometimes quite involuntarily.

Saleh at this time seemed disposed to do his duty. The money (thirty dollars) that had been extorted the day before for *siyar* to the Hamoumi, who had not yet turned up, and given to the soldiers, was by them put into Saleh's keeping, as he had a box that could be locked. In the night Talib came to Saleh and said: 'Six Hamoumi are here; give me the money for them.' 'Wait till morning,' said Saleh, 'and I will give it you before Mr. Bent, Imam Sharif, and everybody,' but when he offered it to him then, he said, 'No, keep it.'

We had gone a little ahead next morning, February 21, Talib, Imam Sharif, and I, with the needful escort, my husband having to ride a camel as his horse's back was sore, and had proceeded an hour on our road when—'Bang!' went a gun high up in the rocks, to our left, near the village of Kouna or Koutna, and 'bang!' went another; so we stopped, and with some hesitation five of the soldiers and some of the Jabberi went forward, getting round behind the shelter of some trees. There were seven men up in the rocks, and a tower in the village was crowded. They constantly fired from both places. The camels soon came up, and we all dismounted and stood together with our animals, Basha, Zubda, and Mahsoud close by. This shooting and parleying went on for half an hour. We thought at first that they would only fire over our heads, but a bullet struck the ground very near us.

We could not make out what it was all about. There were so many different suggestions made as to the cause; some said the people of the village wanted to come with us as *siyara*, and some that they wanted to fight the Hamoumi, who had lately taken their camels.

Our men shouted, '*Siyara! Siyara!*' and the men on the tower, 'Come no nearer!' 'By my God you shall not come on!' 'We are fighting and we will slay him who dares to stir a step!'

Talib said, 'Now we can go neither backward nor forward,' and amazed us by asking for no money.

At last the soldiers came back from the village and told us to advance, so we mounted and rode through the village amidst uncomplimentary remarks from the scowling inhabitants. We were told some people had gone on to intercept us, and accordingly about half a mile farther there were more shots, this time to our right. We of course came to a standstill, but Talib, in spite of the shooting, rushed at Mahsoud's bridle and dragged Imam Sharif down into the river bed, calling excitedly to the rest of us to hurry on. We passed safely, and you may be sure looked in every rock and bush for enemies.

Hardly a quarter of a mile on, and where the valley is about three hundred yards wide, there was a small tower to our left, and we saw a lot of men rushing into this and appearing on the battlements. We knew they would shoot at us and I was watching for the puff. The first shot threw up the earth nearly two yards from my horse's nose, and the next seemed to say 'tshish!' just at the back of my neck. It went just between my husband and Imam Sharif, who were on foot behind me.

Everyone ran as fast as the rocky ground let them, to some trees out of sight of that tower, but not knowing whether we were not going to meet with more shooters, we always had our revolvers ready, though no one knew that; our safety lay in being unarmed in the enemies' eyes; we kept them for worse need.

The sheikh of Kouna said his name was Abdullah-bal-Jabbeli, of the tribe of Obathani. There are two other small tribes, Zedin—Sheikh Ebenadon, and Shibim—Sheikh Bengadem.

After that last firing there was no more that day, and we slept peacefully at Naïda, which we reached about 12.30, and where the inhabitants were quite friendly, bringing us all the food we asked to buy. The valley seemed to come quite to an end, but took a sudden turn eastward just before we reached the village. It is rather a pretty place, but the spot on which we were encamped was dreadfully dirty, and we were so afflicted by dust-storms, that our books were covered while we read, and the colour of our clothes and bedding obliterated, and we had to tie our hair up in handkerchiefs to keep it clean.

We always had quilts of turkey-red or some other cotton, for when we lay down our beds often became sandy, and the quilts could easily be shaken or brushed, and besides protected the blankets from burrs and grass-thorns. We were by ourselves in the afternoon when Talib came quite alone, and with an air of secrecy, to ask for his eleven dollars for that day's camel hire. I rushed out to the kitchen and brought Matthaios as a witness. Then Talib asked for two dollars, and when my husband began to call Saleh, he said he did not want them and went away. He was soon back again, however, with Saleh, to ask if my husband wished to pay any more for *siyara* of the people we were coming to. My husband said 'No,' and after some talk Talib said he would not ask it if my husband did not wish. I told Talib that the very next thing he would get would be my husband's money-bag, so he retired. Later he came for thirty dollars to send to some people that night, but my husband told him to send his own men for them, and not afterwards to say he had paid a messenger; the money would only be paid into those people's own hands. We lay down with no great certainty of peace for the morrow, when we expected to reach Ghaida.

All, however, went quietly that day, much to our relief. My husband had been induced to pay a rupee to send a scout up the mountain to look behind rocks and bushes for dangers, but we passed on our way completely unmolested by the shepherdesses, young and old, who were all we met with in the shape of human beings.

The valley became narrower, we rose higher, and the cliffs were cavernous. Sometimes the valley seemed quite to finish up, but then it always took a turn again. Much of the way was over large, round stones, most horrible for the horses.

We passed a water-place two hours after we left Naïda, though Talib had made us stop there because, he said, there was no water within a day's journey, and we found ourselves stopped at Rahba, two hours at least before Ghaida, where we expected to be, Talib still sticking to it that we should be at Sheher in three more days. He only asked for four annas for coffee to drink at the great tomb of a wali, Sheikh Salem-bin-Abdullah Mollah el Mohagher, who is buried near a mosque and a tank, the footbath of cattle, from which we drank pea-green water, boiled and filtered of course. Altogether Rahba is a pretty village, but much exposed to wind. The tribes thereabout are Mahri, Gohi, and Salbani.

February the 23rd was a weary day. Talib had asked leave to go to Sufeila to arrange something with the sheikh, soon after our arrival at Rahba, saying he would not be away long. He did not go all day, but at night said he was now going, and would take sixty rupees *siyar* then, but was told we would take it ourselves. In the morning the Hamoumi refused to load up, saying they had not been paid the twenty-seven dollars. Talib was absent, but being fetched said he was keeping the money, as otherwise the Hamoumi might leave us anywhere they liked. In the meantime the soldiers, according to their habit, instead of keeping their weapons for our safeguard, once more gave up their swords and guns to the Hamoumi. They always were pledging them to our enemies, as an earnest that we would do what they wanted.

The Hamoumi loaded the camels, on the oath of Talib that they should have the money that night at Sufeila, a place that we were to pass, and which the day before we were told it was impossible to reach in one stage. They swore to take us to Bir Baokban. We started about ten o'clock, and at eleven the camels were stopped at Sufeila, and the men said they would wait a quarter of an hour, to which my husband consented. They then began to lead the camels away to feed, so my husband stoutly said that if they did that he would get other camels. Neither he nor any of us knew how or whence these other camels could be procured, but it had the desired effect, and they left the camels sitting among their loads. Saleh was sent to arrange with the wretched little sheikh, and remained away till after two o'clock. A soldier was sent to fetch him, and then arose a tremendous uproar. First they said we should stay where we were, then that we should go only a short distance, and on a different way to that already settled. After that we were told we could not go to Al Figra or Al Madi, as these were recognised places for murders, and we were told the same of Ghail Babwazir; also a good many different numbers of days were mentioned for our journey.

My husband said he would camp at Sufeila, but they quickly loaded up for Bir Baokban, they said. The sheikh was given fifteen dollars, and he told us he would send four of his sons with us.

I must say that after those four or five hours of being stared at and called bad names, I was pretty tired. We none of us remarked that three of the soldiers, all the Jabberi, and the four sons stayed behind.

I was riding with Imam Sharif, two Indians, four soldiers, and the groom leading Zubda, whose back was still sore, when we came to a fork in the way. The soldiers asked a passing man, 'Which is the way to Ghail?' The man looked puzzled; so were we. I said, 'We want to know the way to Bir Baokban.' 'No, no! Ghail,' said the soldiers, and when I said 'Baokban!' again they laughed scornfully. Our *kafila* came up, and I rode to my husband and told him I was sure we were being led out of our way.

We were guided down a rocky slope into a valley not more than 200 feet wide, with thick woods up each side, and a sandy bottom. Here we were stopped by a good many shots from each side, and retreated a little, without turning our backs, and then looked about for the four sons. There was another row of course, and my husband said we would return to Sufeila; but we were told at last that we might pass, so we did, and one of the shooters soon joined us and asked for a rupee for coffee, but was refused, and then said he would let us go to Bir Baokban if he got a rupee, but he did not insist. We now thought it well to ask where we were, and were told that it was Hadbeh, a place we had never heard of before. My husband said we should return to Sufeila, and carried off a string of camels. There was a great consultation, amid much roaring and shouting. I rode fast to the head of the *kafila* to see what was happening, my husband still going back with about six camels, the others going on, they said, to Bir Baokban. I then galloped back over the stones to the soldiers who were behind, and said, 'Your sultan has placed you under our orders; go and get those camels back.' 'No, no,' they said, 'it is quite safe to go on,' and ran back as hard as they could.

I then rode back quickly to my husband, and found him in abject distress; one of his camels had shed its load, and was seated on the ground. The soldiers remained behind, sitting on a bank. After a long council, we determined to go on to a village close by, where we joined the other camels. We had barely time to set up the tents before dark, and our store of bread and charcoal stood us in good stead. The Indian party were dreadfully late getting to bed. Dismay reigned supreme amongst us all.

Saleh came in to our tent and said, 'The man who shot at us says, "You cannot go on to-morrow. To-day we only shot our bullets in the air, but to-morrow we shall shoot at you."'

We thought of going back to Sufeila, and sending to the sultan of Sheher for help, but where could we find a messenger? When we were in bed, Saleh came and said two men with the matches of their guns alight were standing by our tent; some of those that had shot at us, and said they wanted four or six annas, as they were returning to Sufeila. They refused to take four then, so my husband said they had better come about it in the morning.

Morning revealed that these were some of our own camel-men, who were just pretending to be the shooters in order to get money, and also we found out that Talib had employed the shooters to give us the fright, in order to delay us, that the Jabberi and the soldiers might have a feast at our expense in the village, and time to eat it. They did not reach camp till eleven.

Next morning the soldiers brought my husband twelve of the fifteen dollars the sheikh had received (being part of the original thirty, said to be for the three other tribes of Hamoumi), saying that he was a very wicked man, as he had not sent his four sons, so they had only left him three dollars for the feast. Hardly had my husband put this by, when Talib came and had to be given thirty-six dollars for *siyar* to the Mahri. Plainly we were in their hands, and had to pay whatever Talib chose, as we might be hemmed in at any moment. We felt as if we were in a net.

The eleven dollars camel-hire which we had kept out having gone to make up this sum, and the camel-men refusing to load without it, we had to unpack again to get it for them.

Sufeila, where we had endured such a disagreeable delay, is on the tableland, 3,150 feet above the sea-level, with excellent air, excellent water, palm and other trees, and would make a first-class sanatorium for Aden. It is ten miles inland from Sheher as the crow flies.

About 8 o'clock next morning we started, not knowing precisely whence or whither, and determined to keep together as much as possible. We followed for miles the bed of a stream, which collects all the water from this part of the akaba, and gradually develops into Wadi Adim, the great approach to the Hadhramout. There is a fortress on a hill 3,500 feet above the sea-level, the highest point in this part; Haibel Gabrein being 4,150 feet, and near Dizba the highest point is 4,900 feet. After some miles on the akaba, we plunged into a valley about 200 feet wide, and wooded with palms; the earthen cliffs were about 60 feet high, and the bed sandy.

By this time we neither had a liking for valleys, cliffs, trees, nor people. We did not feel pleased at being led straight across the valley to a band of armed men, in a most unpleasant situation for us if they meant mischief. These were only Jabberi travelling, and they were told that we were friends of the sultan of Sheher, and not going to stay a minute. I suppose they would have fired if we had not been introduced to them. We were glad to reach Bir Baokban at 11.30. It is a well in a bare place at the mouth of a valley. Talib did not wish to stay there, for the water is brackish, and he wanted us to go on before the camel-men came up, but we waited, and they and the Jabberi had a loud and angry quarrel, and we were told there was no water nearer than Al Madi, and some of them wanted to stop at a place half-way to Al Madi and send for water. We could make neither head nor tail of it. Talib then asked my husband which he wished to do, for so it should be; but as he knew it was a case of 'You may do as you like, but you must,' answered to that effect, 'Whichever Talib liked, we were in his hands and could not choose.' After great hesitation we encamped in a windy, dusty, but rather pleasant place near Bir Baokban.

There were many tombs on the way. One had three upright stones, which the Hamoumi camel-men touched, and then kissed their fingers.

They cheerfully told us that many caravans have been robbed here, and men murdered; pleasant news for us.

We asked them why we had been fired on, and they said that the people believed we poisoned the wells. The soldiers came and shouted at us a good deal, saying, 'Why do you hire Bedouin to protect you? Are we not here? Do you not trust us?' We soothed them with flattering words, and then Talib came and extorted nine more dollars.

In the morning we had to pay three dollars to three men who said they had seen four men, which four men ran away. We were informed that we were to pass through three tribes that day, and should have a good deal of trouble on the way to Dizba, the place half way to Al Madi. As a matter of fact we were pretty sure that these later scares were only got up to frighten more money out of our pockets. The soldiers were told to go in front, but they often sat down and lit a fire for their water pipe, got behind, or rode a camel.

Though we went up and down a good deal, it was not too steep to ride all the way, and though there were watchings and scoutings, we saw neither man nor beast, nor any habitation of the three tribes. As we went along my husband was told that an old woman (whom we never saw) had come and said that the men of Al Madi would not let us pass, and that we must write to the sultan of Sheher to send us two hundred soldiers.

There is water at Dizba, though we were told there was none till Al Madi. We encamped in a sheltered spot, a sort of pot between low hills. We ought, according to the solemn contract, to have been at Sheher by that time. We talked over the plan of sending to Sheher, and decided that doing so meant much pay to the messenger, thirty or forty more dollars *siyar*, and, what was worst, four days' delay; it would also cost forty-four dollars in camel-hire; so we decided that it was far better to push on, for our delay would only give time to more enemies to gather round us. It would likewise be far cheaper, and so it subsequently turned out.

From being hypocrites we now became liars, and my husband said he had not so much money left, and that he had already paid four rupees to send men on the morrow. There was some talk of our all going by night and getting past Al Madi, but in that case our own men would only fire on us to frighten us. Next we heard that there was no village at Al Madi where we could buy forage; we had but little left, though plenty of dried bread. Then three Jabberi came and said they were getting lame, and wanted eight dollars to buy a donkey out of their food-money, but my husband said he had paid so much for *siyara* that he had not enough to pay that till we reached Sheher.

There was an idea that they would shoot round us in the night, for they spoke of the dangerous situation in which we were, and wanted six or eight dollars to pay for scouts on the hills, but went away when my husband said he would see about it in the morning. In case they did we determined to remain silent in our beds that they might be unable to locate us, and in that case they would not fire at our tents for fear of hitting us.

We had a very cold night; the dew in the morning was streaming off our tent in heavy drops.

Talib said, 'The people of Al Madi do not want money, but our lives and souls.' We did not think they meant to kill us, but only to frighten money out of us. We also overheard some conversation about our lives and baggage being in peril. We had not far to go, but the way was very intricate.

At sunset we three had a great council, and sent for Saleh; the soldiers, having been flattered, were fetched too, as we now thought we had them on our side, and we threatened to ruin them and their families, or to give them good bakshish if they did well by us. My husband said we had decided that in future he would not give another pi (not to eat, but there are a good many pies in an anna and also pice), but that, as the camel-men spoke of stopping between Dizba and Al Madi, we would have some food ready to eat on the journey and get the soldiers to force them on; and, if we had to stay, to load the horses and start the following morning to Sheher. The soldiers agreed on promise of a good sheep next day; the Hamoumi camel-men were promised coffee and sugar, so they agreed also.

When they were all gone, Saleh, to our unbounded amazement, said that Seid and Talib had confided to him 114 rupees, on account of his having the locked box; so he brought them to us, and amid shouts of laughter they were engulfed in our bag.

By the bye, we actually had two of the Al Madi people with us, so we ought to have been safe; or what is the good of *siyara*?

In the morning an awful object met our view. This was a soldier, a very ugly black man, who was dragged along on his knees by his arms and shoulders to our tent. He had been struck by the cold, his companions said. He seemed to be perfectly helpless, and to have no control or use of any muscles save those which were at work making the most horrible grimaces. I ran to the kitchen and fetched our tea, to the rage of Matthaios, who said he had no more water to replace it, and that as it was we could not have a cupful each. It was poured down his throat in a very rough way, but refused to stay. My husband gave him some of an unknown medicine, that he said was specially used for such cases, and this brandy just trickled out of his mouth, so they dragged him away to their own fire, still in a kneeling position. They then opened his jacket and burnt him a good deal with a hot sword, and he was given tepid water to drink, which stayed down very well. When we were about to start, he was held upright by two men. A thick square shawl was put rather carelessly over his head with the fringe over his face, and pushed back off his shoulders, to allow his arms to come out through an *abba*, a kind of cloak with armholes, which was also put over his head. They came out so high up of course, that the hands stuck out on a level with his ears. High up under his elbows, and far above his waist, a turban was wound, and a muffler was put round his neck and mouth; he hobbled along with two supporters and leaning on a spear, with the shawl streaming on the ground like a train—a very absurd sight. In about an hour he was quite well.

Talib, not knowing of our little plan of going with the Hamoumi to Al Madi, came and told us how very dangerous Al Madi was, and that it would be far better to go by Ghail Babwazir, if only the camel-drivers would agree. If they would not, he would put all our most necessary things, *i.e.* our money, on his own camel, and we would ride secretly off together. It is needless to say we did not consent, as it would have been 'Good-bye Talib and money!'

Then Ali, the chief of the camel-men, came and said he would not go unless he got six secret dollars for himself and six for the others, and said he would (like Ananias and Sapphira) swear he had only six. Imam Sharif and Saleh again perjured themselves in our behalf to such an extent that my husband and I could hardly sit by, but we must speak the language of the country, I suppose.

From Dizba we passed over very high ground, 4,300 feet, with a cold refreshing wind from the sea. It seemed to us a healthy climate. In a little narrow pass is a rude tomb near the rough stone cabin of a sainted lady called Sheikha, where our soldiers and camel-men made their devotions.

I had a very uncomfortable ride, for on the way we saw an aloe of a kind we had not seen before, and which proved to be new enough to obtain the name of *Aloe Luntii*. The botanist sawed off the head of it (which is growing now in Kew Gardens), and we knew he dared not try to take it on his camel, as the men always quarrelled over every weight that was added to the load; so I told him to go on and leave it, as if he did not care for it, and then I tied it to the off-side of my saddle, and had to ride hanging heavily on my left stirrup, as otherwise I should have been over-balanced, and my horse would have got a sore back. On arrival, I dismounted in a quiet place, put the aloe down with my jacket thrown on it, and later fetched it into the tent, under cover of my feminine draperies, and at night it was smuggled into some package. On one occasion, when no one had been riding for some days past, a felt saddle-cloth somehow was left behind by us, so one of our own men was forced to carry it in his hand till I discovered it, and tied it to my saddle, for he was not allowed to put it on a camel. I tell this to show how very disobliging they were to us.

Mariala is the name of a disgusting pool or cistern of the very dirtiest water, on a bare and lonely hillside, where we were exposed to wind and cold, and where we encamped in much the same state of perplexity as usual.

Soon after our arrival my husband was asked for eight dollars to send fifteen men up the hills to look for murderers; he refused, then the camel-men said they would not start without six men to go ahead, but that was refused too.

Next morning we started for Al Madi. We wound up and down, over bare ground, and could see no danger for miles. At a point on the highland we waited for the camels to come up; they came and passed to the southward on a well-trodden path. Talib called out to them to stop, and said that he would not go that way, and that we should not, and that the men were taking us into danger. He pointed to the south-west, but we did not like parting from our baggage. Talib then asked my husband which way he pleased to go.

'Which is the best?' he asked.

'I do not know,' said Talib.

'Very well,' said my husband, 'we will follow the camels.' On we all went in great doubt, and the Jabberi told us awful stories of the Hamoumi intentions. We had five armed Jabberi, seven soldiers, and twelve Hamoumi, all armed, including two little boys.

The soldiers, so brave the night before, said: 'We can do nothing— we are afraid. If we fired a gun, or if they fired, hundreds of people would come, and they would kill us.'

They never either raised their weapons or their tongues in our defence. They said the sultan of Sheher would not be able to go himself or send soldiers into these parts, and that the Al Madi people wished to decoy us to Al Madi and kill us. The Jabberi said the same, and Talib again wished us to ride off with him.

The Hamoumi said it was all Talib's fault, for he owed a great deal of money at Al Madi, and was afraid of going thither.

The Hamoumi then said they would take us to Ghail Barbwazir or Barbazir or Babwazir, but we must keep it a secret from the Jabberi and the soldiers.

Saleh said to them, 'My dear friends, tell me the truth. Where are we going? I also am an Arab and a Moslem, and I swear by my Koran and my religion, that we will give you forty dollars, and spend two days in Ghail Babwazir, during which you will have your eleven dollars a day; and we will engage you on to Sheher, and give you good bakshish, and a good character to the sultan and two nice turbans.'

We gasped in amazement at this.

'Oh!' said Saleh, 'I only read them something from the preface of the Koran! We are not bound at all. If I had to swear falsely on the Koran, I should have to be given a great many guineas!

We never knew the name of the place where we slept that night.

Talib came in the morning and said he could not persuade the Bedou Hamoumi to go to Ghail Babwazir. We told him that they had agreed to do so, and he was very angry at our having settled anything without him. Then Ali said he could not go in two days; so he was led aside and privily threatened with public betrayal as to having taken twelve dollars and saying he only had six. Then they all wanted payment in advance, but the same threat to Ali availed to avert this bother and we set out, told that we should go as far as Gambla.

We had, after, all, to part from the camels, which went a more roundabout way, while we climbed down 1,000 feet over very steep rocks, with the use of hands as well as feet, the horses being with us, to a place not very far from water. The horses were sent to fetch a little, while we awaited the camels more than half an hour, and ate some food we had with us.

The horses had been badly off and had only bread and dates, for the camel-men would sell us no forage. When they arrived they said we must stay where we were, and there was a fierce row as usual. They also demanded their eleven dollars, but gave up sooner than unload, as we said we would not stop.

At one time, when we had been waiting a long while for the return of those camels which had gone to fetch skins of water, Talib caused our horses to be saddled, mounted his camel, and started, but my husband would not go on to Gambla, when the camel-men had refused to go there. Then we all lay down on rough stones, scorching in the sun for hours, wondering what would happen and whether we could get any farther that day, but at length we suddenly were invited to start.

We had a very steep climb up on foot and then down, and pitched our tents for the night in a very bare little hollow. We were very sorry for the horses; it was sad to see them turning over the stones, and we longed for some real horse food for them.

The soldiers sent a letter to Sheher to announce our arrival, and they wished to send for more soldiers, but we begged them not to do so, as they were quite useless.

Seid-bin-Iselem in this lonely spot came to Saleh and wanted some money to buy something, where there was no one to sell. Saleh said the money was still in his box, and to make his words good smuggled it in again, in a most clumsy but quite successful way.

Ali's secret had twice to be threatened, next morning, for different reasons before we could start, and then they all roared that they would none of them carry our chairs. We all travelled on foot still, as there was much climbing to do. We climbed down 2,000 feet, very steep in parts, to Gambla.

Gambla is a verdant and palmy place where we could buy so much food for our hungry horses that at length my Basha turned his back on his big pile, and came with long green streamers hanging from his sated mouth to doze beside me.

There was a struggle, of course, to stay the night at Gambla, and we were told we could not reach Ghail Babwazir till very late, but we said we did not care how late, and Ali was once more privately drawn aside, and again threatened about the twelve dollars, so it was agreed we should go on.

We waited, however, a long time, and seeing no camels collected to load I said very loud, 'Call all the Hamoumi together here, and tell Ali that the very last moment has come.'

Ali rushed about, and soon had us on our way.

CHAPTER XV

RETRIBUTION FOR OUR FOES

We reached Ghail Babwazir in three hours, at half-past five, passing through several oases. It is a large town. Some children, as I came round a corner, cried, 'Let us flee! here is a demon' (*afrit*).

All the guns of our escort were fired, and we were ushered into a house, where there was a good-sized room with some matting.

We were all very tired, hot and hungry, but alas for Arab hospitality! No coffee was brought, not even water, and when our servants asked for water and wood—'Show us first your money' was the answer they got.

We had a very public visit from the governor, who is called sultan, and who asked us if we had had a pleasant journey, and wondered how we could have been so many days on the road.

He was told of all our troubles, and took the Hamoumi, Mohammad, who shot at us, a prisoner, and his *jembia* (or as they say in Southern Arabia *ghembia*), without which he is ashamed to be seen, was given into my husband's custody.

Our expedition all passed a peaceful night, thankful to be in security after eighteen days of anxiety, never knowing what ambushes we might be led into; but Talib we heard did not sleep at all and was quite ill from fright, as contrary to his wishes he was, said the sultan, to be taken to Sheher with us on the morrow.

Ghail Babwazir is an oasis or series of oases of rank fertility, caused by a stream the water of which is warm and bitter, and which is conducted by channels cut in the rock in various directions.

Acres and acres of tobacco, bananas, Indian corn, cotton, and other crops are thus produced in the wilderness, and this cultivation has given rise to the overgrown village.

The stream was discovered about five hundred years ago by one Sheikh Omar, and before that time all this part was waste ground.

This fertilising spring rises under a hill to the east, where a large reservoir has been dug out. Above on the hill are some Arab ruins, places where things were stored, and there is a road up. Canals cut some twenty feet deep, like the *kanats* of Persia, conduct the water to the fields. The chief product is tobacco, known as Hamoumi tobacco.

Our roof happened to command a view of the terrace where a bride and her handmaidens were making merry with drums and coffee. In spite of the frowns and gesticulations of the order-keeper, who flourished her stick at us and bade us begone, we were able to get a peep, forbidden to males, at the blushing bride. She wore on her head large silver bosses like tin plates, her ears were weighed down with jewels, her fingers were straight with rings, and her arms a mass of bracelets up to the elbow, and her breast was hidden by a multiplicity of necklaces. Her face, of course, was painted yellow, with black lines over her eyes and mouth like heavy moustaches, and from her nose hung something which looked to us like a gold coin. The bride herself evidently had no objection to my husband's presence, but the threatening aspect of her women compelled us reluctantly to retire.

On the 29th we set out for Sheher, or Shaher Bander as it is called, a most cheerful set of people, at least as far as our own immediate party was concerned; some of the others had little cause for pleasant anticipations.

We were in advance of the baggage camels, riding our horses and donkey, and accompanied by Talib, without his dagger, on his camel. Matthaios, the Jabberi, and the soldiers surrounding the prisoner Mohammad, attached by a long rope to my husband's horse, an arrangement not invented by my husband, but which we enjoyed very much, and no wonder, after all we had suffered!

The servants all thought that as soon as might be after getting to Sheher we should take ship for Aden, and many were the plans made for vengeance upon Saleh once he was safe in our clutches on board that ship.

We, however, had quite another design, which was that my husband and Imam Sharif and I should go off to Bir Borhut, if the safety of our lives could in any way be guaranteed, we taking only Noura, one of the Indian servants, as our own attendant. Of course the others would be with their master.

Several times we went by small passes through gypsum hills, lovely to behold, and twice we passed water, not so bitter as Ghail Babwazir. We had plenty of up and down hill, but never had to dismount. The way was, for the most part, arid and uninteresting. Four years before, in these passes, the Hamoumi had attacked a caravan and killed nine men, taking eighty camels and 2,000 rupees. They must have had *siyara*, though, from some tribe. Each tribe has its fixed tariff. The Hamoumi have twenty-seven dollars, the Jabberi seventy, the Tamimi one hundred, &c., and when this sum is paid, if you have only one of each tribe with you, you are safe.

When we had gone two-thirds of our way we reached a palm-shadowed village called Zarafa. Here we went into a house to eat our luncheon and obtain some coffee, which had to be prepaid.

We reached Sheher about four o'clock. The last three miles, going eastward, were close along the shore at low tide. It was quite delightful, and we were very much amused at all the crabs we put to flight.

We were very glad to dismount in the middle of the town, at the gate of an old castle, and were shown up into a room about 50 feet by 30 feet, with a good many chairs, tables, and sofas, arranged stiffly, and all dusty. Indian cotton carpets covered the floor, and there was a great number of very common lamps with lustres.

We waited wearily nearly an hour, while the Sultan Hussein Mia and his brother, Sultan Ghalib Mia, put on their best clothes, and at last we became so out of patience that my husband sent a message to the wazir, asking him to be kind enough to send a man to point out to us a spot where we might pitch our tents, and an answer then was returned that the sultans were coming. When they appeared, very gorgeous, our letter from Aden was given, with that from Sultan Salàh of Shibahm, and my husband requested leave to make a camp. Sultan Hussein looked round him and asked if this room would not do? Imam Sharif explained to him that we were rather a large party for such accommodation (the whole of our expedition being then present in the room), that we should require separate apartments, and, therefore, would prefer a private house. We were given tea in crockery of the commonest kind; I had an odd cup and saucer which both leaked badly, and I feared my cup would fall into four pieces, but they had come from afar, and I dare say the sultans would be astonished at the care we take of cracked cups from foreign parts.

We were then led on foot quite to the other side of the town, where there was a 'summer-house' partly constructed and partly furnished, the builders were on one side and we on the other. We had a room with a carpet, a settee, and two little tables, and set up our own beds and chairs. We had rather a good dinner served by an Indian butler who could talk English, so we had hopes of being very comfortable. The summer-house at that time consisted of two very long rooms back to back, and several rooms at each end projecting so as to form a verandah for each of the long rooms. The back one was quite unfinished then, and upstairs there were only rudimentary walls traced out, three or four feet high. There was a great square wall surrounding a piece of desert in process of being transformed into a garden; the sea sand came quite up to the wall.

We found the heat intense, so we had our tent somehow fastened up on the roof to sleep. All the sides had to be tied up for coolness, but the defences against mosquitoes and fleas were very stifling. Goats had been kept on the roof, and hence the fleas. We could only stay there till sunrise, and then had to betake ourselves to our suffocating room, to find the flies wide awake. We had to use our mosquito curtains by day on their account. In Shibahm the mosquitoes are awake by day only, and at Aden both by day and night.

Imam Sharif found great favour in the eyes of the two sultans, who asked him to supper every day. The conversations he had with them about us, and the letters they had received from their cousin at Shibahm, did us far more good than the letter from the wali of Aden. They said this gave them no idea other than that my husband was 'only a merchant' or a person of that rank. They were very hospitable to us while we were in their town.

They examined into our complaints with regard to the treatment we had experienced on our journey. Mohammad, who had shot at us, and Ali, the one who had extorted the money from us, were both imprisoned, and this money was made to pay for our last two days' journey. Talib was forced to repay the thirty dollars and sent to summon the heads of those villages which had fired upon us, his sword being taken from him as a disgrace, and all were to wait in Sheher, till after Ramadan was over, to be judged.

This, of course, was pleasing to us; however, no money could repay us for the anxiety of this journey under the protection of the Jabberi, and we considered it as quite the worst experience we had ever undergone in the course of any of our travels.

On reflection we could attribute these troubles neither to any indiscretion on our part, nor to neglect of care on the part of the sultan of Shibahm.

We have always been perfectly polite in respecting the prejudices of the inhabitants of the countries through which we have travelled, never, on the one hand, classing all non-Europeans as 'natives' and despising high and low alike as inferior to ourselves in intelligence and everything else, nor, on the other, feeling that, having seen a few men, not quite as white as ourselves, in no matter what country or continent, we thoroughly understood how to manage 'these niggers.'

Sultan Salàh did, assuredly, his very uttermost to secure our safety and comfort, quite disinterestedly. He absolutely refused to take a sum of money, saying, 'I want nothing, I have plenty.' When we determined to have some money melted and to have a silver-gilt present made for him, he heard of our vain inquiries for a non-existent jeweller, and earnestly begged that we would do no such thing. 'He loved the English, and only asked that my husband would mention him favourably to the English Government'—and this favourable mention has gained him nothing.

If when my husband asked that a reliable interpreter should be recommended to him, he had been sent a man favourably disposed towards ourselves, and capable of inspiring respect in others, instead of a little clerk, aged twenty, from a coal-office, a fanatical Moslem who hated his employers, we should have been in a much better position, and have been able to pass on from the Jabberi to the Hamoumi, whereas travelling with the Jabberi through the Hamoumi country we had to encounter their enemies as well as our own.

Sheher is a detestable place by the sea, set in a wilderness of sand. Once it was the chief commercial port of the Hadhramout valley, but now Makalla has quite superseded it, for Sheher is nothing but an open roadstead with a couple of *baggalas* belonging to the family of Al Kaiti, which generally have to go to Hami to shelter, and its buildings are now falling into ruins, since the Kattiri were driven away. Why anyone should choose such a place for a town, and continue to live in it, is mysterious. It is a place so unpleasant with flies and fleas, that the inhabitants often go to sleep on the seashore. The doors of the houses are very prettily carved all over, also the cupboards, and lintels to doors; we tried to buy some but could not. They have texts from the Koran carved on them. We were not allowed to buy them for fear we should work magic with them.

There is a very picturesque mosque with a sloping minaret, white domes, palm-trees, and a well, and hard by a house we saw a miniature mosque—a sort of doll's house—built for children who play at prayers. They can just crawl into it. It is hung with lamps, and the children make mud pies of various shapes, which they put in it. Especially during Ramadan they are encouraged to play at mosque, and the lamps are lit up every evening. It is 3 feet high and 3 feet square, and has its little dome, minaret, and parapet like other mosques.

There is an imposing gateway to the town—but built in a kind of Romanesque style which does not suit Arabia—with long guard-houses on each side, and various quaint weapons and powder-flasks hung upon it.

Ghalib, the eldest son and heir of the chief of the Al Kaiti family, ruled here as the vicegerent of his father, who is in India as *jemadar* or general of the Arab troops, nearly all Hadhrami, in the service of the Nizam of Hyderabad. Ghalib was quite an oriental dandy, who lived a life of some rapidity when in India, so that his father thought it as well to send him to rule in Sheher, where the opportunities for mischief are not so many as at Bombay. He dressed very well in various damask silk coats and faultless trousers of Indian cut, his swords and daggers sparkled with jewels, in his hand he flourished a golden-headed cane, and as the water is hard at Sheher, he sends his dirty linen in dhows to Bombay to be washed. He was exceedingly good to us, and as we wanted to go along the coast for about eighty miles, to get a sight of the mouth of the Hadhramout valley near Saihut, where it empties itself into the Indian Ocean, he arranged that the chief of the dreaded Hamoumi tribe should personally escort us, so that there might be no further doubt about our safety.

Sultan Hussein had married a daughter of Sultan Salàh two years before, when she was eleven years old.

The Al Kaiti family have bought up property all round the town, and talked of laying out streets and bringing water to Sheher. We heard that one brother had to have all his share in money, and had twenty-two lacs of rupees, about 150,000*l.*

We became very tired of Sheher before we finally left, having to stay a week, while arrangements were made for our onward way, and on account of Ramadan no communications could be held with anyone, or business be done till sunset. We seemed all day to be the only people alive, and then at night we could hardly sleep for the noise.

Our only pleasures were walks at sunset along the sand, picking up lovely shells and watching the crabs, and we used to sneak out as quietly as we could for fear of being pursued by soldiers. Our little walks were very much shortened when we had an armed escort dogging our steps. Once we got a mile away but were fetched back for fear of the Hamoumi, Sheher being quite on the frontier. There is a round, black basaltic mountain which they call the Hamoumi mountain. The Hamoumi tribe occupy nearly all the mountainous district east of Sheher, between the Hadhramout valley and the sea, and they are reported to be very powerful. Next to them come the tribe of Mahra.

Even Sultan Ghalib himself cannot ride far out of his capital unprotected, because the Hamoumi are his foes.

We tried to get leave to go to Saihut in the Mahri country, but that was impossible, and at last it really was settled that we should go to Bir Borhut and Kabr Houd. We were highly delighted, and fear broke out badly again among the servants, who dreaded the very name of those places. They gladly took permission to remain behind. All arrangements about *siyara* were made, and we were never to stop more than one night anywhere, and to return by a different way, and the day of departure was settled; but the day before that fixed, it became apparent that we Christians could by no means be permitted to go near Kabr Houd, and that the time occupied for the journey would now be thirty-one days, and we must wait till after Ramadan. It was to be a mere journey without our seeing anything that we wanted to see, and it was getting very late and hot, and we did not feel we could spend so long a time for so little; therefore we gave up all idea of seeing Bir Borhut and Kabr Houd that year. It was to have cost us 670 dollars, at seven to the pound sterling.

By the way, Maria Theresa dollars are always spoken of as *reals*. You have to buy them dear, two rupees and a varying amount of annas, and are told they are very hard to get. They are tied up in bags, and you may very well trust the banker for the number of coins; but if you are wise you will examine them all, for any dirty ones, or any that are the least worn or obliterated, or that have any cut or mark on them, will be rejected and considered bad in the interior. When you return to civilisation you hasten to the banker to change these dollars, and you sell them cheap, for you are told that there is now little demand for dollars, they are quite going out of use and rupees only are used—quite a fable. No matter how many extra annas you may have paid, the dollar only passes for two rupees in the interior. We lost 1,100 rupees on this one journey between our departure from Aden and our return to Aden.

We next settled to go to Mosaina along the coast, and still to start on the appointed day. Therefore we were up betimes (what little baggage we were to take being bound in bundles the day before), packed our beds, and then we waited; it was not certain till four o'clock that no camels were coming. No one could do anything, as the sultan had no power beyond his own dominions, and the camel-men were all foreigners.

However, next morning seven camels came and we were quickly on the road, causing great terror to the crabs. When I say the road I mean the sand at low tide.

We had the chief of all the Hamoumi with us, a very old, rich, and dirty man, but most precious to us as a safeguard. Two of his sons were kept as hostages in Sheher till we should return in peace.

We also had the governor of Kosseir with us, as well as men of the various little tribes whose country we were to traverse, as *siyara*. The camels and *siyara* cost twelve dollars. The camels were hired by the job, twelve days, so it would not pay them to dawdle.

We had told the sultans how Saleh had behaved and asked them to keep him under their eyes till our return, and this is how we managed without him as interpreter. We talked English to Imam Sharif, he talked Hindustani to his Afghan servant Majid, Majid talked his own tongue to an Afghan whom we annexed at Sheher, and he could speak Arabic. We got on very well, but as such a party had to be assembled to say important things, we had to struggle to express simple things ourselves.

CHAPTER XVI

COASTING EASTWARD BY LAND

The journey was delightful, nearly all the way by the edge of the sea, past miles and miles of little mounds thrown up by the crabs in making their holes: daily they make them, and they are daily washed away by the tide. They live in holes higher up, but these are refuges for the day while they are scavenging in the sea. They were nearly under the feet of the horses. Near Sheher we passed the mouth of the Arfa river, where there is water, and near it are horribly smelling tanks where they make fish oil.

We had to make a deviation of two miles inland to cross the estuary of the Wadi Gherid, and then go down to the sea again, but the last mile was over a low cliff covered with a smash of huge shells. It must be a furious place in a storm. We passed a wretched hamlet consisting of a few arbours and a well, whose waters are both bitter and salt.

Hami (hot), where we stopped, is sixteen miles from Sheher. It is most picturesquely situated at the foot of some low spurs, volcanic in nature, and is fertilised by a stream so very hot that you can hardly put your hands in it; indeed, in the tanks where it is collected in large volume, it is quite impossible. It is much cooler in the little irrigation channels, which have hard beds from the incrustation of the sulphur. The water is very nasty when hot, but much better when it cools. We did not enjoy our tea at all in Hami. We were encamped in a delightful spot under both date and cocoanut-trees, and hot baths were a pleasure to everyone. I had to wait a long time till mine in the tent was cool enough.

There was a great flutter when we arrived on the scene, for there were a large number of women and girls bathing. They did not seem to mind their own relations seeing them, but on our approach they rushed into their blue dresses and fled.

This sulphureous stream makes the crops grow prodigiously, and we walked through fields of jowari and Indian corn as high as our heads. At our camp we had a delicious sea-breeze, but in our walks abroad we got an occasional whiff of the little fish which were being boiled down to make oil for lamps and colours used in ship-painting.

We paid a visit to the governor of Hami, who received us on the roof of his house, where many were assembled, and scarcely had he greeted us when they all fell to praying, the mollah standing in front to lead, and all the others standing in a row behind. After that they gave us coffee with no sugar, followed by tea with far too much, and they pressed us to stay with them and partake of their evening meal, but we declined politely and retired to our camp.

On March 11 we started for Dis without any rows or brawls whatever. Dis is fifteen miles off. We never went down to the shore at all that day, but travelled over a barren, undulating country which runs out to sea and forms Ras Bagashwa. We went for half a mile close above the sea on a cliff 20 or 30 feet high, with many shells, some in an ordinary state, some half petrified, and some wholly so, but none embedded in the stone. After travelling three hours and a half we passed over and amongst a range of low hills, a volcanic jumble with earths of all colours, seams of gypsum stuck up edgeways, and many other things.

I used once to sigh and groan over not having brought a geologist with us, but I was wiser by that time. It was enough to think of his specimens and their transport, to say nothing of the responsibility for his safety. Still my husband and I often wished we knew more of geology than we did.

When the geologist does visit these parts he must make a special bargain with his camel-men, not based on his apparent, present, visible baggage, but upon what it may expand to. He might arrange to pay at the end according to the results of his journey. On one of the dreadful days with the Jabberi, the man whose camel carried the botanical boxes positively refused to load up, on account of having seen stones with lichen put in; and but for the fact of his being last and that all the other camels had started, we might have had to throw the things away.

There was nothing to see at Dis but a sudden oasis of fertility caused by a *ghail*, but the report of an inscription led my husband a long wild-goose chase. The district is very populous, and from the old forts near it evidently has been and is a very prosperous place.

We had a great many patients, and were nearly driven wild with starers.

To avoid the crowd we pitched our tent tight up against a field of sugar-canes, but so anxious were the populace to see me, that the whole field was trodden down and no one seemed to mind. There were perpetual shouts for the 'woman' to come out. On this part of the journey, as well as in the Hadhramout, I was always simply spoken of as the *Horma* (plur. *Harem*) and never as *Bibi* (lady).

There were some very light-skinned Arabs at Dis, with long dark hair, which they dress with grease, wearing round their neck a cocoanut containing a supply of this toilet-requisite for the purpose. Most of them affect red plaid cotton turbans and waist-cloths, a decided relief to the eye from the perpetual indigo.

We had a very damp night, not from rain but from dew, though there is more rain in this part than in the interior.

We had an uninteresting march next day, over desert and many stones, up and down hill, past a village called Ghaida, and went somewhat out of our way to see a rock with bitumen or asphalte oozing out of it. We went fifteen miles and encamped near Bagashwa on the margin of a large and pretty pool made by recent rains, with bushes round it. Though pretty, this pool was not clean. Almost before we could dismount the camels were unloaded and in it, my horse immediately followed, and likewise all the camel-men, and by the time our vessels could be unpacked to fetch the drinking water, the soldiers were washing their clothes, consequently our water was turbid and of mingled flavours.

Later my husband took a bath, and said he felt as if he was sitting in warm oil.

My horse, for two days after this, was afflicted with a mysterious bleeding from the mouth which we did not till then discover was caused by three leeches under his tongue. We did not like to put the bit in, so the immense iron ring which was usually round his chin hung round his neck and clanked like the clapper of a bell, while the nose was thrust through that part meant for his ears.

Some pastoral Bedouin were encamped near here, whose abodes are about the simplest I ever saw: just four posts stuck in the ground with a roof of mats to afford some shelter from the sun; on this roof they hang their cooking utensils, their only impedimenta when they move. One old woman was boiling a pot of porridge, another was grinding grain on a stone, another was frying little fish on a stick, whilst the men were engaged in picketing the kids on a rope with a very loose noose round each little neck, and preparing the oil-cakes for their camels. We had just sunlight left to photograph them, and perpetuate the existence of this most primitive life. Young camels are reared here.

We were so lucky as to discover a scorpion that had travelled in our tent from Dis, before it could do us harm.

That day one of the Bedou soldiers came to me and asked me in a confidential sort of whisper, 'Are you a man or a woman?'

We were five hours on our journey to Kosseir (11 miles), which was our next stage, over stones first, then over heavy sand to the shore again. There were not so many shells, seaweeds, corals, crabs, madrepores, sponges, and flamingoes as we had seen near Sheher, but hundreds of seagulls sitting in the shallow water, and quantities of porpoises. The lobster-shells which lie about are a beautiful blue mixed with red.

The great stretch of basalt which runs for fully fifteen miles along the coast, with Kosseir in the middle, caused us to mount on to the rocks some little distance before reaching Kosseir, and when we got quite near we sat on a rocky hillock, contemplating the town and awaiting our *kafila*, that we might arrive with all the dignity due to the governor. All our baggage was on five camels and the old sultan of the Hamoumi on the sixth, so we really need not have had the seventh. That dirty old Bedou owns many houses in Ghail Babwazir and other places.

The governor was a very thin old man very like Don Quixote, his scanty hair and beard dyed red with henna. He had been governor five years before, and was now reappointed at the request of the town, so great were the rejoicings, manifested by the firing of many guns. Some came to meet him at the rock, some stayed in the town, some appeared on the tops of the numerous towers, but no matter where they were, one and all, as well as those who came with us, fired off their guns whenever they liked, under our noses, in and from every direction. Our animals did not mind one bit.

The governor and all the foot-passengers arrived in the town with their feet twice the natural size from the clinging mud, through which we had to pass, and which necessitated great scraping of feet and picking out between toes with daggers.

We were most pleasantly received and taken upstairs in the governor's castle to a roofless room with a kind of shed along one side, and here we subsided on mats, very hot, and soon a most powerfully strong tincture of tea with much sugar, ginger, and cinnamon was administered to us; and though the kind old governor was so busy being welcomed by his happy old friends, he was always coming to see that we were properly attended to.

We had our camp in his yard, where we had a very comfortable room, and enjoyed having his wall round us very much.

In the evening we went on the shore and about the town. The town is on a small point and approached from the west it seems to 'lie four-square' and to present a very strong appearance, 'with its yetts, its castle, and a'.' We rode in by the gate on the northern side and were surprised to find that the side towards the sea had no wall, but only four detached towers. There were fishing-boats on the beach, with the planks just sewn together with cords.

The long line of black basalt, jutting into capes here and there, is thought by the Arabs to be formed by the ashes of infidel towns. The tiny port of Kosseir is just a nook where the boats can nestle behind a small, low, natural breakwater of the basalt. Boats lie on either side, according to the wind.

Next we went to Raida, three hours all along the top of the cliff; the old Hamoumi sultan was with us, of course, otherwise there would have been no safety for us beyond Kosseir.

We had a dreadful experience passing the village of Sarrar. The smell from the cemetery was so awful that even the Bedouin had to hold their noses for many yards on both sides of it.

The village of Sarrar only consists of three large mud houses and a good many bamboo shanties.

We were amused by a man whom we met alone, his terror of us was so great. As we approached he lit his match, got his gun all ready, and left the path seeking cover, but our people shouted: 'What good can you do? You are one and we are many, and besides we mean you no harm!' so he came forward, and there was great laughter both at and with him.

Raida is a large fishing village. Certainly there are strange eaters in these parts. The Ichthyophagoi here prefer their fish generally in a decayed state; and one of our Hamoumi soldiers had a treat of lizards, which he popped in the fire to roast and ate whole.

We did not get much farther eastward that year, only two hours farther to Rakhmit, a very uninteresting journey, but we were buoyed up by hopes of some very delightful inscriptions that were described to us: one on the way to Mosaina, to which we were supposed to be going that day, and another in a cave, quite close to Mosaina. When we reached the river-bed at Rakhmit, a spot in the mountains about five miles off was pointed out; so after very much and long consultation with the aged sultan, we decided it would be safer to camp where we were, see Mosaina next day, and return to the same camp. However, when we were quite prepared to go the five miles, it appeared that it might be dangerous. It was in the country of no one then present, so we could have no *siyara*, and the old Hamoumi chief said it would be bad for his sons, the hostages; so this plan had to be abandoned.

Afterwards it was revealed to us that the cave is twenty miles from Mosaina on the akaba, that there is no water near, no village at Mosaina, no means of getting forage; so, as in that case farther progress was useless, as well as impossible, we proposed to return the following day to Kosseir, helping ourselves, if possible, with a boat from Raida.

It took us three hours to return to Raida, where an old seyyid took us into his house and led us to a little clean room, 10 feet by 6 feet, and there we settled down on the matting to rest and have our luncheon till one o'clock, when we started, leaving the baggage camels to follow.

How thankful we were that, tastes differing, there were people in Arabia who could look upon us as harmless and pleasant individuals. Everyone had been nice to us, and we had had no difficulties whatever, and been treated like human beings, just because we had not that horrid little Saleh Hassan with us. The more civil people were to us the more enraged we were with him, and I think if the servants had carried out their threats against him when he should be on the dhow, the masters would not have interfered.

It is fifteen miles from Raida to Kosseir. We were quite determined, after the severe lesson we had had two days previously, to go to windward of Sarrar. When we passed a well there I was requested to detach myself from the party and go and let some women see me, and then the soldiers begged that I would show off Basha prancing about that the women might see that I did not want holding on, and finally they shouted 'Shilloh!' to make him gallop away, amid screams of delight. I dare say these women had never seen a horse. The sultans at Sheher had only three. We had already sent Zubda back to Al Koton. The soldiers were very fond of terrifying my horse, when passing a village and I wanted to stare about, to show him off.

In avoiding Sarrar we got into great difficulties with the loose sand. We went over it half a mile, and when we reached the sea there was so narrow a strip of firm sand that, our animals being too much afraid of the rising tide, we had to make our way up again. We reached Kosseir about half-past five, warmly welcomed by Don Quixote, who gave us coffee while awaiting our *kafila*, which was, to our surprise and delight, only half an hour behind us, not having been fighting with the sand.

We were made more angry with Saleh by finding that water, wood, forage, eggs, fish, and a little milk had been prepared for us beforehand. My night was disturbed by the old Hamoumi chief choosing the eave of our tent just beside my ear to say his prayers. Quiet nights, however, must not be expected in Ramazan.

Next morning we were off at eight, of course dragging the poor wizened old gentleman with us on a camel, two hours (6 miles) up the Wadi Shirwan to see a ruin at the village of Maaber, where there is a running stream.

At the entrance to Wadi Shirwan the ruins are situated. They consist of a large fort, circular on one side and about 40 feet in diameter, built of round, water-worn stones set in very strong cement, dating from the same period as those at Ghail Babwazir.

Evidently the mediæval inhabitants of Arabia chose these two points for good water. Tobacco is also grown here, besides other things. The water is really good and sweet.

We behaved with the greatest temerity in entering these ruins; no one now living had been in before we did. The building is the abode of *jinni*, and no one who goes in is ever able to come out by the same door. We were so fortunate as to be able to do so. On the road we saw a stone, and were told that a *jinni* (or *ghinni* as they are called in Southern Arabia) was bringing this to help to build the fort when he was met by another *jinni* who said, 'Why do you bring stones when the fort is finished?' so he dropped it in disgust.

Jinni are able to get sufficiently near to heaven to hear the conversation of the angels, and there are various incantations to make them reveal the whereabouts of hidden treasures. One called *darb el mendel*, carried on with a handkerchief, is much in vogue.

Maaber nestles under a big pointed rock on the highland, which sticks up aloft, and to which we heard that the Kafirs used to tie their horses. Bottles were stuck into the graves as ornaments, and built on to the tops of buildings.

We rested beneath a b'dom-tree, which showered its little fruits on us, and made as many inquiries as possible in a crowd of starers who were all very polite.

We heard that Wadi Shekhavi is the end of Wadi Mosila. It runs parallel to, and is almost as large as, the Wadi Hadhramout. Ghail Benzamin is the principal town in it.

At last, feeling that our work and our researches were as thoroughly done as in our power lay, we arose and turned our faces toward England.

CHAPTER XVII

COASTING WESTWARD BY SEA

Though we rose so early next morning that we dressed by candle-
light, we were not up nearly so early as Imam Sharif, who, being
sleepy and misled by a candle in our tent, aroused his followers and
made them light their fire for breakfast at midnight. Kind old Don
Quixote and many others walked with us a mile to Ras Dis, where
we were to embark; this is the harbour of the town of Kosseir. Ras
Dis is not near Dis, as Ras Bagashwa runs out between them.
Probably before the interstices of the black rock were filled up there
may have been a decent harbour for small craft. Two forts guard the
way to Ras Dis, and near it are two wali's or sheikh's tombs which
afford perfectly safe store-places to the fishermen. All their gear,
anchors, ropes, sails, wood, fish, and what not are heaped round the
tombs, and none dare touch them.

Having been carried into a filthy boat, we scrambled into a *sambouka*
crammed and stuffed with the baggage—eight passengers, including
the Afghan interpreter.

There was a little deck 3 feet by 4 feet at its widest, where Imam
Sharif and I were packed, the steersman sitting in a little angle,
leaning against my gaiters. About ten o'clock Matthaios began to
make some tea, but soon had to retreat to the bow very sick. My
husband finished this cookery, and from a small hole in the baggage
handed me what little food he could reach, but soon everyone was
expanded over the baggage, no one having room for his legs. Imam
Sharif was soon a wretched heap, and not an appetite was left
among our party but my husband's and mine. We had nothing but a
little *halwa* (a sweetmeat) and no water, till the end of our eighteen
hours' voyage, so we rather envied the others who seemed
unconscious of the smells of cockroaches, bilge-water, and fish oil, as
well as of the great heat, for we had no awning.

The wind was favourable, but there was little of it, and fearing it would fail entirely we planned to land, taking food, which would then be attainable, and the one blanket we each had kept out, not knowing how long we should be at sea, and lie in the sand, but we wasted an hour of great trouble in a vain attempt. The shore was too shelving, so we dressed ourselves in our blankets and settled down to catch bugs. We had seen few by day, but by night they kept us busy, for they swarmed over us with their descendants and their remote ancestors.

Once we saw some operations which made us think we were going to tack, but to our dismay we perceived the captain hovering over his bedding, and found that he had put the ship to bed, and we were meant to be violently rocked in the cradle of the deep till morning; but he was firmly reasoned with, and at two in the morning, worn and weary, we were borne ashore at Sheher.

It being Ramazan, we easily found the Indian cook of the house, and asked for some boiled eggs, but not till four did we get some very nasty fried ones and tea, and then lay down on the floor anyhow, to fight with mosquitoes and fleas, our baggage and beds being still on board; regular quarantine measures were carried out as regards bugs when it came. I felt too weak to stir till luncheon was brought me at twelve, there having been some little difficulty as regarded breakfast.

The horse, donkeys, camels, *siyara* people, and soldiers all came in by land next day.

A period of waiting and hoping for a ship to take us to Aden now set in. Our annoyances were rather aggravated by some Indian converts to Mohammedanism being taught their prayers well within our hearing.

A promising ship was said to have gone to Hami for water, and anxiously we turned our eyes in that direction for three days, till we were in such desperation that my husband went down to find any small boat to take us as far as Makalla, but the ship had come at last and we were able to leave.

Hussein Mia and Ghalib Mia took leave of us with much friendliness and hopes of seeing us the following year, which they did.

Mia is a kind of title.

We were told that the captain had gone on board with the baggage, but we found it covering a vast expanse of sand, live hens, dead foxes, swords, spears, and other strange things making it look very unlike Christian baggage. We also had quantities of cocoanuts, that we might have some palatable water on the voyage. A bargain was made with much shouting in a great crowd, to put us and all belonging to us on board for four dollars.

I was quietly looking on when a man came suddenly behind me and whipped me up, seated me on his shoulder and carried me off into the sea. It required all my balance to keep safe when so suddenly seized. I did not know I was being scrambled for as the lightest person. I hate that way of being carried, with my five fingers digging into the skull of my bearer, with one of his wrists placed lightly across my ankles, while he holds up his clothes with the other; and I do not like being perched between the elbows of two men, whose hands are clasped far beneath me, while I clutch their dirty throats. It is much nicer to be carried in both arms like a baby.

Our ship lay tossing so far out that we had to be put in a good large boat first and as I sat amidships I was well ducked when those who had been pushing the boat off all jumped in, shedding sheets of water from their garments.

Our ship did not look smart; on the contrary it looked so untidy that it had a kind of mossy, woolly, licheny appearance. There was no ladder, so it was rather hard to climb up the side in that uneasy sea. My first care was to scramble up ropes and various other things to survey the little deck, sure that Saleh had taken care of himself. There were two charpoys or stretchers tied one to each side of this little deck, and we determined that Imam Sharif should have one, and the 'botanist' the other. Saleh's things were settled on the latter. I at once ousted them and lay down till the proper occupant appeared, looking evidently anxious to assume a recumbent position.

Saleh then put himself and his property in a place which I told him was inconvenient as no one could pass.

'I only stay here a little while,' he said. 'Mr. Lunt has my place.'

'Your place!' I said. 'How did you get a place?'

'I told the *Nakhoda* to keep that place for me.'

I said, 'Had you first asked Mr. Bent where he wished you to sleep or where he wished Mr. Lunt to sleep?'

'No.'

'Well remember that Mr. Bent is master on board this ship and I am mistress,' I said. 'I have given that bed to Mr. Lunt, and you can go *there*, and as you have a habit of spitting on floors and carpets you will now spit overboard or you will move.' So Saleh began to take a back seat. He was positively afraid to be among the servants.

Any excitement at sea is welcome, so we now began to take a great interest in him and Mahmoud. We were quite anxious as to whether they would be sea-sick or not. You might wonder why we cared, but this is the reason.

If they were sea-sick their fast of Ramazan would be broken, and all their previous fasting would go for nothing; they would gain nothing by going on with it, and might eat as much as they liked.

All the Indian party had taken advantage of the excuse of travelling to eat as usual.

Mahmoud soon broke down and rejoiced greatly thereafter, but Saleh reached the end of the day and his evening meal in safety, but his fast came to an abrupt termination early in the morning.

Does it not seem a wildly funny idea that putting food into your mouth by the back door (the throat) involuntarily should be quite as bad for your soul as voluntarily putting it in at the front door (the lips)?

We started at half-past five and reached Makalla at sunrise the following morning, Easter Sunday, March 25. Our arrival being announced, the Sultan Manassar invited us to see him, and he and his ugly sons were all dressed up again, and we had tea and *halwa*. Saleh kept running about trying to whisper to all the wazirs. My husband kept him under his eye as much as possible, but once he escaped and ran back and begged the sultan for a box of honey and a carpet. He only got the former, so he returned and was very abusive to my husband, saying it was his fault; I told him he could say what he liked at Aden, but had better be quiet as long as he was on the sea with us.

My husband graciously gave permission to ship a cargo of frankincense, and the ship was filled with delightfully sweet, clean bales, on which our luggage and men could be accommodated, and we were glad of the ballast.

We had three more days and nights on the sea, and during the last had a miserable fear of a calm; but at last a fine wind sprang up and we whizzed along, all sitting up in our beds, loudly rejoicing with one another on the prospects of our arrival at the haven where we would be, which took place at sunrise on March the 27th.

I am thankful to say that the work of our expedition was successful in all its branches; but what we should have done without Imam Sharif, Khan Bahadur, I cannot tell. He was the greatest help to us in every way, and it was an untold comfort to have one brave person as anxious to get on as ourselves. I have always been sorry that the map was made on so small a scale—eight miles to an inch. It would have been more useful to future travellers had it been larger. The spelling had, of course, to be according to the ancient Indian method, and not that now recommended by the Royal Geographical Society, to which I have adhered myself.

The year before, when we were embarking for England on board a Messageries steamer at Aden, we noticed an Indian gentleman standing in the angle of the landing of the ladder to let us and our baggage pass, and little we thought how well we should know that Indian gentleman, and he on his side had no inkling how far he would travel, two successive years, with all that baggage around him; it would have been so interesting could we have guessed. Imam Sharif was returning from Zanzibar, and leaving that ship to tranship for India.

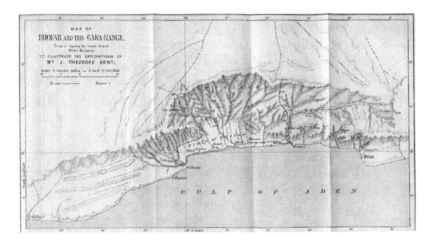

Map of Dhofar and the Gara-Range

Surveyed by Imam Sharif, Khan Bahadur.

to illustrate the explorations of

Mr. J. THEODORE BENT.

Stanford's Geog.¹ Estab.¹, London

London: Smith, Elder & Co.

DHOFAR AND THE GARA MOUNTAINS

CHAPTER XVIII

MERBAT AND AL HAFA

After returning from our expedition to the Hadhramout in 1894 we determined the next winter to attempt the ambitious adventure of making a journey overland right across Southern Arabia from Maskat to Aden. On our way we hoped to revisit the Hadhramout, to explore those portions which we had been compelled to leave unvisited the former winter, and so to fill up the large blank space which still exists on the map of this country. Experience taught us that our plan was impracticable; the only possible way of making explorations in Arabia is to take it piecemeal, to investigate each district separately, and by degrees to make a complete map by patching together the results of a number of isolated expeditions. Indeed, this is the only satisfactory way of seeing any country, for on a great through journey the traveller generally loses the most interesting details.

My husband again, to our great satisfaction, had Imam Sharif, Khan Bahadur, placed at his disposal; and, as the longest way round was the quickest and best, we determined to make our final preparations in India, and meet him and his men at Karachi.

We left England at the beginning of November 1894, and at Aden, where we were obliged to tranship, we picked up our camp furniture, which we had deposited there on our return from Wadi Hadhramout.

Imam Sharif came on board to meet us at Karachi, and we also received a letter inviting us to stay at Government House, where we were most kindly entertained by Mrs. Pottinger, in the absence of her brother, Mr. James, the Commissioner in Scinde. This was very delightful to us, as we had already stayed in Reynolds's Hotel when on our way to Persia.

Matthaios had absolutely refused to come with us for fear we should carry out our great wish of going to Bir Borhut, and indeed the very name of '*Aravia*' was odious to him. Of course, being in India, we had to take two men in his place, and accordingly engaged two Goanese, half Portuguese: one Diego S. Anna Lobo, a little old man, as butler, and the other, Domingo de Silva, as cook. The former could speak English and Portuguese; the latter neither, only Hindustani. We took them back to India with us the following spring, keeping Lobo as our servant during the time of our stay there.

We had a calm and pleasant voyage of three days to Maskat with Captain Whitehead on the B.I.S.N. steamer *Chanda*, arriving just in time to escape a violent storm, which lasted for days, and in its commencement prevented our landing at the usual place. We had to go round a little promontory. There was also a good deal of rain, which cooled the air considerably.

We were the guests of Colonel Hayes Sadler, in his hospitable Residency, and he interested himself kindly in our affairs, giving us all the help he could in our arrangements, as did also Dr. Jayaker, the Indian doctor.

We intended first of all to penetrate into the regions of the Jebel Akhdar, and then to pass through the territory of the Jenefa tribe to Ghubbet el Hashish, which takes its name not from land grass, but from seaweed. There a boat was to meet us and take us westward; in this way we should avoid a stretch of desert which the Bedouin themselves shrink from, and which is impassable to Europeans. We could not procure any information about our journey to the Jebel Akhdar, as it does not appear to be the fashion at Maskat to go inland. However, both our old friend the Sultan Feysul and Colonel Sadler took infinite trouble to arrange for our journey; camels were hired and a horse for me, and the sheikhs of the tribes through whose country we should have to pass were summoned to escort us.

Owing, however, to the illness of some of our party, we were at the last moment obliged to defer the expedition; though we had made all the preparations we could for the great cold we should have to encounter, the change of climate would have been injurious to Imam Sharif and two of his men. As events proved it was fortunate we did so, for the insurrection (which I have already mentioned) broke out almost immediately afterwards, and in all probability we should not have returned alive to relate our experiences.

We next determined to go by sea to Merbat, and thence explore the Dhofar and Gara mountains. The sultan offered us the use of his *batil*, which was preparing to go to Zenghiber, as they call Zanzibar. We found on inspection that it was a small decked boat, with a very light upper deck at the stern, supported by posts. They were busy smearing the ship with fish oil. We were told it might be ready in three days, and we might take seven days or more over the voyage. However, we were delivered from this long voyage, for, unexpectedly, a steamer arrived most opportunely for us.

As it was not the pilgrim season, and as there was no cholera about, we ventured on this steamer, which is one of those that ply under the Turkish flag between the Persian Gulf and Jedda. The captain was an Armenian: in fact, all the steamers belonging to Turkey are run by Armenian companies and manned by Armenian sailors. The captain of the *Hodeida* was not too exorbitant in his demand of 500 rupees to drop our party at Merbat. The steward could fortunately speak Greek.

We left Maskat on Monday, December 17, and had a very calm voyage, but this being our fifth steamer since we left home, we were anxious for a little dry land journeying.

We saw the high mountains all Tuesday, but nothing on Wednesday after early morning. The coast recedes and becomes low where the desert comes down to the sea. We passed the Kouria Mouria Islands in the night. They are inhabited by the Jenefa tribe, who pursue sharks, swimming on inflated skins. On Thursday we passed very curious scenery, a high akaba, just like the Hadhramout, in the background, and for about a mile between this and the sea a volcanic mass of rocks and peaks and crags of many hues. After passing this we were at our destination, and at three o'clock in the afternoon we left the steamer to land at Merbat. We were conveyed to the shore in three boats, one of which was called 'el liebot.' It is only fair that the English who have borrowed so many nautical terms from the Orientals, should now in their turn provide the Arabian name for a boat. Cutters and jolly-boats have taken their names from 'kattira' and 'jahlibot.'

Merbat, which is sixty-four miles from Maskat, is the first point of the Dhofar district after the long stretch of desert has been passed. It is a wretched little spot consisting of some fifty houses and a few Bedou huts, with about two hundred inhabitants. It is built on a tongue of land, which affords shelter for Arab dhows during the north-east monsoon. The water supply is from a pool of brackish water.

The excitement caused by the first arrival of a steamer was intense, and tiny craft with naked Bedouin soon crowded round us; after entrusting us to their tender mercies our Armenian captain steamed away, and it was not without secret misgivings that we landed amongst the wild-looking inhabitants who lined the shore.

We imagined we were being very kindly received when they pointed out the largest building in the place as our habitation, and my husband, Imam Sharif, our interpreter Hassan, and I joyfully hastened thither.

Unfortunately we had no recommendation to the head-man of this place, and he evidently distrusted us, for after taking us to a fort built of mud bricks, which offered ample accommodation for our party, he flatly refused to allow us to have our baggage or our servants therein.

After entering a kind of guard-room, we had to plunge to the right into pitchy darkness and stumble along, stretching out our hands like blind men, each taken by the shoulders and pushed and shoved by a roundabout way to a dark inner staircase, where we emerged into the light on some roofs.

They wanted us to stay where we were, but not wishing to remain without conveniences, we succeeded in getting between them and the door, and then found our way out of the building and rejoined our servants and our baggage on the beach. We flourished our letter to Wali Suleiman in his face; we expostulated, threatened, and cajoled, and passed a whole miserable hour by the shore, seated on our belongings under the blazing afternoon sun, watching our steamer gradually disappearing in the distance. Hemmed in by Bedouin, who stared at us as if we had come from the moon, exceedingly hot, hungry, and uncomfortable, we passed a very evil time indeed, speculating as to what would be the result of the conclave of the old head-men; but at last they approached us in a more friendly spirit, begged our pardon, and reinstated us in the fort with our bag and baggage, and were as civil as they could be. To our dying day we shall never know what caused us this dilemma. Did they really think we had come to seize their fort (which we afterwards heard was the case), and interfere with their frankincense monopoly? Or did they think we had come to look into the question of a large Arab dhow, which was flying the French flag, and was beached on the shore, and which we had reason to believe was conveying a cargo of slaves to one of the neighbouring markets for disposal? Personally, I suspect the latter was the true reason of their aversion to our presence, for the coast from here to Maskat has a bad reputation in this respect, and just lately Arab slave-dhows have been carrying on their trade under cover of protection obtained from France at Obok and Zanzibar. The inhabitants have plaited hair and knobkerries. I believe they belong to the Jenefa tribe.

Finding Merbat so uncongenial an abode, with no points of interest, and with a malarious-looking swamp in its vicinity, and not being able to obtain camels or escort for a journey inland, we determined only to pass one night there, and after wandering about in search of interests which did not exist, we came to terms with the captain of a most filthy baggala to take us along the coast to Al Hafa, the residence of Wali Suleiman, without whose direct assistance we plainly saw that nothing could be done about extending our expedition into the interior. It was only forty miles to Al Hafa, but, owing to adverse winds, it took us exactly two days to perform this voyage, and our boat was one of the dirtiest of the kind we have ever travelled on. In our little cabin in the stern the smell of bilge-water was almost overpowering, and every silver thing we had about us turned black with the sulphureous vapours. These pungent odours were relieved from time to time by burning huge chafing dishes of frankincense, a large cargo of which was aboard for transport to Bombay after we had been deposited at Al Hafa. One of the many songs our sailors sang when changing the flapping sails was about frankincense, so we tried to imagine that we were having a pleasant experience of the country we were about to visit; and even in its dirt and squalor an Arab dhow is a picturesque abode, with its pretty carvings and odd-shaped bulwarks. We were twenty-five souls on board, and our captain and his crew being devout Mohammedans, we had plenty of time and opportunity for studying their numerous prayers and ablutions.

The plain of Dhofar, along which we were now coasting, is quite an abnormal feature in this arid coast. It is the only fertile stretch between Aden and Maskat. It is formed of alluvial soil washed down from the Gara mountains; there is abundance of water very near the surface, and frequent streams make their way down to the sea, so that it is green. The great drawback to the country is the want of harbours; during the north-east monsoons dhows can find shelter at Merbat, and during the south-west monsoons at Risout, but the rest of the coast is provided with nothing but open roadsteads, with the surf always rolling in from the Indian Ocean.

The plain is never more than nine miles wide, and at the eastern end, where the mountains were nearer to the sea, it is reduced to a very narrow strip, a grand exception to the long line of barren waste which forms the Arabian frontage to the Indian Ocean, and which gets narrower and narrower as the mountains approach the sea at Saihut. Tall cocoanut palms adorn it in clusters, and long stretches of bright green fields refresh the eye; and, at frequent intervals, we saw flourishing villages by the coast. Tobacco, cotton, Indian corn, and various species of grain grow here in great abundance, and in the gardens we find many of the products of India flourishing, viz. the plantain, the papya, mulberries, melons, chillis, brinjols, and fruits and vegetables of various descriptions. We anchored for some hours off one of these villages, and paid our toll of dates to the Bedouin who came off to claim them, as is customary all along this coast, every dhow paying this toll in return for the privilege of obtaining water when they want it.

The Gara mountains are now one of the wildest spots in wild Arabia; owing to the disastrous blood feuds amongst the tribe and the insecurity of travel, they had never previously been penetrated by Europeans: all that was known of the district was the actual coast-line. Exciting rumours had reached the ears of Colonel Miles, a former political agent at Maskat, concerning lakes and streams, and fertility unwonted for Arabia, which existed in these mountains, and our appetites were consequently whetted for their discovery.

In ancient times this was one of the chief sources of the time-honoured frankincense trade, which still maintains itself here even more than in the Hadhramout. It is carried on by the Bedouin of the Gara tribe, who bring down the odoriferous gum from the mountains on camels. About 9,000 cwt. of it is exported to Bombay annually. Down by the coast at Al Hafa there is a square enclosure or bazaar where piles of frankincense may still be seen ready for exportation, miniature successors of those piles of the tears of gum from the tree-trunks which are depicted on the old Egyptian temple at Deir al Bahari as one of the proceeds of Queen Hatasou's expeditions to the land of Punt.

The actual libaniferous country is, perhaps, now not much bigger than the Isle of Wight, and in its physical appearance not unlike it, cut off from the rest of the world by a desert behind and an ocean in front. Probably in ancient days the frankincense-bearing area was not much more extensive. Claudius Ptolemy, the anonymous author of the 'Periplus,' Pliny, Theophrastus, and a little later on the Arabian geographers, speak of it, and from their descriptions there is no difficulty in fixing the limits of it, and its ruined towns are still easily identified.

After much tacking and flapping of sails we at last reached Al Hafa, where Wali Suleiman had his castle, only a stone's throw from the beach. Our landing was performed in small, hide-covered boats specially constructed for riding over the surf, and was not completed without a considerable wetting to ourselves and baggage. After so many preliminary discomforts a cordial welcome from the wali was doubly agreeable. He placed a room on the roof, spread with carpets, at our disposal, and he furnished our larder with a whole cow, and every delicacy at his command. The cow's flesh was cut into strips and festooned about in every direction, to dry it for our journey. Our room was, for Arabia, deliciously cool and airy, being approached by a ladder, and from our roof we enjoyed pleasant views over the fertile plain and the Gara mountains, into which we had now every hope of penetrating. We looked down into his courtyard below and saw there many interesting phases of Arab life.

Al Hafa is 640 miles from Maskat in one direction and 800 from Aden in the other; it is, therefore, about as far as possible from any civilised place. Nominally it is under the sultan of Oman, and I may here emphatically state that the southern coast of Arabia has absolutely nothing to do with Turkey—from Maskat to Aden there is not a single tribe paying tribute to, or having any communication with, the Ottoman Porte. Really Al Hafa and the Dhofar were ruled over autocratically by Wali Suleiman, who was sent out there about eighteen years before as governor, at the request of the feud-torn inhabitants, by Sultan Tourki of Maskat. In his small way Wali Suleiman was a man of great capacity; a man who has made history, and could have made more if his sphere had been larger. In his youth he was instrumental in placing Tourki on the throne of Oman, and after a few years of stern application to business he brought the bellicose families of the Gara tribe under his power; and his influence was felt far into the interior, even into the confines of Nejd. With a handful of Arabs and a badly armed regiment of slave origin he had contrived to establish peace and comparative safety throughout the Gara mountains and, thanks to him, we were able to penetrate their fastnesses. Wali Suleiman was a stern, uncompromising ruler, feared and respected, rather than loved.

The wali kept all his prisoners in the courtyard. When we were there he had twelve, all manacled, and reposing on grass mats at night. These were wicked Bedouin from the mountains, prisoners taken in a recent war he had had with the Mahri tribe, the *casus belli* being a find of ambergris which the Mahri had appropriated, though it had been washed up on the Dhofar coast. One prisoner, a murderer, whose imprisonment was for two years, was chained to a log of wood, and he laid his mat bed in a large stone sarcophagus, brought from the neighbouring ruins of the ancient capital of the frankincense country, and really intended for a trough. Another, convicted of stealing his master's sword and selling it to the captain of a dhow, had his feet attached to an iron bar, which made his locomotion exceedingly painful. A mollah prisoner was, owing to the sanctity of his calling, unfettered, and he led the evening prayers, and on most nights—for want of something better to do, I suppose— these prisoners of Wali Suleiman prayed and sang into the small hours of the morning. Day by day we watched these unfortunate men from the roof, and thought we had never seen so unholy a set of men, according to what we heard; they did not look so. Some were morose, and chewed the cud of their discontent in corners; the younger and better-looking ones were gallant, and flirted with the slave girls, helping them to draw up buckets from the well in the centre of the courtyard; the active-minded cut wood for the household, and walked about doing odd jobs, holding up the iron bar which separated their feet with a rope as they shuffled along, or played with the wali's little boy, five years of age, who rambled about among them.

Goats, kids, cocks, and hens, also occupied this courtyard, and the big, white she-ass, the only representative of the equine race as far as we could see in Dhofar, on which Wali Suleiman makes his state journeys to the various villages in his dominions along the coast, and which he kindly lent to me once when we went to visit the ruins.

The ladies of the wali's harem paid me frequent visits, and brought me presents of fruit and embarrassing plates of food, and substances to dye my teeth red (tamboul leaves and lime), but they were uninteresting ladies, and their conversational powers limited to the discussion of the texture of dresses and the merits of European underclothing. On the very first morning they appeared before I was up—that is about sunrise. As I had put them off the evening before, I dared not do so again. My husband sprang out of his bed and got out of their way. I managed to put on a jacket sitting up in bed, and then, finding time allowed, a skirt, and had just got my hair combed down when in they trooped. I knew my shoes and stockings would never be missed, so I felt quite ready for the visit. They wore *bourkos* on their faces, and had on a great deal of coarse jewellery with mock pearls and bad turquoises. Whenever they chose to come my husband had to depart, and I do not think he liked these interruptions.

We were much interested in the male members of the wali's family. His eldest son was paralysed and bedridden, and he had adopted as heir to his position in Dhofar a nephew, who lived in a separate wing of the castle, and had his separate harem establishment. Besides these the wali had two dear little boys, one of twelve and the other of eight, who constantly paid us visits, and with whom we established a close friendship. Salem, the elder, was a fair, delicate-looking boy, the son of a Georgian slave who was given to Wali Suleiman by Sultan Tourki of Oman. Some years ago she ran away with her boy to Bombay, but was restored to her husband, and now has been sent as a punishment to Zanzibar; she is a servant in the house of one of the princesses there. Salem would often tell us that his mother was coming back to him in a year or two, but we thought differently.

The tragedy connected with little Muoffok, the younger boy, a bright, dear little fellow, very much darker than his brother, in fact nearly black, is far more heartrending. About two years before, his mother, also a slave, an African, was convicted of misconduct, and on her was visited the extremest penalty with which the Arab law can punish a faithless wife. In the presence of a large assemblage, the unfortunate woman was buried up to the waist in the sand and stoned to death.

The poor little motherless fellows were constantly on the go, rushing hither and thither, playing with and petted by all; at one time they amused themselves with the prisoners in the courtyard, at another time they teased the Gara sheikhs who sat in the long entrance corridor, and then they came to torment us, until we gave then some trifle, which they forthwith carried off in triumph to show it to everybody. Both the little boys wore the large silver and gold daggers of Oman round their waists, and powder-flasks similarly decorated hung on their backs; and when dressed in their best silk robes on Friday, they were the most fantastic little fellows one could wish to see.

Wali Suleiman was, as I have said, an austere and unlovable man, but he was the man for his position: taciturn and of few words, but these always to the point. Before he would permit us to go forth and penetrate into the recesses of the Gara mountains, he summoned the heads of all the different families into which the tribe is divided to Al Hafa, and gave us into their charge, we agreeing to pay for their escort, their protection, and the use of their camels a fixed sum *per diem* in Maria Theresa dollars, the only coin recognised in the country.

Such palavering there was over this stupendous piece of diplomacy! Wali Suleiman and the Gara sheikhs sat for hours in solemn conclave in a palm-thatched barn about fifty yards distant from the castle, which takes the place of a parliament house in the kingdom of Dhofar. The wali, his nephew, and Arab councillors smoked their *narghilehs* complacently, whilst the Gara Bedouin took whiffs at their little pipes, which they cut out of soft limestone that hardens in the air, and all drank endless cups of coffee served by slaves in huge coffee-pots with long, bird-like beaks, and we looked on at this conference, which was to decide our fate, from our roof, with no small amount of impatience.

Before starting for the mountains we wandered hither and thither over the plain of Dhofar for some days, visiting sites of ruins, and other places of interest, and greatly admired the rich cultivation we saw around us, and the capacity of this plain for producing cotton, indigo, tobacco, and cereals. Water is on the surface in stagnant pools, or easily obtainable everywhere by digging shallow wells which are worked by camels, sometimes three together, and so well trained, that at the end of the walk they turn by themselves as soon as they hear the splash of the water into the irrigation channel, and then they walk back to fill the skin bucket again. The cocoanut-palm grows admirably here, and we had many refreshing draughts of the water contained in the nuts during our hot rides; and in pools beneath the trees the fibre of the nuts is placed to rot for making ropes, giving out an odour very similar to that of the flax-pits in the north of Ireland.

Between Capes Risout and Merbat we found the sites of ruined towns of considerable extent in no less than seven different points, though at the two capes where now is the only anchorage, there are no ruins to be seen, proving, as we afterwards verified for ourselves, that anchorage of a superior nature existed in the neighbourhood in antiquity, which has since become silted up, but which anciently must have afforded ample protection for the boats which came for the frankincense trade. At Takha, as we shall presently see, there was a very extensive and deep harbour, running a considerable distance inland, which with a little outlay of capital could easily be restored.

After a close examination of these ruined sites, there can be no doubt that those at spots called now Al Balad and Robat, about two miles east of the wali's residence, formed the ancient capital of this district. We visited them on Christmas Day, and were much struck with their extent. The chief ruins, those of Al Balad, are by the sea, around an acropolis some 100 feet in height. This part of the town was encircled by a moat still full of water, and in the centre, still connected with the sea, but almost silted up, is a tiny harbour. The ground is covered with the remains of Mohammedan mosques, and still more ancient Sabæan temples, the architecture of which—namely, the square columns with flutings at the four corners, and the step-like capitals— at once connects them architecturally with the columns at Adulis on the Red Sea, those of Koloe and Aksum in Abyssinia, and those described by M. Arnaud at Mariaba in Yemen.

In some cases these are decorated with intricate patterns, one of which is formed by the old Sabæan letters [Symbol: See page image] and X, which may possibly have some religious import. After seeing the ruins of Adulis and Koloe and the numerous temples or tombs with four isolated columns, no doubt can be entertained that the same people built them.

As at Adulis and Koloe there were no inscriptions which could materially assist us; this may be partly accounted for by the subsequent Mohammedan occupation, when the temples were converted into mosques, but besides this the nature of the stone employed at all these places would make it very difficult to use it for inscribing letters: it is very coarse, and full of enormous fossils.

This town of Al Balad by the sea is connected by a series of ruins with another town two miles inland, now called Robat, where the ground for many acres is covered with ancient remains; big cisterns and water-courses are here cut in the rock, and standing columns of the same architectural features are seen in every direction.

With the aid of Sprenger's 'Alte Geographie Arabiens,' the best guide-book the traveller can take into this country, there is no difficulty in identifying this ancient capital of the frankincense country as the Μαντειον Ἀρτέμιδος of Claudius Ptolemy. This name is obviously a Greek translation of the Sabæan for some well-known oracle which anciently existed here, not far, as Ptolemy himself tells us, from Cape Risout. This name eventually became Zufar, from which the modern name of Dhofar is derived. In a.d. 618 the town was destroyed and Mansura built, under which name the capital was known in early Mohammedan times. Various Arab geographers also assist us in this identification. Yakut, for example, tells us how the Prince of Zufar had the monopoly of the frankincense trade, and punished with death any infringement of it. Ibn Batuta says that 'half a day's journey east of Mensura is Alakhaf, the abode of the Addites,' probably referring to the site of the oracle and the last stronghold of the ancient cult.

Sprenger sums up the evidence of old writers by saying that the town of Zufar and the later Mansura must undoubtedly be the ruins of Al Balad. Thus, having assured ourselves of the locality of the ancient capital of the frankincense country—for no other site along the plain has ruins which will at all compare in extent and appearance with those of Al Balad—we shall, as we proceed on our journey, find that other sites fall easily into their proper places, and an important verification of ancient geography and an old-world centre of commerce has been obtained.

The ruins at Al Balad and Robat were last inhabited during the Persian occupation, about the time of the Crusades, 500 of the Hejira. They utilised the old Himyaritic columns to build their mosques. Some of the tombs have beautiful carving on them.

In the ruins of one temple the columns were elaborately carved with a kind of *fleur-de-lis* pattern, and the bases decorated with a floral design, artistically interwoven.

I had dreadful difficulty with a photograph which I took of these columns. I developed it at night, tormented by mosquitoes, and in the morning it was all cracked and dried off its celluloid foundation. I put it in alum, and it floated off half an inch too large in both directions. If I had had a larger plate on which to mount it, it would have been an easy enough job, but I had not, so I was obliged to work it down on to the original plate with my thumbs. It took me seven solid hours, and I had to be fed with two meals, for I could never move my thumbs nor eyes off my work. I felt very proud that the cracks did not show when a magic-lantern slide was made from it.

There was a great deal of vegetation among the ruins. Specially beautiful was a very luxuriant creeper called by the inhabitants *asaleb*. It has a luscious, large, pear-shaped red fruit with seeds which, when bitten, are like pepper. It has large flowers, which are white at first, and then turn pink.

On our way home from Al Balad we stopped to rest under some cocoa-palms, and stones and other missiles were flung up by our guides, so the cocoanuts came showering down in rather a terrifying way. The men then stuck their *ghatrifs* in the ground and banged the nuts on them, and thus skinned them. Then they hacked at them with their swords till they cut off the tops like eggs, and we enjoyed a good drink of the water.

CHAPTER XIX

THE GARA TRIBE

We left Al Hafa on December 29, after waiting six days for camels. There was much difficulty in getting a sufficient quantity, and never before had camels been hired in this manner. It was hard to make the people understand what we meant or wished to do.

When at length the camels were assembled, they arrived naked and bare. There were no ropes of any kind, or sticks to tie the baggage to, no vestige of any sort of pack saddle, and we had to wait till the following day before a few ropes could be procured. A good many of our spare blankets had to be used as saddle-cloths, that is to say under the baggage; ropes off our boxes, straps, raw-hide *riems* that we had used in South Africa, and in fact every available string had to be used to tie it on, and the Bedouin even took the strings which they wear as fillets round their hair, to tie round the camels' necks and noses to lead them.

There was great confusion over the loading, as all that ever yet had been done to camels in that country was to tie a couple of sacks of frankincense together and hang them on. The camels roared incessantly, got up before they were ready, shook off their loads, would not kneel down or ran away loaded, shedding everything or dragging things at their heels. Sometimes their masters quite left off their work to quarrel amongst themselves, bawling and shouting. Though we were ready at seven, it was after midday before we were off, though Wali Suleiman himself superintended the loading.

Camels in Dhofar are not very choice feeders, and have a predilection for bones, and if they saw a bone near the path they would make for it with an eager rush extremely disconcerting to the rider. Fish, too, is dried for them and given them as food (called *kei* by the Gara and *ohma* by the Arabs), as also is a cactus which grows in the mountains, which is cut into sections for them. They are fine sturdy animals, and can go up and down hill better than any camels

217

I have ever seen. The fertile Gara range is a great breeding place for camels, but as there is no commerce or communication with the interior, the Bedouin do not make much use of them themselves, but sell them to their neighbours, who come here to purchase.

My husband, Imam Sherif and I had each a seat on a separate loaded camel, with our *rezais* or *lahafs*—thick cotton quilts—on the baggage; six of the servants rode in pairs while one walked, all taking turns. We went about eight miles westward the first day and considered it a wonderfully good journey. We stopped at the edge of the plain, about half a mile from the sea at Ras Risout, where some very dirty water was to be obtained under a rock.

We passed some ruins with columns four miles west of Al Hafa at Aukad.

The approach to the mountains is up narrow gulleys full of frankincense-trees.

We had a stormy and quarrelsome start next day, after a delay caused by my husband's camel sitting down constantly and unexpectedly, and a stoppage because two possible enemies being descried it was deemed needful to wait till all the camels came up that we might keep together. When they arrived we waited so long that we got up, told them that we did not want to be kept all day on the road, and began to mount our camels, saying we would return to the wali at Al Hafa. In the end they began quarrelling with each other and made peace with us, and next we set off to a place farther north than they had before intended, where there was good water in a small amphitheatre of mountains. We went up a lovely gorge with ferns, trees, and a running stream, as different as possible to the aridity of the Hadhramout.

January 1, 1895, began with a wild-goose chase after some ruins consisting of a circular wall of loose stones about a foot in height, very likely only a sheep pen.

The camels were much quieter and the Bedouin very friendly. We only travelled an hour and a half, having gone round some spurs and found ourselves in a round valley, back to back with that we had left, and about half a mile distant from our last camp. It was surrounded by some very high and some lower hills, and we were just under a beetling cliff with good water in a stream among bulrushes, reeds, and tropical vegetation.

There was a Bedou family close by with goats; they sold us milk at an exorbitant price and asked so much for a kid that we stuck to our tinned meat.

The Gara, in whose country we were now, are a wild pastoral tribe of the mountains, travelling over them hither and thither in search of food for their flocks. They are troglodytes of a genuine kind and know no home save their ancestral caves, with which this limestone range abounds; they only live in rude reed huts like ant hills, when they come down to the plain of Dhofar in the rainy season for pasturage. There is a curious story connected with the Gara tribe, which probably makes them unique in Arabia, and that is, that a few years ago they owned a white sheikh. About the beginning of this century an American ship was wrecked on this coast, and all the occupants were killed save the cabin boy, who was kept as a slave. As years went on his superior ability asserted itself, and gained for him in his later years the proud position of sheikh of all the Garas. He lived, married, and died amongst them, leaving, I believe, two daughters, who still live up in the mountains with their tribe. The life and adventures of this Yankee boy must have been as thrilling and interesting as any novelist could desire, and it is a great pity that the white sheikh could not have been personally interviewed before his death, which occurred over twenty years ago.

Sprenger (§ 449) supposes that the tribal name Gara or Kara corresponds to the ancient Ascites whom Ptolemy places on this coast; but as the Ascites were essentially a seafaring race, and the Gara are a pastoral tribe of hill Bedouin, the connection between them does not seem very obvious. It is more probable that they may correspond to the Carrei mentioned in the campaign of Aelius Gallus as a race of Southern Arabia, possessing, according to Pliny, the most fertile country.

A Gara Forge

As for weapons, the Gara have three, and every male of the tribe carries them. One is a small shield (*gohb*) of wood or shark's skin, deep, and with a wooden knob at the centre, so that when they are tired and want a rest they can turn it round and utilise it as a stool; the second is a flat iron sword with a wooden handle, actually made in Germany, for we saw a dhow arrive from Zanzibar whilst we were at Dhofar which brought a cargo of such swords; the Bedouin purchased them with avidity, and were like children with a new toy for some time after, bending them across their naked shoulders, and measuring them with their neighbours, to see that they were all equally long; handing them safely about by their blades. These swords are simply flat pieces of iron, made narrower at the top to leave a place for the hand to grip them; there is no form of hilt of any kind. They are used to cut down trees, split logs, scrape sticks, and cut meat into joints. They have scabbards covered with white calico, which are not always used, and there are no straps to attach the sword to the person. The third weapon is a wooden throw-stick, made of a specially hard wood called *miet*, which grows in the mountains; it is about a yard long, and pointed at both ends; it is called *ghatrif*. The Gara are wonderfully skilful at hurling it through the air, and use it both in battle and for the chase with admirable precision. They have hardly any guns amongst them, and what they have are only of the long matchlock class; in fact, they do not seem to covet the possession of firearms, as our friends in the Hadhramout did the year before. Every man clutched the sword and ghatrif in one hand very tightly as there was nothing to prevent their slipping, being both pointed.

The little pipes which they use are of limestone, soft when cut and hardening in the air. They are more like cigarette holders than pipes.

The thorn-extractors used by the Gara tribe are like those used by most of the other Bedouin: a knife, a sort of stiletto, and tweezers. They sit down on the wayside and hack most heartily at their feet, and then prod deeply with the stiletto before pulling the thorn out with the tweezers.

Certainly black skins are not so sensitive as white, and though, of course, I do not approve of slavery, I do think a great deal of unneeded pity has been wasted on slaves by people who took it for granted that being men and brothers they had the same feelings as ourselves, either in mind or body. No one with the same feelings as we could go so readily through the burning cure (*kayya*). In Mashonaland I have seen people walking on narrow paths only suited to people who have never learnt to turn out their toes, all overhung with thorny bushes which not only tore our clothes but our skins. The black people only had white scratches as if they were made of morocco leather. If by any chance a knock really brought a bit of flesh or skin off, and blood annoyed them by streaming down, they would clutch up a handful of grass with a dry leaf or stick, and wipe the wound out quite roughly.

We had never put ourselves into the charge of such wild people as the Garas—far wilder in every way than the Bedouin of the Hadhramout, inasmuch as they have far less contact with civilisation. The Bedou of Southern Arabia is, to my mind, distinctly of an aboriginal race. He has nothing to do with the Arabs, and was probably there just as he is now, centuries before the Arabs found a footing in this country. He is every bit as wild as the African savage, and not nearly so submissive to discipline, and is endowed with a spirit of independence which makes him resent the slightest approach to legal supervision.

When once away from the influence of Wali Suleiman, they paid no heed to the orders of the soldiers sent by him, and during the time we were with them we had the unpleasant feeling that we were entirely in their power. They would not march longer than they liked; they would only take us where they wished, and they were unpleasantly familiar; with difficulty we kept them out of our tents, and if we asked them not to sing at night and disturb our rest, they always set to work with greater vigour.

Seventeen of these men, nearly naked, armed as I have described, and wild-looking in the extreme, formed our bodyguard, and if we attempted to give an order which did not please them, they would independently reply, 'We are all sheikhs, we are not slaves.' At the same time they paid the greatest deference to their chief, the old Sheikh Sehel, and expected us to do the same.

Sheikh Sehel was the head of the Beit al Kathan, which is the chief of the many families into which the Gara tribe is divided, and consequently he was recognised as the chief of all the Garas. He was a wizened, very avaricious-looking old man, who must have been close upon seventy, and though he owned 500 head of cattle and 70 camels, he dressed his old bones in nothing save a loin-cloth, and his matted grey locks were adorned and kept together by a simple leather thong twisted several times round his forehead. Despite his appearance he was a great man in his limited sphere, and for the weeks that were to come we were completely in his power.

He had the exclusive charge of me and my camel, which he led straight through everything, regardless of the fact that I was on several occasions nearly knocked off by the branches of trees; and if my seat was uncomfortable, which it often was, as well as precarious—for we all sat on luggage indifferently tied on—we had the greatest work to make Sheikh Sehel stop to rectify the discomfort, for he was the sheikh of all the Garas, as he constantly repeated, and his dignity was not to be trifled with.

The seventeen sheikhs got half a dollar a day each for food, their slaves a quarter.

Our expedition nearly came to an untimely end a very few days after our start, owing, as my husband himself confessed, to a little indiscretion on his part; but as the event serves to illustrate the condition of the men we were with, I must not fail to recount it. During our day's march we met with a large company of the Al Khathan family pasturing their flocks and herds in a pleasant valley. Great greetings took place, and our men carried off two goats for an evening feast. When night approached they lit a fire of wood, and piled stones on the embers so as to form a heated surface. On this they placed the meat, cut in strips with their swords, the entrails, the heads, and every part of the animal, until their kitchen looked like a ghastly sacrifice to appease the anger of some deity. I must confess that the smell thereof was exceeding savoury, and the picture presented by these hungry savages, gathered round the lurid light of their kitchen, was weird in the extreme. Daggers were used for knives, two fingers for forks, and we stood at a respectful distance and watched them gorge; and so excited did they become as they consumed the flesh, that one could almost have supposed them to be under the influence of strong drink. Several friends joined them from the neighbouring hills, and far into the night they carried on their wild orgy, singing, shouting, and periodically letting off the guns which the soldiers sent by Wali Suleiman brought with them.

We retired in due course to our tent and our beds, but not to sleep, for in addition to their discordant songs, in rushing to and fro they would catch in our tent-guys, and give us sudden shocks, which rendered sleep impossible. Exasperated at this beyond all bearing, my husband at length rushed out and caught a Bedou in the very act of tumbling over a guy. Needless to say a well-placed kick sent him quickly about his business, and after this silence was established and we got some repose.

Next morning, however, when we were prepared to start, we found our Bedouin all seated in a silent, solemn phalanx, refusing to move. 'What is the matter?' my husband asked, 'why are we not ready to start?' and from amongst them arose a stern, freezing reply. 'You must return to Al Hafa. We can travel no more with you, as Theodore has kicked Sheikh Sehel,' for by this time they had become acquainted with our Christian names, and never used any other appellative.

We felt that the aspect of affairs was serious, and that in the night season he had been guilty of an indiscretion which might imperil both our safety and the farther progress of our journey. So we affected to take the matter as a joke, laughed heartily, patted Sheikh Sehel on the back, said that we did not know who it was, and my husband entered into a solemn compact that if they would not catch in our guys again, he would never kick his majesty any more. It was surprising to see how soon the glum faces relaxed, and how soon all ill-feeling was forgotten. In a very few minutes life and bustle, chattering and good humour reigned in our camp, and we were excellent friends again.

It was on the third day after leaving Al Hafa that we passed through one of the districts where frankincense is still collected, in a narrow valley running down from the mountains into the plain of Dhofar. The valley was covered for miles with this shrub, the trunk of which, when punctured, emits the odoriferous gum. We did not see any very large trees, such as we did in Sokotra. The Bedouin choose the hot season, when the gum flows most freely, to do this puncturing. During the rains of July and August, and during the cool season, the trees are left alone. The first step is to make an incision in the trunk, then they strip off a narrow bit of bark below the hole, so as to make a receptacle in which the milky juice, the *spuma pinguis* of Pliny, can lodge and harden. Then the incision is deepened, and after seven days they return to collect what are, by that time, quite big tears of frankincense, larger than an egg.

The shrub itself is a picturesque one, with a leaf not unlike an ash, only stiffer; it has a tiny green flower, not red like the Sokotra flowers, and a scaly bark. In all there are three districts in the Gara mountains where the tree still grows; anciently, no doubt, it was found in much larger quantities, but the demand for frankincense is now so very limited that they take no care whatever of the trees. They only tap the most promising ones, and those that grow farther west in the Mahri country, as they produce an inferior quality, are not now tapped at all.

The best is obtained at spots called Hoye and Haski, about four days' journey inland from Merbat, where the Gara mountains slope down into the Nejd desert. The second in quality comes from near Cape Risout, and also a little farther west, at a place called Chisen, near Rakhiout, frankincense of a marketable quality is obtained, but that farther west in the Mahri country is not collected now, being much inferior. The best quality they call *leban lakt*, and the second quality *leban resimi*, and about 9,000 cwt. are exported yearly and sent to Bombay. It is only collected in the hot weather, before the rains begin and when the gum flows freely, in the months of March, April, and May, for during the rains the tracks on the Gara mountains are impassable. The trees belong to the various families of the Gara tribe; each tree is marked and known to its owner, and the product is sold wholesale to Banyan merchants, who come to Dhofar just before the monsoons to take it away.

One must imagine that when this industry was at its height, in the days when frankincense was valued not only for temple ritual but for domestic use, the trade in these mountains must have been very active, and the cunning old Sabæan merchants, who liked to keep the monopoly of this drug, told wonderful stories of the phœnix which guarded the trees, of the insalubrity of the climate and of the deadly vapours which came from them when punctured for the gum. Needless to say, these were all false commercial inventions, which apparently succeeded admirably, for the old classical authors were exceedingly vague as to the localities whence frankincense came. Merchants came in their ships to the port of Moscha, which we shall presently visit, to get cargoes of the drug, but they probably knew as little as we did of the interior of the hills behind, and one of the reasons why Aelius Gallus was sent to Arabia by Augustus on his unsuccessful campaign was 'to discover where Arabian gold and frankincense came from.'

Early Arabian authors are far more explicit, and we gather from Makrisi, Ibn Khaldun, and others, something more definite about Dhofar and the frankincense trade, and of the prince of this district who had the monopoly of the trade, and punished its infringement with death. These writers, when compared with the classical ones, assist us greatly in identifying localities.

The Portuguese knew about Dhofar and its productions, for Camoens, in his Tenth Lusiad, 716, writes:

'O'er Dhofar's plain the richest incense breathes.'

But not until Dr. Carter coasted along here some fifty years ago was it definitely known that this was the chief locality in Arabia which produced the drug.

Myrrh, too, grows in large quantities in the Gara range, and we obtained specimens of it in close proximity to the frankincense-tree. The gum of the myrrh-tree is much redder than ordinary gum Arabic, whereas the frankincense gum is considerably whiter. The commerce of Dhofar must have been exceedingly rich in those ancient days, as is evidenced by the size and extent of the Sabæan ruins on the plain. They are the most easterly ruins which have been found in Arabia of the Sabæan period, and probably owe their origin entirely to the drug trade.

For the first few days of our journey, we suffered greatly from the unruliness of the camels. They danced about like wild things at first, and scattered our belongings far and wide, and all of us in our turns had serious falls, and during those days, boxes and packages kept flying about in all directions. Imam Sharif had his travelling trunk broken to pieces and the contents scattered right and left, and some treasured objects of jewellery therein contained were never recovered. So scarce did rope become during our journey, that the Bedouin had actually to take the leather thongs which bound their matted locks together, to lead the camels with, and rope was almost the only thing they tried to steal from us while we were in their company. At length our means of tying became so exhausted that we had to send a messenger back to buy rope from Wali Suleiman, and obtained a large sackful for two reals.

Our new supply of rope was made of aloe-fibre, barely twisted in one thin strand, and at every camp we had to set up a rope-walk to make ropes that would not break. The Garas were always cutting off short bits to tie round their hair or their necks. The servants, headed by Lobo, had to be very sharp in picking up all the pieces lying about after unloading, or we should soon have been at a loss again.

We originally understood that Sheikh Sehel was going to take us up to the mountains by a valley still farther west, but for some reason, which we shall never know, he refused; some said the Mahri tribe was giving trouble in this direction, others that the road was too difficult for camels. At any rate, we had partially to retrace our steps, and following along the foot of the mountains, found ourselves encamped not so many miles away from Al Hafa.

CHAPTER XX

THE GARA MOUNTAINS

At length we turned our faces towards the Gara mountains, with considerable interest and curiosity, and prepared to ascend them by a tortuous valley, the Wadi Ghersìd, which dives into their very midst, and forms the usual approach for camels, as the mountain sides in other parts are too precipitous. After riding up the valley for a few miles, we came across one of the small lakes of which we were in quest, nestling in a rocky hole, and with its fine boulders hung with ferns and vegetation, forming altogether one of the most ideal spots we had ever seen. That arid Arabia could produce so lovely a spot, was to us one of the greatest surprises of our lives. Water-birds and water-plants were here to be found in abundance, and the hill slopes around were decked with fine sycamores and acacia-trees, amongst the branches of which sweet white jessamine, several species of convolvulus, and other creepers climbed.

The water was deliciously cool, rushing forth from three different points in the rock among maidenhair and other ferns into the basin which formed the lake, but it is impregnated with lime, which leaves a deposit all down the valley along its course. Evidence of the mighty rush of water during the rains is seen on all sides, rubbish is then cast into the branches of the great fig-trees, and the Bedouin told us that at times this valley is entirely full of water and quite impassable.

Next day we pursued our way up the gorge of Ghersìd, climbing higher and higher, making our way through dense woods, often dangerous for the camel riders, and obliging us frequently to dismount.

Merchants who visited Dhofar in pursuit of their trade knew of these valleys, and not unnaturally brought home glowing accounts of their fertility, and thus gained for Arabia a reputation which has been thought to be exaggerated.

In the Wadi Ghersìd, amongst the dense vegetation which makes the spot a veritable paradise, we came across many Bedouin of the Beit al Kathan family tending their flocks and dwelling in the caves. They were all exceedingly obsequious to Sheikh Sehel, and we soon found that he was a veritable king amongst them, and forthwith we gave up any attempt to guide our own footsteps, but left ourselves entirely in his hands, to take us whither he would and spend as long about it as he liked. One thing which interested us very much was to see the greetings of the Bedouin: for an acquaintance they merely rub the palms of their hands when they meet, and then kiss the tips of their respective fingers; for an intimate friend they join hands and kiss each other; but for a relative they not only join hands, but they rub noses and finally kiss on either cheek. Whenever we met a party of their friends on our way, it was a signal for a halt that these greetings might be observed, and then followed a pipe. At first we rather resented these halts; but they take such a short time over their whiff of tobacco, and are so disconsolate without it, that we soon gave up complaints at these delays. They literally only take one whiff and pass the stone pipe on, so that a halt for a smoke seldom lasts more than five minutes, and all are satisfied. Sheikh Sehel met many of his relatives in the Wadi Ghersìd, and his nose was subject to many energetic rubs, and the novelty of this greeting, about which one had vaguely read in years gone by, excited our interest deeply, but at the same time we were thankful we were not likely to meet any relatives in the valley, and to have to undergo the novel sensations in person.

Every afternoon, when our tents were pitched and our baggage open, whole rows of Bedouin would sit outside asking for medicine; pills, of special violence of course, and quinine were the chief drugs required, and then we had many sore eyes and revolting sores of every description, requiring closer attention. As to the pills, we had some difficulty in getting the Bedouin not to chew them, but when one man, Mas'ah by name, solemnly chewed five Holloway's pills and was very sick after so doing, it began to dawn upon them that our method was the right one. Most embarrassing of all our patients was old Sheikh Sehel himself. Fortune had been kind to him in most respects: she had given him wealth and power amongst men, and the fickle goddess had bestowed upon him two wives, but alas! no offspring, and to seek for a remedy for this, to a savage, overwhelming disaster, he came with his head-men to the tent of the European medicine men. It was in vain for my husband to tell him that he had brought no remedy for this complaint. They had seen him on one or two occasions consult a small medicine book, and their only reply to his negative was, 'The book; get out the book, Theodore,' and he had solemnly to pretend to go through the volume before they could be convinced that he had no medicine to meet the case.

It was curious to hear their morning greeting, 'Sabakh, Theodore! Sabakh, Mabel!' The women of the Gara tribe are timid creatures, small, and not altogether ill-looking; in fact the Garas are, as a tribe, undersized and of small limbs, but exceedingly active and lithe. The women do not possess the wealth in savage jewellery which we found to be the case in the Hadhramout the previous year, nor do they paint themselves so grotesquely with turmeric and other dyes, but indulge only in a few patches of black, sticky stuff like cobbler's wax on their faces, and a touch of antimony round their eyes and joining their eyebrows; they wear no veils, and at first we could not get near them, as they ran away in terror at our approach. They have but poor jewellery—silver necklaces, armlets, nose, toe, and finger rings. One evening, when up in the mountains, we were told that a harem wished to see us, and we were conducted to a spot just out of sight of our tents, where sat three females on the ground looking miserably shy, and in their nervousness they plucked and ate grass, and constantly as we approached retreated three or four steps back and seated themselves again. Presently, after much persuasion, we got one of them to come to the tent and accept a present of needles and other oddments, the delight of womankind all the world over. Altogether these Gara women formed a marked and pleasant contrast to the Bedouin women in the Hadhramout, who literally besieged us in our tent, and never gave us any peace.

It is interesting to read in the 'Periplus' (p. 32) a description of this coast and of the high mountains behind, 'where men dwell in holes.' We often went to visit the troglodytes in their cave homes, where we found men, women, and children living with their flocks and herds in happy harmony. The floor of their caves is soft and springy, the result of the deposits of generations of cattle; in the dark recesses of the cave the kids are kept during their mother's absence at the pasture, and though these caves are slightly odoriferous, we found them cool and refreshing after the external heat. In some of them huts are erected for the families, and in one cave we found almost a village of huts; but in the smaller ones they have no covering, and when in the open the Gara cares for nothing but a tree to shelter him. All their farm implements are of the most primitive nature; the churn is just a skin hung on three sticks, which a woman shakes about until she obtains her butter. Ghi or rancid butter is one of the chief exports of Dhofar. They practise too, a pious fraud on their cows by stretching a calf-skin on a stick, and when the cow licks this she is satisfied and the milk comes freely. They have but few pots and pans, and these of the dirtiest description, so when we got milk from them we always sent our own utensils.

In these valleys, by rocks near the streams and under trees, live, the Bedouin told us, those curious semi-divine spirits which they call *jinni*, the propitiating of which seems to be the chief form of religion amongst them. One morning, as we were riding up a narrow gorge beneath the shade of a beetling cliff, our guides suddenly set up a sing-song chant, which they continued for fully ten minutes. '*Aleik soubera, Aleik soubera,*' were the words which they constantly repeated, and which were addressed, they told us, to the jinni of the rocks, a supplication to allow us to pass in safety.

Jinni also inhabit the lakes in the Gara mountains, and it is considered dangerous to wet your feet in them, for you will catch a fever. We could not induce the Bedouin to gather a water-plant we coveted in one of them for this reason. They inhabit, too, the caves where the people dwell, and have to be propitiated with suitable offerings. In fact, the fear of jinni, and the skill of certain magicians in keeping them friendly, are the only tangible form of religion that we could discover amongst them. When at the coast villages they outwardly conform to the Mohammedan customs, but when away in their mountains they abandon them altogether. During the time we were with them they never performed either the prayers or the ablutions required by the Moslem creed, and the only thing approaching a religious festival amongst them that we heard of, is an annual festival held by the Garas in November by the side of one of their lakes, to which all the members of the different families repair, and at which a magician sits on a rock in the centre of a group of dancing Bedouin, to propitiate, with certain formulas, the jinni of the lake. Amongst the Bedouin of the Hadhramout we noticed the same absence of religious observances and the same superstitious dread of jinni, but at the same time I fully believe they have their own sacred places and festivals, which they conceal as much as possible from the fanatical Moslems who dwell amongst them. A Bedouin never fasts during Ramazan, and does not object to do his work during the month of abstinence, but he goes to mosque and says his prayers when occasion brings him to the coast. It seems to me a curious coincidence that in many other Mohammedan countries we have visited we have come across the same story of concealed religion as practised by the nomad races. We have the Ali-Ullah-hi in the Persian mountains, about whose secret rites horrible stories are told; we have the Ansairi and the Druses in the Lebanon, and the nomad Yourouks of Asia Minor, and the Dünmeh of Salonika, about all of whom the strict Mohammedans of the towns tell you exactly the same story that we heard about the Bedouin of Southern Arabia. They are all looked upon as heathen by the Moslems, and accredited with secret rites and ceremonies about which no definite knowledge can be gained; and thus it would seem that throughout the length and breadth of Islam there are survivals of more ancient cults which the followers of Mohammed have never been able to eradicate, cults which no doubt would offer points of vast interest to the anthropologist if it were possible to unravel the mysteries which surround them.

We were for ever hearing stories of jinni amongst the Gara Bedouin, and all we could gather was that when propitiated they are friendly to the human race. Old Sheikh Sehel and his men stuck to it that they had constantly seen jinni, and their belief in them seems deeply rooted. This word is pronounced ghinni in Southern Arabia.

On January 4 we were at Beit el Khatan. We had to climb on foot. The valley became narrower as we went on, and the cliffs at the side were full of long caverns, with great stumpy stalactites and stalagmites, looking like teeth in gigantic mouths. The rocks we had to climb up were very rough and rugged, but where millions of camels' feet in thousands of years had polished them they were quite smooth and slippery. When we got above the woods, all very hot, we were able to ride again, at an elevation of 2,600 feet, on undulating, grassy ground.

We encamped under two large fig-trees, and the weather being cloudy and windy were glad to find a quantity of wood ready gathered, the remains of a night shelter. There was muddy water at a little distance. The climate seems most healthy, in winter at least. Three kinds of figs grow here. Some are little purple ones with narrow leaves, and some large red ones with broad leaves.

Leaving the Wadi Ghersìd we had a beautiful journey. We two enjoyed every minute of the three hours and a half.

We went up the valley through a thick forest of lovely trees. There were myrtles, ilex, figs, acacia, and a quantity of other trees, with climbing cacti and other creepers, and great high trees of jasmin. Sometimes it was hard enough to get through the bushes and under the trees, perched up aloft on our camels. We were down in the river-bed part of the time, and then climbing through the forest to get to the top of the falls. Above the forest rise tiers of cliffs, and there were trees at the top on a tableland, as well as large isolated trees on most of the mountain tops, sheltering many birds.

We had to wait fully an hour for our tent, as the servants' camels were somehow belated, and it was considered to be all owing to the jinni, whose abode we passed. Large white bustards assembled round our camp.

Once we were settled, there was the usual run on the medicine chest. A very nice Bedou soldier, Aman, the head one, was given five pills into one hand by my husband, and as he insisted on grasping his weapons with his other, he had such difficulty in consuming them that I had to hold the cup of water for him to sip from.

Madder trees grow about, and the Bedouin make clothes from the silky fibres.

We ascended a good deal the following day, to a point whence our view extended over the great central desert. It looked like a blue sea with a yellow shore. We then turned a little to the south, then north again, and found ourselves among a quantity of wooded spurs, and on the edge of a deep wooded wadi.

Right up to the tops of the mountains, which reach an elevation of about 3,000 feet, the ground is fertile and covered with grass, on which large herds of cattle feed; clusters of sycamores and limes growing here and there give to the undulating hills quite a park-like appearance. As we happened to be there in the dry season, the grass was all brown and slippery, and there stood around us acres upon acres of hay with no one to harvest it; but after the rains the aspect of the Gara hills must be as green and pleasant as those of Derbyshire. The dry grass often catches fire, and from the mountains in various directions we saw columns of smoke arising as if from the chimneys of a manufacturing district. The country through which we travelled for the next two days is covered with thorny bushes and anthills, and is more like Africa than Arabia. The anthills, though very extensive, were not so fantastic as those we saw in Africa. We were going eastward over high ground; we decided to halt for two nights near a pretty little hole full of maidenhair fern, where there was water. It was nice and clean at first, but even at the end of the first day it was much diminished and very muddy. Travellers like ourselves must be a great nuisance drinking up the scanty supply of water which might last the inhabitants for a long while.

We had hoped to get a good rest after our many days of marching, but while we were here there came on the most frightful hurricane from the north; it blew steadily for two days and nights and put all rest out of the question. With difficulty could we keep our tents erect; when we were in ours we had to be tightly tied in and sit next to the sunniest wall; in the evening when the wind abated a little we used to sit by a large fire, dressed in blankets.

The piercing blasts quite shrivelled up our poor unclad conductors, who crouched in an inert mass round log fires which they made. We were obliged to remain inactive, for they said the camels would not move during this wind, though I believe the cause of inaction rose more from their own dislike to travel in the cold; and so inert were they that we could hardly get them to fetch us water from the neighbouring spring, their whole energy being expended in fetching huge logs of wood to keep the fires burning, and I think they were all pleased when the time came to descend to the lower regions again and a warmer atmosphere.

We were afraid to start before the sun was up for fear the camels would be too cold to move, and he did not visit us very early.

Sheikh Sehel promised to take us across the Gara border into Nejd if we wished; but as it would have entailed a considerable delay and parley with the sheikhs of the Nejd Bedouin, and as we could see from our present vantage ground that the country would afford us absolutely no objects of interest, we decided not to attempt this expedition.

On leaving our very exposed and nameless camping-ground, we pursued our course in a north-east direction, still passing through the same park-like scenery, through acres and acres of lovely hay, to be had for nothing a ton. It is exceedingly slippery, and dangerous foothold for the camels; consequently numerous falls were the result, and much of our journey had to be done on foot.

We and they used involuntarily to sit down and slide and be brought up suddenly by a concealed rock.

To the south the descent is abrupt and rocky to the plain of Dhofar and the Indian Ocean, and the horizon line on either side is remarkably similar, for in the far, far distance the sandy desert becomes a straight blue line like a horizon of water. To the east and west the arid barrenness of Arabia soon asserts itself, whereas the undulating Gara range, like the Cotswold, is fertile, and rounded with deep valleys and ravines running into it full of rich tropical vegetation.

On the second day we began again to descend a hideously steep path, and a drop of about 1,500 feet brought us to a remarkable cave just above the plain, and only about ten or twelve miles from Al Hafa. This cave burrows far into the mountain side, and is curiously hung with stalactites, and contains the deserted huts of a Bedou village, only inhabited during the rains. Immediately below this cave in the Wadi Nahast are the ruins of an extensive Sabæan town, in the centre of which is a natural hole 150 feet deep and about 50 feet in diameter; around this hole are the remains of walls, and the columns of a large entrance gate. We asked for information about this place, but all we could get in reply was that it was the well of the Addites, the name always associated with the ruins of the bygone race. They also said the Minqui had lived in the town. In my opinion this spot is the site of the oracle mentioned by Ptolemy and others, from which the capital of Dhofar took its name. It much resembles the deep natural holes, which we found in Cilicia in Asia Minor, where the oracles of the Corycian and Olbian Zeus were situated. It is just below the great cave I have mentioned, and, as a remarkable natural phenomenon, it must have been looked upon with awe in ancient days, and it was a seat of worship, as the ruined walls and gateway prove; furthermore, it is just half a day's journey east of the city of Mansura or Zufar, where, Ibn Batuta somewhat contemptuously says, 'is Al Akhaf, the abode of the Addites,' and there is no other point on the plain of Dhofar where the oracle could satisfactorily be located from existing evidence. Some time, perhaps, an enterprising archæologist may be able to open the ruins about here, and verify the identification from epigraphical evidence.

When we reached the valley Imam Sharif said: 'We do not know how we got down that place, for all of our feet was each 36 inches from the other foot.' We had such trouble squeezing through the trees, too.

We encamped not at all far from the deep hole, and at first were too hot and tired after our tremendous clamber to look round, but my husband found it in his sunset stroll, and came and called to me to hurry out while light yet lingered in such joyful tones that I asked, 'Is it Dianæ Oraculum?'

Before starting in the morning we went to visit some troglodytes, dirty, but pleasant, and willing for us to see all there was to be seen, and as anxious to see us; indeed, they wished to see more of me than I thought convenient, but fortunately my husband's collar-stud came undone and they all crowded to see his white chest amid shouts of 'Shouf Theodore!' (Look at Theodore).

One of these people had fever and another neuralgia. We found neuralgia pretty common in Arabia. Quassia-chips were given to each to steep in water, but carefully tied up in different coloured cotton bags. Our way was very uninteresting, due south to the sea at Rizat.

My husband's camel required repacking, and he and Hassan managed to lose sight of the rest of the *kafila*. Imam Sharif and I went on without perceiving that the rest had stopped. We had to wait an hour to be found. I dismounted, and sat in a circle of thirteen men. When one of them wished to attract my attention he tapped me on the knee with sword or stick, saying, 'Ya (oh), Mabel!'

One of the first days I heard them consulting what my name might be; several were suggested, but at last they thought it must be 'Fàtema' and to try called 'Ya Fàtema!' I said 'My name is not "Fàtema";' then they asked, and thus they learnt our names.

They said they did not wish us to give them orders of any kind as they were sheikhs; certainly not through the soldiers. 'We are gentlemen, and they are slaves, and if we choose we can kill them. What is it to us? We shall have to pay 400 reals, but we can give a camel each and can well afford it. We are rich.'

I must say these men were often very kind to me.

CHAPTER XXI

THE IDENTIFICATION OF ABYSSAPOLIS

We now pursued our way along the coast-line of Dhofar in an easterly direction. Wali Suleiman entertained us for a night at a farm he had built at a place called Rizat, the land around which is watered by an abundant stream. His garden was rich in many kinds of fruits, and on our arrival, hot and weary from the road, he spread a carpet for us under the shade of a mulberry tree while our camp was pitched, and ordered a slave to pick us a dishful of the fruit, which was exceedingly refreshing. Besides these he provided us with papayas, gourds, vegetables, and all sorts of delicacies to which we had been strangers during our wanderings in the Gara mountains. In this genial retreat Wali Suleiman passed much of his time, leaving behind him at Al Hafa the cares of state and the everlasting bickerings in his harem.

The next morning, refreshed and supplied with the requisites for another journey, we started off again in our easterly course towards Takha, the most important village at the east end of the plain of Dhofar. As we rode across the plain we were perpetually harassed by the thought as to where the excellent harbour could be, which is mentioned by all ancient writers as frequented by the frankincense merchants, and which modern writers, such as Dr. Glaser and Sir E. H. Bunbury, agree in considering to be some little way west of Merbat. Yakut tells us how the ancient ships on their way to and from India tarried there during the monsoons, and he further tells us that it was twenty parasangs east of the capital. The 'Periplus' speaks of it as Moscha, Ptolemy as Abyssapolis, and the Arabs as Merbat; but as there is no harbourage actually at Merbat, it clearly could not be there. So as we went along we pondered on this question, and wondered if this celebrated harbour was, after all, a myth.

It was a most uninteresting ride along this coast: flat, and for the most part barren, broken here and there by lagoons of brackish and evil-smelling water and mangrove swamps. On the way we saw antelopes and foxes with white bushy tails. One night we encamped by one of these river beds on slightly rising ground, and were devoured by mosquitoes, and so pestilent are these insects here that they not only attacked us, but tormented our camels to such a degree that they were constantly jumping up in the night and making such hideous demonstrations of their discomfort that our rest was considerably interfered with.

When we reached Takha, after a ride of fifteen miles, we found ourselves once more amongst a heap, or rather two heaps, of Sabæan ruins, which had not been so much disturbed by subsequent occupants as those at the capital, but at the same time they were not nearly so fine, and the columns were mostly undecorated. There were also some very rough sarcophagi.

The wali of Takha received us well, and placed his house at our disposal, but it was so dirty we elected to pitch our tents, and encamped some little distance from the village. On the following morning the wali sent us with a guide to inspect some ruins round the neighbouring headland which forms one end of the bay, of which Ras Risout is the other. The rock of which it is composed is white in all the sheltered parts and where the path is polished, and nearly black in the exposed parts. When we reached the other side of this promontory, to our amazement we saw before us a long sheet of water, stretching nearly two miles inland, broken by many little creeks, and in some parts fully half a mile wide. This sheet of water, which is called Kho Rouri, had been silted up at its mouth by a sandbank, over which the sea could only make its way at high tide, and the same belt of sand separated from it a fortified rock, Khatiya by name, which must formerly have been an island protecting the double entrance to what once must have been an excellent harbour, and which could be again restored to its former condition by an outlay of very little capital and labour. We were the more amazed at coming across this sheet of water, as it is not marked in the Admiralty chart.

Surely there can be no doubt that this is the harbour which was anciently used by the merchants who came to this coast for frankincense. It would be absolutely secure at all seasons of the year, and it is just twenty parasangs from the ruins of the ancient capital—exactly where it ought to be, in fact—and probably the Arabs called it Merbat, a name which has been retained in the modern village on the sheltering headland, where we landed when we first reached Dhofar. As for the name Moscha—given in the 'Periplus'—it is like Mocha, a name given to several bays on the Arabian coast, and I think we discovered why Ptolemy called it Abyssapolis, as I will presently explain. We ascended the rock at the entrance, took a photograph of the sheet of water, and felt that we had at last succeeded in reconstructing the geography of this interesting bit of country.

The Abyss of Abyssapolis, Dhofar

I hear that the Egyptologists are in search of a harbour to which the expedition to the land of Punt was made under the enterprising Queen Hatasou. Some imagine that this coast of Arabia was the destination of this expedition, and I herewith call their attention to this spot, for I know of none other more likely on the barren, harbourless coast between Aden and Maskat. If we take the illustration of this expedition given in the temple of Deir al Bahari, we have, to begin with, the frankincense trees, the long straight line of water running inland, the cattle and the birds; then the huts which the Bedouin build on tall poles, approached by ladders, from which they can inspect the produce of their land and drive off marauders, look exactly like those thereon depicted. All that we want are the apes, which certainly do not now exist in the Gara mountains, but it is just the spot where one would expect to find them; and in a district where the human race has been reduced to the smallest point, there is no reason why the kindred race of apes should not have disappeared altogether. Apes still exist near Aden.

We had great difficulty in getting the camels to face the water and carry us to the peninsula, the water being half-way up their sides. On climbing up we saw columns lying about, and there had been a wall all round the summit. It had originally been built in courses with roughly squared stones, as we could see near the doorway, but the present wall is of ordinary broken stones.

Leaving the harbour behind us we again approached the mountains, and, after journeying inland for about eight miles, we found the valley leading up to the mountains choked up by a most remarkable formation caused by the calcareous deposit of ages from a series of streams which precipitate themselves over a stupendous wall in feathery waterfalls. This abyss is perfectly sheer, and hung in fantastic confusion with stalactites. At its middle it is 550 feet in depth, and its greatest length is about a mile. It is quite one of the most magnificent natural phenomena I have ever seen, and suggestive of comparison with the calcareous deposits in New Zealand and Yellowstone Park; and to those who visited this harbour in ancient days it must have been a familiar object, so no wonder that when they went home and talked about it, the town near it was called the City of the Abyss, and Ptolemy, as was his wont, gave the spot a fresh appellative, just as he called the capital the Oracle of Artemis.

About a quarter of a mile from the western side of the whole abyss is a small conical mountain, about 1,000 feet high, which looks as if it had once stood free but were now nearly smothered by the petrifaction of the overflowing water. It rises above the level top of the cliffs, and has about a quarter of a mile of abyss on one side, which is only 300 feet in depth, and half a mile on the other. It is all wooded. The larger side and the upper plain is called Derbat, and the smaller Merbat or Mergà.

The three days we spent in exploring the neighbourhood of this abyss were the brightest and pleasantest of all during this expedition. Our camp was pitched under shady trees about half a mile from the foot of the abyss, whither we could wander and repose under the shade of enormous plantains which grew around the watercourse, and listen to the splashing of the stream as it was precipitated over the rock to irrigate the ground below, where the Bedouin had nice little gardens in which the vegetation was profuse. One day we spent in photography and sketching, wandering about the foot of the rocky wall; and another day, starting early in the morning, with one camel to carry our things, we set off to climb the hill by a tortuous path under shady trees which conducted us along the side of the hill, and got lovely glimpses of the abyss on both sides through the branches.

On reaching the summit we found ourselves on an extensive and well-timbered flat meadow, along which we walked for a mile or so. It was covered with cattle belonging to the Bedouin grazing on its rich pasturage. It seemed like the place Jack reached when he had climbed up the beanstalk. At length we came to two lovely narrow lakes, joined together by a rapid meandering stream, delicious spots to look upon, with well-wooded hills on either side, and a wealth of timber in every direction. We lunched and took our midday siesta under a wide-spreading sycamore by the stream, after walking up alongside the lakes for nearly two miles; fat milch cows, not unlike our own, were feeding by the rushing stream; birds of all descriptions filled the branches of the trees, water-hens and herons and ducks were in abundance on one of the lakes, bulrushes and water-weeds grew in them; it would be an ideal little spot in any country, but in Arabia it was a marvel. The trees were loaded with climbing cactus and a large purple convolvulus with great round leaves.

We wanted to get some water-plants, easily to be obtained if anyone would have entered the lake in which they grew, but the jinni or ghinni who lives there (our old friend the Genius of the 'Arabian Nights') was so dangerous that the plants had to be hooked out with sticks and branches tied to strings. Sheikh Sehel maintains that he has seen ghinni in that neighbourhood.

This wide-spreading meadow can be watered at will by damming up the streams which lead the water from the lakes to the abyss, and in a large cave near the edge of the precipice dwells a family of pastoral Bedouin who own this happy valley; before leaving the higher level we went to the edge and peered over into the hollow below, where, far beneath us, was our camping ground among the trees, and in the sun's rays the waterfall over the white cliff gave out beautiful rainbows. We had to cross much swampy ground, and got our feet wet, without catching the inevitable fever.

Imam Sharif camped away from us one night and found that the streams which feed them have their source up in the limestone, about two days' journey from them. The Bedouin are exceedingly proud of them, and in the absence of much water in their country they naturally look upon them with almost superstitious awe and veneration. Perhaps in Scotland one might be more inclined to call them mountain tarns, for neither of them is more than a mile in length, and in parts they are very narrow; yet they are deep, and, as the people at Al Hafa proudly told us, you could float thereon any steamer you liked, which may or may not be true, but their existence in a country like Arabia is, after all, their chief cause for renown. This really is Arabia Felix.

If ever this tract of country comes into the hands of a civilised nation, it will be capable of great and useful development. Supposing the harbour restored to receive ships of moderate size, the Gara hills, rich in grass and vegetation, with an ample supply of water and regular rains, and, furthermore, with a most delicious and health-giving air, might be of inestimable value as a granary and a health resort for the inhabitants of the burnt-up centres of Arabian commerce, Aden and Maskat. It is, as I have said, about half way between them, and it is the only fertile stretch of coast-line along that arid frontage of the Arabian Peninsula on to the Indian Ocean.

Every November a fair or gala is held up here by the side of the lakes, to which all the Bedouin of the Gara tribe come and make merry, and the fair of Derbat is considered by them the great festival of the year. A round rock was shown us on which the chief magician sits to exorcise the jinni of the lakes, and around him the people dance. There is doubtless some religious purport connected with all this, but, as I have said before, it is extremely difficult to get anything out of the Bedouin about their religious opinions; like the Bedouin of the Hadhramout, they do not observe the prayers and ablutions inculcated by the Mohammedan creed, and the Arabs speak of them as heathen, but beyond this we could not find out much. Their language, too, is different from anything we had heard before. They can understand and converse in Arabic after a fashion, but when speaking amongst themselves none of our party, Arab or European, could make out anything they said, and from such simple words as we were able to learn—such, for example, as *ouft* for *wadi*, a valley, *shur* instead of *yom* for day, and *kho* instead of *nahr* for a river—we were led to believe that they speak an entirely different language, and not a dialect as in the Hadhramout.

As we passed through the hay, the Gara had gathered up a lot of it in sacks, which they put under the camels' loads by day and used as beds by night, and between times applied to quite a different purpose. One of these sacks was used as a combined dish and strainer when they boiled their rice. The rice was turned out of the pot, and as soon as the cook had scraped it all out with his hands they sat round, and fed themselves with handfuls of it.

After another day, spent over sketching, photography, and measurements, we felt we had thoroughly explored the neighbourhood of the abyss, so we started back to Al Hafa to prepare for our departure from Dhofar.

It took us three days to get there. We stayed a night on the way on some high ground above one of the swamps, and on the second day stopped to visit Hamran, or Hameroun, where the wali had built a small fort and a farm, which supplied him when at Rizat with butter, vegetables and fruit. He also grew tobacco there.

We found ourselves once more in our old quarters in the castle, where many fleas had been born in our absence, while the flies and mosquitoes were not diminished. The wali had more prisoners. We again visited Robat and the other ruins.

The interests which centred in this small district—the ancient sites, the abyss, and, above all, the surprising fertility of the valleys and mountains, the delicious health-giving air, and the immunity from actual danger which we had enjoyed—combined in making us feel that our sojourn in Dhofar had been one of the most enjoyable and productive of any expedition we had hitherto undertaken, and that we had discovered a real Paradise in the wilderness, which will be a rich prize for the civilised nation which is enterprising enough to appropriate it.

CHAPTER XXII

SAILING FROM KOSSEIR TO ADEN

Our object had been to go across from Dhofar by land to the Hadhramout, across the Mahri country. Wali Suleiman had done all in his power to help us, but without much success, as the Gara were more or less at war with the Mahri, who are a dangerous warlike tribe. When we first left Al Hafa, a message had been sent to the Mahri chiefs to come and arrange about our journey, but on our return we found that only two had come. They said if we would give them 200 reals, *i.e.* about 12*l.*, they would let us go through their country, but they made no allusion to the request that they would arrange with the Minhali, Amri, Kattiri, and Tamimi. As far as we and the wali could make out, they would only have let us go a certain way along their coast, and then we should have been in difficulty about a ship. The reply from the sultan of Jedid was also unfavourable, so we had nothing left but to hire a *batil* and set sail along the coast for Kishin, to the sultan of which place my husband had a letter from the British political agent at Maskat.

We took leave of Wali Suleiman with much regret, and had we foreseen all the disappointments that were in store for us we should, I think, have stayed far longer under his favourable influence. We were sorry afterwards to hear of his death. A rebellion broke out, in which his castle was knocked into ruins, and in the battle he, his eldest son, and little black Muoffok were all killed.

A long sea journey in an Arab batil is exceedingly uncomfortable. We had a cabin in the stern, open all round; a sail was stretched in front to secure our privacy; it was so low that we could by no means stand or even sit up except on the deck, as 3 feet 6 inches was the height of this place. It was roofed over with palm-stalks supported on posts overlaid with matting, so slippery that Imam Sharif and Hassan, the interpreter, had to tie themselves with ropes, as there was nothing to prevent their sliding into the sea. I stayed in my camp bed for six days, as there was nothing else to do. Our servants crowded every space on the outer part of the deck in and on boxes. We had some palm-leaf matting hung on the port and southern side to shield us from the sun, and much rejoiced that we were not deprived by the sun of the glorious views which unrolled themselves along our starboard side.

When morning came, Lobo used to creep in across my husband's feet and bring our basins to our bed-sides, and when our toilette was finished he used to creep in and fetch them, and then creep back, and, spreading the breakfast on the floor, squat in the middle and hand us our food. The gunwale of the batil was only three inches from the level of my bed. Airy as our 'cabin' was, bilge-water was our torment.

We had started on January 23, the weather being cool and overcast, about 11 o'clock, and reached the village of Rakhiout in thirty hours—only forty miles.

We called there to do a civility to the wali, and leave two soldiers there. This is the end of Omani influence, and there is a small fort as a protection against the Mahri. There was a contrary wind and such a violent swell that we rocked and tossed for thirty more hours in front of the small village, whence parties of inhabitants came to stare at us. It is on a small flat space, with high hills and cliffs all round it.

We started at last, and got at least two miles, when we were awakened by a great gale. I was nearly blown out of bed. The sail was taken down, and we were in some danger, as it was feared the mast would give way. We anchored, and the wind seemed to blow from all sides at once; the small boat was nearly smashed against the rudder. The stars were shining brightly all the time.

We started again at dawn, and did not go more than three-quarters of a mile in the whole day, the wind being so contrary. One of the peculiarities of our navigation was that whenever we tacked we went completely round. At sunset we had to cast anchor again, and lie tossing till three, and then went on well.

While at anchor we heard shouts and cries to come to land, but our sailors would do nothing of the sort. They said a single man might often be seen calling that he was wrecked, and asking to be fetched away, but a party of armed men would be behind a rock, and come out and murder the benevolent crew and steal the boat.

It was really delightful in the morning to open my still sleepy eyes and, without moving, to see the lovely picture which seemed to be passing before me—not I before it—of beautiful mountains with their foreground of water, every fold and distance filled up and separated by soft vapours. Then sunrise began to paint the rocks red, and black shadows came and changed their shapes, and presently all became hard and stony looking.

Passing Ras Hamar, which is the next cape to Risout, we had seen easily how it had acquired the name, for it looks like a donkey drinking, with its nose in the water and its ears cocked. This shows particularly from the west. In the pilot book of that sea, it is stated that it is called Hamar, or Ahmar, from its red colour; but it is not red. The two peculiar peaks on its summit are noticed.

The wind died away about nine, and we shook about and went round and round; but in the afternoon we had a good wind, and at noon of the next day (January 28) we were before Kishin.

The sultan was at his village, three miles inland, or, more correctly, in sand—a hot walk. He is a wizened little old man, who can neither read nor write, and was poorly dressed, visitors being quite unexpected.

The village of Kishin, the Mahri capital, consists of a few scattered houses and some Bedou huts of matting and poles placed in a dreary sandy waste, very different from the fertile plain of Dhofar, and more like the surroundings of Sheher.

When my husband asked for the sultan's assistance to go into the Hadhramout, he said: 'No one ever goes that way, it is full of robbers.'

Of course he was civil enough, as my husband showed him the letter from Maskat, but he seemed to have little authority. I think his followers were sorry to see such a likely prize depart unmolested. Those on board were rather alarmed at the length of time consumed in these negotiations.

The old Sultan Salem is father to the sultan of Sokotra, which belongs to the Mahri tribe, and brother to the sultan of Saihut, another robber chief, who is equally averse to admitting Europeans to his dominions. The fact is that these tribes object to European inquiry, as they know they would no longer be able to exist in their present condition.

My husband extracted from him a letter to his brother of Saihut.

After our futile attempts to penetrate into the Mahri country, there was nothing left for us but to start again in our boat for Sheher, and rely on the promises which Sultan Hussein al Kaiti had given us the year before of sending us under safe escort to the eastern portion of the Hadhramout valley, which must contain much of interest, not yet having been explored by Europeans; so we set sail again, and were soon passing country that we had ridden over on camels.

Ras Fartak is the great landmark, but the fine scenery ends at Jedid. Looking back, the rich colouring of the capes, seeming to overlap one another, and the great height, give a most impressive effect. The slopes are adorned with feathery-looking trees, and there are many little sandy beaches, and there were also many deep caverns. For two days we saw hardly an inhabitant.

Between Jedid and Ras Fartak the land is low and recedes, and as we sailed along we decided that it was the mouth of some big valley from the interior, and after careful cross-examination of the sultan of Kishin and our sailors we gathered that this was actually the mouth of the great Hadhramout valley, which does not take the extraordinary bend that is given in our maps, but runs in almost a straight line from west to east, and the bend represents an entirely distinct valley, the Wadi Mosila, which comes out at Saihut.

We were two days getting to Sheher, anchoring both nights; the first, as 'dirty weather' was causing alarm, was a very noisy one, the servants and sailors talking and singing all night to be in readiness. The second night we were put to bed very quietly among the strange and weird stacks of rocks at Ras Dis, and had a heavy shower of rain, which, of course, penetrated our matting roof.

When we reached Sheher, a messenger was sent ashore with a letter to Sultan Hussein, and a message was returned inviting us to take up our quarters in the same unfinished palace where we had lived ten months before. One of the first people to greet us was the *nàkhoda* of the ship on which we had gone to Aden from Sheher. The word *reis* for captain is never used. Ghaleb Mia was at the house to meet us, and we were much interested by finding that the governors of everywhere round about were in Sheher to give up their accounts. He of Hagarein was scowling, but they of Dis, Kosseir, and Haura seemed friendly and pleased to see us. We heard good accounts of various patients, and were especially pleased to hear that the daughter of the governor of Dis, who had for some time been bedridden with a bad leg, had been well ever since our visit—quite cured by Holloway's ointment. The next day there were great negotiations and plannings as to our future course.

Our scheme was that we should go from Sheher to Inat in the Hadhramout valley, down to Bir Borhut and Kabr Houd, and thence eastward to Wadi Mosila, back to Sheher by the coast, and then try to go westward—or, as to us appeared preferable, to go up by the Wadi Mosila to Wadi Hadhramout, and then to try to get to the west without returning to Sheher.

There we stuck for some days, listening to any gossip we could hear, and taking evening walks by the sea, guarded by soldiers. We were told that Sultan Salàh of Shibahm had lost his head wife, the sister of Manassar of Makalla, but had consoled himself by marrying four others about two months afterwards, and had divorced two of them already. The family of Al Kaiti are not very good friends among themselves; a soldier discharged by Salàh of Shibahm is always quickly engaged by Hussein of Sheher, and if Hussein dismisses a servant he is sure of a place with Manassar. They stop each other's letters and annoy each other in many ways, but are always ready to unite if any strange foe assails their family.

Manassar had quarrelled with his wife, the daughter of Salàh, because Salàh, on the death of his wife, had refused to marry a third daughter of Manassar, as his dying wife requested. Hussein had only one wife and no children.

There had been great trouble with the Hamoumi, and only three months before two soldiers had been killed about half a mile from Sheher. Ghaleb Mia and Hussein Mia dared not go to Inbula or anywhere outside their walls without forty or fifty men, and when Salàh's daughter, who is married to the seyyid, came to Sheher, she had to come by a circuitous route, with an escort of five hundred men.

When a Bedou has committed a murder, he runs to the houses of the seyyids, where there is sanctuary, and gets absolution on paying four or five hundred dollars, according to the rank of the murdered man. Thus travelling is difficult unless you have paid *siyar*, and a relation of the *siyara* is kept in prison at Sheher. All this time the behaviour of the sultans and their hospitality to us were very different to what it had been the year before; they sent us no presents of food, nor did they ever invite Imam Sharif to a meal, which they had constantly done when we were last there. Their manner was stiff and constrained, and they said they themselves had been badly treated for their kindness to us and that they were now considered Kafirs themselves. The fact is that all the Mohammedan world was in a state of restless activity, as the jehad, or holy war, was being preached. And now I will tell a most remarkable circumstance, quite the most extraordinary in this book.

Sultan Hussein told my husband *on February 1* that a consul had been murdered at Jedda.

We were most excited about this, and anxiously inquired about it when we reached Aden, but heard that no murder had taken place, *nor did it till May*, when several consuls were murdered.

This proves that it must have been a very long-arranged plan, and that the sultan knew of it and thought it had had time to be carried out. No doubt all this accounted for his bad reception of us.

After a good deal of illusory delay, the sultan declared he could not in any way be responsible for our safety if we went anywhere from Sheher, so we had to bow to the inevitable and put ourselves on board a dhow belonging to Kutch, bound for Aden.

The captain and sailors were all Hindoos, and to our amusement our Mohammedan party were as unclean as ourselves. The crew would not let us touch their fire and water, and filled our vessels themselves without touching them, very good-humouredly, and they made up an extra galley for us by putting some sand in a wooden box, and here Christians and Moslems had perforce to cook together. Of course we did not mind, but there was much laughter at the expense of the others, in which indeed they joined, for they bore their adversity amiably when it brought strange cooking-fellows.

On reaching Aden we still desired to penetrate into the Jebel Akhdar, so looked out for a ship going to Maskat. We could find none, therefore we embarked for India with all our company. I am not going to describe India, but will only tell of our money difficulties.

So ignorant were we and everyone at Maskat as to what money was in use in Dhofar, that we were persuaded that it was necessary to take an immense quantity of small change in the shape of copper coins about the size of a farthing, supposed to be Omani. We had four wooden boxes bound with wire, about 1 foot long and 5 or 6 inches high and wide, delivered to us, all closed up, and said to have a certain sum in each.

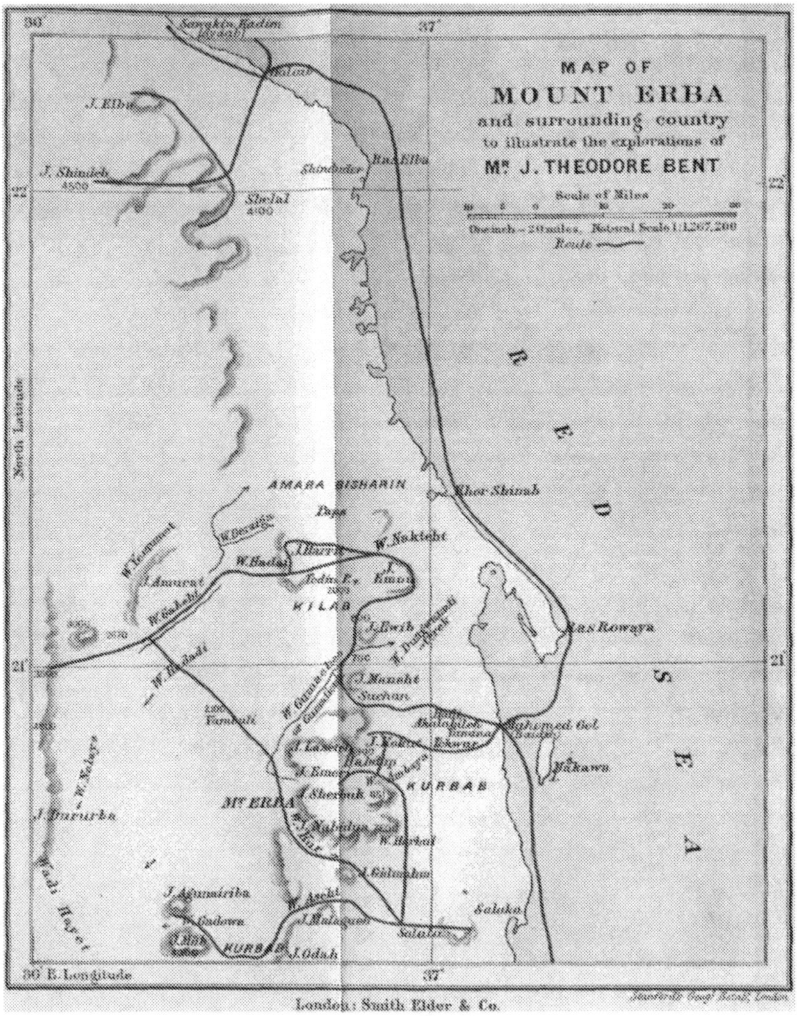

Map of Mount Erba

and surrounding country

to illustrate the explorations of

M^r. J. THEODORE BENT.

Stanford's Geog.^l Estab.^t, London

London: Smith, Elder & Co.

Soon after we set out we opened one of these boxes to get out some money and have it ready, but found in it so many and various kinds of coins, all the same size, that we opened all the boxes, making quite a mound on the ground, to sort out the German East Africa, English East Africa, Zanzibar, and other useless coins, and then packed them neatly up, an awfully troublesome and dirty job. We kept out what we thought would pass, but behold! all were useless; no one would look at anything but Maria Theresa dollars and Indian coins down to two-anna pieces—nothing lower.

All these boxes, therefore, had to return to Maskat, and when paying off the interpreter, Hassan, a most respectable person with large, round, gold spectacles, my husband asked him to be kind enough to take his money in these boxes and change at Maskat. No, he would only have good silver dollars; and sadly he rued his want of good-nature.

We two and Lobo, whom we retained, went to a hotel in Bombay, but Imam Sharif, Khan Bahadur, his four men, our Goanese cook, Hassan, and a certain young Afghan, Ahmet, who had been a sort of odd man and tent-pitcher, went to a caravanserai; and after Hassan's steamer had departed to Maskat, Imam Sharif came and told us the doleful tidings that Ahmet had disappeared with the good silver dollars and the gold watch and chain of Hassan. No doubt he then regretted he had not taken the boxes of copper.

AN AFRICAN INTERLUDE: THE EASTERN SOUDAN

CHAPTER XXIII

COASTING ALONG THE RED SEA

In the winter of 1895, though we still wished to continue our investigations in Arabia, we found it impracticable, owing to the warlike state of the tribes there, so we decided to turn our attention to the other side of the Red Sea, and travel once more in Africa.

Parts of Africa have to be discovered and other parts rediscovered. Each little war and each little journey contributes to the accomplishment of both these ends with surprising rapidity, but the geographical millennium is looming in the distance when the traveller will no longer require his sextant and theodolite, but will take his spade and pruning-hook to cultivate the land this generation is so busy in discovering.

That winter we added a few square miles to a blank corner of the map where re-discovery was necessary, and where re-discovery will go on apace and produce most interesting results, when we have finished conquering the barbarous followers of the Khalifa, and restore law and order to that wide portion of Africa known as the Eastern Soudan; for the Soudan, meaning in Arabic 'the country of the blacks,' really extends from the Atlantic to the Red Sea. Little did we think when we started to explore the western shores of the Red Sea that the explosion with the Dervishes was so near, otherwise I think we should have turned our steps in another direction.

We had with us Mr. Alfred Cholmley, who took numbers of beautiful photographs, and Lieutenant, now Captain, N. M. Smyth, D.S.O., Queen's Bays, kindly attached to our expedition by Colonel Sir F. Wingate, and to his exertions we owe the map.

My husband had always thought it foolish to engage an interpreter unknown to him, on his own responsibility, and would only have one recommended by the official of our Government. The choice made for us on this occasion was not at all successful. He tried to make out that he was the principal leader of the party, and his impedimenta far exceeded ours. He may or may not have been sent to keep us from going more than ten miles from the coast, but no explorer would wish to remain within the limits set down in the Admiralty Chart. My husband found it necessary to dispense with his services when we were at Mersa Halaib, and we got on far better without him.

Our first task was to choose a ship; it was exciting work rowing about in the harbour of Suez in order to find one that would suit us.

A letter from our interpreter had told us we could have one at 120*l*. a month, a sum which our great experience of sailing-boats told us was quite too large. When we started our search, having refused this, we were only shown wretched boats in which we could hardly sit and certainly not stand. We espied one we thought would do, and said nothing at that time, but afterwards my husband and Matthaios went off by themselves and engaged her for 35*l*. a month, and I do not think that a better ship was to be found in Suez—certainly there was none worth 120*l*.

Our boat was an Arab dhow of 80 tons, named the *Taisir*; we at once put her in the hands of a carpenter, who boarded off two cabins for us four whites, in the big, open stern cabin, leaving a sort of verandah in front of them, about 8 feet in depth, where we lived by day. Campbell Bey, who lives at Terre Pleine, pronounced by the English Terry Plain, kindly lent us two water-tanks containing half a ton each.

We embarked late on Christmas night, and by the murky light of lanterns the ship looked most dreary and uninviting; but when we had furnished it, by laying down our tent carpet and beds and hanging sheets of coloured calico over the gaping boards of our walls, and had put up the cabin bags, we were quite snug. We always had to close in our verandah with a sail at night, for when the ship swung round at anchor we were exposed to the north wind.

Our captain, Reis Hamaya, turned out an excellent fellow, as also did the seventeen sailors he had under him; and though at times they would quarrel loudly enough amongst themselves, the only points of discord which arose between them and us always had reference to the length of time they wished to stop in harbour and the length of distance they wished to go in a day. Ill-fed, dirty, unkempt men as our sailors were, we got to like them all, from the elderly dignified Mohammed, who thought he knew more about navigation than the captain, to Ahmet Faraj, the buffoon who played the tom-tom and made everybody laugh; this worthy individual was the recognised leader of all the festivities with which they regaled us from time to time, consisting of very ugly songs and a yet uglier dance, the chief art in which consisted in wagging their elastic tails with an energy which mortals further removed from monkey origin could never hope to approach.

We travelled all the first night, but the second we anchored near Safaia Island, and the third at a place called Sheikh Ganem, in front of the Ashrafi Light, and the fourth day found us at Kosseir, which means 'little castle.' The Government steamer *Abbas*, which had started one day after us and gone straight down 'outside', had only got in two hours before us, and we had been 'inside', through the reefs, and stopped all night, so we thought we had not done badly.

We stayed two nights in the harbour to make our final victualling arrangements. Kosseir, our last really civilised point, is now a wretched place, though twice in its existence it has been of importance, owing to its road connection with Keneh on the Nile. Five miles to the north of the present town are the ruins of the old Ptolemaic one, Myos Hormos (Kosseir Kadim), where the Red Sea fleets in ancient days assembled to start for India; twenty years ago it was a favourite point for the departure of pilgrims for Mecca, and the P. and O. had offices there, which are now turned into camel-stables. Kosseir is waiting for a railway before it can again recoup its fortunes.

There are two mosques of pretty architecture, with courses of dark red stone from Keneh, and white Kosseir limestone; there are also diaper and fretwork patterns; the pillars are similarly decorated and are quaint and picturesque. The tombs of the Ababdeh sheikhs have melon-shaped domes, and there are endless dovecotes, chiefly made of broken old amphoræ built into walls.

Along the whole coast-line from Kosseir to Sawakin one may say that there are no permanent places of residence, if we except the tiny Egyptian military stations, with their fort and huts for the soldiers, at Halaib, Mohammed Gol, and Darour; it is practically desert all the way, and is only visited by the nomad Ababdeh and Bisharin tribes, when, after the rains, they can obtain there a scanty pasturage for their flocks. During the Ptolemaic and early Arab periods the condition of affairs was very different; several considerable towns stood on this coast, now marked only by heaps of sand and a few fallen walls. In spite of its aridity, this coast has a wonderful charm of its own; its lofty, deeply serrated mountains are a perpetual joy to look upon, and the sunset effects were unspeakably glorious, rich in every conceivable colour, and throwing out the sharp outline of the pointed peaks against the crimson sky.

The nature of this coast-line is singularly uniform, and offers tremendous obstacles to navigation, owing to the great belt of coral reefs along it, through which the passage was often barely wide enough for our dhow to pass, and against which on more than one occasion we came in unpleasant contact. The bay of Berenice, for example, was for this reason known in ancient times as ἀκάθαρτος κόλπος, and is still known as 'Foul Bay'; it can only be navigated with the greatest care by native pilots accustomed to the various aspects of the water, which in many places only just covers the treacherous reefs. All boats are obliged to anchor during the night either just inside the reefs or in the numerous coves along the coast, which are caused by the percolations of fresh water through the sandbeds of rivers into the sea, and these prevent the coral insect from erecting its continuous wall.

The rapidly succeeding little harbours formed in the coral reef are called *mersa*, or anchorage, by the Arabs, from *mersat*, anchor.

Sometimes when the coral reef rises above the surface low islets have been formed, with sandy surface and a scant marine vegetation. By one of these, named Siyal, we were anchored for a night, and on landing we found it about three miles in length, some 50 feet in width, and never more than 4 feet above the surface of the sea. On its eastern side the shore was strewn with cinders from the numerous steamers which ply the Red Sea, and quantities of straw cases for bottles, out of which the ospreys, which live here in large numbers, have built their nests. Turtles revel in the sand, and corals of lovely colours line the beach, and at one extremity of the islet we found the remains of a holy sheikh's hut, with his grave hard by. Many such holy men dwell on promontories and on remote island rocks along this coast in sanctified seclusion, and they are regularly supported by the Bedouin and pearl-fishers, who bring them food and water, neither of which commodities is to be found in such localities. Our sailors on New Year's Eve took a handsome present of bread and candles, presented to them by us, to a holy man who dwelt on the extreme point of Ras Bernas, and had a long gossip with him concerning what boats had passed that way and the prospects of trade—*i.e.* the slave trade—in these desert regions. They burnt incense before his shrine, and the captain devoutly said his evening prayer, whilst he of the tom-tom, Ahmet Faraj, stood behind and mimicked him, to the great amusement of his fellows—a piece of irreverence I have never seen before in any Mohammedan country. Still I think our sailors were as a whole religious; they observed their fasts and prayers most regularly during Ramazan, and their only idea of time was regulated by the five prayers. 'We shall start to-morrow at "God is great," and anchor at the evening prayer,' and so forth, they used to say.

It is difficult to estimate how far these coral reefs have changed since ancient days; there is a lagoon at Berenice which looks as if it had been the ancient harbour with a fort at its extremity. Now there are scarcely two feet of water over the bar across its mouth; but all ancient accounts bear testimony to a similar difficulty of navigation down this coast. At the same time, it is manifest that this coast-line is just the one to have tempted on the early mariners from point to point, with its rapid succession of tiny harbours and its reefs protecting it from heavy seas. More especially must this have been the case when the boats were propelled by oars, and in one's mind's eye one can picture the fleets of the Egyptian Queen Hatasou and of King Solomon from Eziongeber creeping cautiously along this coast and returning after three years' absence in far distant regions laden with precious freights of gold, frankincense, and spices. In later days Strabo and Pliny tell us how flotillas of 120 ships proceeded from Myos Hormos to Okelis in thirty days on their way to India, going together for fear of the pirates who marauded this coast, and in those days the settlements on the Red Sea must have presented a far livelier aspect than they do now.

On both shores we find a curious instance of the migration and adaptation of an entirely foreign kind of boat. Some Arabs who have lived in Singapore—and Singapore is as favourite a point for Arab emigration as America is for the Irish—introduced 'dug-outs' in their native harbours, and these have been found so useful in sailing over the shallow coral reefs in search of pearls, that they now swarm in every Red Sea port, and steamer-loads of 'dug-outs' are brought from the Malay peninsula. The Arabs call them 'houris'—why, I cannot think—for a more uncomfortable thing to sit in, when half full of water in a rolling surf, I never found elsewhere, except on a South-East African river.

At the present moment the coast below Ras Bernas and above Sawakin is the hot-bed of the slave trade, carried on between the Dervishes of the Nile Valley and Arabia. Regular Egyptian coastguard boats keep matters pretty clear north of Ras Bernas, and we can testify to their activity, for we ourselves were boarded and searched by one; but south of this, before the influence of Sawakin is reached, there is a long stretch of country where the traffic in human flesh can be carried on undisturbed. Troops of slaves are sent down from the Nile valley to the Dervish country at certain seasons of the year, and the petty sheikhs along the coast, owing a doubtful allegiance to the Egyptian Government, connive at this transport; and the pearl-fishing craft which ply their trade amongst the coral reefs are always ready to carry the slaves across to the opposite coast, where the markets of Yembo, Jeddah, and Hodeida are open to them. This will, of course, be the case until the Dervish power is crushed, and the Soudan opened out for more legitimate trade. As we sailed along we passed hundreds of these pearl-fishing boats engaged in this dual trade, and nothing could be more propitious for their pursuits than the absolutely lawless condition of the tribes by the coast. At Berenice, for instance, there are absolutely no government or inhabitants of any sort. Nominally, one of our Nile frontier subsidised sheikhs, Beshir Bey Gabran, of Assouan, has authority over all the country between the Nile and the Red Sea, but the coast has been visited more frequently by Dervish emirs than by Beshir Bey. One Nasrai, a Dervish emir, is said to have resided in the mountains behind Berenice for some time past, and, with a small following, collects tithes of cattle from the nomads and sees to the safe conduct of slave caravans. The collecting of *yusur*, or black coral, as they call it, a fossilised vegetable growth, is a third trade in which these boats are employed. From this pipes are made, and beads, and the black veneer for inlaying tables.

The navigation of an Arab dhow is no easy task, with its clumsy arrangements for sails, when there is a strong north wind behind it and reefs in every direction. Three men are perpetually in the bows on the look out for rocks, and indicate the presence of danger to the steersman by raising their hands. The gear of these boats is exceedingly primitive. They do not understand reefing a sail, hence they are obliged to have no less than five different sizes, which they are constantly changing as occasion requires. They use a clumsy cogwheel for raising and lowering the sails, and do it all by main force, singing silly little distiches and screaming at the top of their voices as they haul the ropes. The arrangement for baling out the bilge water is extremely laborious. A large trough, with channels on either side, is erected in the centre of the boat, into the middle of which the water is baled by skins from below, and the stenches during the process are truly awful, as the water flows out of either channel, according to the roll of the ship. There was always a large surface of wet wood to dry up.

Leaving Kosseir on the last day of 1895, we reached Ras Bernas on the second day of 1896, stopping, of course, each night, always rolling and tossing about, and always keeping a sharp look out for coral reefs, the watchers shouting advice continually to Reis Hamaya.

We were supposed to owe our safety in getting through some dangerous reefs, with not a yard to spare on either side, and escaping our other difficulties, to the lucky fact of Reis Hamaya's having discovered amongst the plants that my husband had collected in our walks ashore one of the order of *Compositæ*, which he pounced on gladly and hung on the bow of the *Taisir*, as a protection to us.

He pointed out another thing, a shrub called *tuldum*, with tiny yellow flowers on green stalks, good to tie round the arm to make one see far.

Ras Bernas is a long, wandering cape composed of rocky hills of ironstone and silicate curiously blended together, with shoals and rocks, and coral reefs, and sandbanks hanging on to it in very shallow water. It is about twenty-five miles long, and ends in a sandy spit.

We encamped at the head of the lagoon, and spent several days amongst the ruins of this old Ptolemaic town of Berenice, and made sundry excavations there. In its centre is an old temple of the date of Tiberius Cæsar, the hieroglyphs in which are rapidly becoming obliterated. All around is a sea of mounds covered with sand, where the houses stood, mostly built of madrepore, and laid out in streets. On the surface are to be found numerous glass beads, Roman coins, bracelets, &c. and a great number of fragments of rough emeralds. From the celebrated emerald-mines in the mountain behind we picked up fully fifty of these, besides a large quantity of olivines or peridots, cornelians, and crystals, testifying to the wealth of these parts in precious stones in ancient days.

A few startled Ababdeh nomads came to visit us; at first they only inspected us at a distance, but gradually gained courage and came to our camp, and we were able to purchase from them two lambs to replenish our larder.

With its emerald-mines, its harbour, and its great road terminus Berenice must have been one of the most important trade centres of the Red Sea; though, judging from the plans of the streets we made out, the town cannot have been a very large one. In digging we turned up immense quantities of textiles in scraps, fine and coarse, nets, knitted work, as well as weaving, plain and in colours, and bits of papyrus in Greek cursive hand. The wretched Ababdeh tribes were constantly at war with one another, and the Dervish Khalifa could make his authority felt about here with a small handful of resolute men judiciously placed. Nasrai had, I believe, done this for some time past with only thirty men.

The nights here were very cold, the thermometer going down to 46° F. There were a few gazelles about, but we saw no other animals.

The Bedouin brought us large shell-fish in those great shells we see polished at home. When boiled the fish comes out. It is in shape like a camel's foot, and they call it ghemel. In taste it is like lobster and oyster combined, but as tough as pin-wire.

We had a great tossing for three days after leaving Berenice, and stopping every night.

CHAPTER XXIV

HALAIB AND SAWAKIN KADIM

It is hard to imagine anything more squalid than the Egyptian fortress of Halaib, as it is spelt on the map, or Halei as it is pronounced, which was our next halting-place, and from which we succeeded in getting a little way inland. The governor, Ismael, has been there seven years; he and his family inhabit some wicker cages near the small white fort, and gathered round them are the huts of his soldiers and the cabins of a few Bisharin, who live under the immediate protection of the fort. Ismael is possessed of the only patch of cultivated land that we saw during the whole of our expedition, where he grows gourds, peas, and aubergines or brinjols. The man of most authority in the place is Mohammed Ali Tiout, head of the Bisharin tribe of Achmed Orab. He appointed his son, a fine, intelligent young fellow of five-and-twenty, called *the batran* in the local dialect, to act as our guide and protector during our exploration of the Shellal range, which rises some miles inland at the back of Halaib.

The people of this portion of the Soudan between the coast and the Nile Valley, who do not own allegiance to the Khalifa, belong to the Morghani confraternity of Mohammedans; their young religious sheikh, a self-possessed, clever lad of about twenty, lives at Sawakin, and his influence amongst the tribes not affecting Mahdism is supreme. He is devoted to British interests, and no doubt in the present condition of affairs his co-operation will be of great value. The Egyptian Government instructed him to write to the sheikhs around Halaib and Mohammed Gol to insure our safety, and to this fact I am convinced we owe the immunity from danger we enjoyed, and the assistance given to us in penetrating inland from Mohammed Gol. The Morghani have the three cicatrices on either cheek, and as a confraternity they are not in the least fanatical, and are well disposed to Christians; very different to the Arabs we met in the Hadhramout, and very different to the Dervishes with whom they are on such hostile terms.

While at Halaib I paid several visits to the wife and family of the mamour or governor. They were very civil always, and used to kiss me. They looked quite as unsettled in their airy brushwood arbours as if they had not resided there steadily for seven years.

There were three huts about 12 feet by 8 feet, one being a kitchen. There is a brushwood fence all round, part having a shed for the stores and water jars. The wife is a Turk, and has one plain grown-up daughter. There was an old lady who made coffee, and a black maid slightly draped in a sheet once white, but now of a general deep grey, pure black in some parts. I liked getting coffee and ginger best. The first day I had to swallow, smiling, tea boiled and a little burnt.

All the furniture I saw was a 3-foot bed, three Austrian chairs, a very common wooden table, and a little iron one with a new and tight pink cotton cover and petticoat to the ground. All was very clean but the maid.

The kind lady thought her dwelling so superior to mine that she begged me to come and sleep in the bed with her in shelter from the wind; tents, she said, were only fit for men. I did not envy her her home in the drenching rain we had all night and half one day. She wore a string round under one arm, with seven or eight charms like good-sized pincushions or housewifes of different coloured silks.

We made two expeditions from Halaib; the first was to the ruins now known as Sawakin Kadim, which are on the coast twelve miles north of Halaib. As only six camels could be obtained we went by boat ourselves, leaving the camels for the baggage. For this purpose we deserted the *Taisir* and hired a smaller *kattira*, and having gone as near as we could to land, and been in considerable danger from coral reefs, on which we ran suddenly, nearly capsizing, we took to the houri that we had towed astern. It was very like sitting in a bath, and, after the houri, we had to be carried a long way. We encamped not far from the shore, and had to endure a dreadful *khamsin* and dust-storm from the south, with such violent wind that I was blown down, and Matthaios dug our beds out twice with a trowel; and the next day we found the north wind nearly as bad. Why it did not raise the sand I do not know.

Sawakin Kadim is like Berenice, nothing but a mass of mounds, but it must at some time or another have been a much larger place. We excavated one of these mounds, but found nothing earlier than Kufic remains, unless the graves, which were constructed of four large blocks of madrepore sunk deep into the ground, may be looked upon as a more ancient form of sepulture. We opened several, but unfortunately they contained nothing but bones. Originally this town must have been built on an island, or an artificial moat must have been dug round it to protect it on the mainland side; this is now silted up, but is traceable all along. Three large cisterns for water are still in a fair state of preservation, and I am told that a Kufic inscription was found here some years ago. There seems no doubt that this town is the one mentioned by the Arab geographers, Abou'lfida and Edrisi, by the name of Aydab, which was a place of considerable importance between Ras Bernas and Sawakin. There are no traces elsewhere along this coast of any other town, consequently we can fairly place it here. Abou'lfida says: 'Aydab is a town in the land of Bedja; it is politically dependent on Egypt, though some say it is in Abyssinia. This is the meeting-place for the merchants of Yemen and the pilgrims, who, leaving Egypt, prefer the sea route and embark for Yedda. In other respects Aydab has more the aspect of a village than a town, and it is seven days' march north of Sawakin, where the chief of the Bedjas lives.' Counting a day's march at twenty-five miles, this would place it near Halaib, which is 170 miles north of Sawakin. Hitherto on our maps Aydab has been placed near Mohammed Gol, but, as there are no traces of ruins there except the towers to which we shall presently allude, this position for an ancient town is untenable.

Edrisi tells us: 'At the extremity of the desert and on the borders of the salt sea is Aydab, whence one crosses to Yedda in one day and one night. Aydab has two governors, one appointed by the chief of the Bedja, and the other by the princes of Egypt.' From the fact that Aydab is mentioned by none of the earlier geographers it would appear not to have been one of the Ptolemaic settlements, but a town of purely Arab origin. The people of Bedja, so often alluded to by these Arabian geographers, seem to have had considerable power, and to have occupied all the Soudan and as far north as Berenice, being probably the precursors of the Bisharin Amara tribes, which wander now over this desert country. They were the recognised guardians of the old gold-mines which existed in this district, and concerning which I have more to say presently; and though vassals of the Egyptian kaliphs, nevertheless they seem to have had considerable local authority, and to have carried on wars on their own account.

It is a curious fact that in the Aksumite inscriptions we come across an account of wars and victories by the old Ethiopian monarchs over the peoples of Kasuh and Bega to the north of Abyssinia, which peoples Professor D. H. Müller identifies with the people of Kush and the Bedja alluded to by the Arab geographers.

In course of time the Bedjas seem to have disappeared from the face of the earth and left nothing but their tombs and a few ruined towns behind them; and for some centuries it would appear that the coast of the Red Sea north of Sawakin was uninhabited until in later years came fresh colonists from the Nile Valley, whose descendants still occupy it.

The tribal traditions of the district are all that we have now to rely upon regarding the immigration of new inhabitants, and they state that two brothers with their families, one named Amer and the other Amar, came from the Nile Valley near Wadi Halfa, and settled along the coast of the Red Sea; from them are descended the Beni Amer and Amara tribes of Bedouin. These brothers were followed in due course by four other brothers, Ali, Kourb, Nour, and Gueil, from whom the tribes and sub-tribes of the Aliab, Kourbab, Nourab, and Gueilior are respectively descended. These tribes have never been anything but pastoral nomads, living in miserable mat huts, and spreading themselves over the district at wide intervals in search of pasture for their flocks. They entirely disown having anything to do with the remains of buildings and tombs found in their midst.

CHAPTER XXV

INLAND FROM MERSA HALAIB

When we returned to Halaib we encamped preparatory to going inland. Great doctoring had to be done over the hand of Ahmet Farraj, our clown. He had held a large hook overboard, with a bait, but no line, and a shark 7 feet long was caught and hauled on board. The shark bit the man's first finger badly. Various remedies were applied by the sailors in turns—tar, grease, earth, and other things— and it was in a very bad state when brought to us. It was quite cured eventually, but we were afraid of blood-poisoning. When I began cleaning it most tenderly he scraped it out with a stick, and his friends dipped stones in the warm water and soundly scrubbed the surrounding inflamed parts. My husband prescribed a washing all over with hot water and stones. He was afterwards quite a different colour.

Our second expedition was to Shellal. We took two days on our way thither, passing through clouds of locusts—that is to say, they were in clouds on our return, but were young and in heaps when we first saw them. We stayed at Shellal several days, for my husband thought as we could get no further in that direction on account of the danger of the Dervishes, it was as well that we, and especially Captain Smyth, should make as many expeditions thence as possible. We heard so many contradictory reports, but little thought how imminent the war was.

After our somewhat long experience of life on a dhow we were delighted to become Bedou once more, and wander amongst the fine rocky range of mountains, but we were disappointed that our guide would not take us far behind this range for fear of the Dervishes; and, as shortly after the outbreak of the war a party of Dervishes came right down to Halaib, there is every reason to believe that had we gone far inland at this point we might have been compelled to pay the Khalifa a not over-pleasant visit at Omdurman.

Wadi Shellal and the adjacent mountains of Shendeh, Shindoeh, and Riadh form a *cul de sac* as far as camels are concerned, and only difficult mountain paths lead over into the Soudan from here. As far as we could see the country did not look very tempting or promise much compensation for the difficulties of transit. We were taken by the Batran to a few spots where there had been ancient habitations; they probably belonged to the Kufic period, and were doubtless military stations to protect the small hamlets scattered at the foot of these mountains, when Aydab was a place of some importance, from the incursion of hostile tribes from the interior.

Shellal itself reaches an elevation of 4,100 feet; Shindeh, 4,500 feet; Riadh, 4,800 feet; and Asortriba or Sorturba to the south seems, though we did not get its elevation, to be the highest of the group.

Elba Mountains from Shellal

On our return to Halaib we passed a Bisharin encampment, consisting of half a dozen beehive huts made of matting on rounded sticks. The women were weaving rough cloths at the door of one of them, and were dressed in long sheets which once may have been white, but are now the colour of dirt. They had glass beads and cowries tied to their matted locks, and brass and silver rings of considerable size fastened to their noses; the small children ran about naked, with waistbands of leather straps, on which were strung long agate and carnelian beads, with cowrie danglements hanging down in front. They seemed very poor, and the old ladies to whom my husband gave pinches of tobacco were so effusive in their gratitude that for some moments he feared his generosity was to be rewarded by a kiss.

Our net results from the excursions from Halaib were more or less of a negative character. The mountain scenery was grand, and the climate exquisite, but, from our observations, we came to the conclusion that at no time was this country of much use to anybody, and that it never had been thickly inhabited, the existence of Aydab being probably due to its position as a convenient port opposite Arabia for the inhabitants of the Nile Valley. Water is, and probably always has been, very scarce here, and, except after the rains, this country is little better than a desert.

The Bishari of the Akhmed Orab tribe, who inhabit the mountains, are exceedingly few in number, and the Batran told us that all the way from Ras Bernas to Mount Sorturba, just south of Shellal, over which country his rule extends, the whole tribe could muster only about three hundred fighting men. They have the Ababdeh to the north, and the Amara Bisharin to the south, and apparently their relations with their neighbours are usually strained. These tribes are purely pastoral, and cultivate no land whatsoever. They live in huts in groups of from three to six together, and are scattered over the country at wide intervals. They wear their hair fuzzy at the top, with a row of curls hanging down the neck, usually white and stiff with mutton fat. They are medium-sized, dark-skinned, and some of them decidedly handsome. They are girt only with a loin-cloth and sheet, and every shepherd here carries his shield and his sword. Under a good and settled government they would undoubtedly be excellent members of society, but with the Khalifa on one side and the Egyptian Government on the other their position is by no means an enviable one. Their huts are very small and dingy, being constructed with bent sticks on which palm-leaf matting is stretched; inside they are decorated with their paraphernalia for weddings and camel-travelling, all elaborately decorated with cowrie and other shells, the most remarkable of these things being the tall conical hats with long streamers used for dances at weddings, entirely covered with cowrie shells in pretty patterns. The things they use for hanging up food are also prettily decorated with shells and strips of red and blue cloth. The family occupying a hut sleep on mats in the inner part, with the usual wooden African pillows, and around the outer edge of the hut are collected their wooden bowls for sour milk, their skins for water, their incense-burners, and their limited number of household utensils. Often when he goes off to distant pasturages a Bishari will pack up his tent and household gods and leave them in a tree, where he will find them quite safe on his return. They live principally on milk and the products of their flocks, water being to them a far more precious article than milk. They are very knowledgeable in the mountain shrubs and herbs, and pointed out to us many which they eat for medicinal and other purposes; but the only one of these which we appreciated was a small red gourd climbing amongst the mimosa branches, resembling a tomato, *Cephalandra Indica*. This they call *gourod*, their usual word for gourd. Also they are, like the ἀκριδόφαγοι whom Agatharchides places on their coast, large consumers of locusts when in season; they catch them only when they have reached the flying stage, and roast them in the ashes. We often saw clouds of locusts in this district, devouring all the scanty herbage and literally filling the air.

For many years past the Egyptian authority in these parts has been *nil*, and confined only to a few wretched forts on the coast. Dervish raids from the interior and the stoppage of whatever caravan trade there ever was have contributed to the miserable condition of affairs now existing.

One can well understand why these miserable hounded tribes are wavering in their allegiance between the Egyptian Government and the Khalifa, whom they dread, and why they countenance the slave-traders, for the reason that they have no power to resist them.

For all practical purposes it is a wretched country, waterless during a great part of the year, except where some deep ancient wells, scattered at wide intervals over the country, form centres where camels and flocks can be watered; and as we travelled along we were struck by the numbers of these wells which had been quite recently abandoned. But the mountains are magnificently grand, sharp in outline like Montserrat in Spain, and with deep and lovely gorges. Formerly they abounded in mines, and were celebrated for their mineral wealth, and if there is ever to be a revival in this country it will be from this source that hope will come.

We had such strong wind when we went to sea again that we feared we should not be able to start, but we got away after all, rising up early to be dressed before we were shaken about; but we forgot to empty our basins, and they emptied themselves into our beds, and all the luggage banged about and the kitchen things went all over the place, including the 'range,' consisting of two little stoves in paraffin-cans, but we got on splendidly till we began to turn into Mersa or Khor Shinab, as the Bisharin call it; the Arab name is Bishbish.

Khor Shinab is a typical specimen of a *mersa*; it is cruciform, and is entered by a narrow passage between the reefs, about 20 feet across, and runs sinuously inland for about two miles, and is never more than a quarter of a mile wide.

We had the second-sized sail up, but that had to be taken down and a smaller tried; the sheet of this soon gave way, and the sail went up in the air with the block and tore all across. This was a frightful sight, as we were among coral reefs. The sailors flew about, casting off garments in all directions. A smaller sail tore up in a few moments, and we were stuck on a reef. Then the smallest sail of all was taken out of its bag, and that got us off with some grating, the captain and some others standing on the reef on the port side with water half up to their knees, pushing with all their might. There were fourteen fathoms under us to starboard. The little sail soon gave way at the top and fell into the water.

One anchor was sent out in a boat and then another, and when they tried to get up the first it was so entangled that they were a long time over it, and one of the five flukes was broken. We were kept off the reef by poles all this time. That broken anchor was then taken ashore, and we were very thankful to be safe.

The flat ground for miles inland is composed of nothing but madrepore, and is covered with semi-fossilised sea-shells, which have probably not been inhabited for thousands of years. We walked over this for three miles before reaching the first spurs of the mountains, and it is impossible to conceive a more barren or arid spot. Khor Shinab is a well-known resort for slave-trading craft; small boats can easily hide in its narrow creeks and escape observation.

We stayed two days while the sails were mended on the shore, and it was hours and hours before the anchor that was in the reef could be got up and fastened to the dry land. We did try to get out to sea again, but the north wind was raging so we could not do it, and, besides, the sailors were very unwilling to start, as a raven was sitting on the bow.

CHAPTER XXVI

MOHAMMED GOL

At Mohammed Gol, to which port our dhow next conducted us, our prospects of getting well into the interior were much brighter, and our ultimate results beyond comparison more satisfactory than they had been at Halaib. Mohammed Gol is distinctly a more lively place than Halaib, possessing more huts, more soldiers, and actually a miniature bazaar where, strange to relate, we were able to buy something we wanted.

The houses at Mohammed Gol are larger than those at Halaib, and one can stand up in some parts of nearly all of them.

The fort is surrounded by a very evil-smelling moat, and the village situated on a damp plain, white with salt. When we made a camp on shore later we went well beyond this plain.

In the summer season, when the waters of the Red Sea are low, traders come to Mohammed Gol for salt. The salterns are situated on the narrow spit of land called Ras Rowaya; consequently, the people about here are more accustomed to the sight of Europeans, and Mohammed Effendi, the governor, or mamour of the little Egyptian garrison, who is young and energetic, seems far more in touch with the world than Ismael of Halaib. He complained much of the dulness of his post, and passed his weary hours in making walking-sticks out of ibex horns, a craft he had learnt from the Bedouin of Mount Erba, who soften the horns in hot water, grease them, pull them out and flatten them with weights and polish them, using them as camel sticks. The governor gave us several of these sticks, and also presented an ibex-horn head-scratcher to me, remarking as he did so, with a polite gesture, that it was a nice thing to have by me when my head itched. He was a little and very dark man, with a pleasant, honest face, and three transverse scars across his cheeks, each about two inches long. His secretary was yet smaller, and decorated in the same way. The chief of the police was a very fat, good-humoured man, with two little perpendicular cuts beside each eye. These are tribal marks.

There was great palavering about our journey into the interior. Though several travellers had visited the Red Sea side of the massive group of Mount Erba on holidays from Sawakin in search of sport, no one had as yet been behind it, and thither we intended to go. The governor had summoned three sheikhs from the mountains, into whose hands he confided us. The day we first landed I thought I never had beheld such scowling, disagreeable faces, but afterwards we became good friends. My husband and I went ashore the second day, and sat in a sort of audience-arbour near the madrepore pier, and many maps were drawn on the ground with camel-sticks, and we were quite proud that my husband was able to settle it all with no interpreter.

Sheikh Ali Debalohp, the chief of the Kilab tribe, was to take us to his district, Wadi Hadai and Wadi Gabeit, some way inland at the back of the Erba mountains, which group we insisted on going entirely round. He was a tall, fine specimen of a Bishari sheikh, with his neck terribly scarred by a burn, to heal which he had been treated in hospital at Sawakin. He is, as we learnt later, a man of questionable loyalty to the Egyptian Government, and supposed to be more than half a Dervish; this may be owing to the exigencies of his position, for more than half his tribe living in the Wadi Hayet are of avowed allegiance to the Khalifa, and Debalohp's authority now only extends over the portion near the coast. As far as we could see his intentions towards us were strictly honourable, and he treated us throughout our expedition in a much more straightforward manner than either of the other two.

Sheikh number two was Mohammed, the son of Ali Hamed, head sheikh of a branch of the great Kurbab tribe. As his father was too old and infirm to accompany us, he took his place. He was an exceedingly dirty and wild-looking fellow, with a harsh, raucous voice, and his statements were not always reliable. We have reason to believe that his father is much interested in the slave-trade, and therefore not too fond of Europeans; but these sheikhs by the coast are generally obliged to be somewhat double in their dealings, and, when anything can be gained by it, affect sincere friendship for the English.

Sheikh number three bore the name of Hassan Bafori, and is *wagdab* or chief of another branch of the Kurbabs, and his authority extends over the massive group of Mount Erba and Kokout. He is a man who seems to revel in telling lies, and we never could believe a word he said. Besides these head-men we had several minor sheikhs with us, and two soldiers sent by the mamour from his garrison at Mohammed Gol to see that we were well treated. Hence our caravan was of considerable dimensions when we took our departure from Mohammed Gol on February 6.

He of the Kilab tribe, Ali Debalohp, was the most important of them, and he took one of his wives with him; all had their servants and shield-bearers, and most of them were wild, unprepossessing looking men, with shaggy locks and lard-daubed curls, and all of them were, I believe, thorough ruffians, who, as we were told afterwards, would willingly have sold us to the Dervishes had they thought they would have gained by the transaction. These things officials told us when we reached Sawakin; but, to do our guides justice, I must say they treated us very well, and inasmuch as we never believed a word they said, the fact that they were liars made but little difference to us.

Some of the men had very fine profiles, and one was very handsome. Their hair is done something like the Bisharin's—that is, with a fuz standing up on the top, but the hanging part is not curled; the white tallow with which they were caked, made them look as if their heads were surrounded with dips.

I asked why the tallow was put on. One said to make one strong, another to make one see far, and a third reason was that the hair might not appear black.

We had fourteen camels for ourselves and two for the police who came with us. The mamour was in European uniform, with a red shawl wound round his head, and sat on a very smart inlaid saddle which came up to his waist in front and reached to his shoulder-blades. The chief of the police did not come, he being, as he told us, far too fat.

We were to fill all our waterskins from a remarkably fine well of particularly sweet water at Hadi, so we took only a couple of skinfuls with us.

CHAPTER XXVII

'DANCING ON TOM TIDDLER'S GROUND, PICKING UP GOLD'

Little did we dream when we left Mohammed Gol with our rather extensive caravan that behind that gigantic mountain, which though it only reaches an elevation of 7,500 feet, looks considerably higher from the sea as it rises almost directly out of the level plain, we were to find an ancient Egyptian gold-mine, the ruins in connection with which would offer us the first tangible comparison to the ruins which had exercised our minds so much in the gold-fields of South Africa.

Some miles inland on the plain behind Mohammed Gol are certain mysterious towers, some 20 feet high, of unknown origin. They have every appearance of belonging to the Kufic period, being domed and covered with a strong white cement. They have no doors, but have windows high up: some are hexagonal, some square, and they are apparently dotted all along the coast. Whether they were tombs, or whether they were landmarks to guide mariners to certain valleys leading into the mountains, will probably not be definitely proved until someone is energetic enough to excavate in one. They are found as far south as Massawa, but as far as we could ascertain those we saw were the most northern ones. In one we found two skeletons of modern date, with the scanty clothing still clinging to the bones, as they had lain in the agonies of death, poor sick creatures, who had climbed in to die.

The tower of Asafra, which marks the entrance to the Hadi Valley, is about 20 feet high, and is octagonal. It struck us, from its position at the entrance of the valley system to the north of Mount Erba, that its original object had been a landmark which would be seen from the sea; had it been a tomb it would not have had the windows, and had it been either a tomb or a fort it would have had a door. There we halted, and bade adieu to the governors and officials of Mohammed Gol, who had accompanied us thus far. Our parting was almost dramatic, and the injunctions to the sheikh to see to our safety were reiterated with ever additional vehemence, the mamour holding my husband's hand all the time.

Near the well of Hadi are numerous ancient structures of a different nature and more puzzling to account for. Circular walls, from 10 to 14 feet in diameter and 3 feet high, have been built, some in the valleys and some high up on the hills. The interiors of these have been filled with stones, the largest of which are in the centre, and in the middle of these large stones is a depression a foot or so deep. They certainly looked like tombs of some departed race, especially as they were generally placed in groups of two or three, and they resembled the tombs in the north of Abyssinia, except that those are filled with mounds of small stones, whereas these have larger stones and a depression in the centre. The water turned out to be rather like port wine to look at, full of little fish, tadpoles, and leeches. We put alum in a bucket to precipitate the worst mud, then filtered it without making it clear, but it was a tremendous improvement. I think there really was a better water-place near, but we did not find it. Bad as it was, water was taken for three days, as they said we should see none for that time. As a matter of fact, I think the people did not want us to know the water-places.

We had a very warm night at Hadi, our tent, beds, and even clothes swarmed with beetles.

On February 7 we started for Gumatyewa. All day we went among little pointed hills, some, indeed many, marked with most curious veins of ironstone, sometimes in cross-bars. We soon reached a place in the Wadi Gumatyewa, whence a camel to our surprise was sent for water, and was not very long away, so water cannot have been far off. The rest of the camels were unloaded, and we sat and waited under some trees. In fact, we could have camped near water each of the days which we took getting to Hadai.

The sheikhs generally encamped at a little distance from us, and as they were given to nocturnal conversations and monotonous noises which they called singing, we were glad they were not too near.

We gradually ascended as we followed the valleys inland, after the Wadi Iroquis, until on the fourth day we came to a curious narrow winding pass, about six miles long, which just left room between the rocks for our camels to walk in single file. This pass, which is called Todin, landed us on a small plateau about 2,000 feet above the sea-level, where we found a large number of the circular remains. Todin is one of the most important approaches into the Soudan on the north side of the Erba group, and is practicable the whole way for camels, from which we never once had occasion to dismount, though going down might not be so pleasant. Before reaching the pass of Todin we passed a most curious mountain, seeming to block up the valley. It looked rather like a rhinoceros feeding among the acacia-trees.

Taking this country generally, I can safely say it is as uninteresting and arid a country as any we have ever visited. Our way perpetually led through valleys winding between low brown mountains, the dry river beds of which were studded here and there with acacia-trees. Occasionally one got a glimpse of the majestic spurs of Erba, and occasionally a fantastic rock or a hill-slope a trifle greener than the rest would temporarily raise our spirits.

As for water, we had the greatest difficulty about it, and our guides always enveloped its existence with a shroud of mystery. Men would be sent off to the hills with a camel, and return to the camp with skins of water from somewhere, probably from gulleys where rain-water still lay; but until we reached Wadi Hadai, after a ride of six days, we never saw water with our own eyes after leaving Hadi. More water can be obtained by digging. There is a great deal of *Mesembryanthemum* about, which probably supplies the place of water to most of the animals living in these regions. A good many doves came to drink at the water in the evening.

Two days more brought us to Wadi Hadai, where we were to halt awhile to rest the camels. On the hill immediately above us was the circular fort, with its door to the east, to which I shall later allude, and on the plain below was another and smaller Kufic tower, several round buildings, and large stones erected on several of the adjacent hills evidently to act as landmarks. Also here we saw many graves of the Debalohp family—neat heaps of white stones, with a double row of white stones forming a pattern around them, and a headstone towards Mecca, on one of which was a rude Arabic inscription. These tombs reminded us very forcibly of the Bogos tombs in Northern Abyssinia, and evidently point to a kinship of custom.

The place where we stayed in a wood of thorny trees was at the branching of two valleys. We always had cold nights, but our widely spread camp looked cheery enough with eight fires; there were so many different parties.

Once we got into Wadi Hadai we were in Debalohp's country. He was chief of the large and powerful Kilab tribe, half of which owns avowed allegiance to the Khalifa, and the other half, with their chief, is put down as wavering by the Government at Sawakin. Luckily we did not know this at the time, or otherwise I question if we should have ventured to put ourselves so entirely in his hands, with the horrors of a visit to Khartoum, as experienced by Slatin Pasha, so fresh in our memories.

At Hadai for the first time during the whole of our journey our interests were keenly aroused in certain antiquities we found— antiquities about which Debalohp had said a good deal, but about which we had never ventured to indulge any hopes.

Hard by the Debalohp mausoleum was another Kufic tower, though much smaller than those we had seen on the coast, and not covered with white cement, and in the same locality were several foundations of circular buildings very neatly executed in dry masonry, which appeared to have at either end the bases of two circular towers and curious bulges, which at once reminded us of our South African ruins. On climbing an adjacent hill we found a circular fort, evidently constructed for strategical purposes, with a doorway, the ends of the wall being rounded, quite a counterpart of the smaller ruin on the Lundi river in Mashonaland. The analogy was indeed curious, and we talked about it hesitatingly to ourselves, as yet unable to give any satisfactory reason for its existence. On various heights around were cairns erected as if for landmarks, and we felt that here at last we were in the presence of one of those ancient mysteries which it is so delightful to solve.

We had as interpreter from Arabic to Hadendowa, as none of our party understood that language, the sheikh whose name was Hassan Bafori. He brought three coursing dogs with him. We had also with us a certain Annibàle Piacentini as general odd man. He was really Italian, but had lived so long among Greeks in Suez that he was always called Annibale. He talked Greek with my husband, Mattaios, and me, and English with the others, besides Arabic.

We rested our camels and our men at Hadai, and drank of some fresh water from a little pool, the first we had seen in this barren country, which was supplied by a tiny stream that made its appearance for a few yards in a sheltered corner of the valley, a stream of priceless value in this thirsty land. Debalohp suggested to my husband that he knew of some ruins in a neighbouring valley to which he could take him, but it was not without considerable hesitation that he decided to go. A long day's ride in this hot country, supposed to be almost, if not quite, within the Dervish sphere of influence, was not lightly to be undertaken, more especially as he had been on so many fruitless errands in search of ruins at suggestions of the Bedouin, and returned disgusted, and when he mounted his camel next morning, without any hope of finding anything, and sure of a fatiguing day, had a reasonable excuse offered itself, he would probably not have gone. But the unexpected in these cases is always happening. The long ride turned out only to be one of three hours. Wadi Gabeit was somewhat more fertile and picturesque than any we had as yet seen, and as a climax to it all came the discovery of an ancient gold-mine, worked in ages long gone by doubtless by that mysterious race whose tombs and buildings we had been speculating upon.

Diodorus, in his account of an old Egyptian gold-mine, describes most accurately what my husband found in the Wadi Gabeit. For miles along it at the narrower end were the ruins of miners' huts; both up the main valley and up all the collateral ones there must have been seven or eight hundred of them at the lowest computation. Then there were hundreds of massive crushing-stones, neatly constructed out of blocks of basalt, which had been used for breaking the quartz, lying in wild confusion amongst the ruined huts, and by the side of what once was a stream, but is now only a sandy, choked-up river-bed. On a high rock in the middle of the valley he found a trifle of a Greek inscription scratched by a miner, who had evidently been working the rich quartz vein just below it.

On an eminence behind the valley was another of the circular forts in ruins, similar to the one on the hill above Wadi Hadai, intended evidently for a look-out post to protect the miners at work below. Burnt quartz and refuse of quartz lay around in all directions, and on either side of the valley, stretched for a mile or more, were seams of the auriferous quartz just as it had been laid bare by the ancient workers. There was no question for a moment that he had come across the centre of a great mining industry, lost in these desert valleys behind the mighty wall by which Mount Erba and its spurs shuts off this district from the Red Sea littoral.

Naturally he felt rather startled at being confronted with this unexpected discovery, and in the short space of time then available it was impossible to grasp it all. So he rode back joyfully to tell the news to his party at Hadai. He told Debalohp that he had decided that we should move our camp thither, and stay as long as it was possible.

Difficulties again confronted us. Our two Kourbab sheikhs did not want to go. Sheikh Mohammed Ali Hamid was anxious to get on to his own country, and Sheikh Hassan Bafori quite set his face against our going at all, and Debalohp himself had to be firmly spoken to. An extra present to him was what finally helped us, and at length we all made a start on the following day to my husband's new El Dorado.

We had become rather confused as to dates, and there was a difference of two days that we could not be in unity about. Before setting out for Wadi Gabeit we consumed for breakfast the artificial horizon that Captain Smyth had used for taking our latitude the night before. It was very good; it was golden syrup instead of quicksilver.

Wadi Gabeit was just a trifle better than the country we had passed through, having finer trees in the valley beds; and here we saw the first colony of natives since leaving Mohammed Gol, consisting only of three huts of pastoral Kilabs, which will give an idea of how sparsely this country is inhabited. Debalohp's huts were certainly somewhere in the vicinity of Hadai, not more than an hour away, but for some reason known only to himself he would not take us there, though he went there himself every night, and when he joined us on our way to Wadi Gabeit he brought with him another wife, having evidently had enough of the other's company on his journey from Mohammed Gol.

Their camping arrangements were never luxurious. The Mrs. Debalohp used to hoist a mat on a spear, to keep off the wind. Mr. Debalohp used to lie on another mat in the open, surrounded by his weapons.

The huts we saw were made of sail-cloth, and were very neat inside. There is a passage all round where pots and baskets are kept, and within that a square room made of matting with a mat floor. One side of this is the sleeping apartment, and is entirely hung round with meat-safes, dancing hats, and camel trappings, all adorned with shells and beads. The huts are so small that it must be difficult to lie at full length.

I bought a gazelle-trap from these people. It consisted of a circle of thin sticks, 6 or 7 inches across, bound round and round with bark. Between the bindings are set little thin sticks like a wheel, but crossing each other thickly in the middle. This is put under a tree over a hole, the noose of a long rope laid round it and the rope tied to the tree; the whole is covered with earth. When the gazelle comes to eat he steps into the hole. By the time he has disengaged himself from the trap he is caught in the noose, and a cross stick, 3 or 4 feet long, tied about a foot from the end of the rope, prevents him getting through bushes.

A short time before reaching our goal we were met by a small band of natives, who tried to stop our advance with menaces, which we were determined neither to understand nor recognise. Possibly they were some of the Kilab tribe, who owned allegiance to the Dervishes; possibly they were actuated by the inherent dread the Moslem has of Christian enterprise reaching their secluded vales. However, our show of firearms and determination to go on had the effect of intimidating them, and after a somewhat feeble hostile demonstration and many palavers, we found ourselves comfortably established in our tents in the heart of the ancient industry, and peacefully distributing medicines from our chest to our whilom foes.

The encounter was amusing to look back on afterwards, but by no means so at the time; the yelling and brandishing of spears and shields and the parleying of Hassan Bafori and Mohammed Ali Hamid, who went forward, and the earnest wishes for the presence of Sheikh Ali Debalohp, who had gone round by his home to join us later. We and our camels were led back, but we dismounted and went nearer in a body, and then our firearms were distributed, and my husband, saying he would wait no longer, went past them, we all following. He fortunately knew the way. After a bit our camels came, and we were soon in the Wadi Gabeit. Knowing where the water was, in a little rocky pool, my husband went straight over to it, and ordered that the water-skins should be filled at once, in case of any difficulties. My husband and I and Mr. Cholmley went for a little walk round a small hill, and then I said I would go back alone to the small, oval valley. Just round a corner I came face to face with all the enemy, on foot and on camels.

I walked smiling to the worst old man, grasped his hand, and wished him a happy day. He started back, wrenched away his hand, waving me away, though Hassan tried to make him shake hands. The soldiers rushed forward, and I sat on a rock laughing at him, and saying I wanted to look at them. They all seated themselves close by. Captain Smyth, who had gone around making a reconnaissance, now arrived, his servant Hamid having galloped back on a camel to fetch him. He thought I was the only survivor. I told him the story before them, and imitated the old gentleman, pointing him out, and they all laughed when I asked how we could be afraid of them when they were so much afraid of me.

They all shouted 'Peace! peace!' (salaam! salaam!) 'aman! aman!' (mercy!)—and subsequently came in a body to our tent to impress upon me that *I* need fear no longer—we were friends.

The real truth was that we were now very near, if not quite in, the territory of that branch of the Kilab tribe which owns allegiance to the Dervishes; when Captain Smyth rode ahead next day to take observations from a hill called Darurba, Mohamed Ali Hamed, who accompanied him, made him dress up in a sheet and pretend to be an Arab woman when they came in sight of some people whom he declared to be Dervishes.

We were told of a native who had lately found a gold nugget whilst digging in the sand. The veins of quartz, particularly on the southern side of the valley, are very marked, and the chiselling by which the miners had followed up their veins could easily be seen; it would appear that the workings here had been of a very extensive character, and the output of gold in some remote period must have been very large.

We were conducted to a hill about two miles from our camp, where there are old cuttings in the quartz, some of them going a considerable depth underground, and blocks of quartz were still standing there ready to be broken up; also we saw several crushing-stones here, but there were no traces of miners' huts, so presumably the quartz was removed to the valley below.

On the rocks near the cuttings we saw many rude drawings, one of a parrot and several of gazelles, evidently done by the workmen with their chisels.

In referring to records of the ancient gold-mines of Egypt, we find that a mine existed in the Wadi Allaki, some days south of Komombo, in the Bishari district. This mine was visited and identified by MM. Linant and Bonomi; there they found an excavation 180 feet deep, handmills similar to ours, and traces of about three hundred miners' huts, also several Kufic inscriptions on a rock. The mines, Edrisi tells us, were twelve days inland from Aydab. We must therefore look elsewhere for a notice of another mine nearer the Red Sea. Edrisi makes two mentions of these mines of Allaki, in one of which he says they are in a deep valley at the foot of a mountain; in another he alludes to them as on an open plain. On turning to Abu'lfida, we find him relating 'that Allaki is a town of Bedja; the country of Bedja is in the neighbourhood of the Red Sea. One finds there pearl-fisheries which do not give much profit, but in the mountain of Allaki is a mine of gold, which covers the cost of working. The mountain of Allaki is very celebrated.' Hence it would seem that two different spots are alluded to both under the name of Allaki, from both of which gold was obtained, one inland and one near the Red Sea. Professor de Goeje, of Leyden, the greatest authority on early Arabian literature, pointed out to my husband further discrepancies in the distances from Aydab to the gold-mines of Allaki in early Arab geographers, and suggests that the mines found by MM. Bonomi and Linant and ours, though several hundred miles apart, may have belonged to the same reef, and have been known by the same name.

In M. Chabas' 'Inscriptions des Mines d'Or' we have a very interesting dissertation on an ancient Egyptian plan of a gold-mine on a papyrus in the museum of Turin, of the time of Seti I., which he thus describes: 'Unfortunately, the name of the locality, which the plan gives us under the form *Ti, ou, oi*, the phonetic signs of which form a confused combination, does not give us any clue. We must therefore limit ourselves to the conclusion that this map, the most ancient that exists in the world, represents to us an auriferous vein in a desert mountain situated to the east of Higher Egypt, and very near the Red Sea. The shells spread on the path leading to it are a proof that the sea is very near; we can only think of the Red Sea, the shores of which abound in coral, in sponge, and shells variegated with the most beautiful colours.'

There seems every probability that the mine discovered by my husband was the one illustrated by the most ancient plan in the world, and, curiously enough, the Greek inscription we found seems to give a combination of vowels closely resembling the name given on the plan. On Egyptian inscriptions we constantly read of the gold of Kush, and that the prince of Kush was always interfered with in his works by the want of water, and from the Arab geographers we learn that they were finally abandoned by the caliphs owing to the want of water for washing purposes, and as far back as the reign of Usertesen we get illustrations of their washing process. Diodorus gives us a vivid description of the gangs of captives and convicts employed in these mines, and the miserable cruelty with which they were goaded on to work until they died of fatigue. He also gives some interesting details as to the processes of abstracting gold, which tally well with what we saw on the spot. 'They burn the quartz and make it soft,' which will account for the quantity of burnt quartz which we saw; and again, 'they take the quarried stone and pound it in stone mortars with iron pestles.' Mr. Rudler examined the specimens of quartz we brought home, and describes it as 'vein quartz, more or less ochreous with oxide of iron suggestive of auriferous quartz,' and told us that, unless we were going to start a company, there was no necessity to get it assayed; for archæological purposes the presence of gold was sufficiently established.

Will this mine ever be available again for those in search of the precious mineral? is the first question that suggests itself. Unfortunately being no gold expert, I am absolutely unable to give an opinion as to the possibilities of the still existing quartz seams being payable or not, but there is abundance of it both in the Wadi Gabeit and in the collateral valleys, and it is improbable that the ancients with their limited knowledge of mining could have exhausted the place. Specimens of quartz that my husband picked up at haphazard have been assayed and found to be auriferous, with the gold very finely disseminated; an expert would undoubtedly have selected even more brilliant specimens than these. Against this the absence of water and labour seemed to us at the time to negative any possible favourable results; but, on the other hand, the mine is so conveniently near the sea, with comparatively easy road access, that labour might be imported; and such wonderful things are done nowadays with artesian wells that, if the experts report favourably upon it, there would be every chance of good work being done, and these desert mountains of the Soudan might again ring with the din of industry.

The morning after we reached Wadi Gabeit an express messenger reached us from Sawakin, bidding us return to the coast at once, as we were supposed to be in considerable danger. Dervish raids were expected in this direction, and the authorities were evidently afraid of complications. A solemn palaver forthwith took place, at which our three sheikhs showed that they thought little of the supposed danger, and said that, though we were nominally in Dervish country at the time, there was no armed force near of sufficient strength to attack us. So we decided, and backed up our decision with a promised bribe, to stay another night in Wadi Gabeit, and to continue our course round Mount Erba, as we had originally intended, and with us we kept the messenger of woe with his gun and spear as an additional protection.

CHAPTER XXVIII

BEHIND THE JEBEL ERBA

We left Wadi Gabeit next morning, and on the following day another messenger from Sawakin met us with a similar mandate; but as we were now journeying in a presumably safe direction we annexed him too, and went on our way rejoicing. Personally we felt that we knew the condition of the country better than the authorities of Sawakin, who had never been there. If our sheikhs had meant treachery they would long ago have put it into practice; our two Kourbab sheikhs, whose property is in and around Mohammed Gol, were ample guarantee for our safety; and, moreover, the country was so absolutely destitute of everything that we gave the Dervishes credit for better sense than to raid it.

Our first day's march was dreary in the extreme, over country covered with dark shale, just like a colliery district without the smoke, and with the faintest possible trace of vegetation here and there.

It was at this juncture that we lost our little dog, a pet that had journeyed everywhere with us; when search failed we gave it up for lost, and drew mournful pictures of the dear creature dying in agonies in the desert, foodless and waterless. The clever animal nevertheless retraced its steps, how we know not, to Mohammed Gol in five days, without food and with very little water, over the desert paths we had come—a distance of about 120 miles—and terrified the governor out of his wits, as he naturally thought it was the sole survivor of our expedition. It made its way straight to the jetty and swam to our dhow, the *Taisir*, and was picked up by our Arab sailors more dead than alive. After resting and feeding on the dhow for two days, the dog jumped overboard once more, and went off by itself to the mountains for three days in search of us; when this failed it returned again, and reached our dhow the night before we did, and was ready to welcome us on our return with a wildly demonstrative greeting. We eventually gave it to a sergeant at Sawakin, and have reason to believe that it is at present taking part with its regiment in the Soudan campaign.

That day, Sheikh Mohamed Ali Hamed, who was riding a loaded camel, came to me so much disgusted with the smell of a box covered with black American cloth, that he asked me if it were not made of pig-skin. The people are so ignorant of what pig-skin looks like that they often handle it without knowing, otherwise they would not touch it.

It was a distinct disappointment to us only to see the mountains of, and not to be able to penetrate into, the Wadi Hayèt, owing to its occupation by Dervish tribes. On excellent authority we heard that there were numerous ruined cities there, especially at a spot called Oso; that it was more fertile than the parts through which we had passed; that the Mogarra mountains were higher than Erba; and that it was well watered. Apparently this important Soudanese valley takes its rise in Bawati, to the south of Erba, and, after making first a bold sweep right through the heart of the Soudan, it reaches the sea to the north of Mount Elba, some twenty miles north of Halaib. This wadi will form an interesting point for exploration when the Soudan is once more settled, and if these statements are correct it will be of considerable importance in the future development of the country. As for the valleys near the coast, unless they prove rich in minerals they can never be of much value to any one. In Wadi Gabeit, the only industry now carried on by the very few inhabitants, except the rearing of flocks, is the drying of senna, which grows wild here in considerable quantities. They cut the branches and lay them out to dry on levelled circles; these they take down to the coast and export to Suez.

We were now sixty miles, as the crow flies, from the sea. We were terribly afraid we should be made to go by a lower way between the mountains and the sea, in which case our journey would not be of nearly such great value in map-making, but at last my husband persuaded the sheikhs, saying he would sign, with all the rest of us, a paper to protect the heads of Sheikhs Ali Debalohp, Hassan Bafori, and Mohamed Ali Hamed, which we did.

They said they did not themselves expect any danger. Had they done so they would never have let our camp extend over so much ground, with no concealment as regarded fires and shouting, nor would they have let their camels wander so far afield.

The first place after Wadi Gabeit that we camped at was Hambulli, four hours distant. The thermometer was down to 50° in the night.

There was another letter from the mamour and another from Sawakin and a most tremendous lot of consultations, and at last my husband sent a letter to the mamour: 'Your Excellency,—I have decided to go by Erba and Sellala and hope to reach Mohammed Gol in a shorter time by that route.'

By this time we were in the Kourbab country, in that part under Sheikh Hassan Bafori, who governs a branch of the tribe. We liked the mamour's messenger, Sheikh Moussa Manahm, who came on with us, very much. Four hours of very desert journeying was our portion the following day. We were a good distance from water, but some was obtained by digging, thick with sand and earth. We had thus far carried water from Wadi Gabeit. We travelled six hours, wandering through desert valleys, in which everything was dried up, with clumps of grass in it as black as if they had been burnt, and as if they had not seen rain for years. All the valleys to the west of Mount Erba seem to be arid except Gumateo or Gumatyewa, a big valley which must have water near the surface, which runs all along at the back of the range, with arid hills from 500 to 1,000 feet on either side of it. Vegetation is more abundant, and masses of arack-trees (salvadora), supposed to be the mustard-tree of the Bible, grow here, the wood of which is much esteemed for cleaning the teeth. Wadi Gumateo seems to be a favourite nursery for camels. On our way we passed many camel mothers with their infants, feeding on the arack and other shrubs. At the upper end of this valley, where we encamped for a night, Mount Erba, with its highest peak, Mount Nabidua, stands out in bold and fantastic outline. It is a remarkable range as seen from this spot, shutting off like a great wall the Soudan from the Red Sea littoral.

It was a most beautiful place and there was plenty of wood, so we could have fine fires at night and burn some charcoal for future use.

On February 18 we had a much more enjoyable day, for we were winding about among the mountains. Twice we had to dismount to walk over passes. One was exceedingly fine, with bold and stupendous cliffs.

There were several groups of huts in the Wadi Khur, which we next reached.

There is much more vegetation here, many tamarisks and other shrubs giving delightful shade. Wadi Khur is the nursery for young donkeys, many of which, we were told, from time to time escape to the higher mountain, and have established the race of wild asses to be found here. The valley has a good many pastoral inhabitants, and in the side gorges are deep pools of lovely water in natural reservoirs, in which we revelled after our somewhat limited supply further inland. Up these gorges we found bulbs, rushes, and water-plants. At our camp here our men busied themselves in decorating their locks prior to reaching Sellala. Mutton-fat is beaten in the hands till it becomes like lard, and this material the hairdresser dabs at the curly wigs of his patients; those whose curls become the whitest and stiffest deem themselves the finest.

As we were going through a very narrow gorge, where Wadi Khur has changed into Khor (gorge) Khur, some stones were bowled down from above, without hitting any part of our caravan. There was a great deal of shouting from the principal sheikhs to the offenders, and they desired one of the soldiers to fire off his gun, which he did. Sheikh Hassan did not half like the laugh that rose against him when I said, 'Last time it was Sheikh Ali Debalohp's men, and now it is yours.'

We encamped while still in the Khor Khur, but the sheikhs would not allow the tents to be put near the rocks, fearing disaster, and in the morning Sheikh Hassan was in a great hurry to be off, coming and shouting 'Al khiem! Al khiem!' ('the tents!') to hasten us out of them and let them be packed. We had had to carry water from the last place. It had been so clear and clean when we had it in our own buckets. It had taken more than four hours to fetch with camels, but what we carried on was put into dirty skins, full of the mud of the place before, so it was horrible and a great disappointment; we had to wait for more.

When we left this camp we were led to suppose we should reach Sellala, said to be an oasis, in about two hours and a half; but it took us an hour to get out of the Khor Khur, winding among high rocks with most beautiful shapes and shadows, rounding Jebel Gidmahm, which was on our left, and then we entered a very hideous wadi called Amadet. The floor of it was very up and down, and high rocks and little hills stood about, whereas the wadis are for the most part flat in the middle. But all round this ugly wadi there were high and fantastic mountains, range behind range.

After that there was a narrow khor called Rabrabda, and finally a great sandy desert, where the hills were comparatively low, through which we marched for several hours, always looking out for the oasis, where we promised ourselves great enjoyment, intending to spend a few days in so nice a place. When at last we reached Sellala, which Ali Hamid's son had led us to believe was a perfect Paradise, instead we found a wretched arid spot, with one deep and well-constructed well, probably of considerable antiquity, surrounded by many mud drinking-troughs, around which were collected a large number of camels.

All our promised verdure resolved itself into a few mimosa-trees and desert plants, and we encamped in great discomfort in a raging sandstorm, quite out of patience with our guide for his deceit. The wind was very wild and cold. We did not enjoy Sellala at all. Our tent had to be tied up in a tiny sandy cleft, and a huge boulder was under my bed. We had only two winds to trouble us there, though, instead of all four, which were raging outside. About 200 yards from the well was Ali Hamid's village, a collection of some six or eight huts, in one of which dwells old Ali Hamid himself, the aged sheikh of this powerful branch of the Kourbab tribe; and the only evidence that we had of greater prosperity was that the women here wear gold nose-rings and have long gold earrings and more elaborate ornaments hanging from their plaited hair.

Ali Hamid looked very old and decrepit. He had a long hooked nose and exceedingly unpleasant face, and when we saw him we quite believed him to be, as they say, a hardened old slave-dealer. Perhaps the most remarkable fact about him was that he had a mother living, a wizened old crone who inhabited a tiny hut at Mohammed Gol, and reputed to be 135 years old by her friends, though I question if she was much over 90. Old age is rare among these nomads, and hence they make the most of any specimen they can produce.

We sat in the village for some time, and purchased various camel ornaments—tassels which they hang from their necks, and curious adornments decorated with cowries, which they place before the covered awning beneath which great ladies conceal themselves when on a camel journey.

Ali Hamid's son took us the next day on fast-trotting camels to visit some graffiti on basaltic rocks about eight miles distant. Here we found representations of animals chiselled on the hard rocks, similar to those we saw in Wadi Gabeit; we could recognise gazelles, camels, and elephants, and we thought the artist also had intended to depict giraffes, mongooses, and other strange beasts. Scattered amongst these animals are several Sabæan letters, the two [Symbol: See page image] (ya) and [Symbol: See page image] (wa) being very conspicuous. These scribblings were evidently done by the miners who were on their way from the coast to Wadi Gabeit, having landed at a convenient little harbour close by called Salaka. There is also one of the ruined towers not far from this spot, and the letters point to the fact that some of the miners here engaged must have been of Sabæan or Southern Arabian origin.

Sheikh Ali Hamid came often to see us, with many other sons, besides Mohamed, who had travelled with us, and a few of the latter's children, clothed and naked. They used to sit in a semicircle round the door of our tent.

Of course an exchange of gifts took place, and we were sent a sheep and a huge basketful of milk. The basket was shaped like a vase, a foot in diameter. A very nice inhabitant of the forbidden Wadi Hayet came to see us, Sheikh Seyyid Ta'ah. He gave us useful information as to the geography of his neighbourhood and the course of the valley.

Captain Smyth went off from Sellala with Sheikh Mohamed to take a peep into Wadi Hayèt, and on February 22 we left the place without any regret and turned northward. There are five Sellalas, and one is really an oasis. The splendid mountains of Erba had been quite obscured by the sand, though there had been a magnificent view of them when we arrived.

On the way we passed three more of the tall towers similar to those we had previously seen, and felt still more convinced that they were connected with the gold industry in the inland valley, and had been built to mark the roads conducting in that direction.

We tried to find a sheltered nook to encamp in when we reached the mountains, but in vain. We stayed at Harboub, and were nearly stifled by the dirty dust that blew into the tents. The water was very clear and soft.

We continued northward for two hours and a half, and then turned westward up the steep Wadi Ambaya.

Wadi Ambaya is the chief valley of Mount Erba, and it runs right into the heart of the mountain. Up this we were conducted by Sheikh Hassan, in whose territory we now found ourselves. This valley is fairly well inhabited by pastoral people; they live in huts dotted about here and there, which are difficult to recognise from their likeness in colour to the rocks surrounding them, which they would almost seem to have been made to mimic. The slopes of Erba provide pasturage for a large number of flocks at all seasons of the year. Nabidua, the highest peak of the range, reaches an elevation of 7,800 feet; Sherbuk and Emeri are not much lower, and the outline of the rugged peaks is exceedingly fine. Up in the higher parts of this range there are a great number of ibex, several of which fell to Captain Smyth's rifle, but we did not care much for the flesh. The natives hunt them with dogs of a breed said to be peculiar to these parts.

Our camp in Wadi Ambaya was a delicious spot, amid fantastic boulders and rich vegetation. On climbing up the gorge beyond us we came across a stream with running water, forming deep green pools among the rocks, and to us, after the arid deserts we had passed through, this spot was perfectly ideal; and the people, too, who dwell up in the higher ground, look infinitely healthier—lithe, active men, who leap like goats from rock to rock, each with a sword and shield. There are several valleys in Erba penetrating into the heart of the mountains, but Ambaya is the principal one.

In the outer part of the valley, which is rather open, is a way into the Wadi Addattereh, where we had already been. It was a tremendous scramble to get up the gorge, and our tents were perched on rocks, and Matthaios was delighted with his nice clean kitchen in the middle of the gorge. He rigged up some sticks to hang a cloak up as a shade. The servants had plenty to do preserving antelopes and ibex heads, and burning charcoal and washing.

We were here made glad by Captain Smyth's safe return, and after staying three days we returned to the mouth of our wadi, and then went on toward the north, and after five hours camped under some large trees near a well of very good water, called Tokwar.

We finished our journey into the Wadi Koukout at 8 o'clock next morning, having to leave the camels and squeeze on on foot. It is a veritable frying-pan. We had hardly room to pitch our tents, or to get into them when pitched, by reason of the big boulders and steep hollows where water swirled about. There was good water quite close.

We had another messenger from Sawakin, Hassan Gabrin, to guide us by land, or, if we went by sea, to say we should go quickly.

The morning after our arrival we started very early to visit Koukout, a mountain really separate from Erba, but looking like a spur of it, the highest peak of which is only 4,000 feet above the sea. Here again one penetrates into the mountain by a curious gorge, with deep pools of water, the rocks about which are, if possible, more fantastic than those of Erba. One comes to chasms, over which the water flows, which look like the end of all things; but by climbing up the side of these one finds the gorge continuing until the very heart of the mountain is reached, where is a little open ground well stocked with water and green. High up here we spent a few hours at a pastoral village, where we found the women busily engaged in making butter in skins tied to a tree; these they shake until butter is produced. They store it in jars, and take it to Mohammed Gol to exchange for grain, but they eat very little except the products of their flocks, and, like the Abyssinians, they do not mind eating meat raw.

We saw some interesting domestic features in this mountain village. The children are given toy shields and spears, with which to practise in early life; and we found here several long flutes with four notes each, the music of which is weird and not unlike that of the bagpipes, and well suited to the wild surroundings.

Here, too, they play the ubiquitous African game, munkala or tarsla. Two rows of six holes are dug in the ground, and in these they play with counters of camel-dung a mysterious game which I never can learn. Here they call it *mangola*, and it is played all down the East Coast, from Mashonaland to Egypt, and also, I hear, on the West Coast; it seems a general form of recreation throughout the Dark Continent, and has been carried by Africans to all parts of the world to which they have wandered. Here they were playing with holes in the sand, but one often sees them dug in marble blocks, or on rocks, or in pavements.

There are two games—the game of the wise and that of the foolish; the former, like chess, requires a good deal of thought.

Flute-players in the Wadi Koukout, Soudan

Sheikh Hassan Bafori's mother resided in this village, so old that she looked like the last stage of 'She,' but no one said she was as old as old Ali Hamid's mother.

I think the weaving arrangements were quite the most rude I have ever seen.

The yarn had been wound over two sticks about 20 feet apart, and that stick near which the weaving was begun was tied by two ropes, each a foot long, to pegs in the ground. The other was simply strained against two pegs. At this end a couple of threads had been run to keep the warp in place. There was no attempt to separate the alternate threads so as to raise each in turn. There was a stick raised 4 or 5 inches on two forked sticks to separate the upper and under parts of this endless web of 40 feet. The weaver sat on her goat's-hair web, and never could get the shuttle across all the way. It consisted of a thin uneven stick, over a foot long. She had to separate twelve to fifteen threads with her hand, and stick in a pointed peg about 10 inches long, while she put the shuttle through that far; then she beat it firm with this instrument and went on as before, patiently.

The shepherd boys looked very graceful, playing on the long flutes with four notes. One of these flutes belongs to each hut. We were interested, too, in seeing men making sticks out of ibex horns. They cover the horn with grease, and put it in hot water or over the fire to melt and soften it, and then scrape and scrape till it is thin enough and able to be straightened. The ibex-horn hairpins are made with six or seven bands of filigree round them. The women's camel-saddles have great frameworks of bent sticks, nearly as large as some of the huts, to give shelter, and are very smart indeed on a journey.

On leaving Koukout, Sheikh Hassan took us to his well at Tokwar again, a deep and presumably ancient well, near which he has his huts; and from there to a spot called Akelabillèh, about four miles from Tokwar, and not far from our original starting-point of Hadi. Here we found slight traces of gold-working. About half a dozen crushing-stones lay around, and a good deal of quartz refuse.

Probably this was a small offshoot of the more extensive mines in the interior which had not repaid continued working.

A rapid ride of three hours from Akelabillèh brought us back again to Mohammed Gol and the close of our expedition, for already the first murmurs of disturbances with the Dervishes were in the air, and the mamour of Mohammed Gol and the officers at Sawakin affected to have been very anxious for our safety. We, however, being on the spot, had been in blissful ignorance of any danger, and further considered that the country we had traversed was not the least likely to be raided by any sensible people, desert and waterless as it was for the most part, and would offer no attractions in the shape of booty, except in the fastnesses of Mount Erba itself. Not one inch of the ground was under cultivation, and the few inhabitants were the poorest of the poor, and I think this is the only expedition we have ever made in which we never once saw such a thing as a hen or an egg.

By the by, at the huts near Tokwar we rejoined Sheikh Ali Debalohp, who had been invited by Sheikh Hassan to stay a night, and with due permission from my husband he was able to do so. We saw the sleeping arrangements. On the ground was a piece of matting large enough for both to sleep on, and another bit a yard high, supported by sticks, round the three windiest sides.

They were busy playing with a large lizard, of which they seemed to be afraid, and which had a forked tongue and very long teeth. It had a string round its neck, and was kept at bay with a sword.

We reached Mohammed Gol the quicker that we had no foot passengers. All had scrambled on to the camels, and so we were by twos and threes on our animals.

The little mamour Mohammed Effendi was delighted to see us, and we were soon drinking tea in his public arbour, surrounded by a crowd of now smiling faces—the very same faces which had scowled upon us so dreadfully when we first landed. We and our little dog Draka were equally delighted at once more meeting.

We found the south wind blowing, if it can be said to do so in a dead calm—prevailing would perhaps be a better word. The madrepore pier had been nearly swept away, and the houses near the water were flooded.

We settled into our ship again that evening.

Next day was pay-day, and my husband and Matthaios went ashore with more than 40*l.* to distribute. The three big sheikhs, by the advice of the mamour, were given 2*l.* apiece; the soldiers got ten shillings each—far too much, he said; Mohammed Ismail, Sheikh Hassan Gabrin, Sheikh Moussa Manahm, Mohammed Erkab, and one Akhmet, a great dandy, had five shillings each.

Besides this, other presents were given. Sheikh Ali Debalohp had a quilted cotton coverlet, and Mohammed Ali Hamid the same and a cartridge-belt; Sheikh Hassan Bafori a blanket, a smart silk keffieh and a sword-belt; and the mamour an opera-glass and a silk blanket, besides minor things; all seemed very well satisfied. They certainly were all very nice to us.

The secretary gave me a tremendously heavy curved camel-stick of ebony, and the mamour besides a head-scratcher, which he had made me himself from an ibex horn, a stick of ibex horn, and seven and a half pairs of horns.

We were weatherbound yet another day, everything damp and sticky. The south wind seems to me to have a very mysterious scooping and lifting power; no other wind lifts sand and water along as this one does. The wind began to freshen up towards night and got as far as the east, and by morning was blowing strong north by east.

My husband had, as usual, to go out and stir up Reis Hamaya and tell him we must be off. He seemed as much surprised as he always was. We had a farewell visit from the little mamour, and off we set for a very rolly voyage. The whole day we rolled with the smallest sail, everything banging, beds jostling, but we were glad no longer to feel wet and sticky as regards our clothes, bedding, and the whole ship. Our last night on board was not the least exciting.

We had stopped near Darour amongst reefs of coral.

Every night when we cast anchor the ship used to turn round so that the north wind blew full on us and our cabins, but this night it whizzed round so violently as to drag the anchors, and we went back on to a reef—only a little, though, but enough to alarm all on board. The anchors had to be got up and taken by boat to fix into another reef. It was necessary for all the gentlemen and servants to assist the sailors in hauling us off the reef. It was very hard on the sailors, for their supper was smoking hot, ready for them after their day's fast, and the poor fellows had to work till 9 o'clock, doing the best they could for the safety of the ship.

We went to bed, however, with the unpleasant knowledge that we were not very tightly fastened up, and the uneasy feeling that we might drag in the night, and not without making some little preparation in case of a swim.

We were all safe in the morning, but almost the first thing we did, as we sat at breakfast, was to grind over a reef, more than the length of the keel.

We duly reached Sawakin in the afternoon of March 4, where Hackett Pain Bey, who was acting-governor, kindly lent us two accommodation in the Government House, and we said farewell to the *Taisir*, its cockroaches, its mosquitoes, and its mouse; and the ship had immediately to be turned over on her side for repairs— needed, as the coral reefs had done a good deal of damage. Reis Hamaya was enchanted with a gift of the cabins with their padlocks, and I am sure they soon became very dirty holes.

Though we were scolded for our pains, our approving consciences told us how pleasing to the British Government those pains had been, and how glad it was of some map beyond the Admiralty chart.

Eight days after our arrival the news of the declaration of war came to Sawakin.

We were offered a passage to Suez in the *Behera* (which means delta), but as an ordinary steamer came in, and we did not know how long the *Behera* might be waiting for troops, we thought it better to make our way northward at once. We reached Cairo just in time for Captain Smyth to be rewarded for his hard work, while with our expedition, by being ordered off to the war by Sir F. Wingate, who, with the Sirdar, was starting that night; Captain Smyth was to follow in two days.

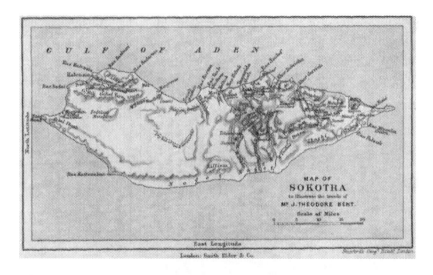

Map of Sokotra

to illustrate the explorations of

Mr J. THEODORE BENT.

Stanford's Geog.¹ Estab.¹, London

London: Smith, Elder & Co.

We felt very proud, and now he has the Victoria Cross, because 'At the battle of Khartoum Captain Smyth galloped forward and attacked an Arab who had run amok among the camp-followers.

Captain Smyth received the Arab's charge and killed him, being wounded by a spear in the arm in so doing. He thus saved the life of one, at least, of the camp-followers.'

THE MAHRI ISLAND OF SOKOTRA

CHAPTER XXIX

KALENZIA

As we had been unable to penetrate into the Mahri country, though we had attempted it from three sides, we determined to visit the offshoot of the Mahri who dwell on the island of Sokotra.

Cast away in the Indian Ocean, like a fragment rejected in the construction of Africa, very mountainous and fertile, yet practically harbourless, the island of Sokotra is, perhaps, as little known as any inhabited island on the globe.

Most people have a glimpse of it on their way to India and Australia, but this glimpse has apparently aroused the desire of very few to visit it, for the Europeans who have penetrated into it could be almost counted on the fingers of one hand. During recent years two botanical expeditions have visited it, one under Professor Balfour, and one under Dr. Schweinfurth, and the results added marvellously to the knowledge of quaint and hitherto unknown plants.

We passed two months traversing it from end to end, with the object of trying to unravel some of its ancient history so shrouded in mystery, and learn something about its present inhabitants.

Mariette Bey, the eminent Egyptologist, identifies Sokotra with To Nuter, a place to be bracketed with the land of Punt in the pictorial decorations of the temple of Deir el Bahri, as resorted to by the ancients for spices, frankincense, and myrrh; and he is probably correct, for it is pretty certain that no one given spot in reach of the ancients could produce at one and the same time so many of the coveted products of that day—the ruby-coloured dragon's blood (*Draco Kinnabari* of Pliny), three distinct species of frankincense, several kinds of myrrh, besides many other valuable gum-producing trees, and aloes of super-excellent quality.

It is referred to by the author of the 'Periplus' as containing a very mixed and Greek-speaking population drawn together for trading purposes, trafficking with Arabia and India. Abu'lfida, Africanus, and other writers, Arabic and otherwise, mention Christianity as prevailing here, and Theodoret, writing in the beginning of the fifth century, speaks of the great missionary Theophilus as coming from the island of Diu to teach Christianity in India.

Cosmas Indicopleustes calls the island Dioscorides. He visited it in the sixth century, and accounted for the Greek-speaking population he met with by saying that they had been placed there by the Ptolemies. El Masoudi considered the Greek a purer race in Sokotra than elsewhere.

As far back as the tenth century Sokotra was a noted haunt of pirates from Katch and Gujerat Bawarij, from a kind of ship called *barja*.[11]

Traders came from Muza Lemyrica (Canara) and Barggaza (Gujerat).

Ibn Batuta gives an account of a certain Sheikh Said of Maskat being seized by Sokotran pirates, who sent him off empty-handed to Aden.

Marco Polo describes the catching of whales for ambergris. El Masoudi[12] says the best ambergris comes from the sea of Zinj in East Africa: 'The men of Zinj come in canoes and fall upon the creature with harpoons and cables, and draw it ashore and extract the ambergris.'

In the inscription of the Nakhtshe Rustam, near Persepolis, which we saw when in Persia in 1889, thirty countries are named which were conquered by Darius, the Akhemenid, amongst them Iskuduru, *i.e.* Sokotra.

Though it is Arabian politically, Sokotra geographically is African. This is the last and largest of a series of islands and islets stretching out into the Indian ocean, including the little group of Abdul Kerim. Some of these are white with guano.

Darzi, Kal Farun, Sambeh, and Samboyia are the names of some of the smaller ones. Sokotra itself is situated about 240 miles from Cape Guardafui, and is about 500 miles from Aden.

The latitude of the island is between 12° 19' and 12° 42', and the longitude between 53° 20' and 54° 30'. It is 72 miles long from east to west, and 22 miles wide from north to south. There is a coral reef nearly all the way from Africa to beyond Ras Momi.

According to the Admiralty charts the water between the islands and the mainland is 500 fathoms deep, but among the islands nowhere is it deeper than 200 fathoms.

It is an island that seems to be very much in the way as far as navigation is concerned, and many shipwrecks have been occasioned by its being confused with the mainland, one being taken for the other. The wreck of the *Aden*, and the great loss of life resulting from it, which took place so soon after we were there, is still fresh in our memories.

Our party consisted of Mr. Bennett, who was new to Eastern life, our old Greek servant, Matthaios, and two young Somali, Mahmoud and Hashi. They could talk a little English, but generally talked Arabic to us and Matthaios. We were told before starting that Mahri, or Mehri, was the language most in use, and we nearly committed the serious error of taking a Mahri man from Arabia, who could also speak Arabic, as an interpreter, but fortunately we did not do so, as he would have been quite useless, unless he could also have talked Sokoteriote.

We found it no easy matter to get there. First we were told we should, if we attempted to go by sailing-boat, have to coast to Ras Fartak, on the Arabian coast, and let the monsoon blow us to Sokotra, and this seemed impracticable. Finally we arranged with a British India steamer, the *Canara*, that it should 'deviate' and deposit us there for a consideration.

The ss. *Canara* promised to await the arrival of the P. and O. steamer before leaving Aden, and would, for one thousand rupees (62*l*.), take us to Sokotra and remain four hours. After that we were to pay thirty rupees an hour, and in no case would she tarry more than twenty-four hours. If landing were impossible, we were to be carried to Bombay.

We were landed in a lifeboat, through the surf at the town of Kalenzia, which lies at the western end of the island. It is a wretched spot, a jumble of the scum of the East; Arab traders, a Banyan or two, a considerable Negroid population in the shape of soldiers and slaves, and Bedouin from the mountains, who come down with their skins and jars of clarified butter, to despatch in dhows to Zanzibar, Maskat, and other butterless places.

Butter is now the chief product and almost the sole export of the island, and Sokotra butter has quite a reputation in the markets along the shores of Arabia and Africa. The sultan keeps a special dhow for the trade, and the Bedouin's life is given up to the production of butter. Nowhere, I think, have I seen so many flocks and herds in so limited a space as here.

Kalenzia (the place has been spelt in so many ways that we took the liberty of spelling it phonetically as we heard it pronounced) has an apology for a port, or roadstead, facing the African coast, which is the most sheltered during the prevalence of the north-east monsoon. Separated from the shore by a bar of shingle is a lagoon, fed by the waters coming down from the encircling mountains, which reach an altitude of 1,500 or 2,000 feet. The lagoon is very prettily embowered with palms and mangroves, and the waters are covered with wild duck, but it is a wonder that all the inhabitants do not die of fever, for the water is very fetid-looking and they drink from nothing else. I believe this is the water which is supplied to ships. The shore is rendered pestiferous by rotting seaweed, and the bodies of sharks, with back fin cut out and tail cut off, which are exposed to dry on the beach. We preferred the brackish water from a well hard by our camp until we discovered a nice stream under the slopes of the mountains, about three miles away, to which we sent skins to be filled. This stream is under the northern slope of the Kalenzia range, and near it are the ruins of an ancient town, and as the water trickles on towards the lagoon it fertilises the country exceedingly, and its banks are rich in palms and other trees. The abandoned site of this old town is infinitely preferable to the modern one, and much healthier.

We were received in a most friendly way by the inhabitants, and hoped that, as we were English and the island was to some extent under British protection, we should be able to proceed inland at once. Our nationality, however, made not the slightest difference to them, and we were told we must encamp while our letters were taken to the sultan, who lives beyond Tamarida, and await his permission to proceed farther. The eight days we had to remain here were the most tedious of those we spent on the island.

One of our amusements was to watch boat-building accomplished by tying a bundle of bamboos together at each end and pushing them out into shape with wooden stretchers.

They have enormous lobster-pots, 6 feet to 8 feet in diameter, made of matting woven with split bamboo, in patterns something like the seats of our chairs. The men often wear their tooth-brushes tied to their turbans; a sprig of arrack serves the purpose.

Whilst at Kalenzia we must have had nearly all the inhabitants of the place at our tent asking for a remedy for one disease or another; they seemed to be mostly gastric troubles, which they would describe as pains revolving in their insides like a wheel, and wounds. The Sokotra medical lore is exceedingly crude. One old man we found by the shore having the bowels of a crab put on a very sore finger by way of ointment. A baby of very tender age (eleven months) had had its back so seared by a red-hot iron that it could get no rest, and cried most piteously.

The poor little thing was wrapped in a very coarse and prickly goat-hair cloth, and its mother was patting its back to stop its cries, quite ineffectually, as you may well imagine. I spread some vaseline on a large sheet of grease-proof paraffin paper and applied it most gently. Its whole family then wrapped it up in the goat-hair cloth in such a way as to crush and put aside the dressing, and the mother laid it on its back, though I had warned her not to do it, on her knees, and jumped it up and down. The baby was none the better, but all around seemed pleased, and I could only sadly think that I had done my best. I find the grease-proof paper most valuable to spread ointment for man and beast where rags are scarce.

One old lady, with an affection of the skin, would only have the 'bibi' as her doctor, so she came to me with a good many men to show her off, but would have nothing to do with my husband. I said the first treatment must consist in a thorough washing all over with warm water and soap: but behold! I heard there was no soap in the island, so halves and quarters of cakes of Pears' soap as well as whole ones, were distributed as a precious ointment.

They have no soap, no oil, no idea of washing or cleansing a wound, and cauterisation with a hot iron appears to be their panacea for every ailment.

A favourite remedy with them here, as in Arabia, is to stop up the nostrils with plugs fastened to a string round the neck to prevent certain noxious scents penetrating into it; but, as far as we could see, they make no use whatsoever of the many medicinal herbs which grow so abundantly on the island.

The women of Kalenzia use turmeric largely for dyeing their faces and their bodies yellow, a custom very prevalent on the south coast of Arabia; they wear long robes, sometimes dyed with indigo, sometimes of a bright scarlet hue. The pattern of their dress is the same as that worn in the Hadhramout, *i.e.* composed of two pieces of cotton cloth wide enough to reach the finger-tips and with a seam down each side. The front piece is longer than in the Hadhramout, coming down to within a foot of the ground, but the train is also very much longer, and must lie more than a yard and a half on the ground. These ladies get good neither from the length nor the breadth of their dresses, for as the train evidently incommodes them, they twist the dress so tightly round their bodies that the left side seam comes straight or rather lop-sidedly behind and one corner of the train is thrown over the left shoulder all in a wisp. There is nothing to keep it up, so down it comes continually, and is always being caught up again. I never saw a train down, except once for my edification.

Their hair is cut in a straight fringe across the forehead and is in little plaits hanging behind. They wear a loose veil of a gauzy nature, with which they conceal half their faces at times. Silver rings and bracelets of a very poor character, and glass bangles, complete their toilet, and the commoner class and Bedou women weave a strong cloth in narrow strips of goat-hair, which they wrap in an inelegant fashion round their hips to keep them warm, sometimes as their only garment. They do not cover their faces. From one end of Sokotra to the other we never found anything the least characteristic or attractive amongst the possessions of the islanders, nothing but poor examples of what one finds everywhere on the south coast of Arabia and east of Africa.

Many weddings were going on during our residence at Kalenzia, and at them we witnessed a ceremony which we had not seen before. On the morning of the festive day the Sokotrans, negro slaves being apparently excluded, assembled in a room and seated themselves round it. Three men played tambourines or tom-toms of skin called *teheranes*, and to this music they chanted passages out of the Koran, led by the 'mollah'; this formed a sort of religious preliminary to a marriage festival; and in the evening, of course, the dancing and singing took place to the dismal tune of the same tom-toms, detrimental, very, to our earlier slumbers. The *teherane* would seem to be the favourite and only Sokotran instrument of music—if we except flutes made of the leg-bones of birds common on the opposite coast, and probably introduced thence—and finds favour alike with Arab, Bedou, and Negro.

The people here did not torment us by staring at and crowding round us. They came only on business, to be doctored, to sell something, or to bring milk wherewith to purchase from us lumps of sugar.

The houses are pleasantly shaded amongst the palm groves, and have nice little gardens attached to them in which gourds, melons, and tobacco grow; and in the middle of the paths between them one is liable to stumble over turtlebacks, used as hencoops for some wretched specimens of the domestic fowl which exist here, and which lay eggs about the size of a plover's.

Though a poor-looking place it looks neat with its little sand-strewn streets.

It contains a single wretched little mosque, in character like those found in third-rate villages in Arabia; Kadhoup or Kadhohp possesses another, and Tamarida no less than two; and these represent the sum total of the present religious edifices in Sokotra, for the Bedouin in their mountain villages do not care for religious observances and own no mosques.

Owing to the scarcity of water in the south-western corner of the island we were advised not to visit it; the wells were represented to us as dry, and the sheep as dying, though the goats still managed to keep plump and well-looking. Perhaps the drought which had lately visited India may have affected Sokotra too; and we were told before going there that a copious rainfall might be expected during December and January, for Sokotra gets rain during both monsoons; but during our stay on the island we had little rain, except when up on the heights of Mount Haghiers.

One day we two went some distance in the direction of the mountains, and came on a large upright rock with an inscription upon it, evidently late Himyaritic or Ethiopic, and copied as much of it as was distinguishable. Not far off was the tidy little hamlet of Haida. The walls of the yards there are circular.

Farther on, behind the village of Kissoh, are the ruins of an ancient village with a long, well-built, oblong structure in the middle, possibly a tomb; and it was behind this again that we found the good water that we drank afterwards.

There must once have been a large population, to judge by the way the hills are terraced up by walls, and the many barren, neglected palm-trees about among the old fields.

The Kalenzia range of mountains is quite distinct from Haghier, and is about 1,500 or 2,000 feet high. We could find no special name for it. They call it Fedahan, but that is the generic Sokoteriote word for mountain.

The highest peak is called Màtala.

We were very glad when a venerable old sheikh named Ali arrived bringing us a civil letter from the sultan and saying he had been sent to escort us to Tamarida.

[11] Elliot, i. 65.

[12] i. 136.

CHAPTER XXX

ERIOSH AND KADHOUP

After four days waiting for camels, and the usual wrangling over the price and casting lots for us, which here they do with stones instead of wood as in Arabia, we started late on Christmas Day, going of course only a short way. As all were mounted on the baggage we could trot all the way; the camels were not tied in strings. The first night we stopped at Isèleh, an interesting place at the entrance of Wadi Gàhai below Mount Lèhe Diftom, about two hours from Kalenzia, whence at night we could see the numerous fires of troglodytes high up on the sides of the mountains; and were able next day to ride nearly all the way, except over a pass to Lim Ditarr, a depression in the hills sometimes filled with water, though there was none for us. A little was fetched, but we had to keep the water from our evening wash to serve next morning. This depression had in former times been used as a reservoir, for we could detect the remains of a stone embankment, a good deal despoiled for Moslem tombs.

Our onward journey took us past a lovely creek, called Khor Haghia, running two miles inland, with silted mouth and overhanging yellow and white rocks. The bright blue water and green mangroves made a brilliant picture.

About a quarter of a mile inland there is a deep pot of salt water, evidently left behind by the ocean when it receded from the shores of Sokotra; it is about 200 feet across, and has its little beach and seaweeds all complete, with its trees and bushes in its cliffs.

We lunched at the brackish well of Dia, and at sunset reached the hideous plain of Eriosh, or Eriush, which has a flat surface of rock, about a quarter of a mile in extent and partly covered with dried mud, and of such soft stone that we could easily cut into it with pebbles. It is covered with purely Ethiopic graffiti, almost exactly similar to those we saw on the steps of the church and on the hillsides around Aksum in Abyssinia—long serpent-like trails of Ethiopic words, with rude drawings interspersed of camels, snakes, and so forth. Riebeck, who went inland from Itur, says these are Greek. Conspicuous amongst them are the numerous representations of two feet side by side, frequently with a cross inserted in one of them; there are many separate crosses, too, on this flat surface—crosses in circles, exactly like what one gets on Ethiopic coins. We met with another inscribed stone to the east of the island, bearing similar lettering.

Hard by this flat, inscribed surface are many tombs of an ancient date. These tombs, which are found dotted over the island, bear a remarkable resemblance to the tombs of the Bedja race, once dwelling on the shores of the Red Sea to the north of Sawakin, and subject to the Ethiopian emperor; they consist of enormous blocks of unhewn stone, inserted in the ground to encircle and cover the tombs, and this forms another link connecting the remains on the island with Abyssinia.

The Plain of Eriosh, Sokotra

When the Abyssinian Christian monarchs conquered Arabia in the early centuries of our era, and Christianised a large portion of that country, they probably did the same by Sokotra, and, inasmuch as this island was far removed from any political centre, Christianity probably existed here to a much later period than it did in Arabia. Marco Polo touched here, and alludes to the Christians of the island.

In speaking of two isles near Greater India, inhabited respectively by men and women, he adds: 'They are Christians, and have their bishop, subject to the Bishop of Socotora. Socotora hath an archbishop not subject to the Pope, but to one Zatuli, who resides at Baldach, who chooseth him.'

F. Xavier said among other things 'that each village had a priest called *kashi*. No man could read. The *kashis* repeated prayers in a forgotten tongue, frequently scattering incense. A word like Alleluia often occurred. For bells they used wooden rattles. They assembled in their churches four times a day, and held St. Thomas in great veneration. The *kashis* married, but were very abstemious. They had two Lents, and fasted from meat, milk, and fish.'

When Padre Vincenzo the Carmelite visited the island in the seventeenth century he found the last traces of Christianity. 'The people still retained a perfect jumble of rites and ceremonies, sacrificing to the moon, circumcising, and abominating wine and pork. They had churches called *moquame*, dark and dirty, and they daily anointed with butter an altar. They had a cross, which they carried in procession, and a candle. They assembled three times a day and three times a night; the priests were called *odambo*. Each family had a cave where they deposited their dead. If rain failed they selected a victim by lot and prayed round him to the moon, and if this failed they cut off his hands. All the women were called Maria.' Of this there is now no trace. Both Sacraments had died out.

This debased form of Christianity existed as late as the seventeenth century. The island was one of the places visited by Sir Thomas Roe in 1615.

It is needless to say that all ostensible traces of our cult have long ago been obliterated, and the only Sokoteri religious term which differs in any way from the usual Mohammedan nomenclature is the name for the Devil; but we found, as I have already said, the carved crosses on the flat surface at Eriosh, and we found a rock at the top of a hill to the east of the island which had been covered with rude representations of the Ethiopic cross. Scattered all over the island are deserted ruined villages, differing but little from those of to-day, except that the inhabitants call them all Frankish work, and admit that once Franks dwelt in them of the cursed sect of the Nazarenes. We felt little hesitation in saying that a branch of the Abyssinian Church once existed in Sokotra, and that its destruction is of comparatively recent date.

If we consider that the ordinary village churches in Abyssinia are of the flimsiest character—a thatched roof resting on a low round wall—we can easily understand how the churches of Sokotra have disappeared. In most of these ruined villages round enclosures are to be found, some with apsidal constructions, which are very probably all that is left of the churches.

Near Ras Momi, to the east of the island, we discovered a curious form of ancient sepulture. Caves in the limestone rocks have been filled with human bones from which the flesh had previously decayed. These caves were then walled up and left as charnel-houses, after the fashion still observed in the Eastern Christian Church. Amongst the bones we found carved wooden objects which looked as if they had originally served as crosses to mark the tombs, in which the corpses had been permitted to decay prior to their removal to the charnel-house, or κοιμητήρια, as the modern Greeks call them.

We stayed two days at Eriosh to study the *graffiti* and tombs.

Water had to be fetched from Diahàmm, which we afterwards passed. It was brackish. I have heard *riho* said for water, but *diho* was mostly used, and certainly the names of many water-places began with Di. I remember my husband answering the question where we should camp by calling out in Arabic 'Near the water.' This was echoed in Sokoteri, '*Lal diho.*'

We took five days in getting from Kalenzia to Tamarida, and found the water question on this route rather a serious one until we reached Mori and Kadhoup, where the streams from the high mountains began. Mori is a charming little spot by the sea, with a fine stream and a lagoon, and palms and bright yellow houses as a foreground to the dark-blue mountains.

Kadhoup is another fishing village built by the edge of the sea, with a marshy waste of sand separating it from the hills; it possesses a considerable number of surf-boats and canoes, and catamarans, on which the fishermen ply their trade. Just outside the town women were busy baking large pots for the export of butter, placing large fires around them for this purpose. The Sokotrans are very crude in their ceramic productions, and seem to have not the faintest inclination to decorate their jars in any way. There were quantities of flamingoes on the beach.

We encamped at the foot of the hills, with a watery and sandy waste between us and the village.

There are the foundations of some curious unfinished houses near Kadhoup, also assigned to the Portuguese; but there appears to me to be no reason whatsoever for ascribing these miserable remains to the builders of the fine forts at Maskat, the founders of Ormuz and Goa, and the lords of the East up to the seventeenth century.

The mountains here jut right out into the sea, forming a bold and rugged coast line, and the path which connects the two places is as fine a one to look upon as I have ever seen.

We had read a very awe-inspiring account of this path by Lieutenant Wellsted, and so were quite disposed to believe all our camel-drivers told us of the awful dangers to be encountered. They had formed a plan whereby their Kadhoup friends might come in for some of our rupees. We were not only to pay for camels, but also for a boat. Some, at least, of the camels were sure, they said, to fall into the sea from the cliffs, and our possessions, if not our lives themselves, might be lost. They said that we ought to send our baggage by boat, even if we risked the mountain path ourselves.

We assured them that we had landed in Sokotra (which they pronounce Sakoutra) to see the island, and not to circumnavigate it. Others could pass, so we could.

Their last hope was in my hoped-for faintheartedness. They watched till I was alone in the tent, and, having recounted all the perils over again, said:

'Let the men go over the mountain, but you, O Bibi! will go in a boat, safely. You cannot climb, you cannot ride the camel, no one can hold you; the path is too narrow, and you will be afraid.'

That being no good, old Sheikh Ali came. He was anxious, poor old man, to be spared the exertion, and eventually rode all the way, except when there was no room. He said I should go in a boat with him; he would take care of me and give me musk (which he called misk) when we reached Hadibo. He often promised misk, but I never got any; and here I may remark that I have frequently heard Maskàt pronounced Mìskit in Arabia amongst the Bedouin of the East.

We really did feel very adventurous indeed when we started. I rode my camel a quarter of a mile to the foot of the ascent. No one else thought it worth while to mount, but I was comfortably carried over a muddy creek.

The Kadhoupers did get some rupees, for we were attended by twelve men carrying bamboo poles 10 or 12 feet long.

It really was a stiff climb, but we had a good deal of shade, and when we reached our highest point there was a pretty flat bit with scattered trees and grass, about half a mile, I think. The twelve men had to carry the baggage slung on the poles for a quarter of a mile or so, where the overhanging rocks made the path too narrow for loaded camels. It was quite high enough for their heads, and we had plenty of room. It was marvellous to see the camels struggling along this road, and awful to hear their groans and the shouts of the camel-men as they struggled up and down and in and out of the rocks; and the hubbub and yelling over a fallen one was simply diabolical.

We had the most tremendous clambering down soon after that, the baggage being again slung on the poles, and the camels came clattering down, with many stones, and looking as if they would rush over straight into the sea.

When we got near the sea, say about 50 feet above it, we, on foot, diverged from the camel-track, which goes more inland, and followed a very, very narrow, washed-away path. This I think must have been the one described by Wellsted, for we were never, till we reached this part, near the sea, though possibly had we fallen we might have rolled over down a slope.

The views inland up the rugged yellow crags, covered with verdure and studded with the quaint gouty trees, are weird and extraordinary, and below at our feet the waves dashed up in clouds of white spray. Though we had heard much of the difficulties of this road and the dangers for foot passengers, and we were told of the bleaching bones of the camels which had fallen into the abyss below, we experienced none of these hardships. We certainly saw the bones of one camel below us, but none of ours followed its example; and we revelled in the beauty of our surroundings, which made us think nothing of the toilsome scramble up and down the rocks.

As we left the mountain side and approached the plain of Tamarida, we passed close by what would seem to have been an ancient ruined fort on the cliff above the sea, evidently intended to guard this path.

CHAPTER XXXI

TAMARIDA OR HADIBO

Certainly Tamarida is a pretty place, with its river, its lagoon, and its palms, its whitewashed houses and whitewashed mosques, and with its fine view of the Haghier range immediately behind it. The mosques are new, and offer but little in the way of architectural beauty, for the fanatical Wahhabi from Nejd swept over the island in 1801, and in their religious zeal destroyed the places of worship; and the extensive cemeteries still bear testimony to the ravages of these iconoclasts, with their ruined tombs and overturned headstones.

We encamped on the further side of a good-sized stream or little river, having it between us and the town of Tamarida or Hadibo; and this was really a protection to us at night, for the inhabitants of that neighbourhood are terribly afraid of certain jinni or ghinni, which abide in the stream, and will not go near it at night. Indeed, we remarked that it was considered by Hashi and Mahmoud, the two Somali servants, a wise precaution to draw all the water and bring up the washing, which was drying, in good time of an afternoon.

They had heard such fearful stories that they were very much afraid of being bewitched while in the island, though I doubt whether I and my camera were not nearly as alarming.

They had heard how a Sokotran man had turned a woman of Maskat into a seal and forced her to swim over to Sokotra in that shape. We were told that this story is perfectly true!

This evil reputation of the islanders is very persistent. Marco Polo says: 'The Sokotrans are enchanters, as great as any in the world, though excommunicated by their prelates therefor; and raise winds to bring back such ships as have wronged them, till they obtain satisfaction.'

It is only just to say we had no need to fear such honest and friendly people.

Sultan Salem of Sokotra, the nephew of old Sultan Ali of Kishin, the monarch of the Mahri tribe, whom we had visited two years before on the south coast of Arabia, governed the island as his uncle's deputy. He had a castle at Tamarida of very poor and dilapidated appearance, which he rarely inhabited, preferring to live in the hills near Garriah, or at his miserable house at Haula, some eight miles along the coast from Tamarida. Haula is as ungainly a spot as it is possible to conceive — without water, without wood, and invaded by sand — quite the ugliest place we saw on the island, its only recommendation being that during the north-east monsoons the few dhows which visit the island anchor there, since it affords some sort of shelter from the winds in that direction, and Sultan Salem has a keen eye to business.

His Majesty came to visit us, shortly after our arrival at Tamarida, from his country residence, and favoured us with an audience in the courtyard of his palace, with all the great men of the island seated around him. He was a man of fifty, with a handsome but somewhat sinister face; he was girt as to his head with a many-coloured *kefieh*, and as to his waist with a girdle supporting a finely inlaid Maskat dagger and a sword. His body was enveloped in a clean white robe, and his feet were bare.

His conversation, both then and when he returned our visit at our camp, on which occasion he received a few presents, was solely about the price of camels and how many we should need. He did not ask us one other question. He talked little Arabic, being of the Mahri tribe.

We gave him an Enfield carbine of 1863.

On the plain behind Tamarida there is a conical hill about 200 feet high called Hasan, which has been fortified as an Acropolis, and was provided with cemented tanks. These ruins have also been called Portuguese, but they looked to us more Arabic in character.

When one has seen the very elaborate forts erected by the Portuguese on the coasts of the Persian Gulf and East Africa one feels pretty confident in asserting that they took no steps to settle themselves permanently in Sokotra; in fact, their occupation of it only extended over a period of four years, and the probability is that, finding it harbourless, and worth little for their purposes of a depôt on the road to India, they never thought it worth their while to build any permanent edifices.

In the neighbourhood there is a hill where the English are said to have encamped, and where there are traces of a more ancient civilisation, probably Portuguese. There are walls of small stones, cased with cement, and, inside them, a tank with conduits.

Opposite to this hill, and across the stream, is a ruined village, only one house of which is still inhabited; it has circular walls and a circular paddock adjoining it for cattle.

It is, perhaps, annoying to have to add another to the list of the many tongues spoken in the world, but I think there is no room for doubt that Sokoteri must be added to that already distracting catalogue.

Though Sokotra has been under Mahri rule probably since before our era—for Arrian tells us that in his day the island of Dioscorida, as it was then called, was under the rule of the king of the Arabian frankincense country, and the best days of that country were long before Arrian's time—nevertheless, the inhabitants have kept their language quite distinct both from Mahri and from Arabic. Of course it is naturally strongly impregnated with words from both these tongues; but the fundamental words of the language are distinct, and in a trilingual parallel list of close on 300 words, which my husband took down in the presence of Mahri, Sokoteri and Arabic speaking people on the island, we found distinctly more in the language derived from an Arab than from a Mahri source.

In subtlety of sound Sokoteri is painfully rich, and we had the greatest difficulty in transcribing the words. They corkscrew their tongues, they gurgle in their throats, and bring sounds from most alarming depths, but luckily they do not click. They have no word for a dog, for there is not a dog on the island; neither for a horse nor a lion, for the same reason; they seemed surprised at the idea that there might be such words in their language; but for all the animals, trees, and articles commonly found there they have words as distinct from the Arabic and Mahri as cheese is from *fromage*.

At Tamarida we annexed a respectable man called Ammar as interpreter. He was familiar with all the languages spoken in the island, and daily, when the camp was all pitched and arranged, my husband used to produce a long list of Arabic words, and Ammar used to sit on his heels and tell the Mahri and Sokoteri equivalents, the words, however, being for the most part shouted out in chorus by numerous bystanders. I have since added the English, and the vocabulary will be found in an appendix.

It was most difficult to get an answer as to anything abstract.

For instance, 'clothes' would be asked, and Ammar, after inquiring if white clothes were meant, or blue, or black, or red, and being answered 'any clothes,' would give a list of garments of various shapes.

'Age' was a question that caused a great awkwardness, I am sorry to say.

'Well,' answered Ammar, 'it might be anything—seven, fifteen, seventy—anything!'

After the greatest invention and planning on our part, we unhappily thought to put the question in this form:

'How do you say "What is your age?"'

'*My* age,' said Ammar, '*mine*—well'—with evident annoyance and great hesitation—'I'm thirty-five—*not* old—not *old* at all.'

He is really quite fifty.

On such occasions there had to be a tremendous conversation with the bystanders.

Theodore Bent Making the Vocabulary at Fereghet

I will not say more of the language than that instead of our little word *I* the Sokoteri is *hemukomòn* and the Mahri *evomúhshom*.

I wish we could speak confidently about the origin of the so-called Bedouin, the pastoral inhabitants of the island, who live in the valleys and heights of Mount Haghier, and wander over the surface of the island with their flocks and herds.

It has been often asserted that these Bedouin are troglodytes, or cave-dwellers pure and simple, but I do not think this is substantially correct. None of them, as far as we could ascertain, dwell always or by preference in caves; but all of them own stone-built tenements, however humble, in some warm and secluded valley, and they only abandon these to dwell in caves when driven to the higher regions in search of pasturage for their flocks during the dry season, which lasts from November till the south-west monsoon bursts in the beginning of June.

Whilst we were on the island the season was exceptionally dry, and most of the villages in the valleys were entirely abandoned for the mountain caves.

The Bedou is decidedly a handsome individual, lithe of limb like his goats, and with a *café-au-lait*-coloured skin; he has a sharp profile, excellent teeth; he often wears a stubbly black beard and has beautifully pencilled eyebrows, and, though differing entirely in language, in physique and type he closely resembles the Bedouin found in the Mahri and Gara mountains. Furthermore, the mode of life is the same—dwelling in caves when necessary, but having permanent abodes on the lower lands; and they have several other striking points in common. Greetings take place between the Arabian Bedouin and the Sokotran Bedouin in similar fashion, by touching each cheek and then rubbing the nose. We found the Bedouin of Mount Haghier fond of dancing and playing their *teherane*, and also peculiarly lax in their religious observances; and though ostensibly conforming to Mohammedan practice, they observe next to none of their precepts; and it is precisely the same with the Bedouin whom we met in the Gara mountains. There is certainly nothing African about the Sokotran Bedouin; therefore I am inclined to consider them as a branch of that aboriginal race which inhabited Arabia, with a language of its own; and when Arabia is philologically understood and its various races investigated, I expect we shall hear of several new languages spoken by different branches of this aboriginal race, and then, perhaps, a parallel will be found to the proudly isolated tongue of this remote island.

The Bedou houses are round, and surrounded by a round wall in which the flocks are penned at night; flat-roofed and covered with soil, and inside they are as destitute of interest as it is possible to conceive—a few mats on which the family sleep, a few jars in which they store their butter, and a skin churn in which they make the same. The plan of those houses that are oblong is that of two circles united by a bit of wall at one side, the door being at the other. In one house into which my husband penetrated he found a bundle hanging from the ceiling, which he discovered to be a baby by the exposure of one of its little feet.

Everything is poor and pastoral. The Bedouin have hardly any clothes to cover themselves with, nothing to keep them warm when the weather is damp, save a home-spun sheet, and they have no ideas beyond those connected with their flocks. The closest intimacy exists between a Bedou and his goats and his cows; the animals understand and obey certain calls with absolute accuracy, and you generally see a Sokotran shepherdess walking before her flock, and not after it. The owners stroke and caress their little cows until they are as tame as dogs.

The cows in Sokotra are far more numerous than one would expect, and there is excellent pasturage for them; they are a very pretty little breed, smaller than our Alderney, without the hump, and with the long dewlap; they are fat and plump, and excellent milkers.

The Bedou does very little in the way of cultivation, but when grass is scarce, and consequently milk, he turns his attention to the sowing of jowari in little round fields dotted about the valleys, with a wall round to keep the goats off. In each of these he digs a well, and waters his crop before sunrise and after sunset; the field is divided into little compartments by stones, the better to retain the soil and water; and sometimes you will see a Bedou papa with his wife and son sitting and tilling these *bijou* fields with pointed bits of wood, for other tools are unknown to them.

We hired our camels for our journey eastwards from the Arab merchants who live at Tamarida or Hadibo; they are the sole camel proprietors in the island, as the Bedouin own nothing but their flocks; and excellent animals these camels are, too, the strongest and tallest we had seen. Of our camel-men, some were Bedouin and some were negroes, and we found them on the whole honest and obliging, though with the usual keen eye for a possible bakshish, which is not uncommon elsewhere.

The eastern end of Sokotra is similar in character to the western, being a low continuation of the spurs of Haghier, intersected with valleys, and with a plateau stretching right away to Ras Momi about 1,500 feet above the sea-level. This plateau is a perfect paradise for shepherds, with much rich grass all over it; but it is badly watered, and water has to be fetched from the deep pools which are found in all its valleys at the driest season of the year, and in the rainy season these become impassable torrents, sweeping trees and rocks before them; and the hillsides up to the edge of the bare dolomitic pinnacles of the Haghier range are thickly clothed with vegetation.

Three considerable streams run from southward of Mount Haghier, fertilising three splendid valleys, until the waters, as the sea is approached, lose themselves in the sand. To the north there are many more streams, and inasmuch as the sea is considerably nearer, they all reach it, or, rather, the silted-up lagoons already alluded to.

By the side of these streams innumerable palm-groves grow—in fact, dates form the staple food of the islanders. And out of the date-tree they get branches for their hedges, stems for their roofs; the leaf provides them with their sleeping-mats, and, when beaten on stones, with fibre, with which they are exceedingly clever in making ropes. Our camel-men were always at it, and produced, with the assistance of fingers and toes, the most excellent rope at the shortest possible notice. They also make strong girdles with this fibre, which the slaves, who are employed in fertilising the palm-trees, bind round their bodies and the trees so as to facilitate their ascent, and provide them with a firm seat when the point of operation is reached. They weave, too, baskets, or, rather, stiff sacks, in which to hang their luggage on either side of the camel.

A Sokotran camel-man is a most dexterous packer. He must first obliterate his camel's hump by placing against it three or four thick felt mats or *nummuds*, and on this raised surface he builds all his luggage, carefully secured in his baskets, with the result that we never, during any of our expeditions with camels, had so little damage done to our property, even though the roads were so mountainous and the box-bushes were constantly rubbing against the loads. The camels are very fine specimens of their race, standing considerably higher than the Arabian animal, and when mounted on the top of our luggage, above the hump thus unnaturally raised, we felt at first disagreeably elevated.

Whilst on the subject of camels and camel-trappings, I may add that each owner has his own mark painted and branded on his own property. Some of these marks consist purely of Himyaritic letters, whilst others are variants, which would naturally arise from copying a very old-world alphabetic original. I take these marks to be preserved by the steady conservatism of the Oriental; we copied many of them, and the result looks like a partial reproduction of the old Sabæan alphabet, and they may be seen in an appendix.

Scattered over Sokotra there are numerous villages, each being a little cluster of from five to ten round or oblong houses and round cattle-pens. I was informed by a competent authority on the island that there are four hundred of these pastoral villages between Ras Kalenzia and Ras Momi, a distance of some seventy odd miles as the crow flies; and from the frequency with which we came across them during our marches up only a limited number of Sokotra's many valleys, I should think the number is not over-estimated. If this is so, the population of the island must be considerably over the estimate given, and must approach twelve or thirteen thousand souls; but owing to the migratory nature of the inhabitants, and their life half spent in houses and half in caves, any exact census would be exceedingly hard to obtain. The east of the island is, however, decidedly more populous than the west, as the water supply is better. We were constantly passing the little round-housed villages, with their palm-groves and their flocks.

CHAPTER XXXII

WE DEPART FOR THE LAND'S END—*i.e.* RAS MOMI

After leaving Tamarida we spent a night at a place the name of which has been variously spelt. We decided to spell it Dihelemnitin. It has otherwise been called Dishelenata, &c. It is a lovely spot, at the confluence of two streams in a wood of palms, and we had a nice little flat field to camp in. When I say a field, I mean a wall-supported place once used as such. We saw very little cultivation except gardens at the villages, and the palm-trees were for the most part quite neglected. Near Tamarida we saw just a few fan-palms, and one I remember looked very odd, as it still retained every leaf it had ever had, and looked like a yellow tower, with the green leaves at the top. All the rest were bristling, withered down to the ground.

In South Arabia people are punished if they steal each other's palm-leaves, as the ribs are valuable for many things as well as the leaves themselves, but here there are no restrictions of that kind.

There was a good deal of climbing up and down to Saièhen, our next camp. While we stayed there my husband went about everywhere that he was told there were ruins or supposed inscriptions, but saw nothing worth mentioning except the inscribed crosses already alluded to.

At first, after leaving Saièhen, we kept along the lower ground for some time, passing by Garriah Khor, a very long inlet or lagoon which stretches inland for at least two miles. We dismounted at Dis'hass, where, we were told by Ammar, 'the English once had houses.' It was a mass of ruins.

We went over a pass about 2,500 feet high, and up and down two sets of hills to a level plain about 1,500 feet high, extending all the way to Ras Momi. As we ascended we passed a peak 2,000 feet high, called Gòdahan, which has a great hole in the middle of it, through which a large patch of sky is visible. We encamped near it, close to the hamlet of Kit'hab, in a wood of palms and various other trees, full of those pretty green and grey birds, half parrot and half dove, whose beauty, however, did not save them from our pot.

From this place and even before we reached it we had very little personal use of our camels, the clambering up as well as down was so severe.

There is behind the peak of Gòdahan a curious flat ridge, raised not very many feet above the plateau, which is called Matagioti, and is perfectly honeycombed with fissures and crevices, offering delightful homes for people of troglodytic tendencies. Huge fig-trees grow in these crevices, and dragon's-blood trees, and large herds of cows and goats revel in the rich carpet of grass which covers the flat surface of the plateau. Unfortunately, this rich pasture ground is only indifferently supplied with water. We obtained ours from two very nasty holes where rain-water had lain, and in which many cattle had washed; and when these dry up the Bedouin have to go down to the lower valleys in search of it. Before we left it had assumed the appearance of porter.

There was a great deal of lavender growing about and numerous pretty flowers, and we found many shells in that place. It was so very cold that we had a fine bonfire to dine by, and the dew that night was drenching, pouring off our tents like rain in the morning.

As Ras Momi is approached the country wears a very desolate aspect; there are no trees here, but low bushes and stunted adeniums covered with lichen, and looking just like rocks with little bushes on them; very little water, but plenty of grass.

We encamped near the hamlet of Saihon, where, though there was no appearance of a mosque, there was not only a mollah but a doctor. The former was so free from fanaticism as to send us a present of a lamb.

The inhabitants were very friendly to us, and let us go into their houses and watch their occupations. The women were busy grinding limestone to make pots; and we obtained a very dirty little bag full of a kind of organic substance like small white stones, which is ground to powder, mixed with water into a whitish paste, which after a little time turns red. I think they paint the pots with it.

They were pleasant looking folk with quite a European cast of countenance, mostly ugly, and some with scanty beards, and reminding us strongly of the old frieze of the Parthenon sculptures in the Acropolis Museum at Athens. Really, they were just like them except for their colour, which is chocolate brown. We could not help thinking of the 'Moskophoros' when one came up to look at us with a lamb round his neck. We settled there for several days, not being able to go nearer Ras Momi for reasons connected with water. I cannot think it could have been really pleasant to the people of Saihon that we should have drunk up nearly all their water, and only left a little the colour of coffee behind us.

We suffered badly while there from two things; firstly from the dreadful kind of grass upon which we were encamped, and secondly from a regular gale of wind.

The grass, a *pennisetum* I believe, is one we knew and hated in Mashonaland. The seed is like a little grain of very sharp oats, well barbed, which carries behind it into your clothes a thread like a fish-hook, about 2 inches long.

As for the wind, when we came home one afternoon we found Matthaios in a most dreadful state, fearing the tents would be down. He was trying to get the outer flies off alone, and was delighted when my husband and I, the only two other experienced tent-dwellers, came to his assistance. For days we might as well have lived in a drum, for the noise of this tempest.

There was a little round enclosure to keep goats in; we knew that Hashi and Mahmoud had taken this as their home, and we were satisfied that no matter which way the wind blew they were sheltered; but one evening before dinner we heard that Mahmoud was ill with fever. We both went to see that he was comfortable, and my husband took him some quinine.

We found Hashi had put him to bed on the windy side of the enclosure, with a hard, stiff camel-mat under him, one over his body, and a third on his head. We soon moved him and wrapped him in blankets, and my husband having got some sacks and other things as a pillow, Hashi put them on the top of Mahmoud's head. We built up a waterproof tent over him, but soon had to unpack him, as the village doctor appeared on the scene, demanding a fee of two annas from my husband.

He began by making several slashes on the top of his head and cupping him with a horn, which he sucked, gave him some medicine, and having spent a little time blowing in different directions, settled down, crouching over the patient, waving his hand as if making passes to mesmerise him, and muttering a few words alternately with spitting, slightly and often, in his face.

Our joint efforts were successful in the recovery of Mahmoud, who was well next day.

It is curious that in this somewhat wild and at present uninteresting locality we found more traces of ruins and bygone habitations than are found in any other part of the island. About five miles from Ras Momi, and hidden by an amphitheatre of low hills on the watershed between the two seas, we came across the foundations of a large square building, constructed out of very large stones, and with great regularity. It was 105 feet square; the outer wall was 6 feet thick, and it was divided inside into several compartments by transverse walls. To the south-east corner was attached an adjunct, 14 by 22 feet. There was very little soil in this building; and nothing whatever save the foundations to guide us in our speculations as to what this could be. Other ruins of a ruder and more irregular character lay scattered in the vicinity, and at some remote period, when Sokotra was in its brighter days, this must have been an important centre of civilisation.

None of the natives would help us to dig in this place. They are very much afraid of the Devil, and think the ground under the ruins is hollow and that there is a house in it. At one time hopes were held out that the sacrifice of a goat might avert danger, but, after all, we and Matthaios had to do the best we could in the way of digging. We always carried tools with us. My part consisted in tracing out the walls with the trowel and moving stones.

My husband and I found it most difficult next day to take the measurements in the high wind.

From Saihon my husband climbed up a steep and rugged mountain to a ruined village on a strong place called Zerug. Ammar's family mansion was near: a cave containing three women, some children, and large flocks of goats, kept in the cave by a wall; it is heated at night, and very stuffy.

Before leaving this corner of the island we journeyed to the edge of the plateau and looked down the steep cliffs at the eastern cape, where Ras Momi pierces, with a series of diminishing heights, the Indian Ocean. The waves were dashing over the remains of the wreck, still visible, of a German vessel which went down here with all hands some few years ago, and the Bedouin produced for our edification several fragments of German print, which they had treasured up, and which they deemed of fabulous value. Ras Momi somewhat reminded us of Cape Finisterre, in Brittany, and as a dangerous point for navigation it also resembles it closely. Near the summit of one hill we passed an ancient and long disused reservoir, dug in the side of it, and constructed with stones; and during our stay here we visited the sites of many ancient villages, and found the cave charnel-houses already alluded to.

We lunched in a sort of cave, behind some huts on the opposite side of the valley, if such it may be called, from the bone caves, and were put to the rout by a serpent, which evidently liked the water in a little rocky pit in the mouth of the cave. It was horrible stuff, but we had brought water for our tea with us. Our supposed foe was slain. The serpent was very pretty, fully a yard long, black and salmon-coloured, and with a very tapering head and tail. It was said to be poisonous, but we thought it could not be.

The hills all about Ras Momi are divided into irregular plots by long piles of stones stretching in every direction, certainly not the work of the Sokotrans of to-day, but the work of some people who valued every inch of ground, and utilised it for some purpose or other. The miles of walls we passed here, and rode over with our camels, give to the country somewhat the aspect of the Yorkshire wolds. It has been suggested that they were erected as divisions for aloe-grounds; but I think if this was the case traces of aloes would surely be found here still. Aloes are still abundant about Fereghet and the valleys of Haghier, but near Ras Momi there are none, and it is hard to think what else could grow there now; but these mountain slopes may not always have been so denuded.

CHAPTER XXXIII

MOUNT HAGHIER AND FEREGHET

After leaving our camp at Saihon we took a path in a south-westerly direction, and after a few days of somewhat monotonous travelling we came again into the deeper valleys and finer scenery of the central districts of the island. Through them we made our way in the direction of Mount Haghier.

Sokotra without Mount Haghier would be like a body without a soul. The great mass of mountains which occupies the centre of the island rises in many jagged and stupendous peaks to the height of nearly 5,000 feet. At all seasons of the year it catches the fugitive sea mists which so rarely visit the Arabian coasts, and down its sides flow sparkling streams and bubbling cascades. The Ghebel Bit Molek (a name which, by the way, sounds as if it had an Assyrian origin) is the highest peak. It is very sheer and unapproachable at its summit, and though only 4,900 feet high will give trouble to the adventurous crag-climber who is bent on conquering it. Then there are the Driat peaks, the Adouna peaks, and many others piercing the sky like needles, around which wild goats and civet cats roam, but no other big game.

In the lower ground are found quantities of wild donkeys, which, the Bedouin complained, were in the habit of trampling upon and killing their goats. Whether these donkeys are naturally wild or descendants of escaped tamed ones I am unable to say. Some are dark and some are white, and their skins seemed to be more glossy than those of the domestic moke. The Bedouin like to catch them if they can, with the hope of taming them for domestic use.

The glory of Mount Haghier is undoubtedly its dragon's-blood tree (*Dracænia cinnabari*), found scattered at an elevation of about 1,000 feet and upwards over the greater part of Sokotra. Certainly it is the quaintest tree imaginable, from 20 feet to 30 feet high, exactly like a green umbrella which is just in the process of being blown inside

338

out, I thought. One of our party thought them like huge green toadstools, another like trees made for a child's Noah's Ark. The gum was called *kinnàbare*, but the Arab name is *kàtir*. The Sokoteri name is *edah*.

Vegetation in Sokotra

It is a great pity that the Sokotrans of to-day do not make more use of the rich ruby-red gum which issues from its bark when punctured, and which produces a valuable resin, now used as varnish; but the tree is now found in more enterprising countries—in Sumatra, in South America, and elsewhere. So the export of dragon's blood from its own ancient home is now practically *nil*.

If the dragon's-blood tree, with its close-set, radiating branches and stiff, aloe-like leaves, is quaint—and some might be inclined to say ugly—it has, nevertheless, its economic use; but not so its still quainter comrade on the slopes of Mount Haghier, the gouty, swollen-stemmed *Adenium*. This, I think, is the ugliest tree in creation, with one of the most beautiful of flowers: it looks like one

339

of the first efforts of Dame Nature in tree-making, happily abandoned by her for more graceful shapes and forms. The swollen and twisted contortions of its trunk recall with a shudder those miserable sufferers from elephantiasis; its leaves are stiff and formal, and they usually drop off, as if ashamed of themselves, before the lovely flower, like a rich-coloured, large oleander blossom, comes out. The adenium bears some slight resemblance, on a small scale, to the unsightly baobab-tree of Africa, though it tapers much more rapidly, and looks as if it belonged to a different epoch of creation to our own trees at home.

Then there is the cucumber-tree, another hideous-stemmed tree, swollen and whitish; and the hill-slopes covered with this look as if they had been decorated with so many huge composite candles which had guttered horribly. At the top of the candle are a few short branches, on which grow a few stiff crinkly leaves and small yellow flowers, which produce the edible fruit. This tree, in Sokoteri *kamhàn*, the *Dendrosicyos Socotrana* of the botanist, is like the language of the Bedouin, found only on Sokotra, and is seldom more than 10 or 12 feet in height. It is a favourite perch for three or four of the white vultures which swarm in the island, and the picture formed by these ungainly birds on the top of this ungainly tree is an odd one.

To the south of Mount Haghier one comes across valleys entirely full of frankincense-trees, with rich red leaves, like autumn tints, and clusters of blood-red flowers. No one touches the trees here, and this natural product of the island is now absolutely ignored. Then there are the myrrhs, also ignored, and other gum-producing plants; and the gnarled tamarinds, affording lovely shade, and the fruit of which the natives, oddly enough, do know the value of, and make a cooling drink therewith. Then there are the tree-euphorbias, which look as if they were trying to mimic the dragon's blood, the branches of which the natives throw into the lagoons so that the fish may be killed, and the poisonous milky juice of which they rub on the bottoms of their canoes to prevent leakage.

Such are among the oddest to look upon of Sokotra's vegetable productions. Wild oranges, too, are found on Mount Haghier, of a very rich yellow when ripe, but bitter as gall to eat; and the wild pomegranate, with its lovely red flowers and small yellow fruit, the flannelly coating of which only is eaten, instead of the seeds, as is the case with the cultivated one.

The vegetable world is indeed richly represented in this remote island, and one could not help thinking what possibilities it would offer for the cultivation of lucrative plants, such as tobacco, which is now grown by the natives in small quantities, as is also cotton; and perhaps coffee and tea would thrive on the higher elevations.

The Bedouin would bring us aloes both in leaf and in solution, in hopes that we might take a fancy to this venerable Sokotran production. Now a very little of it is collected, and everybody takes what he likes from the nearest source, whereas, I believe, in former times, when aloes were an object of commerce here, the plantations were strictly divided off by walls, and the owners jealously looked after their property.

The way the aloe-juice is collected is this. As the Abyssinians do when they are going to wash clothes the aloe-gatherers dig a hole in the ground and line it with a skin. Then they pile old leaves, points outward, all round till the pressure makes the juice exude. This at first is called *taïf diho*, or *riho*, both of the latter words used for water, though the former is the most usual. It is left till it is firmer and drier, and this takes about a month. Then it is called *taïf geshisha*. When it has dried for about six weeks it is nearly hard, and called *taïf kasahal*. It is exported in skins. The collection of dragon's blood is carried on just like that of the mastic in Chios. The drops are knocked off into bags. The drops which come off unbroken are the most valued, and called *edah amsello*. Then the nice, clean, broken bits are picked out, and called *edah dakkah*; the refuse, with bits of dirt, bark, and leaves stuck in it, *edah*. This is made up into cakes with a little resin and sold very cheap.

My husband as usual made a botanical collection, and I believe it contained a few novelties; but for further particulars on the flora of Sokotra and the trees thereof I must refer you to Professor Bailey

Balfour's very huge and equally interesting book. We were so fortunate as to have it with us, and it added much to our pleasure.

Our way was over broken ground, with little of interest save the lovely views over mountain and gorge and the many dragon, frankincense, and myrrh trees, past an open space in which is the village of Jahaida, where the inhabitants had cultivated some little fields, to Röshi, where there was no village but a good deal of water. We encamped in a cattle-pen, the camel-men making themselves a capital house with floors, walls, and sides of the thick mats of the camels. These mats are really like hard mattresses, nearly 1 inch thick, and very stiff, about 1 yard long by 2 feet wide.

We always tried to encamp in a field if we could, as then we were sure of some earth for the tent-pegs. After three days, during which I do not think our guides knew their way very well, we went over a steep pass, up and down, into the deep valley of Es'hab. We had wandered about a good deal backwards and forwards over stony wolds, and the men all disagreed as to the direction, and we had scrambled up a valley off our road to see some supposed inscriptions, a much more dangerous place than the Kadhoup road.

The Es'hab valley, with its rich red stone dotted with green and its weird trees, forms an admirable foreground to the blue pinnacles of Haghier—tropical and Alpine at the same time.

The climbing was most tremendous, up first and then down very steeply, all over large sharp loose stones, till we reached the water, the camel-men leaning backwards holding their camels by their tails with all their might by way of putting on the drag. When we reached the valley we gladly mounted our camels, and squeezed through woods, and often were nearly torn off. We encamped in a sweet place, with a stream and shade and a most fragrant carpet of basil, some of which we had in our soup, and some of which was carried on for future use. We found the management of our milk-tins rather difficult. We often had to resort to them, for, surrounded though we were by herds of cattle, the supply of fresh milk was very irregular: sometimes we could have more than we wanted and at others none at all. It is pretty dear, too, in Sokotra, as so much is used up for the *ghi*.

The Breakwater at Fereghet

On January 17 we forced our way on through more woods, the peak of Toff seeming to fill up the end of the valley, to the Wadi Dishel, and crossed over to the Wadi Dikadik, where we settled near a wide river in a beautiful grassy spot, with many trees entwined with monkey-ropes, rejoicing that on the following day we should reach Fereghe, or Fereghet, where we intended to rest some time. We had heard from Ammar a delightful description of it, and as we have so often been disappointed under such circumstances we said we would take all possible enjoyment out of the pleasures of hope beforehand. But really this time we had everything we expected, including a wide rocky river, enabling us to bathe, develop photographs, and set up a laundry.

Fereghet was, in fact, a most charming spot. Here our tents were pitched beneath wide-spreading tamarinds, and we could walk in shade for a considerable distance under these gigantic old trees. Fereghet, moreover, was the site of an ancient ruined town which interested us exceedingly: walls, 8 to 10 feet thick, had been constructed out of very large unhewn boulders externally, filled with rubble, to check the torrent, which in the rainy season rushes down here carrying all before it to the sea. These walls, showing much skill in keeping a straight line, are clearly the work of an age long gone by, when weight-moving was better understood than it is at present, and doubtless the ruins of Fereghet may be traced back to the days when Sokotra was resorted to for its gums. The fine old tamarind-trees had done much to destroy the colossal wall, only about 100 feet of which now remains, still about 5 feet high; but there are many other traces of ruins and a small fort of later date. It is likely enough that Fereghet was a great centre of the trade of the island, for frankincense, myrrh, and dragon's blood grow copiously around, and the position under the slopes of Haghier, and almost in the middle of the island, was suitable for such a town.

We opened a tomb not very far from Fereghet with a great block of stone over it, 6 feet long by 3 feet thick; but the ill-conditioned relatives of the deceased had placed nothing therein save the corpse; and we were annoyed not to find any trace of inscriptions near this ruined town, which might have thrown some light on the subject. All I feel sure of is that the Portuguese did not build this town, as it is commonly asserted. In fact we did not see any building on the island which can definitely be ascribed to that nation.

Below Fereghet the valley gets broader and runs straight down to the sea at the south of the island, where the streams from Mount Haghier all lose themselves in a vast plain of sand called Noget, which we could see from the mountains up which we climbed.

This is the widest point of the island of Sokotra, and it is really only thirty-six miles between the ocean at Tamarida and the ocean at Noget, but the intervention of Mount Haghier and its ramifications make it appear a very long way indeed.

The island to the east and to the west of its great mountain very soon loses its fantastic scenery and its ample supply of water. The most remarkable peak we could see from Fereghet was Adouna. The topmost point of this mountain is split. We saw this clearly afterwards, when we continued our journey up the valley, but from Fereghet, I found it out by seeing a small cloud passing through it. To look at the mountains you would think they were made of black stone with a few patches of red lichen, but really these patches of red are the natural rock showing amongst the fine black lichen which covers the mountains.

The channels of the water in the river-bed are shown by this blackness, and the water looks like an inky stream.

Beyond Fereghet we were near a river the water of which was very low. The main bed of the water-channel was all black, and above this was a coat of white over the blackened stones, and as the remaining pools were all white, I suppose that some white tributary continues flowing later than the black stream.

The few Bedouin who live round Fereghet were in constant contact with our camp, as you will understand when you know that our tent was pitched exactly on their high road—a little narrow path. They behaved most kindly in going aside. The women used to bring us aloe plants just torn up, and seemed much disappointed at finding that we did not find any use for them.

We heard from them that there is only one leper on the island and he lives alone in the hills.

Our sheltering tamarind-trees, wide-spreading and gnarled, abounded in doves; some were small ones like ours, and some of the parrot kind, whose cawing was far from sedative. We enjoyed wandering in the shade of the fig-trees, wild and unprofitable, the date and other trees. Around us stood the relics of a bygone race of men, who had ill-naturedly left us no inscriptions on stone, and no clue to tell us who they were. Mountains hemmed us in on every side, and any little wind was very refreshing, for we were only about 400 feet above the sea-level, and quite sheltered from our now only too-well-known north-east monsoon. On a kind of promontory by a deep pool in the river is a building of stones and mortar, later in style than the wall and equally inexplicable, probably a fort.

It is impossible to describe the fantastic beauty of the delightful Fereghet. We were quite sorry to leave it on January 24. We rode a little way along the river, passing a single fan-palm-tree, very tall and bare, and then had another great climb up and down. We passed a good many old tombs, which had been opened. They were made of large slabs. We found one in the evening not far from our camp, so we opened it the following morning before starting. After a great deal of trouble with the pickaxes and crowbar nothing was found but bones. We measured the top stone, 6 feet 5 inches by 2 feet 10 inches and 1 foot 5 inches thick.

We next scrambled up a wooded mountain, steep enough, but nothing to the downward scramble. There was no particular road: one had to stick one's heels into trailing masses of sharp chips and blocks of red stone and let them slide as short a way as they would. The booted portion of our party began to feel great anxiety as to foot-gear. We wondered if our boots could possibly last to Tamarida where we had left a good deal of baggage, *i.e.* clothes that we had needed on the steamer. We used to apply the gums of various trees to the soles and toes to retard consumption. The camels sat down and slid, or looked as if they were doing so; the camel-men, holding the tails, nearly lay on their backs; but we reached the river safely, encamped there, and rode most of next day up a valley, crossing the water often. We had to wind in and out of clumps of trees, sometimes lying on our camels to get under branches, and finally, after going through thick woods, stopped at the foot of some mighty mountains.

Though many of our camps on Mount Haghier and the expeditions therefrom were very delightful, I think this one, called Yehazahaz, was decidedly the prettiest. It was low down on the southern slope of Mount Haghier; our tents were pitched in a grove of palm-trees at the meeting of two rushing streams; tangled vegetation hung around us on every side, and whichever way we looked we had glimpses of granite peaks and rugged hill-sides clad with dragon's-blood. The village was quite hidden by trees and creepers, but its inhabitants were away on the higher pasturage, and our men occupied the empty tenements.

Dragon's-Blood Trees at Yehazahaz

We stayed there a couple of days, and the first evening as we were sitting in our tent after tea, a tremendous noise and shouting proceeded from the direction of our kitchen. This proved to be occasioned by the discovery of some long-suspected sugar thieves. They were the three youngest of our camel-drivers. They were all tied to a palm-tree with their arms round it, and Ammar began scourging them with a rope. I begged them off; my husband thought I had been foolish, particularly as the scourging had not been ordered by him. The boys certainly did not seem to mind it a bit. However, the elder men consulted and Ammar brought a rupee next morning as a fine, which my husband thought it right to accept.

The red mountains here assume a greyish-white appearance. The land shells seemed to grow larger on the tops of the mountains. We found some about 3 inches in length.

On leaving Yehazahaz there was no riding for us, but a climb afoot straight up a steep pass and down across a river and over a second pass. The way was mostly rough and through woods, but there were a few little grassy bits. We descended only about 100 feet and pitched our tents on a flattish, spongy piece of grass, near a pretty streamlet overhung with begonias and many other flowers, at a spot called Adahan, where a sort of pass winds its way between the granite peaks. We were encamped for several days at an elevation of close on 3,000 feet above the sea-level. Here, when the mist came down upon us, we were enveloped in clouds, rain, and wretchedness; but the air to us was cool and invigorating, though I fear our scantily clad attendants found it anything but agreeable.

There were drawbacks, too, to the enjoyment of our mountain camps in the shape of several kinds of pernicious grasses, which grew thickly round our tent, and the seeds of which penetrated relentlessly into everything. Grass thorns invaded our day and night raiment, getting into places hitherto deemed impregnable, and the prickly sensation caused by them was irritating to both body and mind.

From Adahan one could easily ascend to the highest ground; though perhaps one ought not to say easily, for climbing is no joke up here, through dense vegetation and rocky gullies. Looking down into the gorges, we enjoyed some splendid effects, and were constantly reminded of the Grand Corral of Madeira.

There were many trees and flowering shrubs, rocky needles, and pinnacles all around us, and a view of the ocean to the north; and by climbing up we could catch sight of the ocean to southward too.

My husband tried to ascend the highest peak in the island—Driate it is called by the Bedouin—but when he had gone as far as possible the peak soared above him about 400 feet sheer and impracticable, quite bare of vegetation. An Alpine Club would find plenty of amusement in Sokotra. The bottoms and sides of the valleys, filled with bulbous plants and rank vegetation, enormous dragon's-blood-trees, the long valleys of Fereghet and Yehazahaz winding their way to the coast, the rugged mass of Bit Molek, and the view over both seas make, my husband said, as interesting a natural view as it is possible to conceive. The clouds had fortunately rolled themselves up for the occasion.

We had, however, during our stay so much wet that we had a special fire to dine by, and by it a very rudely constructed clothes-horse to dry our dripping garments. Our kitchen fire was the constant resort of the Bedouin of the neighbourhood, coming to see us and bring provisions to sell. We had plenty of milk and one day bought a tiny calf for three rupees. The camel-men who skinned it tried to keep the head as their perquisite, but Matthaios secured it and put it in our soup. To our surprise the two Somali servants, Hashi and Mahmoud, would in consequence eat none of the soup nor any meat. They usually ate anything that was going.

A lame Bedou brought us some green oranges and potatoes, which were really the roots of a convolvulus: they were not bad when baked in the ashes, but hard when boiled. He also brought us a sweet herb which they use to stuff pillows with. The greetings of the Bedou always amuse us; they first put cheek to cheek and then rub noses in the most matter-of-fact way, so we may infer that this mode of salutation is in vogue in the Mahra country. It was pleasant to be among such friendly people, who had no horror of us and did not even seem much surprised at seeing us there, and to be able to go off quite alone for a scramble so safely.

CHAPTER XXXIV

BACK TO THE OCEAN

After several days at Adahan we climbed down northward. Our journey was only three miles along a very narrow valley, but we made much more of it climbing after plants and shells. We stopped at the first little flat place that would hold our tents, a sort of small shelf more than knee-deep in that awful grass; and though we really enjoyed that camp for two days, pain was our portion all the time. The scenery was magnificent, and all the more striking that the mountains, having cast off their lichen covering, gleamed out in their glowing red. All round us there was such steepness that it was a work of great difficulty to set up my camera anywhere.

We had a very steep descent after that over sharp stones to the plain, my husband and I, as usual, when on foot, starting before the others, and though we were sorry when we finally quitted the mountains, we were glad enough to find ourselves on our camels again, to be carried to Suk, where we decided to stay, as we heard that the sultan's boat was there and the sultan himself was not so very far off. We wished to engage the ship for our return to Aden.

Before leaving the s.s. *Canara* my husband had begged the captain to take a letter to Bombay requesting that the B.I.S.N. Co. would send a steamer for us, and let us know about it by some dhow. A dhow had arrived from Bombay with no letter for us, but with news of the plague: so we became afraid that if the plague prevented the steamer from coming and we waited for it, we might have to stick on Sokotra during the whole of the south-west monsoon. My husband therefore began parleying about sailing-boats and had sent Ammar from Adahan, and the sultan had sent his captain up to meet us.

Dr. Schweinfurth sees in the present name of Sokotra a Hindoo origin, and the survival of the Hindoo name Diu Sukutura, which the Greeks, after their easy-going fashion, changed into Dioscorides. This is very ingenious and most likely correct. When the Portuguese reached the island in 1538, they found the Arab sheikh dwelling at the capital called Zoko, now in ruins, and still called Suk, a survival doubtless of the original name.

The old capital of Zoko is a delicious spot, and the ruins are buried in groves of palm-trees by the side of a large and deep lagoon of fresh water; this lagoon is only separated from the sea by a narrow belt of sand and shingle, and it seems to me highly probable that this was the ancient harbour where the boats in search of the precious products of the island found shelter. The southern coast of Arabia affords many instances of these silted harbours, and the northern coast of Sokotra is similar, many of the lagoons, or *khors* as they call them, being deep and running over a mile inland. The view at Suk over the wide lagoon fringed with palm groves, on to the jagged heights of Mount Haghier rising immediately behind, is, I think, to be placed amongst the most enchanting pictures I have ever seen.

Extensive excavation at Suk might probably bring to light some interesting relics of the earlier inhabitants of this island, but it would have to be deep, as later edifices have been erected here; and labour and tools would have to be brought from elsewhere.

The present capital is called Tamarida by Arabs and foreigners, and Hadibo by the natives, and its construction is quite of a modern date; the name is apparently a Latinised form of the Arabic *tamar*, or date fruit, which tree is largely cultivated there.

Much is said by old writers about the Greek colonists who came to Sokotra in ancient times, but I cannot help thinking that the Hellenic world never carried its enterprise much in this direction, for, if the Greeks did, they have left no trace whatsoever of their existence there.

I should think few places in the world have pursued the even tenor of their way over so many centuries as Sokotra has. Yakut, writing seven hundred years ago, speaks of the Arabs as ruling here; the author of the 'Periplus' more than one thousand years ago tells us the same thing; and now we have a representative of the same country and the same race governing the island still.

Sokotra has followed the fortunes of Arabia; throughout, the same political and religious influences which have been at work in Arabia have been felt here. Sokotra, like Arabia, has gone through its several stages of Pagan, Christian, and Mohammedan beliefs.

The first time the island came in contact with modern ideas and modern civilisation was when the Portuguese occupied it in 1538, and this was, as we have seen, ephemeral. Then the island fell under the rod of Wahabi persecution at the beginning of this century, as did nearly the whole of Arabia in those days. In 1835 it was for a short time brought under direct British influence, and Indian troops encamped on the plain of Tamarida. It was then uncertain whether Aden or Sokotra would be chosen as a coaling station for India, and Lieutenant Wellsted was sent in the *Palinurus* to take a survey of it; but doubtless the harbourless condition of the island, and the superior position of Aden in that respect, caused the decision in favour of Aden.

The advantages Aden afforded for fortification and for commanding the mouth of the Red Sea influenced the decision, and Sokotra, with its fair mountains and rich fertility, was again allowed to relapse into its pristine state of quiescence, and the British soldier was condemned to sojourn on the barren, burning rocks of Aden, instead of in this island paradise.

Finally, in 1876, to prevent the island being acquired by any other nation, the British Government entered into a treaty with the sultan, by which the latter gets 360 dollars a year, and binds himself and his heirs and successors, 'amongst other things, to protect any vessel, foreign or British, with the crew, passengers, and cargo, that may be wrecked on the island of Sokotra and its dependencies,' and it is understood that the island is never to be ceded to a foreign power without British consent.

A more peaceful, law-abiding people it would be hard to find elsewhere—such a sharp contrast to the tribes on the South Arabian coast. They seem never to quarrel amongst themselves, as far as we could see, and the few soldiers Sultan Salem possesses have a remarkably easy time of it. Our luggage was invariably left about at night without anyone to protect it, and none of it was stolen, and after our journeys in Southern Arabia the atmosphere of security was exceedingly agreeable.

The only thieves were the white and yellow vultures who sat on guard around our kitchen and were always ready to carry off our meat, and made many valiant attempts to do so.

Money is scarce in the island, and so are jealousies, and probably the Bedouin of Sokotra will remain in their bucolic innocence to the end of time, if no root of bitterness in the shape of modern civilisation is planted amongst them.

It is undoubtedly a providential thing for the Sokotran that his island is harbourless, that his mountains are not auriferous, and that the modern world is not so keen about dragon's-blood, which is still called 'the blood of two brothers,' frankincense and myrrh, as the ancients were. A thing we regretted very much in leaving Sokotra was the delightful peace of travelling without an armed escort, which we had not enjoyed for years; we knew we should soon be travelling again with soldiers in Arabia.

There is a wretched hamlet of Somali at Suk, which had been visited by us from Hadibo. We had only one night at Suk, and in the morning my husband and Matthaios went off on foot to Haulah or Haulaf to see the boat. This is where the sultan lives. I believe the boat was actually at Khor Dilisha. They did not think it would have been so far or they would have taken camels. It was a three-mile tramp in the sand.

My husband and Matthaios came back from Haulah very hot and tired, not having seen the sultan; he was sleeping or praying all the time, the mode in which Moslems say 'not at home'—in short he was keeping out of the way. They described the boat as everything that was delightful, though people not so well accustomed as we were to voyaging in these ships might not agree with them, but it was impossible to come to terms. They had had a very stormy interview with the sultan's captain, who said that 1,000 rupees was the lowest price. My husband said he had paid no more for the steamer, and we had all had beds provided and food; 800 was his highest price.

The sultan has a miserable house in a very uncomfortable spot, surrounded by a few huts belonging to fishermen, who go out on little rafts made of bundles of palm-leaf ribs to drop the traps for fish.

The Haghier Mountains from Suk
(*From a water-colour sketch by Theodore Bent*)

We then moved to Hadibo again, going along the shore, and encamping quite in a different place to that in which we were at first; we were in a nice date grove by the lagoon and close to the beach. We now commenced a time of dreadful uncertainty as to how or when we could leave the island.

Hearing nothing from the sultan, Matthaios was sent on a camel to offer 800 rupees, and returned most indignant, 2,000 being the lowest price asked, *i.e.* 124*l*. Later the captain came, agreed to the 800, and said my husband must pay 400 at sunset to get wood and water. As the men never came for the money till we were in bed, they were sent off till next morning, when they came very early and asked for paper to write the contract. My husband produced some, with pen and ink. They said they could only write with a pencil, but when that was got the captain said 500 must be paid: he did not want it himself, nor yet the sultan, but the sailors did; my husband then said he would complain to the Wali of Aden, and they all suddenly departed, and the captain, we heard, went to Kadhoup, where there was another boat, in order to prevent its owner spoiling the sultan's bargain.

Two days after we had a message to say we were to pay the whole 800 rupees at once, that the sultan was coming to fetch it himself, and that we should positively start that day.

No sultan came, but next day a very affectionate letter from him said he would come round with the ship at sunset. We had to forgive his non-appearance that time, as there was such a storm that we could not, in any case, have passed the surf. Next day he came by land to the castle, where we had seen him, and sent to ask my husband to bring the money; so he went, attended by myrmidons bearing money-bags, pen, and paper, but as the sultan would not sign the contract, the money was brought back. At midday there was an apology sent with two lambs and a little calf, and at sunset the sultan really arrived at our camp, signed the contract, and carried off the money; so we left next day.

We had plenty to do, so were quite occupied all this time. I used to develop photographs, for I had my dark tent set up. I had awful trials to bear. The water was so warm that the gelatine frilled in spite of alum, and what was worse, when I put the negatives in the hyposulphate of soda they ran off their supports like so much hot starch. Some I saved, but I never dared do more than carefully dip them in the 'hypo,' and even then it seemed to froth up at once. I had a good many negatives marked by this, and had to smooth off the bubbles with my hands, regardless of their colour, and I had to work at night for coolness.

We had very little milk while there; none till the last two days. A man was drinking a bowlful in our camp, and this is the surprising way in which he did it: he dipped his hand in and sucked his fingers (not clean ones at first), and so continued till he had finished it all up. Our visitors used sometimes suddenly to hurry off to pray, choosing a bit of damp sand, and when they returned some of the sand was sticking to their foreheads. The longer that sand stayed on the better, as it was considered a sign of a religious man.

We had an anxious battle with white ants also. A basket was nearly devoured by them, but our best steamer raiment was preserved by the inner lining of American cloth, though they were sitting on it in sheets. We had remarked in South Africa that they never eat mackintosh. The basket was brushed over the sea, steeped in the lagoon, and inundated with boiling water. This was the only thing attacked of all that we had left behind when we were in Hadibo the first time.

Our brown ship, 70 feet in length by 15 wide, did really look a very 'mere nutshell' to go 500 miles over the great ocean in, but it was far, far better than some we had been in.

From the deck Sokotra looked almost too beautiful to leave.

The weather was very rough, the sailors not nearly ready, and it was midday before we started. By this time all the servants were prostrate, and my husband had to get the sailors to help him in setting up our beds, and arranging the baggage in the place between decks astern, which was 3½ feet high, and, as the beds had to be tied to each other, 2 feet apart, as well as to the sides of the ship, we had to bend low and step high when moving about. The two Somali servants managed wonderfully to take it in turns to be well after a bit, but Matthaios was one of the worst, so food was a difficulty and his wrath was great when, Mahmoud having made us tea like ink, he found the tea canister empty. We had rough weather enough, but the wind was favourable. We were always afraid of falling off our seats at meals, for we were perched anywhere, on anything we could get, round our kitchen box as a table. Bruises alone were not the cause of our terror, but the fact is that the sailors were always shaking their raiment and making those searching and successful investigations, accompanied by that unmistakable movement of the elbows and backs of the thumb-nails, which literally 'give one the creeps.'

The captain had a compass, but no other instrument of any kind, and none of the sailors seemed to know the way. They showed us islands, which we knew to be such, as the African coast, and Cape Guardafui where we knew it could not be.

On the third evening we saw the Asiatic coast, and at sunset we saw the jagged Jebel Shemshan very far away, and of course hoped to see it nearer next day. But when we woke in the morning, my husband went out to see the cause of the unusual rocking of the ship and still more unusual silence, and found everyone asleep and the ship lying to out of sight of any land.

The captain said they imagined we had passed Aden in the dark, and thinking they should soon be among rocks or coral-reefs had stopped; a dreadful uproar then arose, and everyone on the ship shouted different directions for steering. My husband desired them to steer north that we might find land, as none of them had any idea of our longitude. At last we saw a steamer, presumably from Aden, and getting north of her and steering west we at length had Africa on our port side again, and reached Aden by the following sunrise, though it took us till two o'clock to get into port.

BELED FADHLI AND BELED YAFEI

CHAPTER XXXV

EXPERIENCES WITH THE YAFEI SULTAN

In the same year, 1897, soon after our return thither from Sokotra, we left Aden to explore the Yafei and Fadhli countries. Our preparations for this expedition were made under quite different and much happier circumstances from those which attended our last journey from Aden to the interior of Arabia, *i.e.* the Hadhramout. We received every help that could be given us by General Cuningham, Colonel Hayes-Sadler, Captain Wadeson, and, indeed, everyone from whom we asked assistance was most kind. We took with us only our servant Matthaios, the Greek, Musaben, an elderly man from the Aden troup, as jemadar or manager of the soldiers and go-between generally; and three or four soldiers. No interpreter was necessary, I am glad to say, this time.

We left Sheikh Othman on February 28, 1897, for our nine hours' ride to Bir Mighar, sorry to have to make so long a journey the first day. At first we went past pretty gardens and villas, but soon left these traces of civilisation behind us, and the way went through desert, sometimes salty, sometimes sandy, sometimes bare, and sometimes with low bushes, now straight, and at others wending among sand-hills with cliffs to leeward, and ribbed and rippled like water. In some parts every trace of path is smothered by sand, and quicksand also must be warily avoided. We passed the ruins of an old town near Sheikh Othman, and five miles on, Imad, a wretched-looking collection of brushwood huts around a dar, or tower, still in English land.

This place is, about Christmas time, the scene of a fair to which all the neighbouring tribes gather, so a good study can be made of the native tongues.

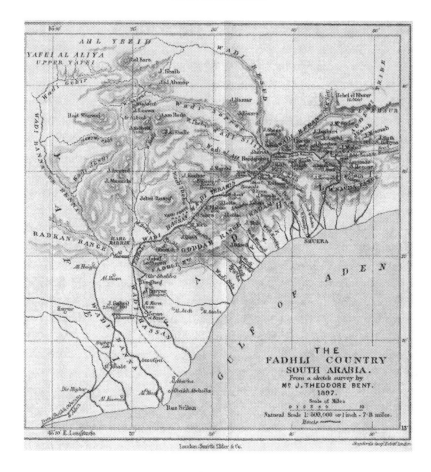

The Fadhli Country South Arabia

From a sketch survey by

Mr J. THEODORE BENT.

1897.

Stanford's Geog.¹ Estab.¹, London

London: Smith, Elder & Co.

A few patches of ground had the sand scraped off into banks, and were awaiting rain to sow some crops for fodder, but looked as if they had been waiting a long time. This caravan road across the Abyan is very old; its monotony is inexpressible, for the nine hours to Bir Mighar. At the sixth hour the road to Hawash goes off to the left. As we approached the well of Mighar the signs of population increased, and a few scrubby acacias grow near. There are two wells a mile apart; the farther, where we encamped, was once protected by a fort, now in ruins. A few years ago a hundred Yafei surprised the Fadhli, and sacked the fort, which has not since been repaired. Many parties of travellers were gathering round this well for the night; one husband and wife who took alternate charge of a baby slung in a straw cradle and a goat; another pair with their household goods, baby, and many fowls on a camel, while they were each laden with more fowls.

We passed a cold night, and were very tired; our things, having been packed on board the baggalla in which we came from Sokotra, were not in marching order. We only made a short journey of six miles next day past Al Khabt, which was just the same sort of place as Imad. We had to take a most circuitous route to reach it, and it was hard to realise that all the banks we wound amongst were fields waiting for rain. Hagheri Ask, our next halt, was even a yet more wretched hamlet—about six reed huts, and about as many goats and jackal-like dogs.

Our tents were most unsteadily pitched on sand. There is a good well, and there has been a village here 'from the first,' as the Arabs say. There are many traces of antiquity; and numerous pieces of glass, good pottery, and bangles lie about. There are three ruined tombs and some smaller ones of mud bricks, and they make mud bricks there still. The villages of the Abyan are most poverty-stricken places.

The first day we had our camels loaded with jowari, and at Bir Mighar we took up fuel. From Hagheri Ask to Kanfar is about six miles, and we spent two hours over it. Trees became more numerous, good large ones, chiefly arrack and acacia, and a few small fan-palms. There were quantities of birds' nests, in every way a contrast to ours; for, instead of warm woolly ones, safe from wind and rain in the innermost recesses of our soft-leaved, easily climbed trees, these were loose open-work airy little baskets, dancing on the outer tips of the thorny branches. The scenery in the desert part was much improved by mirages of beautiful blue lakes and streams, nearly under our feet. Once, on the journey, we thought the piping times of peace had come to an abrupt end. The army of three became a vanguard, one who was riding having very suddenly turned himself into infantry, the guns were taken out of their calico bags and cocked, but the supposed enemy turned out to be only six or eight men carrying great rolls of skins and huge dry gourds for sale, so the rifles were packed up again. Some had Martini-Henrys and one or two of the camel-men had matchlocks.

Castle at Kanfar

Since leaving the British Empire we had been in the Fadhli country till we reached the Wadi Banna, or Benna, the boundary between the Beled Fadhli and Beled Yafei, then winding indeed was our way, for we were in thick wood; swords and daggers had to be used to cut a path, and we were brought to a standstill more than once, with our heads bent under trees, not daring to lift them. It would be easy for the inhabitants to stop an enemy's attack here. The smell of the arrack is not at all pleasant. Two Fadhli were once directed into the Banna bed by the Yafei of Al Husn, and when they were in the wood they set fire to it and burnt them. The inhabitants do not venture off the path. There are quicksands in some parts of the wadi.

We encamped not far from the town of Kanfar, amongst some large arrack bushes on the sand, and surrounded by mounds scattered over with bits of glass. There has been a succession of towns here, and the present one is situated on large mounds near some somewhat ruinous forts. It would take an immense quantity of digging to come on Himyaritic remains. Many gold coins are found, and set on the jembias; our old Musàben had two on his dagger, about four hundred years old. We were told that Boubakr-bin-Saïd, sultan of the lower Yafei, was to come in two days to keep the feast of a saint, Wali Abdullah-bin-Amr, who is buried here. In the meantime we surveyed our surroundings while awaiting his coming. The ground under the arrack bushes is perforated through and through by rats with bushy tips to their tails, as far as the utmost branch extends. Sometimes we felt our feet sinking, and discovered we were walking over the site of a vanished bush. There is an old ruined castle, with pretty herring-bone patterns and open-work windows. The principal well, a little distance from the town, is very close by the present fortress, where the sultan lives. There is a gunpowder factory of a primitive kind, for there is plenty of saltpetre to be found close by. We went all about the village quite comfortably with a couple of Yafei guards, and the people were civil. We saw curious ovens, like pots with lids, and oxen returning with the dustpans they use for scraping the sand off the cultivable soil, and many preparations for the feast in the way of food and very smart new indigo-dyed clothes. Photography, sketching, and unpacking the gifts for the sultan occupied our time. The mosquitoes were awful.

The sultan came to visit us very suddenly on the afternoon of his arrival—a rather handsome, sly-looking man. He wore a purple velvet jacket embroidered with gold, and a many coloured turban and waist-cloth forming a petticoat to his knees and leaving his fat legs bare. His complexion is of a greenish brown. His first question was as to my husband's age, that of the Wali of Aden, and of various other officials. He brought some honey and made himself most agreeable till we spoke of going to Al Kara. He then immediately began to speak of danger. He read the letter of introduction with more discretion than I have observed in any of the Arab sultans I have seen. Instead of reading to a crowd of slaves, he banished all but one very confidential, though dirty man, who was lame and carried a long lance adorned with silver bands, and read this letter and one previously sent. When he left, my husband told him the sooner he sent a message as to the possibilities of going to Al Kara the better it would be for him; and we also told Musàben to tell the Bedouin there would be money for them, and also to mention to the sultan that we had a gun that he might hope for.

It appeared, after much fruitless negotiation, that the sultan was determined to cheat the Bedouin. He arrived very soon after breakfast, *i.e.* before seven, and demanded 500 rupees for himself, which he immediately lowered of his own accord to 400 rupees, and gave us to understand danger would be averted if we paid this sum. He carried off 100 rupees for coffee and a bundle of turbans and other garments. No one but Musàben was to know of the money, and the fat parcel he himself stuffed into the clothes of his dirty confidant, explaining to us and them that he should only show an aluminium box as his sole gift, and walked off holding it ostentatiously between his finger and thumb. Later we walked round the castle, and were let into the courtyard. The sultan saw us from a window in his tower, and beckoned us up. We had to go through gateways on all sides of the tower, so that they can quite command the entrance. We went up a high winding stair to a room about 10 feet square, where we sat on the floor and had coffee with cloves and no sugar, and a coarse kind of sweetmeat. His first question was, 'Where is the gun?' I said, 'Where is Al Kara?' So he laughed merrily, and said, 'You shall not go to Al Kara till I have the gun.' So I told him he should not have the gun till we had been. He then told my husband he must pay 1,000 rupees and the gun first, and he would manage the Bedouin; but my husband said he would pay afterwards, and not more than 400 rupees. So this conversation went on, and we left. Musàben was surprised that we had been admitted.

We spent our days taking long walks in the cultivated fields, stepping on banks between the canals, or *abrs*. There were many trees, and acres of dukhan grown for making oil, gilgil, and other crops; and the shade, the birds, the greenery, and water made it a pleasant relief from the sandy mounds. The workpeople are slaves of the subordinate race of Hagheri. There are really very few Arabs. Watchmen or scarecrows, with long canes, stand on high platforms scattered about. The old well has very-much-worn stones round its mouth, and had once an extensive building over it. Corn is ground in a mill made from the hollowed trunk of a tree, with a camel going round and round. It was amusing to see the little children with their arms held aloft bound up in leaves to their elbows, to keep their hands nice, as they had been dyed with henna for the festival.

Jebel Gabeil is the acropolis of the ancient Kanfar, about 200 feet high and a quarter of a mile long, with a double fort on the top, containing an area of about 100 square yards. The outer wall is built of fine large stones, and the interior has a beautiful foundation, evidently Himyaritic, and commands an extensive view. The tomb of the saint whose feast it was is surrounded with tombs, all in disrepair, but covered with very pretty carved wood. The procession passed our camp both going and coming, and was an interesting sight. Quite early I was begged to come out and see crowds of women and girls, who had come to visit me with their new clothes, some indigo-dyed and some of red ingrain. They wear the same shape as in the Hadhramout, but do not cover their faces. They have a good deal of jewellery, and paint their faces yellow. I did not see any of the fantastic patterns I saw in the Hadhramout on the faces. First came four men with lances, dancing to and fro, then the sultan on a camel, dressed in red and purple and gold, and after him about thirty soldiers. A large white and red flag followed. On his return the sultan stopped and delivered a short address, the bystanders assenting by shouting 'Nahm! Nahm!'

The sultan came constantly, always raising his demands.

One afternoon he came and said 'Where is the gun?'

'Under that bed; you cannot have it now.'

'I should like to see the cartridges,' said the sultan.

'They are packed up.'

My husband then did what might seem rude here but is all the fashion there: he walked out of the tent and went off a little distance with Matthaios and Musàben to have a consultation; and the sultan got up and stood craning his neck and trying to listen, but I chattered and babbled to him to prevent his doing so, and finding he could hear nothing he said in a very cajoling sort of tone:

'Al Kara is such a very nice place! you would like to see it,' and asked me just to let him see the gun and some more clothes, and when my husband returned begged for more money; but he put on an air of great indignation and impatience and said:

'When we say a thing once it is enough,' and when the sultan began again he said 'Bas!' (Enough!) so loud that his majesty hastily departed.

Finally, when he could not get what he wanted, and we saw it was not safe to trust ourselves in the hands of so shifty a man, he became so insistent that my husband told him 'he had seen enough of him; he might leave our camp; we would not travel with him.' Off went the sultan in such a hurry that he left his stick behind, and sent us a message that we were not to pass another night in his country. We sent back a message that we would not stir till morning. When the sultan was gone we had tea, and I was talking to a dirty little boy of five called Boubakr and a bigger one called Ali, to whom I was giving lumps of sugar dirtied by the journey. We were laughing well at the sultan, calling him all sorts of names expressing our scorn of his meanness, when to our amusement we found these were his sons. He came himself about dawn next day to say we were to go back over the Wadi Banna, and not the shortest way to the part of the Fadhli country, which is beyond the Yafei, unless we gave him more money. We would not speak to him ourselves, so he had to talk with the servants (who were continuing packing) all the while, and, we let him see the greatest amusement on our part. Musàben was most anxious to go on, but the difficulties delighted Matthaios, as he was so frightened that he wished to go back at any price. When we did go, about six o'clock, we only went a very little way in the prescribed direction, then turned round, and took the path we desired, our army now being a rearguard, rushing up hillocks to watch for pursuers. We reached Al Khaur, a village with many ruined castles, and camped in frightful dust. The Wazir Abdullah bin Abdurrahman had been sent by the Fadhli sultan to welcome us. He proved a very agreeable travelling companion. He is young and refined looking.

We saw a great deal of cattle about. There is a sheer rock overhanging the village 1,000 feet above the plain. My husband ascended Jebel Sarrar to see the ruins. A fine paved road, protected by forts, climbs up past a curious square stone said to be full of money, and goes zigzag through a narrow gully like the walls at Zimbabwe. My husband having heard of the stone from the wazir, very much astonished the guides by pointing it out to them and saying 'There is money in that stone.' At the top there is a very strong fortress with many walls, and three cisterns just like the smaller of the tanks at Aden, with steps down into them, all covered with cement. This has been a very strong fortification, protecting and overlooking the whole of the Abyan from Jebel Goddam beyond Shukra to Jebel Shemshan at Aden. The Abyan is the low plain by the sea.

The following day we started for Dirgheg. The country is all irrigated by water brought from Masana by a channel called Nazai. At the corner of the Wadi Hassan the *abrs* branch off in every direction. The sources belong to the Yafei, and the Fadhli pay them annually 25 Maria Theresa dollars, a basket of dates, and a turban for the sultan, but the management is in the hands of seyyids in *inam* for ever, they being supposed to be neutral, for fear a war might produce a drought. Still, in time of war the water often is cut off. The banks of the abrs were full of castor-oil bushes, cotton, myrtle and tamarisk, all smothered with a pretty creeper covered with yellow flowers and little scarlet gourds.

Dirgheg lies just on the left bank of the Wadi Hassan in an almost desert place. There are many dars, or towers, where the wealthy

Arabs, of whom there is a considerable population, live. The servile tribe of Hagheri live in reed huts; we saw them threshing gilgil and vetch. There are a market and a few shops. I had no trouble about taking photographs. Once, however, one of our attendants asked a man to move out of my way and gave him a little push. Out he pulled his ghembia, and there was a scrimmage very dangerous to my camera and its appurtenances, as they were going to be used as weapons of defence by our attendants. I rushed into the midst, and they stopped fighting to tell me not to be afraid, and peace was restored. I think it requires some courage to plunge out of the tent into the burning sand with the camera, but it never seems so hot once one is out. We were given over by our soldiers to the charge of two inhabitants of Dirgheg, and were quite elated at hearing on other authority than our own, 'They can speak Arabic.'

Dirgheg

We had on our return to the camp the delightful pleasure of a letter from Sultan Boubakr, making another try for the gun, and saying he would come and take us to Al Husn. The messenger was fetched, and scornfully told by my husband that it was too late; we would not think of travelling with so bad a man. I said, 'You have a great thief for your sultan, and a great liar,' and told him all about the money and clothes he had secretly taken; so, no doubt, he had to disgorge some after all. Musàben laughed very much, and said my imitation of the sultan's manner was so good he must get two sheikhs to hear the Bibi mimic the Yafei sultan. The Yafei messenger was much interested. I told the whole story, and how we had gone round three trees and departed our own way, adding, 'The sultan could see us from his own castle'; and he said, 'Yes, he did.' We told him all his conduct was written down and sent yesterday to the Wali of Aden, so now he might be sorry and frightened. We said we had been treated well by all the other Yafei we had met, but the sultan wanted to cheat both them and us. Indeed, it grieved us to hear the kind Yafei spoken of with horror and detestation by the Fadhli, but no doubt they have a different point of view to ours.

We went to another village called Abr Shebba, more under the mountains. We were shown about very civilly, and taken to the door of a large dar, and asked if we wished to go in. We did not know if we were wanted, so made an indefinite answer. There was a difference of opinion, and at last they said the Bibi should go in; so I crossed the court and entered the house, and had hardly done so when my hand was seized, and I was dragged by a man through black darkness upward and round and round. I stepped high, and, as quickly as I could, rushed after him. At the third round I saw a little light shining on the roughest possible shallow earthen steps, and was pulled into a little room, where I was greeted with cries of amazement by some women, and then continued my way unaided to the top of the tower. The parapets were ornamented with gazelle horns. After some time I wanted to go down, but I was on my way taken to a large room where manners demanded I should settle down for coffee. Every one was very kind, and for greater friendliness a naked baby four months old was placed in my hands. When I wished to return it it was made to sit on my knee. It soon kindly cried, and was, to my joy, removed. It had never in its life been completely washed, though several large spots and trimmings had been painted on its head. My husband joined me at last, and had coffee too.

The first thing next morning, before our departure to Al Ma'a, another letter came from the Yafei sultan about Al Husn; but the messenger was told that once was enough to see that great thief (*harami*), and he could take the letter back. It was fourteen miles to Al Ma'a, and took us six hours. We passed up the Wadi Hassan, and saw Al Husn in the distance. We did not go quite to the corner where the Wadi Hassan turns east. It is considered too near the Yafei frontier to be safe, and the Fadhli always used a narrow pass called Tarik al Kaha, going round Mount Gherash. It gets narrower and steeper as it goes on zigzagging up slabs of shale, with only room for one camel at a time. There are any amount of ambush places, especially on the north side. The pass goes uphill, west to east, and the steepest end is at the east. A spur runs out west on the north side about 50 feet high, convenient to shoot over. The approaches are quite open. It leads through Wadi Goddam to Wadi Hassan, and at the entrance to Wadi Hassan, Fadhli Bedouin are for ever stationed to watch for Yafei attacks on a tiny jutting hill. Three men of ours, sheikhs who had come to meet us, galloped forward to explain to them who we were, and ascertain that all was safe. They fired a gun over our heads. There were a few baboons about. We saw several little heaps of stones, and were told they marked spots where Fadhli had been shot by Yafei. A very large heap is formed by those who pass the valley safely for good luck. We also passed the tomb of a seyyid with four large smooth stones at the top anointed with oil for the Ed. Before we reached Al Ma'a the river-bed narrowed in from the other side, and along the raised bank at short intervals were watch-towers of the Yafei. At Al Ma'a they are quite close, about half a mile off at most. The country was still very arid and barren, but the mountains very fine.

Al Ma'a is a wretched hamlet, which has seen very much better days. There are high ruined castles, destroyed by the present sultan, as Al Ma'a and its head-men were once in revolt. Now there are only three or four Arab houses and a collection of reed huts. The valley is about two miles wide, and there are four or five Yafei towers near. Our escort were very much afraid. They said that the Yafei might shoot us, though a cannon would be necessary, and lay the blame on the Fadhli, so they would by no means let us camp anywhere but in a most disgustingly dusty place next the village; and they kept sharp watch all night, talking much. The towers protect the approach to the Wadi Theba, which here goes up or comes down from Al Kara. The country round is in a perpetual state of ferment, like Germany in the Middle Ages, every one on the look-out for attacks from enemies.

CHAPTER XXXVI

AMONG THE FADHLI

We were up and off before the sun rose, our party being increased by Sultan Salem, brother to the Fadhli sultan. He was twenty, and though not dark in colour, has woolly hair. He and the soldiers and the wazir, Abdullah bin Abdurrahman, rode at some distance to our left, between us and the dangerous Yafei towers. The Goddam or Kadam range, which separates the Wadi Yeramis from the Abyan, is a mass of arid peaks, none reaching to more than 2,000 feet. A road leads from Al Ma'a across the mountains to the sea at Asala.

We reached Karyat el Maksuf about ten, the valleys getting narrower and more woody and grassy as we approached. There is an ancient fort on a hill 650 feet above the valley, and about 1,300 above the sea, with a glorious view over the Goddam range to the sea. There is another ruin of a round fort on the left of the valley. We went on a mile to a delightful place, where there were trees, water, and reeds, and beautiful views through shady glades to the mountain peaks, and many cattle. We wished to remain there, but were told it was better to get on to Naab, as there was a little danger. We quite understood that danger was a bogey to prevent us keeping them from a town, and we pointed out that the Yafei were not likely to come down a light-coloured mountainside with only a few tamarisks into a valley half a mile wide; so my husband firmly said we would stay on the clean sand. Here we saw many baboons. The first ruin is probably Persian or later Arabian. The second one, which is a mile further up the Wadi Yeramis than the first, is evidently Himyaritic, and protected the first town after Banna on the way to the Hadhramout. It is circular, crowning a hill 300 feet high, and enclosing a space of 50 yards in diameter. On the north-east side it is protected by five square towers, and has one gate to the south. It was the acropolis of a large town, lying in all directions, but chiefly to the north-east. It has evidently been a place of considerable strength, as the Wadi Yeramis is only half a mile wide here. There is a regular stream of water in a narrow channel, and the whole valley is green and fertile.

Old Na'ab (*By Theodore Bent*)

Before we entered this narrow part of the valley, it was curious to see below the peaked mountains a flat-topped effusion of basalt, called *borum*, advanced forward.

We made a very early start next morning, and gradually got into a thick low wood, but where the Wadi Yeramis widened out there were only tamarisks. Our ascent was rapid, and after about an hour we turned due east, this part being very bare-looking, though there were a good many horrid acacias and also euphorbias with rounded trunks. We soon burst upon a lovely plain all mapped out in fields and abrs. It is six miles to Naab, and we took three hours. We passed through full two miles of this fertility, with three or four villages— Souat, Nogat, Arrawa, and Old Naab, with mosque, minar, and a fine old house all tumbling into ruins. Wadi Yeramis is much opened out here, and the lower part is bounded by the basalt in walls about 200 feet high, sometimes with mounds within them again, and hillocks of the same formation as the high mountains. This cultivated paradise is the property of Sultan Ahmet bin Salem, brother to Sultan Saleh of the coast, and may be said to be the pick of his whole dominions.

Arrawa, or New Naab, has twenty-four shops, and the sultan gets half a real (or Maria Theresa dollar) on all merchandise-camels going up to the Beled Yafei. There were many bales of merchandise in a sort of Custom-house when we arrived at this great centre of inland traffic. We encamped on the opposite side of the wadi from the town of Arrawa, which is perched on a raised plateau of earth banks. When we halted, and had climbed up, there was a line of people waiting to salute us. We and Sultan Salem walked in front, our eleven men with guns walked behind, singing a *merghazi*, or salutation song, of which I have a copy. We halted again, and they fired ten salutes; then we advanced again, Sultan Salem leading, when twenty of the local sultan's soldiers came forward and kissed his hand and shook ours. Then there was a refreshment of five or six cups of coffee and ginger, very weak, on the floor in a tower. There was milk in the first cups, but it became exhausted. We never saw the sultan all the time we were there, for they said he had a wound in his leg.

The earthen cliffs are about 30 feet high, and we had to go a very roundabout way to get up them by very narrow gullies. My husband went up a hill, Yerad, just behind Naab, with an old Arab fort on it above the Yeramis, which ends here; then begins Wadi Reban, with a clear course north-east for three miles, then north, and then a long stretch east again. There was a lovely view over the Yafei mountains on the north and Goddam range on the south. A Bedou, Abdallah, who went with him told him all the names. Though he could understand when the Bedouin talked to him, he could not understand two talking together. Abdallah said he had been a soldier in the sultan's service, but when my husband asked how long he answered, 'Four, five, six years. I have never had it written down.' The Bedou gave my husband some food called *kharou*, roast millet seeds put in a mug with boiled milk, not at all bad.

The Sultan Salem bin Saleh's old abandoned castle had some nice decoration about it. They left it because there were so many jinni (*i.e.* ghosts) in it. Our informant had not seen them, but only heard of them.

March the 12th my husband went up what he thought was the highest mountain of the Goddam range, Minzoko, just behind Naab, and made it 2,000 feet, but considered when he got to the top that its neighbour Haidenaab was 300 or 400 feet higher. The Tarik Minzoko goes between them.

The sultan sent to our camp some bowls of food, soup, and a fowl cut up and cooked in gravy, very rich with oil and onions. It would have been good but for the stuffy, bitter taste of myrrh, which they like so much to put in their food. He also sent us red cakes of millet bread.

A poet of Naab made a *merghazi* on us during our stay, about our treatment by the Yafei sultan: how he had demanded money of us and how he had bidden us return to Aden. This was thought so excellent by everybody that my husband was forced to take a copy of it from dictation and Sultan Salem took a copy back to Shukra.

Our party was now increased by another 'prince,' Sultan Haidar, son of the sultan of Naab, a person delightful to contemplate. He was got up in Bedou style; his hair, fluffy and long, was tied back by a fillet and stuck out in a bush behind. He had a curious countenance and very weak eyes. He was wrapped in a couple of large blue cotton cloths with very long fringes, half a yard at least. The cotton is plastered with indigo, even beyond the dye, and when calendered, as the clothes are when new, gleam purple and red. The richer you are the bluer you are, and Sultan Haidar was very blue indeed. The curious thing about these blue people is that, as the prominent parts of the face and body are the darkest, there is an odd inside-out effect.

While in Naab we had our usual number of patients, but the one we were most interested in was a woman who had a dreadfully sore foot. The foot was very much swollen, and there was a sore on her instep and ankle in which one could nearly put one's fist. This had never been washed, though it had been going on for some years, and it had a dressing composed of half a pound or so of dates stuffed into it. The poor creature lay on a sort of bedstead or *charpai* in a tidy little house consisting of one room and lighted only by the door.

My husband set off at once half a mile back to camp to fetch the necessary relief and I waited, sitting on a cloak that someone rolled up on the floor, for there was not even a carpet to sit on. I was afraid of various insects, but I could not rudely stand, and I should have had to stand a good time as my husband had a mile to walk.

When he returned he syringed the sore with Condy's fluid and I cleaned it with bits of wadding, and the woman with her nails in a way that made me shudder, but she did not seem to hurt herself. Then we put on zinc ointment. She drew her bedding from under her foot so that the water streamed through the bed to the floor, which was earthen and below the level of the door. There was a big puddle, of course, and I feared they would have mud to contend with, but a woman soon came with a basketful of dry sand, and by constantly brushing it up when wet into a palm-leaf dustpan quickly cleaned up all the mess.

We went daily to attend to this foot and at last, if not much better, it was improved by becoming thoroughly clean, foot, leg and all, and its poor owner was cheered and looked much brighter herself.

We left her all the zinc ointment we had remaining to use first; a milk-tinful of ointment, composed by me from pure lanoline, vaseline, and zinc powder, to go on with, and some grease-proof paper to spread it on, a lot of tabloids of permanganate of potash and directions to pour it from a water vessel, very clean.

Before the family would undertake to receive these final instructions we had to wait while some elderly persons were fetched, reputed wiseacres evidently, and it was like teaching a class. The poor things, with such earnest faces, were determined to make very sure they all thoroughly understood what to do. An old man took each thing and handed it to the husband, telling him how to use it, and we all consulted as to the best niches in the roof in which to stow the things safely. They, at least, longed for us to stay, and we felt sorry to go. One feels so helpless face to face with such misery. I do hope she got well.

The first day we visited this house a great crowd came after us, but they were turned out with sticks and fastened out in a very ingenious way.

Most of the houses are surrounded by a fence of prickly brushwood, in which is an entrance 3 or 4 feet wide. Outside this stands, on its head, with its root in the air, a bush. The root has a rope of twisted palm-leaf attached to it. You enter and pull the rope. The bush stands on its side then and blocks up the entrance; the rope is secured inside to a bar which is fixed across the threshold and no one can pass this strange and thorny gate. The bush is, of course, wider than the gateway.

Certainly Arabians are not all that one expect. I never can believe that Mohammedans in general can consider dogs so very unclean, when they have so many about them, and one tribe in the Soudan is called Kilab (dogs). We used to hear also that they all shaved their heads, leaving one lock only for Mohammed to draw them up into

Heaven. Instead of this they do all kinds of things to their hair, and the only people I ever saw with one lock were the Yourouks in Asia Minor, and I think it was only a fashion.

Fadhli at Shariah, Wadi Reban, with Curious Sandal

Some people think that all the rude efforts of aborigines and uncultivated tribes are inspired by truer wisdom than are the results of science and civilisation, and amongst other things, turbans are pointed out to us as an instance of the good sense of people in hot climates, who know how necessary it is to protect their heads from the sun. If so, why do some cover their heads with turbans and some not? and why do those who wear turbans take them off to cool their heads in the sun, and some accidentally leave a bit of head exposed when they put the turban on without ever finding it out? Some never cover the middle of the head at all, but only wind the turban round. My theory, which may be wrong, is that it is really worn for ornament, as a diadem in the original sense of the word, just tied round the head as a mark of dignity.

Once or twice, our camp being on the far side of the valley from the town, we managed to give the slip to the spearman who otherwise would have accompanied us, and sneaked up a very narrow little wadi, where we found a good many flowers and enjoyed this very much.

Wild beasts live in holes in these hills, and on the extreme top of the mountain my husband ascended, was found a big goat that had been killed in the wadi the night before. A little hairy animal called *ouabri* was brought to our camp.

When we left Naab we turned into the Wadi Reban to Shariah—three hours and ten minutes, seven geographical miles, four north-east and three north—and ascended 350 feet. Wadi Reban is a quarter of a mile wide near Naab, but after two miles opens out; and there are gardens, and now and again running water appears, and plenty of trees. At the fourth mile, near a fort, we turned sharply to the north, past Jebel Riah, where Wadi Riah comes in, and then reached a wide open space, where Wadi Silib joins in. Jebel Shaas was beyond us, very high, and Wadi Ghiuda to the right. This large open space is girt with mountains 500 to 5,000 feet high, and is a great junction for the waters from Wadis Reban, Silib, and Ghiuda. It was once exceedingly populous; there are here no less than four old villages called Shariah; two considerable towns were perched on the rocks, forming gates to the Wadi Silib, and two others at a great elevation on the opposite side. The cause of the decrease in population in Arabia must be the constant inter-tribal warfare and the gradual filling up of the valleys with sand. Great banks of sand 20 feet high line the river-beds, and wash away with the heavy rains, which contribute to the silting up. This country must have been very fertile to have supported the population, for the four towns must have been large. The stone buildings alone would make any one of the four larger than most towns in Arabia to-day, and there must have been the usual hut population. We had a very pleasant camp among trees, and had a steep scramble to the ruins.

An enthusiastic geologist would have enjoyed our next day's journey immensely; we went through such a strange weird volcanic valley—not a wadi, but a sheb, narrower and shallower. The road is called Tarik Sauda. The strata of the rocks are heaved up at a very steep angle, and we had to ride along smooth rocks, sometimes without any trace of a road at all among the stones; sometimes we had to make very great windings amongst heaps and hillocks of all sorts of different-coloured earths. Hardly a green thing was to be seen, and altogether the whole place looked dreary and desolate; but we were much interested in this day's journey among the great scarred and seamed volcanic mountains. We ascended 650 feet—very difficult indeed, travelling about seven miles in four hours; the steepest part is called Akaba Sauda. We reached the headwater of the Wadi Ghiuda at the top of the akaba, 2,000 feet from sea level. Naab is 1,000 feet above sea level; thence to Shariah is 350; and thence to Ghiuda, 650. We passed Dogoter and M'Haider, mere names. We encamped on a waste of stones; no tent-pegs could be used, and it was windy and cold.

There are gazelle in this part and we had some for dinner.

Now was our time to send by Musaben to the camp of the sultans three very gay blankets for them and Abdullah-bin-Abdurrahman. The long name of the wazir's father had constantly to be on our lips on account of his dignity, for they are like the Russians in that respect—common people's fathers are not mentioned. The name was marvellously shortened to B'd'rahman. We were thought to be in danger that night, and did not make a very early start, as we had to load up water; and we two climbed down 350 feet into the Wadi Ghiuda, that I might take photographs. It was so pretty, with pools of water and creepers hanging on the trees.

The sultans, meanwhile, sat up in their beds of leaves wrapped in their blankets. How absurd it seems that two princes and a prime minister should have to sleep out because two English choose to travel in their country! Not a word of thanks did we ever get for those blankets, but they were evidently much appreciated, for their recipients sat on their camels wrapped over head and ears in them in the blazing sun.

CHAPTER XXXVII

FROM THE PLAIN OF MIS'HAL TO THE SEA

We joined the camels on the way, and after two hours of stones ascended the very steep Akaba Beva. The view from the hills above—about 2,500 feet—is splendid, all the Yafei mountains and the Goddam range ending at Haide Naab, and giving place to the higher mountains of Rekab and Ghiuda. We descended, but not much, into the lovely Wadi Hadda, full of trees smothered with a kind of vine with thick glossy indiarubber-like leaves; then we went on straight up Akaba Hadda to the huge plain of Mis'hal, full of villages, but ill-supplied with water. There are only some very bad wells for the cattle, and they have to fetch drinking-water from afar, from Ghenab and Lammas. We engaged a Bedou's camel to keep us supplied, while resting our own. The plain is 2,700 feet above the sea. The sheikh's name is Mohommod-bin-Nasr Nakai; this is the first time we heard this pronunciation of the Prophet's name. He was determined to give us a grand reception. Sheikh Seil had gone forward to announce us from Ghiuda, and he came to meet us on his pony down both akabas—a fearful journey.

We always liked Sheikh Seil very much. He was the sheikh of Dirgheg. His hair and his shaggy chest were not white, but a lovely sky-blue. In that part of the world old people's hair is not dyed red with henna, as it is in other parts of Arabia and Asia Minor and in Persia, so the effect of the indigo can be seen.

From a distance we could see the preparations. There was a long line on the sandy plain of between two and three hundred Bedouin, naked save for a blue scarf round their waists, with dagger, powder-horn, &c., stuck in. Some had guns, matchlocks, and some had spears. They mostly had their long hair tied up and sticking out in a fuz behind, as funny a long line of men as ever one saw.

We dismounted, nearly a quarter of a mile off, and all our party advanced hand-in-hand, fourteen besides ourselves and Matthaios, we being the only ones who did not know the words in which to chant our response to the welcoming shout. This they interrupted occasionally by the high gurgling sound they are so fond of, constantly coming out of the rank, one or other, and firing a gun and retiring. The blue-bearded Sheikh Seil galloped up and down in front of us, twirling his spear. We stopped 150 yards from them, and after much more firing the spearmen began to parade before us in a serpentine way, two and two, backwards and forwards, zigzag, and round and round the gunners, gradually getting nearer and nearer to us, and dragging the gunners after them, with a red flag, a seyyid, and their sheikh, Mohommod-bin-Nasr, between them. When they got quite close they welcomed us, and we said 'Peace' to them. They passed us so many times that we could see and notice them well. Some were very tall; one who was very lame led his tiny little boy. The lancers danced very prettily, having a man a little way in front of them executing wild capers and throwing up his spear and catching it, singing all the while songs of welcome. We could not understand more than some allusions, which assured us they were composed for the occasion. After many gyrations they retired to their former place, and then a herald came forward and made a solemn address of welcome.

Village of Mis'hal

Then our turn came, and we sent forth a line of men with Sultan Haidar in it to sing and let off guns. When the two lines met they shook hands and kissed, the sultans and seyyids being kissed on the forehead and the upper part of the leg. When they returned to us all our party joined hands to go to our camp, now ready, a good distance off, all keeping step in a kind of stilted, prancing way, singing. The spearmen in front danced with all manner of light and graceful antics, and we were nearly stifled with the dust; and the din was so appalling that we arrived quite dazed at our tents after this welcome, which had lasted fully an hour. We were the first white people who had been at Mis'hal. I tore my camera from its case to take a photograph before the people left us, and it did better than I could have expected in such a crowd, with no sun and so much whirling dust. The town consists of a low square dar and a collection of brushwood arbours, so slight that there is no pretension of concealing anything that goes on inside. We were very thankful for a large pot of coffee and ginger, sent by a sultan, and a fat lamb. The princes ventured to leave us in charge of Abdullah-bin-Abdurrahman, and abode in the tower. Sultan Haidar went home from here.

The tableland of Mis'hal is approached by three akabas: (1) Sauda, to 2,000 feet; (2) Beva, to 2,500 feet; (3) Hadda, to 2,750 feet. The Nakai tribe live here, and are on friendly terms with their neighbours the Fadhli—a sufficiently rare circumstance in this country. The Nakai chief can put four hundred men in the field to help the Fadhli. The Markashi were at war with them; they live in the Goddam range, and had been giving the sultan trouble lately.

The road to Shukra most frequented is the Tarik el Arkob; eastward goes the road to the Hadhramout, over the plain. Northward is the mountainous country of the Aòdeli tribe, where they told us 'it is sometimes so cold that the rain is hard and quite white, and the water like stone.' The plain is ten or fifteen miles long, by about four or five miles at its broadest. If irrigated it would yield enormously. The well is of great depth, but the water very bad. My husband ascended a mountain about 3,000 feet high, but only 400 feet above the plain, with a most remarkable view of the Aòdeli mountains, about twenty miles away, towering up to a great height—far higher than the Yafei range, which Mr. Tate gives as 7,000 feet: these are probably 10,000 feet. The range must run for thirty or forty miles from east to west, with few breaks and no peaks. We were not well the last day at Mis'hal.

The Aòdeli women paint red lines under their eyes and down their noses and round their foreheads with a kind of earth-dye which they call *hisn*. Sometimes there is a round spot on the forehead and red triangles on the cheeks. One woman had her face literally dyed scarlet all over. She had a heavy necklace of beads and carried the sheep-skin coat, that she could not wear in the hot plain, rolled up and laid on her head. It is curious how dissatisfied dark people seem to be with the colour of their skins, so often trying to lighten it; the fairness of the English is in some places attributed to the soap they use.

We took advantage of the curiosity of the Aòdeli, who had just arrived with a *kafila*, to make them stay in our camp and question them. The El Khaur mountains look most fascinating to see only from a distance: they are inhabited by lawless tribes owing allegiance to no man, and, having no wholesome fear of the Wali of Aden before their eyes, would murder any traveller who ventured among them; they are all Bedouin. The Aòdeli are a very large tribe, and say they have 4,000 men for war; the Markashi can put 500 or 600 in the field; and the Fadhli 2,000. Lauda, the chief town of the Aòdeli, is much bigger than Shibahm; there are many Arabs. The sultan is Mohamed-bin-Saleh. It is six hours from Mis'hal—thirty-four miles—and is situated below the mountains. Above it is El Betha—Sultan Saleh. Belad el Megheba, in the upper Yafei country, is under Sultan Hakam Mohamed-bin-Ali. Sabad el Baida Resass (where there must be lead) is not under the Turks; El Aòdeli live there. Neither is Sahib Lauda under the Turks; the inhabitants are Augheri. This has a very soft guttural—the Arabic *ghin*.

Our next stage was Bir Lammas, about four miles off, mostly across the monotonous plain. We passed four dars and villages. In time of war the Fadhli sultan comes and occupies one of these dars. We met sheikhs walking with little battle-axes on long poles—weapons in war, and in peace used for chopping wood, at all times emblems of their rank. The plain at length broke away, and we got into the narrow, and not very deep, wooded Wadi el Mimin. It has very precipitous sides of basalt, brown in colour, and making a very untidy attempt at being columnar. Bir Lammas is a great, and I must add, very dirty, halting-place for caravans going to Shukra, on the Tarik el Arkob, to El Kaur and the Wadi Hadhramout.

Plain of Mis'hal and Aòdeli Tribe

We were two nights at Bir Lammas. I was too ill to go about at all, but I could not resist going out to see some baboons which came to look at us from the low cliffs. I am sure their leader must have been 4 feet long without his tail.

My husband, who went for a climb, came to pretty close quarters with a striped hyena.

We were encamped about 380 yards off from the well, and thought it a very pretty place, with acacia-trees and creepers hanging in long trails and making arbours of all of them. The women do all the work here, having to fetch water from Bir Lammas and Ghenab for Mis'hal. The children, up to fourteen years of age, tend the flocks, and the men stroll about or sit in very warlike-looking conclaves, with guns and spears. Young children have wooden jembias to accustom them to their use, and it is funny to see tiny urchins of three or four hurling reeds at each other in imitation of their elders with more deadly weapons. The Bedouin seem born in an element of war; one we heard of had lasted fifteen years, but was happily now stopped for a little while.

On a hill near the plain, about half a mile from Bir Lammas, there are ruins of good style, probably of the Ashabir period of Hamdani.

We were to ride five hours to the next water after Bir Lammas. I felt it would be an awful journey, as I was becoming more and more inert, but I was able to jump on to my camel as usual. I begged my husband to tell me as each hour passed, being quite determined never to ask too soon, but every time I did ask it turned out to be only twenty minutes from the last time.

We were soon out of Wadi Lammas, and went over stony plains with basalt scattered over them, and no possible place to encamp, which I was keenly on the look-out for. We went through a curious little pass, not high, but a very narrow cutting just wide enough for us to ride through, for 300 yards, and then we had to wind down steeply at the other side over rocks. I began to feel that I had no control over my legs and I hardly cared to change my position for going up or down hill, and once when my camel slipped down about 5 feet, I started to fall off headlong, but a Bedou caught me by my leg and held me on. If I had fallen, as the path was very narrow, the camel would surely have stepped on me. I should certainly have cracked my skull first. Camels are not like horses—they do not object to stepping on people.

A late sultan of Shukra fell from his camel and was trampled on, and 'though the Koran was read to him, and *herris* or talismans were put on him, his breath would not stay in him, but came out in half an hour.' *Herrises* are put on camels to make them strong; my husband's camel had one, of which its master was very proud.

At last we came to the Wadi Samluf, and I begged that we might stop and have a camel fetched for water. I had to be dragged from my camel, and laid in the cinder-like sand till the tent was pitched, for, as my malarial fever was constant, and I had no tertian intervals, I lost my strength completely. Both my husband and I, and several others were very ill, and we were not strong enough to get at our medicine chest. The water was very bad. The Sultan Salem and other grandees camped at the more dangerous open mouth of the valley.

The place where we pitched the tents was very pretty. There were trees and very fantastic peaky rocks against the sky, and a great step about 3 feet high, which had once been a wave of basalt, black on the yellow sand.

The camel-men used to spread their beds and light their fire on this sort of stage by night, but they spent the day under the trees.

The last night we were in the Wadi Samluf there was a great noise— guns firing, parties going out to reconnoitre, and shouting—but it turned out that the new-comers who arrived at such an unseasonable hour were sent by the sultan of Shukra to welcome and escort us.

From this spot I had to be carried to the sea, seventeen miles, on my bed, which was strengthened with tent-pegs and slung on tent-poles. From the little sultan downwards there was not one who did not help most kindly. We went down gently 3,000 feet. I cannot describe this journey, except that it was so very winding that I seemed to see the camels meeting and passing me often. Fortunately the crossing of the low hot Abyan was short.

I dreaded the journey, as I thought my bearers would not keep step, but they did wonderfully well, though of course they had no path to walk in, for two men and the bed were far too wide for any path there was. I saw one man double up his legs and go over a boulder 3 feet or 4 feet high; and they kept me very even too, and only dropped my head once; the bearers changed as smoothly as if they were accustomed to it, and were always saying something kind to me.

I was not pleased at first at being carried off very suddenly head first, but it was certainly sweeter not having all those men in front of me, and I rejoiced in a delicious sea-wind, which blew stronger and stronger, and just seemed to keep me alive. I was very grateful to them, and took good care never to ask if we had still far to go.

How glad I was to find myself in a rushing, roaring, rabble rout of men, women, and children tearing along beside me!—not a thing I generally like, but now it told me of the end of my weary journey. I was deposited on my bed in a tower, tent-pegs and poles removed, and left with a spearman on the doorstep to keep off intruders. The rest of our miserable fever-stricken party came in half an hour later. The sultan of the Fadhli came to our tent to see us—a pleasant-faced mustard-coloured man; and also his wife, the daughter of an Aden sheikh, a very handsome woman. They were very kind in sending milk, watermelons, and any little luxury they could. The sultan lived in a fine brown building with a stunted tower, a glorified Arab house, but nothing like those in the Hadhramout. They send sharks' fins to China from here, as well as from Sokotra and the Somali coast. This is probably Ptolemy's Agmanisphe Kome. It is just the right distance from Arabia-Emporium, *i.e.* one day; so we found it. There was the greatest difficulty in getting a boat, for none of the ships wished to go to Aden, for fear of quarantine, as they would be supposed to be coming from the plague-stricken Bombay. My husband promised 100 rupees for every day, and the sultan compelled a captain whose baggala was loaded for Mokalla to take us to Aden, by refusing to give him his papers otherwise.

Our last moments at Shukra were spent lying on the sand with our heads on a bag, and sheltered by a little bit of sacking on three sticks. The sultan sat over us on a high chair, saying very polite things. We were lifted on board our ship at three o'clock, and from the ship admired Shukra, which looked very picturesque in the evening haze, with its towers, its few trees, and its many-peaked Goddam mountains behind. We reached Aden at three next afternoon. This is all I can write about this journey. It would have been better told, but that I only am left to tell it.

APPENDICES

a

I

LIST OF PLANTS FROM DHOFAR MOUNTAINS, SOUTH-EAST ARABIA, COMMUNICATED BY J. THEODORE BENT, ESQ., TO KEW GARDENS, MAY 1895.

209.	Farsetia near longisiliqua, Dene.	102.	Hibiscus micranthus, L.
12.	Farsetia? (too young)	142.	Hibiscus Trionum, L.
193.	Diplotaxis Harra, Boiss.	66.	Senra incana, Cav. wild cotton
	Dipterygium glaucum, Dene. var.	46.	Malvaceæ, cfr. Senra
163.	Ochradenus baccatus, Delile	206.	Cochorus antichorus, Raesch
195.	Capparideæ		Cochorus trilocularis, L.
132.	Ionidium, n. sp.	80.	Grewia asiatica, L.
186.	Polygala near hohenackeriana, F.& M.	181.	Grewia populifolia, Vahl
114.	Polygala near javana, DC.	54.	Boswellia Carteri, Birdwood
201.	Tammarix mannifera, Ehrenb.	118.	Acridocarpus orientalis, A. Juss.
5.	Frankenia pulverulenta, L.	194.	Dodonæa viscosa, L.
155.	Cleome brachycarpa, Vahl	92.	Vitis quadrangularis, Willd.
1.	Cleome quinquenervia,	137.	Balsamodendron

DC.

Opobalsamum, Kunth

65. Gynandropsis pentaphylla, DC.

93. Indeterminable

60. Capparis spinosa, L.

128. Moringa aptera, Gaertn.

201. Cadaba (incomplete)

3, 79. Zizyphus Spina-Christi, Lam.

136. Cadaba longifolia, R.Br.

185. Celastrus senegalensis, Lam.

208. Polycarpea spicata, W. & A.

30, 199. Ruta tuberculata, Forsk.

156. Gypsophila montana, Balf. fil.

116. Tribulus alatus, Delile

173. Gossypium Stocksii, Mast.

4. Tribulus terrestris, L.

82. Pavonia

Zygophyllum album, L.

Pavonia near glechomœfolia, Ehrenb.

17. Fagonia arabica, L.

39. Abutilon graveolens, W. & A.

Fagonia Luntii, Baker

61, 225. Abutilon indicum, Don.

68. Fagonia, n. sp. near Luntii and latifolia

232. Abutilon near indicum, Don.

157. Acacia Senegal, Willd.

127, 135. Abutilon fructicosum, G. & P.

205. Acacia verugera, Schweinf.

212. Sida humilis, Willd.

69. Cassia, n. sp., near C. holosericea, Fres.

151. Hibiscus vitifolius, L.

22. Indigofera? (incomplete)

73, 150. Withania somnifera, Dunal (Muscat)

16.	Indigofera arabica, J. & S.	16.	Hyoscyamus muticus, L.? (Muscat)
36.	Indigofera paucifolia, Delile	140.	Dæmia extensa, R.Br.
9, 103.	Indigofera argentea, L.	71.	Dæmia cordata, R.Br.
226.	Psoralea corylifolia, L.	230.	Pentatropsis cynanchoides, R.Br.
213.	Argyrolobium roseum, J. & S.	154.	Adenium obesum, R. & S.
170.	Rhynchosia minima, DC.	104.	Azima tetracantha, Lam.
74.	Sesbania punctata, Pers.	141.	Salvadora persica, L.
13, 84.	Tephrosia purpurea, Pers. (Muscat)	162.	Plumbago zeylanica, Linn.
47.	Papilionaceæ, not determinable	97.	Vogelia indica, Gibs. (V. arabica, Boiss.)
146.	Oldenlandia Schimperi, T. And.	199.	Anagallis latifolia, L.
122.	Anogeissus	106.	Jasminum officinale, L.
143.	Woodfordia floribunda, Salisb.	13.	Statice axillaris, Forsk.
48.	Pimpinella Tragium, Vill.	115.	Trichodesma
182?	Cephalandra indica, Naud.	168.	Hyoscyamus n. sp.
200.	Cucurbitaceæ (flowers racemosa, male)	15.	Arnebia hispidissima, Forsk.
11.	Cucumis prophetarum, L. (Muscat)	126.	Cordia Rothii, R. & S.
222.	Mollugo hirta, Thunb. (M. Glinus, A. Rich.)	1.	Heliotropium undulatum, Vahl
15,	Trianthema near T.	86.	Heliotropium ovalifolium,

175.	pentandra, L.		Forsk.
158, 223.	Eclipta erecta, L.	12.	Heliotropium drepanophyllum, Baker
25, 232, 220.	Vernonia cinerea, Less.	121.	Heliotropium zeylanicum, Lam.
51, 3.	Vernonia atriplicifolia, J. & S.	21.	Lithospermum callosum, Vahl
196.	Conyza stricta, Willd.	125.	Ipomæa blepharosepala, Hochst.
37, 9.	ex parte Blumea Jacquemonti, Clarke	214.	Ipomæa (indeterminable)
9.	ex parte Pluchea	112.	Ipomæa purpurea, Lam.
7.	ex parte Pluchea	227.	Ipomæa hederacea, Jacq.
190.	Gnaphalium luteo-album, L.	144.	Ipomæa obscura, Ker.
40.	Microrhynchus nudicaulis, Less.	119.	Ipomæa palmata, Forsk.
228.	Pulicaria arabica, Cass.	61.	Ipomæa biloba, Forsk. (Pescapræ)
171.	Pulicaria leucophylla, Baker		Ipomæa Batatas, Lam.
81.	Pulicaria sp.	229.	Ipomæa near Lindleyi, Choisy
192.	Carthamus (Kentrophyllum)	147, 148.	Ipomæa (Capitatæ) sp.
188.	Echinops spinosus, L.	63.	Convolvulus arvensis, L.
35.	Centaurea near Calictrapa, L.	55.	Convolvulus (Rectæ)
221.	Lactuca (Ixeris)	64.	Cressa cretica, Linn.

235.	Lactuca orientalis, Boiss.	113.	Hypoestes verticillaris, R.Br.
233.	Lactuca cretica, Desf.?	83.	Ruellia?
160, 234, 109.	Lactuca? (too incomplete)	107.	Ruellia patula, Jacq.
149.	Solanum nigrum, L.	50, 184.	Ruellia spp.
23.	Solanum melongena, L.	110.	Acanthus sp.
6.	Solanum xanthocarpum jacquinii, Dunal	87.	Barleria acanthoides, Vahl
96.	Barleria Hochstetteri, nus	95, 174.	Barleria spp.
166.	Neuracanthus?	100.	Neuracanthus?
108.	Ruttya (Haplanthera speciosa Hochst.)	61.	Halocnemum fruticosum, Moquin
224.	Justicia debilis, Vahl		Cornulaca monacantha, Delile
91.	Justicia simplex, D. Don.	101.	Chrozophora obliqua, Vahl
145.	Justicia sp.	139.	Dalechampia scandens, L.
14; 72.	Lippia nodiflora, Rich.	57, 131.	Acalypha indica, L.
187.	Striga.	231.	Croton near C. sarcocarpus, Balf. fil.
11.	Striga orobanchoides, Benth.	90.	Euphorbia arabica, H. & S.
237.	Striga hirsuta, Benth.	120.	Jatropha spinosa, Vahl
167.	Scrophularia?		Jatropha villosa, Mull. Arg.
2.	Linaria macilenta, Dene.		Jatropha lobata, Mull. Arg.
76, 85.	Lindenbergia fruticosa,	165.	Phyllanthus sp.

Benth.

78.	Orobanche cernua, Loefl.	9.	Phyllanthus sp. (Muscat)
183.	Lantana salviæfolia, Jacq.	172.	Phyllanthus, sp. rotundifolius, Linn.
111.	Lindenbergia? (incomplete)	81.	Phyllanthus (Muscat)
238.	Herpestis Monnieria, H. B. K.	180, 105, 133.	Phyllanthus
164.	Lavandula setifera, T. And.	159, 210.	Ceratopteris thalictroides, Brong.
	Coleus aromaticus, Benth.?	75.	Cheilanthes farinosa, Kaulf.
152.	Orthosiphon near Kirkii, Baker	59.	Adiantum caudatum, Linn.
79.	Orthosiphon tenuiflorus, Benth.	59.	Nephrodium odoratum, Baker
191.	Ocimum menthæfolium, Hochst.	56.	Pteris longifolia, Linn.
198.	Teucrium (Stachyobotrys)?	218.	Chara hispida, Linn.
169.	Teucrium (Pohlium)	71, 123.	ex parte Commelyna Forskalie, Vahl
10, 27.	Digera arvensis, Forsk.	123.	ex parte Commelyna albescens, Hassk.
177, 178.	Celosia trigyna, L.	203.	ex parte Scirpus littoralis, Schrad
34.	Achyranthes aspera, L.	203.	ex parte Juncellus laevigatus, C. B. Clarke
98.	Pupalia lappacea, Moquin	138.	Eleocharis capitata, R.Br.

5.	Boerhaavia ascendens, Willd.	41, 134.	Cyperus rotundus, Linn.
14.	Boerhaavia elegans, Choisy	28.	Cyperus conglomeratus, Rottb.
24.	Boerhaavia plumbaginea, Cav.	189.	Asparagus racemosus, Willd.
89.	Boerhaavia (leaves only)	217.	Naias minor, All.
4.	Cometes abyssinica, R.Br.	219.	Naias major, All.
67.	Euphorbia n. sp. (cultivated at Kew from Hadhramout)	153.	ex parte Pancratium tortuosum, Herb.
236.	Euphorbia cuneata, Vahl?	153.	ex parte Hæmanthus arabicus, Roem.?
42.	Euphorbia cactus, Ehrenb.	94.	Typha angustifolia, Linn.
197.	Euphorbia adenenis, Deflers	31.	Juncus maritimus, Linn.
129.	Euphorbia sp.	216.	Potamogeton pectinatus, Linn.
2, 53.	Euphorbia indica, Lam.	211.	Potamogeton natans, Linn.
37.	Aristolochia bracteata, Retz.		Panicum Crus-galli, Linn.
88.	Forskohlea tenacissima, L.	176.	Cynodon Dactylon, L.
4.	Ficus salicifolia, Vahl	204.	Phragmites communis, Trin.
51, 70, 130.	Chenopodium murale, L.	52.	Latipes senegalensis, Kunth.
38.	Amarantus Blitum, L.	44.	Salsola verrucosa, M. B.
161.	Polygonum glabrum, Willd.	20, 215.	Suæda fruticosa, Forsk.

4.   Suæda baccata, Forsk.?

49.	Aristida caloptila, Boiss.	26.	Panicum geminatum, Forsk.
45.	Pennisetum cenchroides, Pers.	18.	Æluropus litoralis, Parl. var. repens.
32, 202.	Sporobolus spicatus, Vahl	32.	Heleochloa dura, Pers.
29.	Eleusine ægyptiaca, Pers.	43.	Apluda aristata, Linn.

II

A LIST OF THE LAND AND FRESHWATER SHELLS COLLECTED IN SOKOTRA BY MR. AND MRS. THEODORE BENT

By Edgar A. Smith, F.Z.S., Assistant Keeper of Zoology, British Museum.

Previous to the researches of Mr. and Mrs. Bent, only forty-eight land and freshwater molluscs had been recorded from Sokotra. In addition to twenty-three of these species, they were fortunate in obtaining eleven new forms, some of them very remarkable. These have been described and figured by the writer in the 'Journal of Malacology,' vol. vi. pp. 33-38, plate v., figs. 1-9. and in the 'Bulletin of the Liverpool Museum,' vol. ii. No. 1, p. 12. The British Museum is much indebted to Mrs. Bent for the donation of this valuable collection.

A. Terrestrial Species

1.	Buliminus Passamaianus	16.	Stenogyra insculpta, n. sp.
2.	Buliminus Balfouri	17.	Stenogyra decipiens, n. sp.
3.	Buliminus mirabilis, n. sp.	18.	Stenogyra Jessica
4.	Buliminus Bentii, n. sp.	19.	Stenogyra adonensis
5.	Buliminus rotundus, n. sp.	20.	Ennea cylindracea, n. sp.
6.	Buliminus socotorensis	21.	Succinea sp.
7.	Buliminus semicastaneus	22.	Otopoma Balfouri
8.	Buliminus Balfouri	23.	Otopoma complanatum
9.	Buliminus hadibuensis	24.	Otopoma clathratulum
10.	Buliminus fragilis	25.	Otopoma conicum
11.	Buliminus fusiformis	26.	Tropidophora socotrana

12. Buliminus acutus, n. sp.   27. Lithidion marmorosum

13. Buliminus innocens, n. sp.   28. Lithidion Bentii, n. sp.

13a. Buliminus Theodoræ, n. sp. 29. Cyclotopsis radiolata

14. Stenogyra socotrana   30. Auricula socotrensis, n. sp.

15. Stenogyra enodis

B. Freshwater Species

31. Melania tuberculata 32. Planorbis sp. 33. Planorbis sp.

III

We bought in Aden a fragment of alabasteroid limestone, said to have come from the Hadhramout. It is broken on all sides. It is part of a perpendicular series of sunken square fields, on each of which is represented in flat relief a sitting or lying goat or chamois with enormous horns. My fragment has two complete goats and parts of another above as well as below. The goats look to the right, and there are some cuttings which may have been part of an inscription on the surface of the stone to the right of the column of goats. The squares are 4 inches high by 3½ inches wide—10 centimetres by about 9.

Fragment of Alabasteroid Limestone

That these goats must have some significance is clear from their likeness to the following objects in the Hof Museum at Vienna, and figured in 'Süd Arabische Alterthümer,' by Prof. Dr. D. H. Müller. The first is the lower part of a slab, complete on three sides with a plain surface down the middle, and columns of goats in squares just like that described above, on either side, the goat facing inwards. In neither of these cases can one know how many goats were originally represented.

The second is an architectural fragment composed of alabasteroid limestone (yellowish in colour), 0.120 centimetres high, 0.202 long, 0.15 thick (so far as it remains).

It represents seven chamois (or goats) lying in a row. The heads are coarsely formed, the eyes like knobs, and the bodies of the two animals which are outside are indicated in profile. The original use of the object is uncertain, but, in any case, it must have been a topmost ornament, for the under-side, though regularly smoothed, is not polished like the other surfaces, and therefore cannot have been meant to be seen.

The trough which we brought from Al Gran is of the same stone as the former objects. It is 2 feet long by 11 inches wide and 4 inches high. It has an inscription containing a dedication to the God Sayan or Seiyin running all round it and finishing on one side of the top. In the top there is a depression sloping towards a spout, which is now broken off all but an inch. The depth of the depression is from one quarter to half an inch, and the channel in the spout runs down to three-quarters of an inch. Prof. Dr. D. H. Müller has kindly translated this inscription, which appears to represent it as an altar. He thinks it must be for frankincense, but I think it must have been for some liquid. The inscription on the end opposite the spout is worn by marks of ropes being dragged against it.

Sabæan Antiquities

1. The Seal of Yarsahal (front view).

2. Copper Seal with Sabota on it.

3. A Pottery Stamp (back view).

4. An Alabaster Lamp.

5. Alabaster Mace Head (?)

6. A Pottery Stamp (front view).

7. The Seal of Yarsahal (side view).

8. An Alabaster Lamp (bottom).

9. Fragment of a Himyaritic Inscription.

We bought an object of fine alabaster in Aden. It was said to come from the Hadhramout. It seems like a seal or stamp and has a hollow round the back, with spouts in either of the short sides. It had been used as a lamp when we obtained it. There is a kind of handle or tube pierced through to the front, probably for suspension.

In the same illustration are also part of an earthenware stamp and the seal of *Yarsahal, the younger of Shibahm,* with its golden setting, and a copper seal with *Sabota* on it.

IV

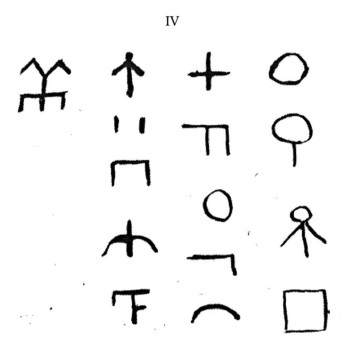

Letters Distinguishable of an almost obliterated inscription near
Haidi village, near Kalenzia, Sokotra, copied by Theodore Bent

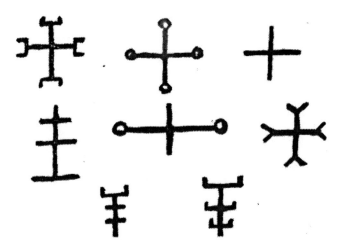

Crosses at *Dihaiterere* on the hill Ditrerre, a spur of Hamar, Sokotra. A perfect mass of crosses, the various shapes of which, on the rocks, were copied by Theodore Bent

Shape of a piece of wood from bone cave at Minèsha, Ras Momi, Sokotra

Sokotra camel marks, collected by Theodore Bent, 1897

V

SOKOTERI AND MAURI WORDS COLLECTED BY THEODORE BENT IN THE ISLAND OF SOKOTRA, HE ASKING THE QUESTIONS IN ARABIC

The transliteration of the second, fourth, and fifth columns is according to the system of the Royal Geographical Society.

English	Dialect used in South Arabia but not in all instances confined to it	Literary Arabic	Mahri	Sokoteri
Fort	Ḥisn	Ḥisn	Hazn	Husn
Spring-fountain	'Ain	'Ain	Mayou	Neshodehin
Pickaxe	Kismah	—	Kasm	Esher
Friend	Ḥabīb	Ḥabīb	Mahabba sidi	Mahabba habiba
Moon	Kamar, Bedr	Qamar, Badr	Kubkob, Warra	Kubkob, Ehri
Funeral	Ghināzah	Ganāzah	Ghinozet	Ghineza
Game (prey)	Ṣaid	Ṣaid	Nehàmel melbetzà	Tahari
Give me	Aṭini	'Aṭini	Zemi	Endakhemu
Glass	Kizāz	Qazāz	Logut	Arashi
Glorious	Galīl	Galīl	Anno	Lubak

Hair	Sha'r	Sha'r	Shuf	Thlef
Half	Niṣf or Nus	Niṣf	Nuss	Nuss
Where	Fein	Fein	Fein	Fein
What	Eish or Ei	Esh	Heshendi	Inimdi
No matter	Mal'eish	—	Laktlela	Bithiokhthi
Thank you	Katterkhair ak	Katharkhair ak	Katerkhair ak	Tarmunkete
Stand here	Stanni hinna	—	Sarbuhun	Takozha'a
Straight	Dogri	Dughrī	Hebkalaze rom (or Hepka)	Torrnà
Blessed	Umbārrak or Mubārrak	Mubārak	Umbarrak	Umbarak
Stop	Wakkaf	Waqqaf	Solop	Tzullebaha
Hammer	Shākoush, Hafir	—	Efeie	Taferra
Hang	Shanak	Shanaq	Azab	Khlanak
Hand	Yad	Yad	Hed	Ed
Anchorage	Mèrsa	Marsā	Moïsi	Moïsi
Headache	Wagà er ras	Waga'-ar-rās	Abkos erayhe	Ellak ade
Often	Ketiran-Tamèlli	Kathīran	Yehoda mekin	Denafakin
Oil	Zeit	Zait	Shigar	Shigar
Onion	Baṣal	—	Bosalet	Basahal
Water	Moya	Miyāh	Hamou	Diho Riho
Mountain	Ghebel	Gabal	Ghebel	Fèdehan

Milk	Leben	Laban	Khlof	Khlof
Stone	Ḥagar	Ḥagar	Hoben	Oben
Bread	Khubs	Khubz	Khobs	Eshere
Date	Nakhl	Na<u>kh</u>l	Nakelet	Tamari
Man	Ragul	Rajal	Reigh	Eik
True	Shagara	<u>Sh</u>ajar	Shighered	Sherehom
Far	Baïd	Ba'īd	Dahak	Sherehek
Near	Garīb	Qarīb	Garib	Sheiki
Well	Bir	Bir	Bir	Abahur
Sheep	Ghanem	Ghanam	Kheoz	Oz
Horse	Khail	Khail	Ferehe	Khail
Camel	Gemel	Gamal	Berr[13]	Berr
Sea	Bahar	Baḥr	Dorum	Denhem
Sand	Raml	Raml	Battar	Shimeh
Garment	Toub	—	Beraka	Farak berekà
Move	Shihl	—	Shilleil	Tizàminha
Before	Kabl	Qabl	Ksobba	Goddam shei
Name	Ism	Ism	Hemukōmn	Mormùkshom
Bed	Ferash	Firāsh	Juderi	Gudere
Sun rises	Sherug esh shems	Sharūg-ush-shams	Skerkot Nayoum	Sherkot Nashom
Light	Kafīf	<u>Kh</u>afif	Dernekfif	Manghena
Gold	Dahàb	Tahab	Deheb	Deheb
Iron	Ḥadīd	Ḥadīd	Hadid	Hadìd
Silver	Fadda	Faḍḍaḍ	Derehem	Derahin
Cloth	Kamash	Qumāsh	Dizhid	Shöd'hem

Cloud	Sahal	Saḥābah?	Afoùr	Hehour
Judge	Kadi	Qādī	Kadi	Kaldi
Take	Emsak *or* Emsik	Imsāk	Elkof	Telö
Satan	Shaiṭān	Shaiṭan	Shaitan	Markush
Difficult	Sabi	Sabi'	Sabi	Marhere
Evening meal	Asher	'Ashā	Izhhè	Teloimö
Midday	Dohr	Dhuhr	Tohr	Vohr
Place	Makan	Makām	Mèkon	D'half
Face	Wagh	Wajh	Weggi	Fenè
Faith	Din	Dīn	Dīn	Izalīhen
Family	Ahl	Ahl	Oher	Dehihkag'-haiho
Fat	Semen	Samn	Mahar	Hammi
Feast	Eid	'Id	Eid	Ayed
Fever	Humma	Ḥummā	Dighilo	Ghiohör
Little	Khalìl	Khalīl	Ihnil (*or* Eint)	Herèrhen, *or* (Ererihen)
—	Melane	—	Millè	Millì
Finger	Aṣbu' aṣabe'	Uṣbu', Aṣba'	Asba	Esba asali
Flea	Barghùt	Bargauth	Gheròse	Gheroz
Fool	Khailak	Aḥmaq	Khailak	Diddo
Saddle	Sarga	Sarga	Zmel	Zmel
Dog	Kelb	Kalb	Kelb	Not known; no word
Sheep	Kharūfa	—	Tiwit	Te'eh

Salt	Melḥ	Malḥ	Milhoda	Milh
Knife	Sikkīn	Sikkīn	Ais	Sari
Fish	Semek	Samak	Seit	Zode
It is necessary— you must	Lāzim	Lāzim	Lazerom	Na'ah
Enough	Bas	Bas	Bas	Ta'ad
One	Wāḥad	Wāḥad	Tat	Tat
Two	Itnein	Ithnaīn	Tro	Tra
Three	Talāta	Thalātha	Saratit	Talele
Four	Arba'	Arba'	Arbote	Arbaa
Five	Khamsa	Khamsa	Khams	Khamse
Six	Sitta	Sitta	Itìt	Sitta
Seven	Saba'	Saba'	Ibeìt	Saba
Eight	Tamania	Thamānia	Timminè	Tamania
Nine	Tissa'	Tisa'	Zeit	Testa
Ten	'Ashera	'Ashara	Aserait	Ashera
Twenty	'Ishrin	'Ishrīn	Asherin	Ishrin
One hundred	Mia	Miat	Mieit	Mia
Work	Shugh	Shaghl	Fìsa	Mahalèh
Wound, sore	Gurrèh	Garūh	Sob	Gourèh
Pain	Waggà	Waga'	Debkhos	Erlakh
Medicine	Dàwa	Dawā	Dewar	Tofin-i-dewar
Sun	Shems	Shams	Hayoum	Shehem
Ready	Ṭaīr	Ṭaīr	Akabìt	Souèdon
Butter	Zùbda	—	Makozo	Gotomìne

I	Àna	—	Hèmukom òn	Evumuksham
You	Enta	Antam	Minesmuk	Minmuksham
He	Hū	Hū	Hou	—
Rope	Ḥabl	Ḥabl	Keit	Enkhar
Son, boy	Welèd	Walad	Aghiēn̄	Mukshin
Daughter	Bint	Bint	Aghinot	Fèrhin
Woman	Horma	Ḥurma	Haremet	Azhè
Wood	Hattab	Ḥaṭab	Hatab	Tirob
Strong	Kawi	Qavī	Musireh	Musirak
War	Harb	Ḥarb	Harb shehen	Harb shehen
More	Kamàn	Kam-min Lawa	Ashishfisa ʼ, Fileh'nicit eh, Riàh	Ta'alt'hefisa, Feleh'ntodèh Dā
Price	Tamàn	Thaman	Soueh	Tetenà
Meat	Laḥm	Laḥm	Tiwë	Tà
Leg	Rigl	Rijl	Serein	Thlaub
Blood	Dam	Dam	Douri	Durr
Allah	Allah	Allah	Allah	Allah
Deaf	Toursh	Ṭursh	Yehomallah	Doufé
Houses	Bouyoūt	Buyūt	Bouyout	Keke
Seaweed, grass	Ḥashīsh	Hashīsh	Mareh	Röd
Servant	ʼAbd	ʼAbd	Hoyur	Embaha
Slave	Gulam	Ghulam	Gulma	B'thlekum
Tall, long	Ṭawīl	Ṭawīl	Tawīl	Ep

411

(Plural)	Atwàl	Aṭwāl	Tawil	Dihom
Stars	Nagoùm	Nagūm	Negoun	Kabkap
Lesson	Dars	Dars	Kerì	Mukerè
Truth	Hak	Ḥaqq	Hak	Hak
Without truth	Bidùn hak	Bidūn haqq	Hammuk hak	Ekmunk hak
In the house	fi'l beit	fi'l bait	be beit	Tofok, diè min kar
In the night	fi'l leil	fi'l lail	be leil	billeilhe
In the road	fi'l tarīk	fi'l tarīq	be haron	orun
Heal	Shāfī	Shāfī	Bekhairgh	Bekhaeraghe
Heart	Kalb	Qalb	Kalb	Elbi
Heaven	Samā	Samā	Simma	Simma
Heavy	Takil	Ṭhaqil	Takil	Eddak
Heel	Akab	'Aqīb	Akonosh	Konosh
Pig	Khansir	—	Khansir	Khansir
Horn	Karn	Qurn	Kon	Kon
Ready	Ḥadir	Ḥadhir	Hader	Hader
Imperfect	Nākis	Nāqis	Nakuss	Biziankazank bidinya
Impossible	Ghair mumkin	Ghair mumkin	Ghair numkin	Ghair numkin
Possible	Yimkin	Imkān	Yumkin	Yumkin
Indigo	Nīl ṇedal	Nīl	Nihl	Nil
Infant	Ṭifl (iṭfāl pl.)	Ṭifl, Iṭfâl	Atfal	Atfal
Infidel	Kāfir	—	Koffer	Keffer
Ink	Hibr	Hibr	Indud	Medad

Intellect	Akl	'Aql	Okul	Akal
Interpreter	Tergumàn	Targumān	Makaddam	Dehane makaddam
Island	Gezīra	Gazīrah	Gezeira	Gezeira
Jew	Zahoūdi	Yahūdī	Yahoude	Yahoude
Kick	Rafos	—	Erkella	Taràkad
Intelligent	Fahīhm	Fahīm	Fehemdi	Fehem
Kill	Katal	Qatal	Ilbedda	Talata
Kind	Laṯīf	Laṯīf	Altehf	Altuiphin
Arms	Sillah	Silāḥ	Shki	Shko
Soldier	'Askar	'Askar	Askęr	Asker
King	Malik	Malik	Moli	D'hemmel
Arrive	Waṣsala	Waṣala	Wassel	Gidda
Matting-bag	Zambīl	—	Zạṃbil	Zambil
Wise	'Alamah	'Ālim	Alamah dimondi	Dimondish alemah
Cut	Ightsal	—	Hanmel kosorn	Nerdober
Journey	Safar	Safar	Nehassol	Insofar
Tired	Ta'b, Ta'ban	Ta'b-Ta'bān	Ketlak	Resak
Tribe	Kabīla	Qabīlah	Kabila	Kabela
Now	Dilwakhti	Dhi'l waqti	Leasar	Leasar
Learn	Ta'alem	—	Mollum	Ma'alem
Tent	Khīmah, Kheim	Khīmah	Arzhlìt	Stirìht
Sword	Seif	Saif	Keit	Keòttaha
Summer	Shitta	—	Kazem	Kébhor

Right, South	Yemèn	Yamīn	Gezĕmhine	Tiozeminhah
Left, North	Shemàl	Shamāl	Shemīn	Shemin
East	Shark	Sharq	Shurakot haioum	Shom
West	Garbis	Gharb	Ghizote	Attabon
Late evening	Mogreb	Mughrib	Mogareb	Mogareb
How are you	Kheifalak	—	Besherhelt	Alghiorg
To walk	Masha	—	Mehèklaz erom	Entòholnà
Yes	Ewa	Ayyawā	Herrì	Herrì
No	Lā	Lā	—	Deh
Key	Mifta	Miftāh	Mîftàh	Miftàh
To tie	Urbut	Yarbuṭ	Urbut	—
Come here	Ta'al hinna	—	Assab	Tazùm
Give me	Gibli, atini	—	Inkalbo, Atini	Tadidbo Habondishoelae
Take hold	Khod	—	Shelùs	Tza
Kneel down (to a camel)	Baraka	Baraka	Hebrekaber	Terburuk
To-morrow	Bukara	Bukara	Bukarèd, Bukerade	Elli
Afterwards	Badèn	Ba'den	M'gori	Enzat
Before	Goddam	Quddām	Fenouni	Adminlefeni
Inside	Dakhl	Dākhil	Keb	Dakhl or Turko

			Khareg or Barrān	Sheraga or Tcherogehte
Outside	Barra	Barrān	Khareg or Barrān	Sheraga or Tcherogehte
Door	Bāb	Bāb	Bob	Terr
Year	Sanna	Sannah	Senate	Ehno
Week	Shahr	Shahr	Warrakh	Tadkleher
Drunk	Sherab	Sharib	Hamontikè	Nerou
Road	Tarìk	Ṭarīq	Haurim	Haurim
Dead	Mut	Mat	Maut	Zami
To-day	El yom	Al Yaum	Imor	Hair
Day after to-morrow	B'ad Bukra	Ba'd bakarah	Bad gehìn	Dishinzomen
Yesterday	Ems	Ams	Imshi	Imshi
Mosque	Mesjid	Masjid	Masjid	Masjid
Priest	Mollah	Mullā	Ma'alim	Ma'alim
Friday	Gumma	Gama'	Ghimata	Gumma
Cross	Salìb	Mīsān	Mison	Mison
Happy	Mahsŏud	Maḥsûd	Laef	Halut
Together	Sawā	Sawā	Nehanaka fakhari	Entafakhari
Buy	Ishteri	Ishtarạ̄	Hamilthtòr	Intergyer
Above	Fok	Fauq	Hàkala	Minali
Below	Ta<u>kh</u>t	Taḥt	Hamenkerat	Inkodediemen
Everything	Kul shei	Kull shai	Haltikalla	—
Evening	Asser	'Aṣar	—	Dinofari
Wild beast	Waḥsh	Waḥsh	Deshìt	Shodhìhm

How much	Kam	Kam	B'kam	Binemshuon
Dom-tree	Nebek	Naba'	Dom	Firehem
Good	Tayib	Ṭaiyab	Ghet	Dìa
Bad	Battal	Baṭl	Khiob	Dià
Nice	Zein	Zain	Ghit	Shikèro
Great	Kebir	Kabīr	Aghus	Shibìb
Greatest	Akbar	Akbar	Aghusa	Shibìhb
White	Abaid	Abyaḍ	Lebanèd	Lebìne
Black	Asoud	Aswad	Hawa	Khalak Ha-he
Old	Kadīm	Qadīm	Dewìl	Tahan
New	Ghedid	Gadīd	Hidin	Gedìd
Cold	Bard	Bard	Gazùn	Habahur
Hot	{ Har	Ḥarr	Hehen	Shehem
_or_	{ Hami	Ḥummā̄	Hanan Hark	Dio denarher
Red	Ahmar	Aḥmar	Ufer	Afer
Green	Akdar	Akdar	—	—
Yellow	Asfar	Aṣfar	Hat'hor	Shedhor
Much	Ghali	Ghalī	Zeboun	Ghali
Cheap	Rakīs	—	Rakis	Rakis
Rich	Ghani	Ghanī	Togìr	Tag
Poor	Fakir	Faqīr	Faker	Faker
Wretched	Meskin	Miskīn	Meskin	Meskin
Father	Abū	Abū	Hebe	Bebe
Mother	Om	Umm	Hamme	Beo
Eat	Akul	Akal	Hamkout	Gebenganeo
Fear	Khāf	—	Linkhaf	Sherboton

416

Angry	Nehm	—	Shuhkof	Daime
Sick	Ayyan	—	Bithell	Giore
Broken, Injured	Maksūr	Maksūr	Tiber	Sheteghen
News	Kabar	Khabar	Kobber	Kabr
Early	Bèdri, Subba	Sabāh	Ksobba	Kasaibeya
Peace	Salaan	Salām	Subbaellah	Alburr
Dirty	Wasakh	Wasakh	Mithkal	Haidek
Clean	Nodīf	Nadhdhaf	Ghihdi	Nodeif
Boat	Merkab	Markab	Merkab	Merkab
Ride	Yerkab	Yarkab	Hamle rekhob	Nirerkab
Rain	Matar	Maṭar	Lehamed	Messer
Crooked	Awwaz	'Awwaj	Nehanellom	Netògher
Finished	Khalas	Khalaṣ	Burneghessen	Tettin
Thus	Kidda	Kaḍā	—	—
Go	{ Yemshi	Yamshī	Suè	Toïke
	{ Rua	Rāh	Ghenī	Toher
Prison	Habs	Ḥabs	Habs	Habs
Present	Bakhshis	Bakhshīsh	Bakhshesh	Bakhshish
Prophet	Nebi	Nabī	Nebe	Nebe
Open	Maftūh	Maftūḥ	Bob fitàh	Ghinatten
Orphan	Yatīm	Yatīm	Aytìm	Esmediafore
Bucket	Dalu	Dalū	Dolu	M'l'hia

To paint	Lauwan, Laun	Lawwan	Laun	Sourah
Palm branches	Saóuf nakhl	—	Safe	Hes el timeri
Parents	Walidein	Wālidain	Hebe wahami	Bebe wavubeyah
Fowl	Dakika	—	Karoun	Ent
Liver	Kabid	Kabid	Kabid	Kabid
Thirsty	Aṯchan	'Aṯshān	Hailuk	Toimek
Hungry	Goàn	Gī'ān	Göak	Sottak
Praise	Ḥamd	Ḥamd	Hamd	Hamd
Slow	Ba'ati	—	Aden abatayah	Aden nau
Christian	Nàzari	Naṣārī	Nazari	Nazari
Immediately	Hàlan	Ḥālan	Lazerom	Na'ah
Myrrh gum	Lobàn	Lubān	Tlahas	Tlahas
Myrrh tree	Leben	—	Mogherate	Emïidu
Knee	Rukbah	—	Bark	Berk
Lame	A'rag	'Arag	Tibere	Gushel
To laugh	Ḍaḥik	Qaḥqaḥ	Istahalk	N'dlahak
Laughter	Ḍiḥk	Ḍiḥk	Ethelhalk	Entlahak
Leg	Saḳ	Sāq	Tharem	Ihlop
Leper	Abraṣ	Ibrāṣ	B'hohg	Behehok
Lift	Urfa	—	Urfah	Dza(minha)
Like (same as)	Mitl-shibh	Mithl	Izdah	Toàha
Lion	Asād; plural,	Asad	Gailar	(No word, because they

	usoŭd			say 'we none in Sokotra')
To dwell	Sakan	Sakan	Nehamel Entowelbo um	N'zohn henna
Lungs	Riah	Ri, ah	Gil't'hori	Geha
Mad	Magnūn	Magnūn	Haiwāl	Mankaina
Mankind	Beni Adam	Banī Ādam	Beni Adam	Makuloka (cf. Makalaka, South Africa)
Magic	Sihr	Siḥr	Saghir	Sahire
Naked	'Aryán	'Uryān	Harket el binad	Esoufai libineben
Napkin	Fòuṭa or Fūṭah	Fauṭh	Foutah	Fotere
Neck	'Unk-Raḳabah	'Unq Raqabah	Ghoti	Rokoba
Needle	Ibrah; plural, ubàr	Ibrah	Makaite	Makite
Noble	Sharìf	Sharìf	Sharif	Sharìf
Noise	Ṣaut	Ṣaut	Aroumeki n or Saut	Metdelhin or Ta'ad'hin
None	Lâ aḥad	Lā aḥad	Hadelabu n	Balheh
Nose	Anf, manakhìr, khoshim	Anf	Nakarinya	Nahare
Hurry	Ishtagil	—	Deghodu m	Denofer
A quarter	Rub'	Rub'	Erbeit	Töman

Bone	'Azm	'Azm	Athail	Sahilla
Feather	Rīshah	—	Thluf	Nefereri
Quilt	Lahàf	Liḥāf	Guderi	Miskal
Lamb	Arnab *or* Erneb	—	Arnab	(They have no word)
Rat	Gard'hom	Gurd<u>hu</u>m	Gihreit	Zadahin
Ruined	Kharàb	<u>Kh</u>arāb	Khaiob	Kharbeni
Purse, bag, pocket	Gaib *or* Kies	Gaib, jaib	Kies	Kies
Idle	Keslān	Kaslān	Fohsel	Aghizdè
Do your work, *or* Mind your own business	Amel Shuglak	'Aml shu<u>gh</u>lak	Amal hagil de felene	Tenofar dishberi
Book	Kitāb	Kitāb	Nektib	Inkotub
Writing	Mektūb	Maktūb	Berklub	Berklub
Honey	'Asal	'Asal	Assal	Assal
Behind	Wàra	Warā	Manghirek	Minherrin
Bitter	Murr	Murra	Hermet	Ajhi
Wielding	Arouz	'Urs	Arouz	Arouz
But	Lākin	Lākin	Lakin	Yakaïta
Caravan	Kàfila	Qāfilah	Shikfilèla	Beghishekfil
Load	Huml	Ḥaml	Hamul	Hamul
Begin	Ibtida	'Ibtidā	Bedihn	Bedehn
Kitchen	Mūṭbūkh	Maṭba<u>kh</u>	Mutabukh	Mulbakt
Bird	Dik	—	Dik	Dik
Dig	Hafar	—	Nehamel	Nehafar

			hafere	
Rest	Rahah	—	Rahah	Tareharhinnaha
Doctor	Ḥakim	Ḥakīm	—	—
Cup	Finjān Kūbayet	Finjān	Finjan Kūbàyet	Finjan Kūbàyet
Skin	Gild	Gild, jild	Geld	Geld
Eggs	Beid, Degade	Baiḍ	Degaghe	Degaghe
Never	Abadan	—	Abadàn	Abadàn
Stream	Ghail	—	Dihib	Thlab
Paper	Warak	Waraq	Werkart	Warraka
Sit	Ghisel Gitez	—	Towel	Tsalleh
Dry	Nashif	Nashshaf	Dehar	Terahat
Read	Karà	Qarā	Ktub	Kteb
Scarce	Nādir	Nādir	Kalèd	Khlahrohb
Roast	Shawa	Shawa	Hamtiwi	Tè
Rob	Sarak	Saraq	Hirrik	Seirek
Room	Oḍa	Oḍah	Hod	Hod
Round	Ḥaul	Ḥaul	Hagìr	Haghia
Root	Aṣl	Aṣl	Asali	Asl
Run	Rakaḍ	Rakaḍ	Houeh	Tshà
Ripe	Mustawi	Mustawi	Mushtawi	Mushlawi
Seal	Khatīm	Khatam	Khatini	Houleh
Riches	Mal	—	Molshè	Inoshinia
Reap	Ḥaṣad	Ḥaṣad	Hazad	Hazd
Beat	Ḍaraba	Ḍaraba	L'bedi	Toghì

421

Nut	Brandouk	—	Brandouk	Brandouk
Obey	Aṭa	Aṭa'	Atawa	Naddub
Order	Amr	Amr	Amr	Amar
Old woman	'Agouz	'Agūzah	Agouz	Khlibip
Ornament	Zena	Zīnat	Git	Tchera
Owl	Boum	Būm	Tlarhitin	Tlarhiten
Castle *or* palace	Kaṣr	Qasr	Ḥazar ed Dowlet	Hăzar Sādahan
Palm of the hand	Kaf-fusa	Kaff	Dehòte	Dehò
Pardon	Ghafar	Ghafar	Netur min el habs	Beligiter min el habs
A little	Shwaya	Shuwaiyah	Musted	Einoshedèhe
Where is the town	Fein el Beled	Fi ain al balad	Hoddehab ed del Felani	Hodde belad
People	Nās	Nās	Haboa	Hohafon
Head	Rās	Rās	Ras	Ras
Blood	Dam	—	—	Musailo
Disordered blood	Dam Kholeil	—	Douri	Durr
Pen	Kalam	Qalam	Kalam	Kalam
Anger	Ghadab	Ghadab	Ghatitali	Hetterhinhi
Pay	Waffa	Wafā̄	Woffehinki	Waffie
Pepper	Filfil	Filfil	Filfil	Tiflfarlo
Perfume	'Iṭr	'Iṭr	Attar	Hal
Perspire	Arak	'Ariq	Deanghalen	Ikimen

Pin	Dabbūs	Dabbūs	Dabous	Dabous
Plague	Ta′ūn	Ṭā′ūn	Duinhaufa l Eikeo	Eiked Ouìhafel
Ugly	Ba′in	—	Behimet	Behimah
Plant	Nabāt	Nabat	Nebhat	Nebout

English	Arabic	Mahri	Sokoteri
What is she doing	Eish yamèlhu	Tum ul aisin	Inempt shüyet
I drink water	Ana sherab moye	Nehamel el tikhe	Ithkellare
You are very kind	Enta latif ketir	Meshiri meikin	Latif beyne
Do you know Mehri?	Enta taraf el Meheri	Arebuk Meheri	Ahruh Mehri
We talk Sokotri	Nahn natàllem el Sokoteri	Nahan natallùm Sokoteriote	Ik n′atalam Sokoteria
Give me another	Gibli waḥad thāna	Hateli tadrhaa	Abouli beladàtis
How many days from here to the sea?	Kam ayo′om min hinna illa el bahr	Kam yom m′boun ta heik	Kam yom menha afta′a
Near the water	Garīb el moya	—	Lal diho

[13] When they wish to warn the camel not to knock against anything in a narrow place they cry 'Berri! Berri!'

LIST OF SOME OF THE ARABIC AND OTHER WORDS
EXPLAINED IN THE TEXT

abba
abr
afrit
ailb
attar
awwal

batil
b'dom
brinjol

ghail
ghasl
ghatrif
ghi
gohb[A]
gourod

habat-assoba
halwa
hárami
horma
helf
herris

jembia

kabila
kadhlb
kafila
kahwa
kattira
kayya
kazbah

kei[A]
kharrad
khawah
kho[A]
kourzan
kutcha

lahaf
loess
luthba

medakdak
madhar
madibash
majilis
mangola
masabam
merghazi
mersa
miet[A]
mis'hap
munkala

nakhoda

ohma
ouft[A]

rack
reis
rezai

saap
salang
sambuka
shabib
shur[A]
sirah

siyar
siyara

tara
tarsla
tawilah

whabba

yusur

zamouta
ziara
ziaret

[A] These words are used by the Gara.

TRAVELS IN SOUTHERN ARABIA AND THE SOUDAN.

With 24 Full-page Illustrations and 5 Maps. Demy 8vo. 18s.

Southern Arabia.

By the late THEODORE BENT and Mrs. THEODORE BENT.

Printed in the United Kingdom by
Lightning Source UK Ltd., Milton Keynes
137873UK00001B/104/A